Class, Capital, State, and Late Development

Studies in Critical Social Sciences Book Series

Haymarket Books is proud to be working with Brill Academic Publishers (www.brill.nl) to republish the *Studies in Critical Social Sciences* book series in paperback editions. This peer-reviewed book series offers insights into our current reality by exploring the content and consequences of power relationships under capitalism, and by considering the spaces of opposition and resistance to these changes that have been defining our new age. Our full catalog of *SCSS* volumes can be viewed at https://www.haymarketbooks.org/series_collections/4-studies-in-critical-social-sciences.

Series Editor
David Fasenfest (York University)

New Scholarship in Political Economy Book Series

Series Editors
David Fasenfest (York University)
Alfredo Saad-Filho (Queen's University, Belfast)

Editorial Board
Kevin B. Anderson (University of California, Santa Barbara)
Tom Brass (formerly of SPS, University of Cambridge)
Raju Das (York University)
Ben Fine ((emeritus) SOAS University of London)
Jayati Ghosh (Jawaharlal Nehru University)
Elizabeth Hill (University of Sydney)
Dan Krier (Iowa State University)
Lauren Langman (Loyola University Chicago)
Valentine Moghadam (Northeastern University)
David N. Smith (University of Kansas)
Susanne Soederberg (Queen's University)
Aylin Topal (Middle East Technical University)
Fiona Tregenna (University of Johannesburg)
Matt Vidal (Loughborough University London)
Michelle Williams (University of the Witwatersrand)

Class, Capital, State, and Late Development

The Political Economy of Military
Interventions in Turkey

Gönenç Uysal

Haymarket Books
Chicago, IL

First published in 2024 by Brill Academic Publishers, The Netherlands
© 2024 Koninklijke Brill NV, Leiden, The Netherlands

Published in paperback in 2025 by
Haymarket Books
P.O. Box 180165
Chicago, IL 60618
773-583-7884
www.haymarketbooks.org

ISBN: 979-8-88890-352-0

Distributed to the trade in the US through Consortium Book Sales and Distribution (www.cbsd.com) and internationally through Ingram Publisher Services International (www.ingramcontent.com).

This book was published with the generous support of Lannan Foundation, Wallace Action Fund, and the Marguerite Casey Foundation.

Special discounts are available for bulk purchases by organizations and institutions. Please call 773-583-7884 or email info@haymarketbooks.org for more information.

Cover design by Jamie Kerry and Ragina Johnson.

Printed in the United States.

Library of Congress Cataloging-in-Publication data is available.

This book is dedicated to my beautiful family, who taught me about love, hope, dignity, and justice, all of which one really fights for

No people wholly despairs, and even if for a long time it goes on hoping merely out of stupidity, yet one day, after many years, it will suddenly become wise and fulfil all its pious wishes.

    KARL MARX (1843)

Contents

Acknowledgements XI
Abbreviations XII
Translations XIV

1 **Introduction**
   Turkey as a Late-Developing Country 1
   1   Dominant Literature on Civil–Military Relations in Peripheries 2
   2   Dominant Approaches to Civil–Military Relations in Turkey 5
       2.1   *Modernisation Theory* 6
       2.2   *Conservative-Liberal Paradigm* 7
   3   Capitalism, Development, and the Military in Peripheries 9
       3.1   *The Contradictions of Capitalism, Unevenness, and Late Development* 10
       3.2   *Late Development in Peripheries* 14
       3.3   *Late Development and the Capitalist State and Military* 18
   4   The State, the Military, and Classes in Turkey: an Overview of the Book 21

2 **The Revolutions of 1908 and 1923, and the State and the Military in Turkey** 24
   1   Late Development and Social Formation in Turkey: the Political Economy of the Late Ottoman Modernisation 25
   2   The Revolution of 1908 and the Military 29
       2.1   *The State and Class Relations in the Twentieth-Century Ottoman Empire* 29
       2.2   *The 1908 Revolution as a Bourgeois Revolution* 32
       2.3   *The Military as the Pioneer and Guardian of the 1908 Revolution* 37
   3   The Bourgeois Revolution of 1923 and the Military 40
       3.1   *The Political Economy of the War of Independence* 41
       3.2   *The Political Economy of the Republican Modernisation* 44
       3.3   *The Military as the Pioneer and Guardian of the 1923 Revolution* 50

3 **The Coup of 1960 and the Guardianship of the Military** 55
   1   Classes and the State in the Post-Second World War Order 55
       1.1   *The Political Economy of the Legacy of the War* 55

		1.2	*The Reconfiguration of Class Relations in the Aftermath of the Second World War* 57

- 2 The State and Classes under *Demokrat Parti*   60
  - 2.1 *The National Economy between 1950 and 1958*   60
  - 2.2 Demokrat Parti's *Hegemonic Project*   63
  - 2.3 *The Political Economy of the Transformation of the Military*   66
  - 2.4 Demokrat Parti's *Hegemonic Crisis and the Military*   70
- 3 The Coup of 1960 and Its Aftermath   74
  - 3.1 *The Coup of 1960 and the Social Classes*   74
  - 3.2 *The Transition to Import-Substitution Industrialisation, the State, and Class Relations*   76
  - 3.3 *The Institutionalisation of the Military's Guardianship Role*   79

4 **The Coup of 1980 and the Reorganisation of the Military**   82
  - 1 The Crisis of the Late 1960s and the Memorandum of 1971   82
    - 1.1 *Class Relations in the 1960s*   82
    - 1.2 *The Hegemonic Crisis of the Late 1960s*   85
    - 1.3 *The Memorandum of 1971*   88
  - 2 The State and Classes in the 1970s   92
    - 2.1 *The Political Landscape and Class Relations in the 1970s*   92
    - 2.2 *The Prolonged Hegemonic Crisis of the Late 1970s*   95
  - 3 The Political Economy of the Coup of 1980 and Its Aftermath   97
    - 3.1 *The Coup of 1980 and Social Classes*   97
    - 3.2 *The Transition to Neoliberalism and Export-Led Industrialisation*   100
    - 3.3 *The State and Classes under* Anavatan Partisi   103
    - 3.4 *The Military's Guardianship Role and Authoritarian Statism*   107

5 **The "Postmodern Coup" of 1997 and Political Islam**   111
  - 1 The Political Economy of the Rise of Political Islam   111
    - 1.1 *The Composition of Islamic Capital*   111
    - 1.2 *Financial Liberalisation and the Formation of Islamic Finance Capital*   113
    - 1.3 *The Rise of* Milli Görüş   116
  - 2 Classes, Crises, and *Milli Görüş*   119
    - 2.1 *The Crises of Financialisation in the Early 1990s*   119
    - 2.2 *The Hegemonic Crisis of the Early 1990s*   121
    - 2.3 Milli Görüş *and Social Classes*   123

    2.4   Milli Görüş *and Secularism*   127
3   The Political Economy of the Process of 28 February   130
    3.1   *The Memorandum of 1997*   130
    3.2   *Social Classes and the Process of 28 February*   133
    3.3   *Classes, the State, and the Military in the Aftermath of the Process of 28 February*   135

6 *Adalet ve Kalkınma Partisi* and the "New Era in Civil–Military Relations"   139

1   The Political Economy of the Rise of the AKP   140
    1.1   *The Economic Crisis of 2001*   140
    1.2   *The Emergence of the AKP*   141
    1.3   *The Rise of the Gülen Congregation*   142
2   The State, Classes, and the Military under the AKP (2002–2007)   144
    2.1   *Classes and the AKP*   144
    2.2   *The Hegemonic Project of Conservative Democracy*   149
    2.3   *The Military and the AKP*   152
    2.4   *The "E-Memorandum" of 2007*   154
3   The State, Classes, and the Military under the AKP (2007–2010)   158
    3.1   *The Ergenekon and the Sledgehammer Trials*   159
    3.2   *The Constitutional Amendments of 2010*   163

7 The Failed Coup Attempt of 2016
Resistance, Crisis, and Restoration   166

1   The State, Classes, and the Crisis under the AKP (2010–2015)   166
    1.1   *The Emergence of Indications of an Economic Crisis*   167
    1.2   *Resistance against Neoliberal Islamism*   169
    1.3   *The Crisis of the Coalition between the AKP and the Gülen Congregation*   172
2   The State, Classes, and the Crisis under the AKP (2015–2018)   174
    2.1   *The Consolidation of Fascism (2015–2016)*   176
    2.2   *The Abortive Coup of 2016*   177
3   The Fascist State and Regime and the Military (2015–2018)   181
    3.1   *The Reorganisation of the Military*   184

8 Conclusion   189

1   From Concrete to Abstract: Late Development, the State, and the Military   191

2 From Abstract to Concrete: State–Military–Society Relations in Turkey 194
3 Concluding Remarks on the Crisis of Fascism 197

References 203
Index 250

Acknowledgements

This book is the extended and updated version of the PhD research I pursued at King's College London. I would like to thank Bill Park for his guidance and support during and after my PhD, and Professor Tim Jacoby for his rigorous comments on my research.

I have met a large number of remarkable scholars and colleagues, whose works I admire and respect greatly, in London, Ankara, Osmaniye, Lancaster, and other cities across the globe. I would like to thank all of these wonderful people with whom my path has coincided. I would like to thank Professor Şebnem Oğuz, whose works have greatly informed my research, for her encouragement; I would like to express gratitude to Dr. David Fasenfest for his help and support; and I would also like to thank Dr. Akif Avcı, who encouraged me to submit my book proposal to Brill, for our conversations.

I express my sincerest gratitude to my Turkish and British families, Canan, Orhan, Ayşe, Ece, Les, and Andy, for their unyielding support and encouragement. I am particularly grateful to my life partner, Dan, for his support, encouragement, and intellectual enthusiasm.

Abbreviations

AKP	*Adalet ve Kalkınma Partisi*, Justice and Development Party
ANAP	*Anavatan Partisi*, Motherland Party
AP	*Adalet Partisi*, Justice Party
CHP	*Cumhuriyet Halk Partisi*, Republican People's Party
DISK	*Türkiye Devrimci İşçi Sendikaları Konfederasyonu*, Confederation of Progressive Trade Unions of Turkey
DP	*Demokrat Parti*, Democratic Party
DSP	*Demokratik Sol Parti*, Democratic Left Party
DYP	*Doğru Yol Partisi*, True Path Party
EOI	export-oriented industrialisation
EU	European Union
FP	*Fazilet Partisi*, Virtue Party
HSYK	*Hakimler ve Savcılar Yüksek Kurulu*, Supreme Council of Judges and Prosecutors
IMF	International Monetary Fund
ISI	import-substitution industrialisation
ITC	*İttihat ve Terakki Cemiyeti*, Committee of Union and Progress
MBK	*Milli Birlik Komitesi*, National Unity Committee
MESS	*Türkiye Metal Sanayicileri Sendikası*, Turkish Employers' Association of Metal Industries
MGK	*Milli Güvenlik Konseyi*, National Security Committee
MHP	*Milliyetçi Hareket Partisi*, Nationalist Action Party
MIT	*Milli İstihbarat Teşkilatı*, National Intelligence Agency
MNP	*Milli Nizam Partisi*, National Order Party
MP	Member of Parliament
MSP	*Milli Selamet Partisi*, National Salvation Party
MUSIAD	*Müstakil Sanayici ve İşadamları Derneği*, Independent Industrialists' and Businessmen's Association
NATO	North Atlantic Treaty Organization
NSC	*Milli Güvenlik Kurulu*, National Security Council
OYAK	*Ordu Yardımlaşma Kurumu*, Military Personnel Assistance Fund
RP	*Refah Partisi*, Welfare Party
SMES	small and medium-sized enterprises
SOES	state-owned enterprises
TISK	*Türkiye İşveren Sendikaları Konfederasyonu*, Turkish Confederation of Employer Associations
TOBB	*Türkiye Odalar ve Borsalar Birliği*, Turkish Union of Chambers and Commodity Exchanges

TSKGV	*Türk Silahlı Kuvvetlerini Güçlendirme Vakfı,* Turkish Armed Forces Foundation
Türk-Iş	*Türkiye İşçi Sendikaları Konfederasyonu,* Confederation of Turkish Trade Unions
TUSIAD	*Türk Sanayicileri ve İş İnsanları Derneği,* Turkish Industry and Business Association
TUSKON	*Türkiye İşadamları ve Sanayicileri Konfederasyonu,* Turkish Confederation of Businessmen and Industrialists

Translations

Assembly (Turkish Grand National Assembly)	*Türkiye Büyük Millet Meclisi*
Association for Fighting Communism	*Komünizmle Mücadele Derneği*
Association for Supporting Modern Life	*Çağdaş Yaşamı Destekleme Derneği*
Atatürkist Thought Association	*Atatürkçü Düşünce Derneği*
breaking of the fast	*iftar*
congregation	*cemaat*
Constitutional Court	*Anayasa Mahkemesi*
Council of State	*Danıştay*
counter-guerrilla	*kontrgerilla*, Turkish *gladio*
Court of Appeal	*Yargıtay*
decree (in the force of law)	*kanun hükmünde kararname*
Directorate of Religious Affairs	*Diyanet*
foundation	*vakıf*
General Staff	*Genelkurmay Başkanlığı*
Grey Wolves	*Ülkü Ocakları*
headscarf	*tesettür, türban, başörtüsü*
holy war	*jihad*
Internal Service Act	*İç Hizmet Kanunu*
Islamic law	*sharia*
Islamic legal ruling	*fatwa*
Military Court of Appeal	*Askeri Yargıtay*
Military Supreme Court of Administration	*Askeri Yüksek İdare Mahkemesi*
Ministry of Interior	*İçişleri Bakanlığı*
Ministry of Justice	*Adalet Bakanlığı*
National Outlook Movement	*Milli Görüş Hareketi*
Nationalist Front	*Milliyetçi Cephe*
natural disposition	*fitrat*
order	*tarikat*
People's Homes	*Halkevleri*
prayer leader and preacher schools	*imam-hatip* schools
preparatory schools	*dershane*
State Planning Organisation	*Devlet Planlama Teşkilatı*
State Security Courts	*Devlet Güvenlik Mahkemeleri*

Special Warfare Department	*Özel Harp Dairesi*
Supreme Council of Arbitrators	*Yüksek Hakem Kurulu*
Supreme Military Council	*Yüksek Askeri Şura*
squat	*gecekondu*
Turkish-Islamic Synthesis	*Türk-İslam Sentezi*

CHAPTER 1

Introduction

Turkey as a Late-Developing Country

> The crisis consists precisely in the fact that the old is dying and the new cannot be born; in this interregnum a great variety of morbid symptoms appear.
> ANTONIO GRAMSCI (1992b [1930])

∴

The research for this book began at the height of the domination of the conservative-liberal paradigm in academia exploring civil–military relations in Turkey. This clique of scholars gave tacit consent to, if not supported, the ruling Islamist *Adalet ve Kalkınma Partisi* (Justice and Development Party, AKP)'s quest to reform and reinforce civilian supremacy over the *modern and secular* Republican military so that its tutelary custodianship would be eradicated. Turkey's long history of military interventions (coups d'état in 1960 and 1980, and memoranda in 1971 and 1997) were claimed to substantiate the need for such reform. At that time, the AKP was in a de facto ruling coalition with the Islamist Gülen congregation, a branch of the religious brotherhood known as the Nurcu congregation and named after its founder, Fethullah Gülen. In July 2016, Gülenist disciples in the military and police allegedly sought to overthrow President Recep Tayyip Erdoğan and the AKP government but failed. The clear inadequacy of conservative-liberal scholars to explain the political role of the military, as well as its later immobilisation by the AKP's growing authoritarianism in the aftermath of the abortive coup of 2016, has underpinned the main aim of this research: to offer a critical/radical examination of state–military–society relations in Turkey, a peripheral country that belongs to the Global South.[1]

---

1 For a short discussion on the emergence of and transition from the concept of the Third World to the Global South in development studies, see Dirlik (2007). Turkey was never formally colonised and hence not a part of the postcolonial bloc represented as the Third World. Turkey has recently been considered an emerging market economy, which further seems to

Critical/radical approaches to civil–military relations in the Global South continue to be significant, timely and relevant. In fact, neither is Turkey the only country to have experienced frequent military interventions, nor are coups d'état things of the past for several countries in the Global South. In this regard, the Turkish military's role in politics and its relations with society have been mostly compared to its counterparts in the Middle East and Latin America, with both regions having been marked with past and recent military interventions, both failed and successful. Nevertheless, all military intervention, ranging from military takeovers to the military's influence behind the scenes, has corresponded with the particular social and historical context of the Global South: existence at the periphery of world capitalism, characterised by unevenness, dependency, and underdevelopment. For this reason, this research proposes a critical/radical perspective to explore state–military–society relations in peripheries, particularly Turkey, in connection with the historical development of capitalist relations and the integration of peripheries into the world capitalist order.

1 Dominant Literature on Civil–Military Relations in Peripheries

The dominant literature on civil–military relations (CMR) is principally centred on the maxim borrowed from Juvenal, the first-century Roman poet: "but who is to stand guard over the guards themselves?" (Juvenal 1998: 140) Mainly drawing upon Weber (1994: 310–311), most CMR literature considers the state to be a political organisation that has successfully claimed "the monopoly of legitimate physical violence within a certain territory". Therefore, it accepts the military as "'organised violence as a legitimate means ... in support of foreign policy objectives ... [and] to cope with domestic disorder'" (Rukavishnikov and Pugh 2018: 123–125). In this sense, it conceptualises civil–military relations as a subject of study to explore the relationship between the government and the military with a focus on civilian control; the relationship between the military and society at large, such as mutual perceptions of military officers and civilians; and the relationship between the government and civil society, including public opinion on and oversight of military spending (Cohn, Coletta, and Feaver

---

complicate its place in the Global South. This book accepts the Global South as a geographical umbrella term to refer to peripheries of the world capitalist system that are characterised with unevenness, dependency, and late development. Contrary to dependency theory, which mainly utilises the notion of periphery (see Wallerstein 2006), this book underlines dynamic class relations and understands peripheries as active subjects of world capitalism.

2018: 711–712). It further proposes typologies of militaries in accordance with the qualitative and quantitative features of civilian and military institutions, as well as the sociopolitical and socioeconomic environment. Such features mainly include the nature and structure of the political system (Perlmutter 1986), including political institutionalisation and stability (Huntington 1973), and political culture (Finer 1969); and the strength and weakness of civilian institutions and the military (Luckham 1971), including the internal organisation of the military (Janowitz 1971).

The dominant CMR literature is fundamentally built on a clear demarcation between domestic and international arenas, as well as among social and economic, political, and military spheres. Based on a duality between the state and civil society, the state is located in the political sphere, and civil society is located in the social and economic sphere, and the political retains its primacy over the economic. The dominant CMR literature implicitly accepts the form of historical evolution of capitalism that took place in the advanced capitalist Western countries as the organic basis of social, economic, and political development and hence the principle of civilian supremacy over the military. This idealisation of the relationship between Western form(s) of capitalism and development, where capitalism is simply reduced to an economic structure, compels the dominant CMR literature to understand discrepancies of state–military–society relations pertaining to underdevelopment in peripheries as inorganic *variations*, or rather *deviations*. For this reason, the dominant CMR literature is inclined to arrive at Western-centric typologies of militaries on the basis of an ahistorical understanding of divergence between the advanced capitalist Western countries and late-developing non-Western countries.

In this regard, the dominant CMR literature draws upon and redefines Rapoport's (1962) notion of *praetorianism* to classify the militaries in peripheries in opposition to the advanced capitalist Western countries (Nordlinger 1977; Perlmutter 1969). Praetorianism, which indicates "systems where a bureaucratically administered professional army ... intermittently deposes governments by extra-legal acts", now refers to "the antithesis of civilian control and a military domination ... 'institutionalised' largely to expand the military's corporate interests at the expense of society as a whole" (Rapoport 2021: 253–254). In this way, the dominant CMR literature—often implicitly—considers the tendency of militaries to intervene in politics as an internal element of underdevelopment characterising state–society relations in peripheries (Cammack, Pool, and Tordoff 1993; Diamond 1989; Diamond, Linz, and Lipset 1995; Roxborough 1979; Shils 1967; Tella 1995). Nevertheless, a rough periodisation of the theorisation of CMR reveals how this dominant literature understands (under)development and its relationship with the political role of the military in peripheries.

The theorisation of CMR coincided with the rise of the discourse on development corresponding to the domination of the modernisation theory, which offered a general framework to understand state–society relations in peripheries in the aftermath of the Second World War (Uysal 2020: 134; see also Escobar 1995). In the context of the Cold War, the United States promoted its hegemonic role as the representative and custodian of the postwar liberal international order and integration of newly independent peripheral countries into the world market economy. In this international context, modernisation theory drew a parallel among modernity, capitalism, and liberal democracy, and associated all of them with development. It understood development in terms of social, political, and economic outcomes of capitalism—particularly liberal democracy, which was assumed to bring about economic and political redistribution and hence convergence between the masses and the elites through political participation—as unfolded in advanced capitalist Western countries, which were the same outcomes it already regarded as quintessential aspects of modernisation (Lipset 1959, 1960; Parsons 1964; Rostow 1991).[2] Therefore, it considered modernisation as an evolutionary, linear, and universal process of development to be adopted by traditional societies of peripheries to achieve Western-style institutions and practices. During this period, the dominant CMR literature was overwhelmingly inclined to tolerate the prominent role the militaries played in peripheries in accordance with the US support for anti-communist authoritarian regimes against the Soviet Union and the socialist camp. To be precise, the dominant CMR literature demonstrated a remarkable tendency to credit military interventions so long as the military officers pursued the capitalist modernisation (Huntington 1973; Janowitz 1964, 1971; Pye 1967). Certain proponents of the dominant CMR literature further considered such military interventions rather transitional until modernity was achieved, after which the political role of the military was supposed to wither away (Janowitz 1971).

The end of the Cold War and the dissolution of the Soviet Union in the early 1990s has emphasised the perceived triumph of liberal democracy while strengthening the hegemonic role of the United States. This transition has reinforced the understanding of links between development, capitalism, and liberal democracy. Therefore, the economic and political underdevelopment underpinning absent/insufficient democratisation has been thought of as the

---

2 Modernisation theory understands development in terms of industrialisation and mechanisation that brings material wealth (economic), rationalisation and secularisation that erases traditional and religious belief systems (social), and centralisation of the state and democratisation that ensures the political representation of citizens (political) (Volpe 2010).

primary element that made peripheries susceptible to military interventions (Acemoğlu and Robinson 2006; Diamond 1997; Lipset 1995; see also Boix and Stokes 2003; cf. Przeworski 1991; Przeworski and Limongi 1997). Meanwhile, the emphasis on modernisation has been replaced by democratisation, indicating political liberalisation and institutionalisation, such as the establishment of universal suffrage, the rule of law, and transparency and accountability mechanisms, all complemented by the strengthening of civil society and political parties. In this regard, the dominant CMR literature has related the question of praetorianism to democratisation which assumes not only political reforms, but also economic restructuring aimed at the consolidation of market economies in peripheries (Diamond and Plattner 1996; Huntington 1991; Linz and Stepan 1996). This has confirmed the reformulation of the main principle of civilian supremacy over the military as the democratic civilian control of the armed forces (Kuehn 2018; Matei 2013). Such reformulation has sometimes been combined with security sector reform indicating development and democratic transition in peripheral countries (Edmunds 2013; Rukavishnikov and Pugh 2018; Schnabel 2015).

2   Dominant Approaches to Civil–Military Relations in Turkey

The dominant literature on CMR in Turkey has been built on apparently opposing but interconnected approaches to state–society relations, namely, modernisation theory and the conservative-liberal paradigm. Their conceptual focus might differ, including on, political institutions and, more broadly, political culture (Akkoyunlu 2007; Demirel 2004, 2005; Sarıgil 2007); ideologies adopted by the state and the military (Brown 1989; Harris 1988, 2011; Narlı 2000); and the international environment (Cizre 2004; Karaosmanoğlu 2000; Karaosmanoğlu and Gökakın 2010; Özcan 2001). Nonetheless, modernisation theory and the conservative-liberal paradigm agree on the significant political, social, economic, cultural, and legal role of the Turkish Armed Forces (TAF). They identify the political role of the Turkish military as "guardianship" (Cizre-Sakallıoğlu 1997; Heper 2011; Narlı 2011), "praetorianism" (Perlmutter 1977; Sarıgil 2011), and "informal or even explicit umpire between competing political parties and political groups" (Janowitz 1971). More importantly, modernisation theory and the conservative-liberal paradigm fundamentally share a similar understanding of development and its relationship with capitalism and with the state and the military. Such a similar understanding paradoxically compels them to arrive at distinct but similar conclusions. Neither approach focuses on development and underdevelopment per se; the question of (under) development remains an implicit element. Both approaches consider the transition to and consolidation of modern capitalism in the advanced capitalist Western countries as an organic process that took place as a result of internal dynamics and brought about social, economic, and political development. This remains in opposition to the supposedly inorganic process of capitalist modernisation pursued by the state, which further lacks any substantial class basis and historical content in its conceptualisation. Such an inorganic process is implicitly perceived as the main cause of underdevelopment. In this regard, modernisation theory and the conservative-liberal paradigm—even though certain proponents might utilise the notion of class as an economic category/market position—converge regarding their Western-centric and ahistorical understanding of the relationship between capitalism and development, and, hence, state–society–military relations in Turkey.

2.1   *Modernisation Theory*

Modernisation theory dominated the literature on CMR in Turkey until the mid-1970s. It dated the process of modernisation in Turkey back to the late eighteenth century, at which time the Ottoman state aimed to modernise the military in order to prevent defeats against European powers and dissolution of the Empire. The modernised factions of the Ottoman civil-military officers, who formed *İttihat ve Terakki Cemiyeti* (Committee of Union and Progress, ITC) in 1889 and *Cumhuriyet Halk Partisi* (Republican People's Party, CHP) in 1923, were understood as the pioneers of the Ottoman and Republican modernisations on the basis of the transition from agricultural production to state-led industrialisation. Since the Republican military emerged as the founder and guardian of secular modernisation beginning in the 1920s, the dominant CMR literature interpreted the military's role in politics as the guardian of the modern secular Republican state (Hale 1994; Harris 1988; Lerner and Robinson 1960; Lewis 1968; Perlmutter 1977).

In the aftermath of the Second World War, Turkey aligned with the Western capitalist bloc, represented by the United States, against the socialist Eastern bloc, represented by the Soviet Union. Turkey's alignment with the Western liberal democracies was combined with the rise of political opposition to the ruling CHP, both of which brought about the liberalisation of politics and the transition to multiparty politics. *Demokrat Parti* (Democratic Party, DP), representing the cities and the villages, emerged as the political opposition to the CHP, which remained the main representative of the modernist civil-military bureaucracy. The dominant CMR literature considered the rise of traditionalism and conservativism of rural masses under the DP in combination with the political impasse of the late 1950s as the main elements that incited the military, the perceived staunch defender of secular modernisation, to undertake the coup of 1960 (Huntington 1973; Lerner and Robinson 1960; Nordlinger 1977).

2.2 Conservative-Liberal Paradigm

Beginning in the mid-1970s, the conservative-liberal paradigm dominated the literature on CMR in Turkey by redefining modernisation and its relationship with state–military–society relations in Turkey.[3] This book utilises the term conservative-liberal to indicate convergence between conservatism and liberalism regarding their understanding of society as an organic whole consisting of self-interested individuals, where the state maintains social order and security and safeguards private property. Based on the implicit assumption in conservatism and liberalism that capitalism brings about social, economic, and political development, the conservative-liberal paradigm perceives development in evolutionary terms where tradition—including religious values—and commitment to individual freedom and flourishing civil society on the basis of market economy are useful and necessary (Garnett 2010; Johnston 2010; Heywood 2017: 24–94).

The conservative-liberal paradigm criticises modernisation theory for promoting illiberal secular modernity that legitimised the role of the military in politics and marginalised conservatism and political Islam/Islamism,[4] which had begun to rise in the mainstream political arena since the 1970s. Mainly drawing upon Weber's (1947: 347–351) conception of "patrimonialism", the conservative-liberal paradigm employs two analytic pillars, namely, state tradition (Heper 1985) and the centre–periphery dichotomy (Mardin 1973), to discuss state–military–society relations in Turkey. The centre consists of the modernist fractions of the Ottoman and Republican civil-military bureaucracy, the secularist political elite represented by the ITC and the CHP, and the industrial bourgeoisie that flourished from the late 1950s. This centre has undertaken an authoritarian and elitist social-engineering project of secular modernisation, which has denied religious sensitivities of the periphery and hence maintained tutelage over the periphery (Kuru 2009; Toprak 1988). The periphery consists of rural notables consisting of landlords, the commercial

---

3   Even though conservatism historically emerged as a resistance to rapid social change conveyed particularly by liberalism in the late eighteenth and early nineteenth centuries, conservatism and liberalism already shared certain fundamental assumptions about capitalism and state–society relations (see Heywood 2017: 24–94).
4   The conceptualisation of illiberal modernity coincides with the advancement of the critique of secular modernity on the basis of its Western-centric origins and characteristics, and its perceived insensitivity to religious people (Bhargava 1998).

bourgeoisie, and local religious constituents; urban and rural workers; and the conservative political elite represented by the DP in the 1950s and *Adalet Partisi* (Justice Party, AP) in the 1960s and 1970s. Since political Islam is thought to emerge as a result of and a response to illiberal modernity (Göle 1997, 2000; Keyman 2010; Mardin 2005; Yavuz 2003), the periphery further consists of the Islamist movements, whose major mainstream representative has been *Milli Görüş Hareketi* (National Outlook Movement). *Milli Görüş* in fact established *Milli Nizam Partisi* (National Order Party, MNP) in 1970, *Milli Selamet Partisi* (National Salvation Party, MSP) in 1972, and *Refah Partisi* (Welfare Party, RP) in 1983, all of which were marginalised by the military. This omnipotent and omnipresent control of the supposedly enlightened and absolutist ruling centre over the periphery indicates the state tradition that constitutes the basis of the tutelary regime of the civil-military bureaucracy, institutionalised through the military interventions (Karpat 1988; Narlı 1999).

In the 1970s and 1980s, the conservative emphasis on the state's authority as the basis for social cohesion has compelled the conservative-liberal paradigm to regard the military interventions of 1971 and 1980 as inevitable and necessary responses to the social and political turmoil of the late 1960s and late 1970s (Tachau and Heper 1983; Evin 1988; Karaosmanoğlu 1993). Beginning in the 1990s, the liberal wing allied with certain proponents of leftism on the basis of perception of the bourgeoisie as the pioneer of the consolidation of liberal civil society as differentiated from the state in the advanced capitalist Western countries (Savran 2006). The supposed lack of a bourgeoisie as the pioneer of capitalist modernisation in Turkey compelled the modernist civil-military bureaucracy to undertake a top-down modernisation, which made the bourgeoisie dependent on the state and established the guardianship role of the military (Başkaya 1999; İnsel 1996; Keyder 1987). Since the memorandum of 1997—also known as the process of 28 February—targeted the ruling RP, it reinforced conservative-liberal paradigm's conception of the military as the bastion of secular modernisation (Demirel 2001; Heper and Güney 2000).

Beginning in the early 2000s, the conservative-liberal paradigm perceived the AKP, whose discourse on conservative democracy supposedly did not challenge liberal democracy (Göle 2012; Öniş 2006; Toprak 2005; Yavuz 2005),[5] as a democratic actor that could confront the tutelary regime and achieve civilian supremacy over the military within the frameworks of the European Union (EU) and the North Atlantic Treaty Organization (NATO) (Belge 2009; Cizre 2004;

---

5 This book borrows the term conservative democracy from the AKP's official discourse (see Akdoğan 2004).

Heper 2005; İnsel 2003; Keyder 2004; Özbudun 2006). The conservative-liberal paradigm further gave tacit consent to, if not supported, the AKP's efforts to reorganise the military through legal and administrative reforms (Sarıgil 2007; Toktaş and Kurt 2010) and political trials and purges in the late 2000s and early 2010s (Aydınlı 2011; Kuru 2012; Polat 2011). Nevertheless, the failed coup attempt of July 2016, combined with the rise of the AKP's authoritarianism beginning in the mid-2010s, has recently immobilised the conservative-liberal paradigm, which has further explained the AKP's authoritarianism with references to the state tradition (Esen and Gümüşçü 2016; Öniş 2015; Özbudun 2015).

3 Capitalism, Development, and the Military in Peripheries

This book recognises a number of critical scholars who have examined the military's role in politics in relation to the economic sources to which it has access (Akça 2013; Akça and Balta-Paker 2013) and class relations (Gülalp 1985, 1987; Savran 2016). These critical works have offered a valuable insight to state–military–society relations in Turkey. Akça's (2013) work is particularly significant in examining the development of organic relations between the military and capital fractions as the economic basis of the political role of the military. Gülalp's (1985, 1987) works are particularly important to understand the military interventions in the nexus of crises of patterns of capital accumulation and class struggle bringing about hegemonic crises. Nevertheless, this book's conceptualisation of late development offers a critical/radical and coherent framework borrowed from historical materialism/Marxism to examine state–military–society relations in Turkey.[6] This book accepts development as a process, a relation, and a structure that conditions social formations in peripheries characterised by unevenness, dependency, and underdevelopment. When development is understood in differential and interactive terms (Rosenberg 2006), state–military–society relations—particularly the role of the military in politics—in peripheries, especially Turkey, become a particular sociohistorical

---

6 This book utilises historical materialism and Marxism interchangeably to indicate the dialectical materialist understanding of history (see Ollman 2003; Politzer 1976), which perceives late development as an integral, whole, and organic structure, relation, and process that is constituted with mutually conditioning phenomena and also determines its parts and moments. This book explores late development as a material reality by abstracting it and understanding the essence of its features and mediations between its features (real abstraction), and later reconstructing the concrete based on the real effects of this real abstraction (see Saad-Filho 2002: 8–10).

form that arises from late development. This book conceptualises late development and discusses the political role of the military in Turkey in relation to the expansion and transformation of capitalist relations on a world scale and the integration of Turkey into the world capitalist system as a periphery.

3.1 The Contradictions of Capitalism, Unevenness, and Late Development

The expansion and transformation of capitalist relations across the globe, as well as the expansion of capital in peripheries and the integration of peripheries into the world capitalist system beginning in the seventeenth century, are inherently uneven processes. Unevenness, "the most general law of the historic process" (Trotsky 2008: 5), arises from the contradictions inherent in the process of capital accumulation, generating competition as an essential element.[7] Competition entails the basic tendency of capital to expand beyond its immediate territory and enhance productive forces (means of production and labour-power) in the pursuit of surplus value. Competition, therefore, becomes the driving force behind the expansion of relations of production and exchange/circulation (commerce and finance) on a world scale through which capital has the drive to accumulate in certain spaces where the conditions necessary for capital accumulation, especially market and labour-power, are reproduced. Competition grants capital the principal tendency to "concentrate in some spaces and, relatively at least, marginalise other locations" (Kiely 2012: 244), leading capital to "grow to a huge mass in a single hand in one place, because it has been lost by many in another place" (Marx 1976a: 777).

Capital accumulation "draw[s] the countries economically closer to one another and level[s] out their stages of development", thereby "set[ting] one country against another, and one branch of industry against another, developing some parts of world economy while hampering and throwing back the development of others" (Trotsky 1957: 19–20). Competition further compels countries that arrived late to capitalism to make leaps forward in development, particularly by adopting the latest advances, mobilising replacement mechanisms, and skipping the intermediate stages. Such leaps usually suffer from the spasmodic and disruptive impact of spatial and temporal pressure, resulting, paradoxically, in the perseverance of traditions. While different social formations "pass through the same development in different forms and tempo" (Trotsky 1972: 116), unevenness manifests itself "most sharply and complexly

---

7 This book accepts the process of capital accumulation as the appropriation and conversion of surplus product into capital in the form of labour-power and the means of production so that further surplus product can be appropriated (Marx 1976a: 725).

in the destiny of the backward countries" (Trotsky 2008: 5). Unevenness leads to *combinedness*,[8] the "drawing together of the different stages of the journey ... an amalgam of archaic with more contemporary forms" (Trotsky 2008: 5). Uneven and combined development (U&CD) indicates developmental discrepancies both within and between societies arising from the interaction of a multiplicity of social formations, and the production of a combination of socioeconomic and sociopolitical forms and relations, which are determined by this interaction of developmentally differentiated societies, within any given social formation (Anievas and Nişancıoğlu 2015: 44–49).[9]

Late development, in this regard, indicates the late development of capitalist relations in temporal terms (latecomer), as well as sociohistorical particularities pertaining to the late development of capitalist relations (Yaman-Öztürk and Ercan 2009: 56).[10] Late development in peripheries of the world capitalist system assume particular forms, relations, and processes of development

---

[8] According to Trotsky (1979: 858), who theorised the dynamics of U&CD, the essential feature of capitalism is unevenness, and *combinedness* "grows out of [unevenness] and completes it". The idea—although in embryonic form—that capitalism is an inherently uneven process can also be found in Lenin (1977: 597): "This process of transformation [of capitalist production] must, by the very nature of capitalism, take place in the midst of much that is uneven and disproportionate: periods of prosperity alternate with periods of crisis, the development of one industry leads to the decline of another".

[9] Certain proponents of Marxism argue that the principle of U&CD accounts for "the transhistorical fact of geopolitical multiplicity" and interaction (Callinicos and Rosenberg 2008: 80). This book argues that U&CD can be best understood within relations, processes, and tendencies of capitalism since capitalist economic, social, and political relations and forms are "historically unique in their capacity to generate both combination and unevenness" (Ashman 2009: 29). Capitalism, contrary to precapitalist modes of production, "inherently and constantly aims at economic expansion, at the penetration of new territories" and the "rapprochement [between] the economic and cultural levels of the most progressive and the most backward countries" (Trotsky 1957: 19). "[O]nce capitalist relations exist in one part of the world, subsequent transitions to capitalism ... cannot follow precisely the same path again" (Ashman 2009: 37). Therefore, the capitalist mode of production has the historically specific disposition of "universalisation and equalisation, on the one hand, and differentiation and fragmentation, on the other" (Allinson and Anievas 2009: 50).

[10] This book recognises that a number of advanced capitalist countries, including Germany, Japan, and the United States, arrived late to capitalism. Nevertheless, the development of capitalist relations in these countries converged with that of the advanced capitalist Western countries, rather than the peripheries. Therefore, this book's understanding of late development absorbs underdevelopment in the sense that "development of parts of the [world capitalist] system" takes place "at the expense of other parts" (Dos Santos 1970: 231). It further redefines underdevelopment in relation to the two countertendencies of expansion of capital: "accumulation and centralisation on the one hand, devaluation and marginalisation on the other" (Selwyn 2011: 439; see also Weeks 1997).

of capitalist relations determined with the opportunities and contradictions of capitalism in general and late development in particular, and the historical conditions of given social formations. Social formations in late-developing countries represent complex and contradictory combinations of "'backwardness'" and "'leaps forward in development'" (Linden 2007: 145–146).

The backward and archaic forms in peripheries have indicated a wide array of structures, relations, and processes that are explained in relation to dependency (Amin 1976; Dos Santos 1970; Frank 1966, 1982), the articulation of modes of production (Laclau 1971; Rey 1971; Taylor 1983), and U&CD (Löwy 2010; Selwyn 2011). This book understands development in terms of the development of productive forces—labour and means of production—since the contradiction between forces and relations of production is the primary motor of history that moves societies forward (Weeks 2018).[11] The advancement of productive forces reduces the labour time necessary for the production and reproduction of labour-power. The socially necessary labour time can be reduced by increasing productiveness of labour in the branches of industry producing the means of consumption and/or the branches providing the constant capital for the production of means of consumption. The relative surplus in production, indicating the growth of productivity through technical progress and hence the decrease in the socially necessary labour time, becomes "the motorforce" of capital accumulation (Weeks 1976: 58).[12] Nevertheless, competition, inherent in the expanded reproduction of capitalism across the world, determines the movement of capital, which fosters or delays technical advancement, efficiency, and productivity, and thus brings about uneven development across industries and regions of capitalist countries (Weeks 1997, 2001). This book defines late development in relation to U&CD while drawing upon and reinterpreting articulation and dependency. In this regard, late development indicates the "amalgam of archaic with more contemporary forms", including

---

11   Marx (1992c: 425–426) underlined such a contradiction.
      In the social production of their existence, men inevitably enter into definite relations … namely relations of production appropriate to a given stage in the development of their material forces of production … No social order is ever destroyed before all the productive forces for which it is sufficient have been developed, and new superior relations of production never replace older ones before the material conditions for their existence have matured within the framework of the old society.
12   The rate of surplus value can be increased by either lengthening the working day and/or intensifying work, or by reducing the socially necessary labour time within a given working day. The former indicates the production of absolute surplus value, whereas the latter indicates the production of relative surplus value (Saad-Filho 2002: 48; see also Marx 1976a: 646).

articulation of capitalist and precapitalist modes of production and dependency, in a given social formation.

Social formation, which indicates the concrete totality and actual site of reproduction of social relations of production (see Wolpe 1980), underlines that a given historical entity is distinctive not only from other contemporary societies but also from "its own past, by virtue of the mode of production dominant in it" (Althusser 2014: 19). The mode of production is "a theoretical concept ... that is never to be found in reality in its 'full' or 'pure' form" (Ayubi 2009: 39).[13] The capitalist mode of production can integrate diverse—including past—forms of exploitation and organisation of labour to produce surplus value. In this sense, social formation indicates "the real system that presumably emerges from and clusters around a specific mode of production ... or a number of 'articulated' modes ..., including the class configuration and other organisations and associations to which such a mode may give rise" (Ayubi 2009: 40). Most significantly, precapitalist forms and relations can be articulated under the domination of capitalist relations of production, indicating backwardness in a given late-developing social formation, where contradictions are resolved on the basis of class relations (Foster-Carter 1978: 51).

The characterisation of late developers with dependency further enables us to explain how certain peripheries, particularly Turkey, could avoid formal colonialism but not dependency on foreign capital in the nineteenth and twentieth centuries.[14] Dependency refers to the conditioning of economies in peripheries by the internationalisation and the expansion of foreign capitals of advanced economies, during which the interests of periphery capital and foreign capital confront and harmonise in a way that responds and corresponds to the interests of dominant foreign capital. Dependency, therefore, denotes the primacy of foreign capital to determine economic relations, particularly patterns of capital accumulation,[15] and hence political forms, in the

---

13   This book accepts the mode of production as the social organisation of relations of production and reproduction (Wright 1980: 325–329).
14   This book refrains from dependency theory even though it utilises the notion of dependency. Dependency theory focuses on the sphere of circulation/exchange and redistribution of value among countries in its attempt to explain the polarisation of the world economy between advanced capitalist countries and peripheries, and underdevelopment in peripheries as a feature of the world capitalist system. Contrary to dependency theory, this book focuses on the sphere of production and class relations reproduced on a world scale (Weeks 1981; Weeks and Dore 1979).
15   Any pattern of capital accumulation is based on particular "economic 'growth model[s]'" and "various extra-economic preconditions" unifying financial, commercial, and industrial capital under the hegemony of one capital fraction (Jessop 1983: 91).

peripheries. On the one hand, this relation of domination between foreign and domestic capital is an "apparently symbiotic relationship" that enables domestic capital to expand its relative autonomy vis-à-vis foreign capital and undertake particular interests, to a certain extent, in contradistinction with foreign capital (Alavi 1982: 174). On the other hand, the primacy of foreign capital can delay the adoption of technical progress as a result of capital's drive for profits (Weeks 1977, 2001). Therefore, the domestic capital accumulation in a late-developing social formation can continue to rely on the production of absolute surplus value, which indicates the primitive state of capitalist social relations (see Weeks 1985: 418–419).

3.2   Late Development in Peripheries

The integration of peripheries into the world capitalist system and the development of capitalist relations in peripheries can be periodised in accordance with the expansion and internationalisation of different circuits of capital and patterns of capital accumulation (Bina and Yaghmaian 1990; Öztürk 2006; Palloix 1974; Weeks 1985; Yılmaz and Yılmaz 2018).[16] This periodisation is important to discuss concrete sociohistorical manifestations of unevenness pertaining to class configurations and state–military–society relations in Turkey. The internationalisation of capital denotes the expansion of capital beyond national borders to appropriate more surplus value for the reallocation of money, obtained through the selling of commodities, to new production when new production within the national borders is unprofitable (Palloix 1977). The internationalisation of capital takes the form of expansion of the circuits of commodity, money, and productive capital. Different phases of internationalisation are dominated by different circuits, shaping the patterns of international competition and entailing "different modalities of uneven development, competition, and interdependence" (Albo 2004: 95).[17]

In the context of Turkey, the uneven expansion of capitalism marked the transition to capitalism between the seventeenth and eighteenth centuries, and the consolidation of capitalism at the point of no return in the nineteenth

---

16 During its basic circuit, industrial capital takes the forms of money capital and commodity capital in the circulation sphere, and the form of productive capital in the production sphere. In accordance with the social division of labour, money capital and commodity capital can assume independent forms, namely, financial capital and commercial capital respectively (Marx 1991: 379–380; Marx 1992a: 133).

17 The internationalisation of different circuits of capital is a continuous and intertwined process. The sphere of circulation derives from the sphere of production, even though the periodisation of capitalism by the forms of capital export accepts a criterion on the basis of the sphere of circulation (Weeks 1985: 423–424).

century. Therefore, this book particularly focuses on the nineteenth and early twentieth centuries to later discuss the emergence of the Turkish military as the guardian of the Republican state. In the nineteenth century, the internationalisation of commercial capital transformed peripheral countries into markets where manufactured commodities were to be sold, and where suppliers of raw material and agricultural products to be used in home production lines were located. The internationalisation of commercial capital integrated peripheral countries into the world capitalist system through free trade and liberal economic policies. Commercial capital accumulation and accumulation based on agricultural production remained the dominant pattern in peripheral countries. Nevertheless, the crises of commercial capital accumulation, such as the Depression of 1873 (Beaud 1984: 117–119), compelled peripheries to undertake measures aimed at industrial capital accumulation, which remained limited in extent (Yılmaz and Yılmaz 2018: 154–155).

By the late nineteenth century, the world capitalist system transformed into the stage of imperialism, "the monopolist stage of capitalism" (Lenin 1974: 266),[18] during which finance capital dominated home and international markets as a social, economic, and political force. Finance capital has assumed different configurations of capital associations in divergent sociohistorical formations. This book approaches finance capital as a power bloc,[19] formed with "the integration of the circuits of money capital, productive capital, and commodity capital under the conditions of monopolisation and internationalisation of capital by means of a series of links and relationships between individual capitals" (Overbeek 1980: 102).[20] In this regard, beginning in the late nineteenth century, the capitalist states representing the expansionist interests of finance capital engaged in economic and geopolitical rivalries and the

---

18   Competition and monopolisation are two intertwined contradictions inherent in capitalism. Competition leads to monopolisation in the pursuit of surplus value but still remains in contradistinction with monopolisation. The process of capital accumulation brings about the "expropriation of capitalist by capitalist, transformation of many small into few large capitals" (Marx 1976a: 777). In this sense, capitalism is "competitive *and* monopolistic" (Beaud 1984: 42).
19   This book utilises the term power bloc to indicate an arena of alliance of capital fractions (Poulantzas 1978: 141).
20   Even though Hilferding (1981) originally conceptualised finance capital, he underlined the primacy of financial capital, as was the case in Germany. As this book will later discuss, productive capital gained its primacy earlier than financial capital in the case of Turkey (Fuat Ercan in Öztürk 2008: 123).

peripheries were dominated and subordinated in the process of the expansion of capital accumulation on a world scale (see Kiely 2010).[21]

The internationalisation of finance capital beginning in the nineteenth century has had a transformative impact on a given late-developing social formation. Beginning in the late nineteenth century, the internationalisation of financial capital enhanced the integration of peripheries into the world capitalist system through debt and credit. This was merged to a certain extent with the dawn of the internationalisation of productive capital, the expansion of which took place mainly in the field of infrastructure, particularly construction and the operation of railways (Sönmez 2005: 28–29). This process was complemented with foreign credits provided by imperialist countries whose productive capital was in the process of expansion. Productive capital's internationalisation primarily through investments in infrastructure rather than manufacturing demonstrated its subordination to the expansion of commercial capital in the late nineteenth and early twentieth centuries.

The internationalisation of productive capital became the dominant circuit in the aftermath of the Second World War, and its expansion in peripheries can be divided into two stages, namely, import-substitution industrialisation (ISI) and export-oriented industrialisation (EOI) (Yaghmaian 1990). Between the late 1940s and late 1970s, peripheries were integrated into the world capitalist system through the globalisation of production and the implementation of ISI policies at home. Productive capital of the advanced capitalist countries expanded to peripheries through partnerships with domestic capital, engaging in the production of nondurable and durable consumer goods, relatively simple industrial machinery, and intermediate goods for the domestic market. Productive capital in the process of internationalisation assumed the forms of commodity capital (intermediate and capital goods) and money capital (foreign credit and aid) aimed at manufacturing.[22] In this regard, the industrial capital accumulation in peripheral countries depended on foreign capital during the period of ISI.

---

21 The differentiation between colonialism and imperialism in relation to capitalism is important for the acceptance of Turkey as a periphery and part of the Global South. Colonialism remains limited to political domination for economic exploitation often through territorial conquest, whereas imperialism encompasses the exercise of political and economic domination not necessarily through direct conquest, but also through influence, including dependency (Gallissot 1999: 189).

22 The circuit of productive capital is "the circuit of industrial capital viewed from a particular perspective ... [and] along the way, capital passes through all three forms" (Bryan 1995: 427).

Export-led industrialisation beginning in the 1980s can be regarded as a response to the crisis of ISI and the transition to neoliberalism based on the free movement of capital and unification of the global market. The integration of peripheries with the world system deepened with the liberalisation of national economies and foreign trade. The expansion of productive capital in peripheries assumed the form of money capital (foreign credit and aid) and productive capital (foreign direct investment). On the one hand, this process continued the dependency of peripheral industrial capital accumulation on foreign capital. On the other hand, it brought about the formation and internationalisation of peripheral finance capital, particularly under the primacy of commodity capital in the form export of nondurable and durable goods, in certain late developers, significantly Turkey. This book considers peripheral finance capital which is in the process of internationalisation as internal capital. Internal capital indicates a particular fraction of capital that retains a basis for capital accumulation in a given social formation and abroad through organic and often dependent relations with foreign capital (Poulantzas 1976a: 23). Internal capital can undertake particular interests that challenge the interests of foreign capital to a certain extent during the process of internationalisation (Luce 2015: 29).

Beginning in the 1990s, peripheries were integrated with the global capitalist system through financial liberalisation and the advancement of globalisation through enhanced financial mechanisms, especially stock exchange, money markets, and derivatives markets, corresponding to the primacy of financial capital. This book borrows from Fine's (2014) conceptualisation of financialisation as the restructuring of capital accumulation that maintains the intensive and extensive accumulation of fictitious (interest-bearing) capital.[23] In this regard, the internationalisation of production and productive capital has advanced the mobility of money and commodity capitals, and the internationalisation of circulation in return has accelerated the internationalisation of production (Öztürk 2006: 295). This process has had a huge impact on the internationalisation of internal capital, particularly that of Turkey, through various mechanisms, including financial inflows and outflows, mergers and acquisitions, joint ventures, and licence agreements.

---

23   This understanding essentially underlines the unity of spheres of production, circulation, and distribution as the basis of capital accumulation to examine the apparently growing asymmetry between the spheres of production and circulation (finance). Therefore, it contrasts with Lapavitsas's (2013) approach to financialisation as the rapid growth of circulation, compared to production, where the sphere of circulation is conceived as an autonomous field.

In the 2000s and 2010s, the globalisation of production and the expansion of internal capital has compelled peripheral capital in certain late developers, significantly Turkey, to assume three main fractions, namely, national, international, and transnational capital. These three capital fractions indicate the integration of each into the stages of production, realisation, and valorisation (Avcı 2022: 8).[24] The national capital fraction operates in one single social formation and produces for the national market. The international capital fraction has a national productive base and produces for the international markets, operating in more than one social formation. The transnational capital fraction operates in different social formations and engages in production relations in different countries, extending the flow and scale of capital. These three capital fractions further indicate differing compositions of capital as well as operations in capital-intensive and labour-intensive sectors, implying the production of relative surplus value production and absolute surplus value respectively.

3.3 Late Development and the Capitalist State and Military

The capitalist state and its military should be conceptualised in relation to late development to understand military interventions as sociohistorical particularities arising from late development in Turkey.[25] This book accepts the state as a form of political organisation that is a "specific material condensation of a relationship of forces among classes and class fractions" (Poulantzas 2000: 129). Different patterns of capital accumulation and hence class alignments manifest different forms of state. The form of the state can be examined "concretely only in [its] combination with forms of [political] regime" (Poulantzas 1978: 317), indicating the nature of legitimate political authority, and its rules and norms. It also depends on the specific relations between dominant classes and class fractions since it is determined by "the concrete articulation of the branches of the repressive ... and ideological state apparatuses", manifesting the crystallisation of "the power relations within the power bloc" (Poulantzas 1976a: 98). The organisation of the military and its relations with

---

24 The national, international, and transnational fractions of capital denote the stages in capital accumulation at which each capital fraction is integrated. The process of capital accumulation consists of three stages: production, involving the extraction and appropriation of surplus value; realisation, involving the transformation of commodities into money through exchange; and valorisation, involving the increase in value through the application of labour in production (Marx 1992a: 108–180). Therefore, this conceptualisation highlights the spatial scale rather than the location of ownership of the firms.

25 The capitalist state arguably mainly consists of the military, since "the superiority of physical force is the decisive factor in social domination" (Liebknecht 1917: 3).

various social classes and their representative civilian governments become a response to and a result of the changes in social, economic, and political structures and processes, which should be discussed in relation to the forms of states and regimes.

The capitalist state manifests class antagonisms and enjoys relative autonomy—whose limits are determined by capitalist relations—vis-à-vis social classes while safeguarding capitalist relations. In this way, the capitalist state can pave the way for changes in economic relations and arrange short-term compromises between and among dominant and subordinate classes while maintaining the long-term interests of dominant classes. By fostering capital–capital and labour–capital contradictions, the expansion of foreign finance capital compels the state apparatus of late developer to be restructured to "take charge of the interest of the dominant imperialist capital in its development within the 'national' social formation" (Poulantzas 1976a: 73). The formation and internationalisation of internal capital under the conditions of dependency further compels the state apparatus of a late developer to internalise the interests of foreign capital as well as internal capital.

The military can be broadly considered as a repressive and coercive state apparatus, whose fundamental role is the reproduction of capitalist social order and class domination. Since the reproduction of capitalist social order is only possible through capital accumulation, the military's main role is to safeguard particular pattern(s) of capital accumulation while maintaining its relative autonomy vis-à-vis social classes (Poulantzas 1973: 40). The pattern(s) of capital accumulation are sustained through hegemony (Jessop 1983), which indicates the organisation of various classes under the political, intellectual, and moral leadership of a particular class or class fraction through coercion and consent. The consolidation of hegemony denotes the formation of a power bloc, which is an alliance of dominant classes, bureaucracy, and executive power under the hegemony of a capital fraction. The crisis in the pattern of capital accumulation that threatens the reproduction of capitalist relations indicates a hegemonic crisis, which requires the transition to a new pattern of capital accumulation through the restructuring of class relations.

A hegemonic crisis can lead to the prolonged failure of the restructuring of a power bloc and the incapacity of all capital fractions to rule, particularly in late developers, due to the devastating impact of the crisis on subordinate classes arising from unevenness,[26] and its impetus to exhaust social classes with

---

26 Unevenness inherent in world capitalism often displaces crisis by "offload[ing] the worst impacts onto those outside the core" (Hanieh 2009: 61).

fierce struggle. The military, representing "the unity of the people" (Poulantzas 1978: 164) and controlling the means of coercion, can intervene in politics as an intermediary to restructure the pattern of capital accumulation and class relations in the last instance. Any military intervention needs to obtain the consent of certain classes and class fractions and coerce the opposing classes and class fractions in order to succeed. Although a military intervention disrupts the established—arguably rather liberal—political order that represents bourgeois domination, it obtains the consent of certain bourgeois fractions.[27] In this regard, military intervention becomes a sociohistorical particularity pertaining to late development.

The place of the military in class structure remains provisional and fragile since the military can be regarded as an order (*Stande*) differentiated from other social classes (Marx 1977a: 50), or a special social category (Poulantzas 1976a: 185). Despite being a repressive and coercive state apparatus, the military itself is not monolithic. Military officers do not own the means of production and sell their labour in exchange for a wage, and thus the interests of the lower and middle ranks tend to converge with those of the subordinate classes.[28] The higher ranks have the authority to make decisions in the name of the capitalist state, and thus they act on the behalf of the dominant classes. This material differentiation constitutes the basis of the emergence of cleavages among and between the upper ranks and the middle and lower ranks in times of hegemonic crises, despite the chain of command. It also constitutes the basic characteristic of any military intervention, whether it is progressive or regressive.[29] In this way, this book examines whether military interventions pioneered by the lower and middle ranks or by the upper ranks broaden and deepen or curtail economic, political, and legal channels through which subordinate classes fight against dominant classes in the context of late development.

---

27 The bourgeoisie indeed agrees that "in order to preserve its social power intact, its political power must be broken" (Marx 1979: 143).
28 See Savran and Tonak (1999) for a discussion on unproductive labour in relation to the reproduction of capitalist social order.
29 There is an immediate necessity to discuss the role of military intervention in its sociohistorical context. In this regard, any military intervention can be progressive or regressive depending on which classes it rests on, the struggles and conditions of subordinate classes, and economic, social, and political relations and forms in that particular historical context (see Marx 1976b).

4   The State, the Military, and Classes in Turkey: an Overview of the Book

Chapter 2 explores the emergence of the military as the guardian of secular modernisation in the late Ottoman and early Republican eras between the nineteenth and early twentieth centuries, during which the capitalist mode of production was consolidated in Turkey. First, it examines the political economy of modernisation of the military, beginning in the eighteenth century, by discussing the uneven and sporadic expansion of capitalist relations in the Ottoman Empire, beginning in the seventeenth century. Second, it discusses the revolution of 1908 in relation to the changing class configuration, where the Muslim bourgeoisie and landlords emerged as prominent classes in the late nineteenth and early twentieth centuries, when the dependent integration of Turkey into the world capitalist system was consolidated. Third, it focuses on the revolution of 1923, during which the military emerged as the subject and object of secular modernisation and hence the guardian of the secular Republican state under the conditions of market-oriented agricultural production (1923–1929) and limited import-substitution industrialisation (from 1929 until the late 1930s).

Chapter 3 explores the institutionalisation of the military's guardianship role following the coup of 1960. First, it examines the state-party regime under the CHP and its dissolution through the transition to multiparty politics in accordance with the dependent integration of Turkey into the world capitalist system during and after the Second World War. Second, it analyses the rise and fall of the hegemony of the DP in relation to the integration of Turkey with the world capitalist system under the hegemony of the United States, as well as the consolidation and crisis of commercial accumulation based on agricultural production. Third, it discusses the coup of 1960 and economic, political, and juridical structures that institutionalised the guardianship of the military in relation to class relations and the transition to import-substitution industrialisation.

Chapter 4 explores the transformation of the military's guardianship role following the coup of 1980 under the conditions of the transition to neoliberalism. First, it discusses the hegemonic crisis of the late 1960s that impacted the CHP and the AP and brought about the memorandum of 1971. Second, it analyses the prolonged hegemonic crisis of the 1970s in relation to the rise of the working classes, the formation of internal finance capital, and the crisis of import-substitution industrialisation. Third, it focuses on the transformation of the military's guardianship role in relation to the transition to export-oriented industrialisation and neoliberalism under the junta of 1980 and its arguable heir *Anavatan Partisi* (Motherland Party, ANAP), both of which articulated Islamic symbols and references to the state ideology.

Chapter 5 explores the memorandum of 28 February 1997 as a response to the prolonged hegemonic crisis of the 1990s and a restoration project to moderate rising political Islam/Islamism. First, it analyses the rise of Islamic capital with a particular focus on the financial liberalisation of the 1990s. Second, it examines the rise of *Milli Görüş* and the RP in relation to the economic, social, and political crises of the 1990s, which were again connected to the financial liberalisation of the decade under the dynamics of unevenness and dependency. Third, it discusses the memorandum of 1997 as an attempt at fine-tuning and domesticating political Islam so that it could not challenge Western hegemony.

Chapter 6 explores the curtailment of the military's guardianship role and the arguable submission of the military to civilian authority in relation to the transformation of the state and the reorganisation of class relations under the AKP. After having discussed the rise of the AKP in relation to the economic crisis of 2001, it examines the AKP's hegemonic project of conservative democracy based on neoliberalism, Islamism, and populism. Second, it focuses on the AKP's aim and failure to maintain the transition to capital-intensive and relative surplus value production in two periods: between 2002 and 2007, when the IMF played a supervisory role; and between 2008 and 2013, when the AKP resorted to measures to postpone crisis dynamics. Third, it examines the so-called e-memorandum of 2007, the Ergenekon and the Sledgehammer (*Balyoz*) trials, and the constitutional amendments of 2010 to discuss the authoritarian transformation of the state apparatus in which the higher ranks of the military and the AKP maintained an agreement.

Chapter 7 explores the transition to an exceptional form of state, particularly the fascist state and regime, under the AKP between the early 2010s and 2018, during which the military continued to play a significant role under the authority of the executive. First, it examines the emergence of indications of an economic crisis, the rise of resistance against neoliberal Islamism, and the crisis of the ruling de facto coalition between the AKP and the Gülen congregation as the processes that promoted the transition to the exceptional state. Second, it analyses the suspension of electoral principles in 2015, the state of emergency in the aftermath of the abortive coup in 2016, and the transition to presidentialism as processes that characterised the exceptional state with fascism. Third, it focuses on the transformation and submission of the military to the authority of the executive.

Chapter 8 offers concluding remarks and a comprehensive overview of the main arguments presented in this book related to state–military–society relations in Turkey in the context of late development. The concluding remarks focus on and relate the current crisis of fascism in Turkey to the currency crisis of 2018–2019 and the complementary political and state crisis under the AKP. In this regard, the concluding remarks offer possibilities for future research as well as opportunities to confront the true nature of the exceptional state and regime currently being restored by the AKP.

CHAPTER 2

The Revolutions of 1908 and 1923, and the State and the Military in Turkey

> Have these gentlemen ever seen a revolution? A revolution is certainly the most authoritarian thing there is; it is the act whereby one part of the population imposes its will upon the other part by means of rifles, bayonets and cannon—authoritarian means, if such there be at all; and if the victorious party does not want to have fought in vain, it must maintain this rule by means of the terror which its arms inspire in the reactionaries.
> FRIEDRICH ENGELS (1988 [1873])

∴

This chapter discusses the emergence of the military as guardian in relation to the late development of social formation in Turkey. The roots of the Turkish military's political role are to be found in the late Ottoman era of the nineteenth and early twentieth centuries as well as the early Republican era, when the capitalist relations of production became dominant in Turkey. For this reason, it approaches Turkey as a late-developing country whose social formation was shaped in accordance with the unevenness that characterises the world capitalist system. It examines Ottoman and Republican state–military–society relations in accordance with the dependent integration of Turkey into the world capitalist system under the dynamics of unevenness and dependency. In this way, it approaches the guardianship role of the military in Turkey as a particular sociohistorical form pertaining to Turkey's late development.

1 Late Development and Social Formation in Turkey: the Political Economy of the Late Ottoman Modernisation

During the seventeenth and eighteenth centuries, the Ottoman Empire was characterised by the uneven expansion of capitalist relations.[1] Geopolitical accumulation based on territorial expansion was interrupted as a result of military defeats, the commercialisation of agriculture was limited to the hinterlands of export, fiscal precarity hampered industrialism, the traditional guild system persisted, and the *âyan* (wealthy local notables) were institutionalised through usury and mercantilism (Nişancıoğlu 2013: 177–184). The social, economic, and political turmoil of the seventeenth and eighteenth centuries further manifested this prolonged and uneven transition to capitalism. This turmoil became visible through decentralisation, since the attempt to integrate the *âyan* into the administrative apparatus through their appointment as tax collectors and governors not only failed but further enhanced their power, by which the *âyan* also had access to means of violence and standing troops (Kasaba 1988: 15). This political and military decentralisation inevitably threatened the legitimate authority of the Sublime Porte (*Bâb-ı Âli*). Therefore, Ottoman modernisation in the late eighteenth century focused on centralisation, particularly the formation of a modern military as a centralised means of violence,[2] to reinstate the power of the monarch, the Sultan-Caliph.

During the nineteenth century, by which time the development of capitalist relations had reached the point of no return in Turkey, inter-imperialist economic and geopolitical rivalry combined with unevenness compelled the Ottoman Empire to become a semi-colony (Ahmad 2008b; Timur 1998), particularly of Britain, France, Imperial Russia, and Prussia (later Germany). The understanding of Turkey as a semi-colony demonstrates that the Ottoman

---

1 There is a wide array of approaches to examine the Ottoman land regime, namely, the tributary mode of production (Amin 1991; Haldon 1993), the Asiatic mode of production (Divitçioğlu 1981; İslamoğlu and Keyder 1977), and the feudal mode of production (Berktay 1987; Boran 1962; Oyan 1998). The Ottoman land regime (*dirlik*) was based on agricultural production and geopolitical accumulation through territorial expansion. In this regard, Ottoman tax farming (*tımar* and later *iltizam*) served to safeguard the hierarchy of property rights over lands, and the inseparable and hereditary linking of peasants to public (*miri*) lands (Uysal 2016: 66–70). Therefore, this book is inclined to characterise the Ottoman land regime with the feudal mode of production (Oyan 2016: 177–178; see also Hilton et al. 1978). Since an extensive discussion of feudalism is beyond its scope, this book prefers to use the term precapitalist in order to consistently and comprehensively characterise the Ottoman social formation.

2 See Uysal (2016: 92–94) on the modernisation of the military in the form of centralisation under the hegemony of Britain and France.

Empire maintained formal independence but could not avoid dependency on and hence domination by the advanced capitalist European countries. Free trade, which was institutionalised through the abolition of the Janissaries in 1826 and the signing of free trade agreements beginning in 1838, played a key role regarding the peripheralisation of the Ottoman economy. Dependency was concretised with the export of agricultural products, such as cotton, silk, and opium, in exchange for the import of manufactured goods, such as textiles made from cotton and wool, and agricultural and other machinery (Kasaba 1988: 47). Dependency through free trade was complemented by the capitulations regime, which indicated economic, political, and judicial privileges that led to the deterioration of the Ottoman economy beginning in the eighteenth century. For example, European merchants paid customs duties at the lowest levels, in many cases paying less than local merchants (Pamuk 2018: 78).

By the late nineteenth century, Ottoman dependency on European capital was clear. The Ottomans attracted funds and direct investments in the production and extraction of primary commodities, such as agriculture and mining, and in infrastructure, such as railroads and ports, to facilitate the marketisation of primary commodities (Pamuk 1978: 92). Meanwhile, the Ottomans began to experience difficulties in repaying foreign debts from the mid-nineteenth century. In 1856, the Ottoman Bank was established under the ownership and control of British capital, with French and Austrian capital later joining. Thus, the Bank served as an intermediary between Ottoman debt and foreign capital (Marois 2012: 45). In 1881, the Ottoman Public Debt Administration (*Düyun-u Umumiye*) was established, allowing a consortium of foreign creditors to supervise revenues, and hence transferring fiscal autonomy and the Ottoman economy to European capital and states. The Debt Administration further attracted additional European capital to invest in railroads, ports, and public utilities (Quataert 2005: 72). For instance, the Régie Company, which was established under the Debt Administration with the support of a consortium of European banks, was one of the biggest foreign investments (Aytekin 2015: 46).

The peripheralisation of the Ottoman Empire was spatially reproduced in the form of the uneven development of capitalist relations in the domestic sphere. During the nineteenth century, the Ottoman Empire largely remained an agrarian society, and the majority of agricultural production remained subsistence agriculture. Nonetheless, the commercialisation and marketisation of agriculture in the hinterland ports of export resulted in the rise of private property rights on land and commercial capital accumulation particularly in southern Anatolia, the coastland of western Anatolia, Thrace, Macedonia, and Thessaly (Kasaba 1988: 26). The Ottoman state apparatus promoted the integration of agriculture with the world market through the establishment of Ziraat Bank, which provided agricultural credits and thus financed agricultural reform in competition with the Ottoman Bank (Hanioğlu 2008a: 136). Precapitalist forms of industrial activity, particularly rural household production and crafts-based urban workshops, declined in competition with mass-produced European manufactures. However, the traditional Ottoman industries, significantly textiles, soon adopted capitalist forms of exploitation, such as the putting-out system and the use of female labour as cheap labour. For instance, workshops in Bursa, Aleppo, and Damascus employed mainly women and children beginning in the mid-nineteenth century (Akkaya 2002a: 132). The decline of the control and power of guilds brought about the development of proto-industrialisation in rural areas of eastern Bulgaria and Tokat (Aytekin 2015: 45). By the late nineteenth century, manufacturing and industry remained remarkable mainly in Istanbul, western Anatolia, the Samsun-Trabzon coastal area, southeastern Anatolia and northern Syria, Damascus, Salonica, and Macedonia (Quataert 2002: 1).

The Ottoman modernisation of the nineteenth century, particularly the *Tanzimat* (Reorganisation) reforms initiated with the declaration of the Rescript of the Rose Chamber (*Hatt-ı Şerif-i Gülhane*) in 1839 during the reign of Abdülmecid I, constituted a significant contribution to the consolidation of capitalist relations. The Rescript sought to transform the political and juridical structures in order to correspond to capitalist relations by safeguarding private property through state guarantee and recognising several fundamental rights and freedoms (Gözler 2000: 30–34). Private property on land was further consolidated with the abolition of confiscation (in cases of unjust enrichment, *müsadere*), and the enactment of the Land Code of 1858 which eased the inheritance, purchase and sale, and mortgaging of lands (Köymen 2007: 69–70). As a result, 70 per cent of all cultivable land became private property (*mülk*) by 1869 (Pamuk 1987: 91). In 1867, the ownership of land by foreign capital for agricultural production was legalised (Quataert 2005: 134). The *Tanzimat* reforms further aimed to establish a modern state and military. The Ottoman state was based on the principle of the unity between religion and state (*din-u devlet*) (Berkes 1998: 9–10), which maintained Islam as an extra-economic mechanism of precapitalist appropriation of surplus, and the Ottoman state as a monarchy ruled by the Sultan-Caliph. The Rescript and *Tanzimat* constituted important but hesitant attempts towards the emergence of a modern state, whose legitimate political authority and rules and norms were to be determined in worldly terms to correspond to capitalist relations. Most significantly, the Rescript hinted at the idea of a modern nation-state, presenting military service as "a binding duty for the protection of the fatherland" (Çöklü 2014: 25). Moreover, military officer-training facilities were combined, and professional and modern military schools emerged through the establishment of the War College in 1846 (Hurewitz 1968: 151).

During the reign of Abdülhamid II, the Constitution of 1876 determined the relationship between state authority and the fundamental rights and freedoms of subjects, and between the executive and legislative branches (Gözler 2000: 42–56). Most significantly, it established the constitutional monarchy by introducing a bicameral system consisting of the Chamber of Deputies and the Senate. The members of the Senate, which was the upper house, were appointed by the Sultan-Caliph, and their background was typically the civilian-military bureaucracy, while rural notables were generally elected to and represented in the Chamber (Akşin 1988: 154–155). Nonetheless, the Constitution limited the Chamber's legislative power by locating it in third place after the Sultan-Caliph and the Senate. The members of the Cabinet were also appointed by the Sultan-Caliph, to whom they were accountable (Kansu 1997: 1–2). Moreover, the Constitution accepted all Ottoman subjects as equal before the law, except in situations pertaining to religious and sectarian issues. Combined with the introduction of a two-house system, this article can be regarded as a remarkable but inadequate step that could "break down the framework of Turkish society and create a new order of things out of its ruins" (Marx 1980: 71). Nevertheless, the Constitution granted the Sultan-Caliph discretionary competence over the functioning of the Chamber. In 1878, Abdülhamid II did not assemble the Chamber, using the Russo-Turkish War of 1877–1878 as a pretext. This marked the end of the first era of the constitutional monarchy, which was soon followed by Abdülhamid II's despotism—often referred to as the Hamidian regime—beginning in 1881 (Ahmad 2003: 42).

The reign of Abdülhamid II enhanced the dynamics of unevenness and dependency regarding the consolidation of capitalist relations. During the Hamidian regime, the Ottoman Empire was submitted to the hegemony of Germany through the modernisation of the Ottoman military under German (previously Prussian) influence, as well as through economic relations, particularly trade, credit, and the construction of railways (Timur 1998: 329–332). Nonetheless, the modernisation of the civil-military bureaucracy had already led to the emergence of lower- and middle-ranking military officers and civil servants intellectually and politically equipped with modern notions of state and citizenship that emerged with the Enlightenment in Europe. The *mektepli* (educated) factions of the Ottoman civil-military bureaucracy and intelligentsia, who were exiled predominantly in Geneva, Paris, and Egypt and could only reach their peers in the Empire subject to the Sublime Porte's censorship and widespread illiteracy, constituted the prominent members of the Young Turks

(*Jön/Genç Türkler*) (Hanioğlu 2001: 3). The same Young Turks, who provided the strongest intellectual and political opposition to the Hamidian regime, were to organise and lead a bourgeois revolution only a decade later.

2   The Revolution of 1908 and the Military

2.1   *The State and Class Relations in the Twentieth-Century Ottoman Empire*

At the beginning of the twentieth century, the Ottoman Empire was characterised by an "amalgam of archaic with more contemporary forms". Regarding classes and class relations, the integration of domestic agriculture with the world market, particularly the marketisation of cotton and tobacco, advanced land tenure and made the ownership of large-scale land widespread in the Empire. Nonetheless, dependency was reproduced in rural areas through the expansion of foreign capital in Ottoman agriculture. Most significantly, the English bourgeoisie owned remarkable areas of land in Izmir and Çukurova (Köymen 2007: 70–71).

Combined with the transformation of the *âyan*, the rise of land ownership brought about the rise of landlords (*ağa*).[3] Landlords, whose members belonged to Muslim and non-Muslim communities, especially Greek and Armenian, owned great areas of land through inheritance, purchase, and merchandise and usury. Since large-scale land ownership was limited to certain regions integrated with the world market, sharecropping and tenancy enabled the persistence of great numbers of smallholders alongside landlords during the consolidation of the capitalist mode of production. The cases of sharecropping and tenancy, where smallholders were both landowners and operators, brought about petty commodity production and did not necessarily result in exploitation and domination. However, distribution of appropriated surplus product in petty commodity production was determined with traditions and customs often embedded in Islam and favoured landlords (Boratav 1980: 21–23). Sharecropping and tenancy legitimised with extra-economic mechanisms of domination represented precapitalist remnants in rural areas that were articulated under the domination of capitalist relations, and hence constituted the basis of the precapitalist nature of landlords.

---

3   Landlords in Turkey differed from capitalist landlords in Britain, on whom Marx's (1991: 1025) examination of capitalist landowners was based, under the conditions of late development.

The integration of agriculture with the world market was related to the expansion of railways, which enabled the rapid and secure transportation of greater amounts of products. The extension of railways to western Anatolia (Izmir–Aydın–Denizli), the Balkans (Bucharest–Varna–Istanbul and Monastir–Salonica), and the Hijaz (Damascus–Medina) contributed to the unification and integration of agriculture, commerce, and industries (Uslu and Aytekin 2015: 95). Nonetheless, the proliferation of railways increased Ottoman dependency on European capital since their construction was undertaken through foreign direct investments, particularly from the British until the late nineteenth century and Germany beginning in the late nineteenth century (Pamuk 1987: 76–77).

Partly in relation to the expansion of the railways, an increasing number of urban areas in Thrace and Anatolia saw the emergence of large-scale industrial enterprises that used imported engines and machines and employed wage workers. First emerging in Istanbul, these enterprises soon spread to western and southern Anatolia, particularly Izmir and Adana, as well as parts of the Balkans, especially Salonica (Pamuk 2018: 148). Meanwhile, European capital remained the owner of the overwhelming majority of large-scale industrial enterprises, since these enterprises were established through partnerships between foreign and Ottoman capital, and the shares of Ottoman capital remained very limited (Uslu and Aytekin 2015: 97). Such Ottoman capital mainly belonged to the non-Muslim bourgeoisie since merchants, traders, and moneychangers among non-Muslim minorities, particularly Armenians, Greeks, Levantine Christians, and Jews, benefited from the *protégé* system in urban areas as well as rural areas that were integrated with the world market (Pamuk 2018: 144; Quataert 2005: 129; Saleh 2021: 215).[4] On the one hand, such partnerships between the non-Muslim bourgeoisie and European capital enabled the non-Muslim bourgeoisie to become the most prominent fraction of the big bourgeoisie. On the other hand, they bastardised the non-Muslim bourgeoisie into the form of a comprador group that represented the interests of European capital, since the non-Muslim bourgeoisie's accumulation of wealth depended on the transfer of surplus value from the Ottoman lands to European states through ownership.[5]

---

4 The non-Muslim minorities in the Ottoman Empire were inevitably divided along class lines. By the early twentieth century, the majority of workers in the large-scale industrial enterprises were also non-Muslim, mainly Greek and Armenian (Uslu and Aytekin 2015: 99).
5 As will be further discussed, this book rejects the portrayal of a national bourgeoisie as a progressive subject that undertakes industrialisation as opposed to a comprador bourgeoisie that reproduces the presence of foreign economic interests (Weeks 2012).

The social, economic, and political upheavals stemming from the advancement of capitalist relations was most significantly observed in the form of the mobilisation of subordinate classes in urban and rural areas. Until the mid-nineteenth century, workers undertook slowdowns, machine-breaking, and complaints as forms of protests. Following the miners' strike in Zonguldak in 1863, workers undertook a series of strikes between 1872 and 1880 in the face of deteriorating economic conditions (Akkaya 2002a: 137–138). Although the despotism of the Hamidian regime suppressed workers' mobilisation beginning in the 1880s, the spring and summer of 1908 saw a growing wave of workers' strikes in ports, trams and the railways, on steamship lines, in coal transportation, bakeries, and factories and railway workshops, as well as in the tobacco, glass, leather, and cement industries (Akkaya 2010: 48). Workers' mobilisation in urban areas was complemented by the mobilisation of peasants in rural areas. By the spring of 1904, peasants started to protest against their tax burden combined with the arbitrary standards imposed through tax-farming by filing official complaints and vacating lands. Between 1904 and 1905, tax rebellions broke out in western and southeastern Anatolia, particularly Izmir and Diyarbakır, and parts of the Middle East, particularly Tripoli. Between in 1906 and 1907, tax rebellions spread to the Black Sea basin, especially Kastamonu, Trabzon, Samsun, and Sinop, and eastern Anatolia, especially Van, Erzurum, and Bitlis (Kansu 1997: 29–72). In this regard, mobilisation and rebellions in urban and rural areas constituted the social basis in which the upcoming revolution of 1908 was rooted.

The last pillar of social turmoil was constituted by rebellions of the lower- and middle-ranking military officers, soldiers, and students. The rebellions broke out in Iskenderun and Skopje, and soon spread to Izmir, Yemen, Beirut, and finally Istanbul (Savran 2016: 151–152). In addition to salary payment difficulties and increasing nepotism in the military under the reign of Abdülhamid II, military officers, like soldiers and students, came from and represented peasant households. Furthermore, military officers and students who were exposed to the intellectual and technological development of Europe through Western education maintained their connections with the Young Turks, who already played a significant role in tax rebellions in the Black Sea basin and eastern Anatolia (Hanioğlu 2001: 91–123). The uprisings of military officers and students represented fragmentation and dissolution within the Ottoman state apparatus, indicating that a revolution was in sight.

In December 1907, opposition groups, including Muslim and non-Muslim associations, held the Congress of Ottoman Opposition Parties, also known as the Second Congress of the Young Turks, whose movement had transformed from an intellectual endeavour into a political organisation between 1889 and

1906, significantly under the flagship of *İttihat ve Terakki Cemiyeti* (Committee of Union and Progress, ITC). The Congress published a manifesto demanding the proclamation of a constitutional monarchy in which all Ottoman constituents were equal regarding duties and rights (Zürcher 2010: 75). While the members of the ITC were already organised in Anatolia and Thrace, and to some extent the Black Sea basin and eastern Anatolia, the ITC branch in Salonica planned and pioneered the revolution in 1908. Owing to their distance, they could avoid the Sublime Porte's surveillance, receiving the support of the rising Ottoman bourgeoisie—as industrialisation and ports characterised the region—including the non-Muslim bourgeoisie and Muslim landlords, and the Salonica ITC branch members were fully aware of the European aspirations regarding domination in Macedonia against crumbling Ottoman rule (Yerasimos 1975: 1051–1052).

The Macedonian question, which was already on the ITC's agenda due to the rise of nationalist and separatist movements and uprisings in the region, triggered the revolution of 1908. During their meeting in Reval (Tallinn) in June 1908, King Edward VII of Britain and Tsar Nicholas II of Russia promoted administrative reforms to favour the Christian population in Macedonia. This compelled the ITC to bring forward a rebellion against Abdülhamid II in July 1908 to avoid a possible Anglo-Russian intervention in Macedonia. The Unionist military officers soon formed armed bands consisting of soldiers and rural locals in close contact with Albanian, Bulgarian, Serbian, and Vlach bandits. This armed rebellion coincided with the demonstrations against Austria-Hungary, since the expansion of Austrian railways through Macedonia was considered a possible Austrian intervention (Zürcher 2010: 31–33). Similarly to the rural classes, the ITC obtained the support of the urban classes in the belief that only a constitutional regime could avert the danger of foreign intervention. On 21 July 1908, a petition demanding the restoration of the Constitution was signed by notables—including landlords and merchants—and clerics and was submitted to the Sublime Porte. On 23 July 1908, the ITC declared "liberty, equality, fraternity, and justice", the slogan of the revolution of 1908. The ITC's de facto control over provinces in Macedonia and Thrace compelled Abdülhamid II to restore the constitutional monarchy on 24 July 1908.

2.2 *The 1908 Revolution as a Bourgeois Revolution*

This book approaches the revolution of 1908 as a bourgeois revolution to discuss the significance and nature of the great transformations that took place between 1908 and 1923 (see Savran 1985; Uysal 2019a). This book defines a bourgeois revolution as a process that aims to consolidate bourgeois social and political order so that the development of capitalist relations cannot be reversed (Engels 1975; Marx 1977b; Marx and Engels 1998). In precise terms, it defines a bourgeois revolution as a political transformation (Callinicos 1989) which achieves the consolidation of a "territorially demarcated sovereign centre of capital accumulation" (Anievas 2015: 843). This understanding of a bourgeois revolution contrasts with the agent-centric approach, which is already implied in the dominant CMR literature on Turkey. The agent-centric approach highlights the weakness or even apparent lack of a national bourgeoisie in Turkey, to render the notion of a bourgeois revolution irrelevant (Hanioğlu 2008a; Keyder 1987; Zürcher 2007). While discussing the presence of a Muslim bourgeoisie as the national bourgeoisie in the Ottoman Empire,[6] this book already accepts the pioneering role of the civil-military bureaucracy during the revolutions both of 1908 and 1923. In 1908, the pioneering role of the civil-military bureaucracy organised in the ITC was already combined with the important role of the intelligentsia[7] and the petty bourgeoisie, including journalists, doctors, and lawyers, in the ITC. The organic relationship the ITC developed with urban and rural social classes by forming guerrilla forces and obtaining support of Muslim and non-Muslim communities further constituted the popular backbone of the revolution.[8] Nonetheless, the pioneering role of the lower- and middle-ranking military officers sowed the seed of the military's emergence as the guardian of modernisation.

Following its victory in the autumn 1908 election, the ITC became the driving force in maintaining capital accumulation and consolidating capitalist relations. Between 1908 and 1913, the ITC fostered capital accumulation through a liberal economy based on free trade, agricultural production for the world market, attraction of foreign investment, and limited state intervention (Boratav 2014: 25–26), all of which further advanced the peripheralisation of the Ottoman economy. To illustrate, 90 per cent of agricultural production

---

6 This book already contrasts with the agent-centric approach through its understanding that the bourgeoisie does not necessarily have to be the conscious agent of revolution (Marx 1977b: 161). The bourgeoisie can further assume non-revolutionary role by "[finding] itself in conflict with the proletariat even before being politically constituted as a class" (Marx 1976c: 332).

7 The intelligentsia, in this regard, can be considered as the organic intellectuals, indicating "the thinking and organising element of a particular fundamental social class ... by directing the ideas and aspirations of the class to which they organically belong" (Hoare and Smith 1992: 3; see also Gramsci 1992a: 5–23).

8 The support of Muslim and non-Muslim communities for the 1908 revolution can be vividly observed through the gatherings of thousands of Turks, Greeks, Armenians, Jews, and Arabs to celebrate the declaration of the constitutional monarchy (see Ahmad 2008a: 89–90; Kansu 1997: 97–114). On the alliance between the Young Turks and the Armenian opposition regarding preparation for the revolution, see also Hanioğlu (2001).

was for export, with barley, figs, opium, raisins, raw silk, raw wool, and tobacco remaining the most important agricultural exports by 1913 (Pamuk 1987: 83–85). Furthermore, railways remained one of the most significant sectors for the expansion of foreign capital. For instance, more than 80 per cent of German investment was placed in railroad construction, concentrated in Anatolia (Pamuk 1987: 79). The expansion of railways further advanced capitalist relations by integrating the Ottoman agriculture with the world market. For example, Eskişehir, Ankara, and Konya provinces in central Anatolia became important sources of barley and wheat for export (Pamuk 1987: 104).

The ITC sought to promote the accumulation of industrial capital to advance productive forces and increase levels of production and economic development. Nevertheless, the rise of nationalism in the Ottoman lands, which brought about the loss of territories in the Balkans, was combined with the comprador role of the non-Muslim bourgeoisie. This compelled the ITC to foster the transition of the small Muslim commercial bourgeoisie to an industrial bourgeoisie. The ITC, in fact, became "'the vanguard party of the Turkish bourgeoisie'" (Ahmad 2008a: 23). The outbreak of the Balkan Wars of 1912–1913 following the Turco-Italian war in Libya in 1911 enabled the ITC to mobilise economic nationalism and statism. Most significantly, the ITC enacted the Law on Industrial Promotion (1913) to provide the industrial bourgeoisie with certain privileges, such as granting concessions and permitting monopolisation (Toprak 2019: 246). The ITC already curtailed the organisation and radicalisation of the working classes by making unionisation difficult and suppressing strikes through the enactment of the Strike Law (1909) to favour capitalists (Uslu and Aytekin 2015: 117). The ITC further sought to consolidate private property rights in land by enacting the Law of Transfer of Immovable Property in 1913 (Ahmad 2008a: 79).

Beginning in 1908, the number of industrial enterprises indeed increased. The fact that more than 80 per cent of industrial enterprises remained in primitive sectors—including food, textiles, tobacco processing, flour milling, leather, wool weaving, and the production of yarn—demonstrated Turkey's uneven and dependent integration with the international division of labour (Boratav 2014: 33). Nevertheless, the ITC articulated elements of anti-imperialism and sought to abolish European hegemony over the Empire. To illustrate, the ITC sometimes supported boycotts against foreign capital, such as the boycott against Austrian goods following Austria-Hungary's annexation of Bosnia and Herzegovina. The boycott replaced the *fez* made in Austria with the Anatolian *kalpak* (Ahmad 2008a: 30–31). The outbreak of the First World War also enabled the ITC to pursue statism and economic protectionism. Most significantly, the ITC unilaterally abolished capitulations in September 1914. In

1916, the ITC regulated taxes on trade and decreased the import of goods that could be produced cheaply in the country (Toprak 1995: 38–39). In 1916, Ziraat Bank was reformed to be able to provide farmers and agriculture industry with credits, land, and animals and machines (Toprak 2019: 221). By 1918, commercial and agricultural banks were established as joint-stock companies in Anatolia, including Ankara, Aydın, Eskişehir, Kastamonu, Konya, and Manisa provinces (Ahmad 2008a: 50–51).

A bourgeois revolution indicates "the removal of backward-looking threats to [the] continued existence [of capitalism] and the overthrow of restrictions to [the] further expansion [of capitalism]" (Davidson 2005: 27). In this sense, it significantly manifests the dismantling of the precapitalist social structure and the "installation of a legal and political framework in which the free development of capitalist property relations is assured" (Jones 1977: 86). In the case of Turkey, the amendment of the Constitution of 1876 in 1909 limited the Sultan-Caliph's powers to secure the constitutional monarchy. For instance, the Sultan-Caliph could only abolish the Chamber in case of a dispute between the Chamber and the Senate after having obtained the Senate's consent and set a future election date within three months. The Chamber was to confirm trade agreements, annexation or cession of a territory, and determination of the fundamental rights and freedoms of the Ottoman subjects (Akşin 1980: 130–132). This amendment was followed by the reforming of commercial law in line with the market economy (Toprak 1995: 81). The transformation of the political and legal framework also corresponded with social transformation. Significantly, the ITC passed the Law on Compulsory Primary Education (1913), since schooling was one of the core pillars of the modern transformation of society (Timur 2012: 145).

The revolution of 1908 contributed to—but could not achieve—the complete separation of state and church and of politics and religion, which was to constitute the basis of the "perfect social revolution" in Turkey (Marx 1980: 72). Most significantly, the ITC curtailed the economic power of the *ulama* (Islamic clergy) and local religious constituents by submitting foundations (*vakıf*) under the authority of the Ministry of Finance in 1916 (Savran 2015: 50).[9] The *ulama* and local religious constituents, which later constituted religious brotherhoods and included Dervish and Sufi lodges, orders, retreats, and cells,

---

9 Certain scholars argue that the *ulama* cannot be regarded as clergy since there is no mediator between individuals and God in Islamic doctrine (Cornell 1999). However, this book considers the *ulama* as Islamic clergy since it represented religious authority, which held economic, political, and juridical political power by appropriating the revenue of the *vakıf* lands and interpreting and applying *sharia* (Berkes 1998: 15).

appropriated the revenue of *vakıf* lands. The *vakıf* lands were part of public lands, linking peasants inseparably and hereditarily to lands, and were exempt from tax and state confiscation (Oyan 2016: 120). In this way, the *ulama* and local religious constituents remained precapitalist remnants among the dominant classes. The ITC further curbed the *ulama*'s political and judicial power by abolishing the place of *Şeyhülislam* (the supreme jurist) in the Cabinet, and placing *sharia* (Islamic law) courts under the authority of the Ministry of Justice (Savran 2015: 50). Nonetheless, the ITC could not abolish the unity between religion and state. Significantly, the ITC established its own *ulama* branch, which was to publish articles in order to legitimise the constitutional monarchy (Hanioğlu 2001: 306).

Related to the previous point, the 1908 revolution could not answer the national question. While the Constitution of 1876 already contributed to the emergence of modern citizenship, accepting all Muslim and non-Muslim subjects as Ottoman, it continued to recognise Islam as the official religion of the Ottoman Empire. This prolonged the *millet* (religious communities) system, which granted cultural and social autonomy to Muslim and non-Muslim communities under their religious leaders. The rise of modern nationalism following the Enlightenment dictated the formation of a nation, which was supposed to be sovereign within a territorially demarcated space where capital accumulation was maintained. This compelled non-Muslim communities to undertake struggles for reform, autonomy, and eventually independence from the imperial system they increasingly found oppressive (Ahmad 2014: 2). The ITC's efforts at the introduction of modern citizenship either could not be implemented, such as the legislation of conscription for the Muslim and non-Muslim communities in 1914 (Timur 2012: 123), or were resisted by the non-Muslim communities, such as the Greeks' and Armenians' defence of capitulations and traditional privileges based on religion (Ahmad 2008a: 27). The ITC further resorted to Turkish nationalism in accordance with its goal to promote the national bourgeoisie, particularly enabling the Muslim bourgeoisie to expropriate and appropriate capital forcibly dispossessed from the Greeks in 1913 and the Armenians in 1915 during forced population movements (Öz 2020: 11–25).[10] This was also apparent in the ITC's populism, coined as "towards the people", aimed at the integration of the Anatolian market and the

---

10   A comprehensive discussion on forced population movements and atrocities pertaining to them, including massacres, ethnic cleansing, pogroms, and genocides, is beyond the scope of this book. Nevertheless, this book considers forced population movements in Turkey to be a form of coercive transfer of wealth from non-Muslim to Muslim communities, and hence a form of primitive accumulation that represents capital accumulation

rise of the Muslim bourgeoisie through the formation of a popular coalition of subordinate classes, Anatolian notables, petty bourgeoisie, intelligentsia, and Anatolian bourgeoisie (Haspolat 2011: 570–571). By 1918, Muslim industrialists constituted an overwhelming majority compared to the non-Muslim bourgeoisie (Hanioğlu 2008b: 98). Consequently, the First World War was to determine the national question through the dissolution of the Ottoman Empire.

2.3 The Military as the Pioneer and Guardian of the 1908 Revolution

The role of the military was significant in terms of the pioneering and safeguarding of the 1908 Revolution. Nonetheless, the military did not remain as a monolithic institution by the late nineteenth and early twentieth centuries. Ottoman modernisation brought about cleavages between the upper ranks and the middle and lower ranks, with their irreconcilable interests, since the former stood upon and represented the Ottoman *ancien régime* which the latter was determined to dissolve and replace with modernity. The 1908 Revolution was launched through the armed rebellion of Niyazi Bey, a middle-ranking Unionist military officer. The rebellion soon turned into an uprising within the Third Army in Salonica, the "most sophisticated unit" spread across Rumelia which contained "the cream of the [War College] graduates" (Turfan 2000: 66), and rapidly spread to the Second Army in Edirne. Even though the higher ranks remained loyal to Abdülhamid II, they could not send regular army units to suppress the rebellion following the Minister of War's advice on the application of the military penal code. The Anatolian reserve divisions, dispatched to Macedonia, ultimately either joined the revolutionaries or did not fire on them (Hanioğlu 2011: 180). In this regard, the declaration of constitutional monarchy was in fact a *fait accompli* mainly on the part of the Unionist military officers, as well the middle and lower ranks.

The cleavage between the upper ranks and the middle and lower ranks further extended to between the *mektepli* and the *alaylı* (unschooled, having risen through the ranks) officers. The higher ranks overwhelmingly consisted of *alaylı* officers, and their interests necessitated the protection of the *ancien régime* as the basis of their legitimate existence. Therefore, it was the middle- and lower-ranking *mektepli* officers who safeguarded the 1908 Revolution. In April 1909, the First Army in Istanbul mutinied in coalition with *alaylı* officers and Islamic theology students, promoting a national union on the basis of Islam against the Ottoman ideal. This counter-revolutionary attempt, which

by forcible dispossession in a hostile conjecture (Karataşlı and Kumral 2019; see also Marx 2018).

called for the rule of the *sharia* and the monarchy, was suppressed by the Action Army (*Hareket Ordusu*), which was mainly constituted with the Third Army and received the support of the Second Army in Salonica and units filled with volunteers (Kansu 1999: 77–125).[11] Abdülhamid II, the most notable representative of the *ancien régime*, was forced to abdicate and replaced by Mehmed V, a weaker ruler in comparison to his predecessor (Uyar 2021: 5). In this regard, the modernised factions of the middle- and lower-ranking military officers became the guardians of the bourgeois revolution.

The role of the military as the pioneer and guardian of the revolution constituted the basis of and legitimised the military's political role, which the ITC enhanced by expanding the military's autonomy. The Ministry of War (*Harbiye Nezareti*) was established in 1908, with its minister being given a place in the Cabinet, and the General Staff was submitted under the authority of the Ministry. As the Ministry was paralysed by political instability, the General Staff assumed most of its duties and became the only authority on military affairs by avoiding political control (Uyar 2021: 5).[12] Meanwhile, the Military Council (*Meclis-i Mehâmm-ı Harbiye*, later *Şûra-yı Askeri*) was established within the Ministry of War to discuss and decide on important military affairs, including promotions of higher-ranking officers (Hanioğlu 2011: 183). Nonetheless, between 1908 and 1912, the civilian wing of the ITC remained in power when it sought to maintain the compliance of the higher ranks with its aim to restructure the military. To illustrate, the ITC dictated the appointment of the fourteen highest commanders in the Ottoman army and required the military personnel in Istanbul to take an oath to "'support'" the ITC in August 1908 (Hanioğlu 2011: 183).

It became clear that the genie had been let out of the bottle when the Unionist officers raided the Sublime Porte in January 1913, using the Balkan Wars of 1912–1913 as a pretext. This raid was in fact a coup d'état which enabled the military wing of the ITC to become the controlling factor in the Ottoman political life. Mahmud Şevket Pasha, who led the Action Army into the city to suppress the counter-revolution in 1913, became Grand Vizier in January 1913; however, he was assassinated in June 1913. His assassination further enabled the ITC to resort to authoritarianism to oppress its political opposition and benefit from more room for manoeuvre, such as through the establishment of

---

11 The counter-revolution of 1909 is also known as the Incident of 31 March (see Kansu 1999: 14–16).
12 Such political instability was characterised by a prolonged period of martial law between 1909 and 1911, and the continuous succession of short-serving ministers of war (Uyar 2021: 5).

Teşkilat-ı Mahsusa (Special Organisation) as a secret intelligence service (Uslu and Aytekin 2015: 142). In 1914, Talat Pasha became the minister of the interior, Enver Pasha became the minister of war, and Cemal Pasha became the minister of the Navy (Hale 1994: 45), all of whom played the most significant roles in the Ottoman Empire's domestic and international relations during the First World War.

As the Revolution of 1908 concretised the dismantling of the Ottoman state apparatus, inevitably including the military, the restructuring of the military was in line with the aim of the revolution at modernisation. In this regard, the political role of the Unionist military officers enabled them to advance the modernisation of the military. To illustrate, the crackdown of the counter-revolution in 1909 was followed by a comprehensive purge of the higher ranks and the *alaylı* officers (Uyar 2021: 6–7). The ITC further established new schools for sergeants to replace the *alaylı* officers and implemented transparent selection processes for officers to be sent to European military academies for further education (Hanioğlu 2011: 183). Nonetheless, the ITC still promoted the modernisation of the military under the conditions of unevenness and dependency. In this regard, the ITC submitted the military particularly to the hegemony of Germany. In fact, *The Nation in Arms* (*Das Volk in Waffen*) by Colmar von der Goltz, a Prussian field marshal also known as Goltz Pasha, remained a compulsory book in military schools and an increasing number of military officers were sent to Germany for further training (Grüsshaber 2018: 11). The ITC further adopted the advice of the German military mission to the Ottoman Empire, such as improving the level of training and courses and rearming the military with modern weapons mostly imported from Germany. Meanwhile, German General Otto Liman von Sanders, the head of the German military mission, was assigned as the commanding general of the First Army in Istanbul, and the members of the Sanders Mission took over key command positions and were granted with extraordinary powers, including over strategic military decision-making (Uyar and Güvenç 2022: 92).

The most significant consequence of the military's role in politics as merged with German hegemony was the decision of the military wing of the ITC to lead the Empire to fight in the First World War on the side of the Germany–Austria–Hungary alliance in October 1914. The fact that the ITC sought to secure an alliance with Britain, Austria-Hungary, Germany, and Russia between 1913 and 1914 demonstrated that the ITC considered that the approaching Great War in Europe would result in the demise of the Empire. Further, the ITC could only secure an alliance with Germany in August 1914 since Germany anticipated favouring Austria-Hungary in the Balkans and inciting a rebellion of Muslims in the Allies' colonies (Hanioğlu 2008b: 90–91). Beginning in January 1914, the

Ottoman General Staff was transformed into "a mere field army headquarters" under the direct command of the German General Staff (Uyar and Güvenç 2022: 98).

The Ottoman Empire's defeats in the Caucasus, the Suez Canal, Syria/Palestine, and Mesopotamia were combined with the collapse of the German army, all of which compelled the ITC to resign and the Empire to surrender in October 1918. This was soon followed by the partition and occupation of Turkey by the Allies, using the Armistice of Mudros (1918) as a pretext.[13] In this sense, the First World War brought about the demise of the Empire. On the other hand, the war enabled the military wing of the ITC to pursue statist and protectionist policies that further consolidated capitalist relations between 1914 and 1918, as previously discussed. More importantly, the Ottoman demise through the Allies' invasion triggered the Turkish war of national liberation, pioneered by the modern factions of military officers, the majority of whom were previously involved with the ITC. In this regard, the bourgeois revolution of 1908 constituted the political and ideological foundation of the bourgeois revolution of 1923, which preserved and transcended its predecessor by bringing about the emergence of a modern nation-state and military.

3   The Bourgeois Revolution of 1923 and the Military

This book considers the revolution of 1923 as a bourgeois revolution that achieved the establishment of the modern nation-state as the sovereign centre of capital accumulation. In this regard, the War of Independence between 1919 and 1922 constituted the first phase of the revolution, which assumed the forms of a war of national liberation and a civil war. The establishment of the secular modern Republic in 1923 and the process of modernisation in the 1920s and the 1930s constituted the second phase of the revolution, which indicated social and political transformation.[14]

---

13   The Armistice granted the Allies "the opening of the Dardanelles and Bosphorus and secure access to the Black Sea" and "the right to occupy any strategic points in the event of a situation arising which threatens [their] security" (Hurewitz 1956: 36–37).

14   The Turkish modernisation has often been associated with laicism, as opposed to secularism, as a result of the subordination of religion to the state and the state's authority to control the clergy (Çitak 2004; Kuru 2009). This book recognises that secularism and laicism are two separate, diverse, complex, contested, and dynamic processes (Davison 2003: 333). Nonetheless, it accepts laicisation as a stage in the process of secularisation that indicates some degree of social conflict and the primacy of political factors in

3.1 The Political Economy of the War of Independence

Following the Armistice of Mudros, Anatolia and Thrace were invaded and partitioned by the Allies, particularly Britain, France, and Italy and their proxies, notably Armenians supported by France in southeastern and eastern Anatolia and Greeks supported by Britain in western Anatolia and eastern Thrace (Mango 1999: 123). The position of dominant classes regarding the partition of Turkey was ambivalent. The Sublime Porte, now represented by Vahideddin (also known as Mehmed VI) on the throne and the Grand Vizier Damad Ferid Pasha—Vahideddin's brother-in-law, appointed by him—sought to secure a foreign mandate in alliance with the Allies to retain the *ancien régime* (Kayalı 2008: 116). The big bourgeoisie in Istanbul supported the Sublime Porte since a foreign mandate was in their interest in the face of the Allies' invasion of Istanbul. *Şeyhülislam* and factions of the *ulama*, local religious constituents, and intelligentsia also supported the Sublime Porte as the *ancien régime* legitimised the continued existence of these precapitalist remnants. Even though factions of notables—including landlords and merchants—remained silent towards, if not welcomed, the French, British, and Italians in western and southwestern Anatolia between late 1918 and early 1919, the Armenian and Greek invasions clashed with the interests of notables. This was because notables had previously seized wealth and lands from the non-Muslim communities that had been deported, had fled, or had been killed during the First World War. British and French support for Greeks and Armenians indicated the imperialist aim to ally with the non-Muslim communities rather than the Muslim communities in Anatolia. To illustrate, the same factions of notables called for Italy to prevent the Greek invasion (Yerasimos 1989: 39). The position of subordinate classes was also irresolute. The actual invasion suppressed the possibility of any resistance among workers, whose more organised fractions in Istanbul and Anatolia already engaged in radical activities against foreign capital through a nationalist discourse. In rural areas, peasants and smallholders continued to be the direct object of exploitation and domination by landlords and local religious constituents rather than the Allies and their proxies.

Nevertheless, landlords and the Anatolian small commercial bourgeoisie as well as workers and peasants remained weak and not radical enough to lead a war of national liberation. To put this differently, neither notables nor subordinate classes developed a fully formed class consciousness or were organised enough to undertake a revolution. The class interests of notables clashing with

---

the course of resolution of the tension between religion and the public sphere (Uysal 2019a: 340–341; see also Baubérot 2001; Wilson 1992).

the interests of subordinate classes further curbed any radicalism. Nonetheless, the interests of the modernised factions of the civil-military bureaucracy were in complete conflict with the partition as the modern military officers and civilian bureaucrats did not have any place in an obsolete *ancien régime* armoured with colonisation (Yerasimos 1989: 22–23). Furthermore, the same modern factions retained the organisational foundation of the ITC, which remained intact despite the flight of the Unionist leaders following the end of the First World War (Ahmad 2003: 48). They also retained the Ottoman army's chain of command and continued presence in important zones in Anatolia even though the Armistice required the immediate demobilisation of the army and disposal of arms and ammunition. To illustrate, the 3rd Corps, 12th Corps, 15th Corps, and 20th Corps did not surrender, and the Sixth Army, Ninth Army, Second Army, Seventh Army, and Yıldırım Army Group transferred their arms and ammunition into the hinterlands to initiate a possible resistance (Türkmen 2001: 37–79).

For this reason, the modern civil-military bureaucracy, particularly the military officers under Kemal's (Atatürk's) leadership, emerged as the pioneers of the war of national liberation that took place between 1919 and 1922, also known as the War of Independence. Since the modern civil-military bureaucracy retained a provisional and fragile position between the bourgeoisie and the proletariat, its approach to dominant and subordinate classes as well as its radicalism remained ambivalent. On the one hand, the revolutionary military officers allied with landlords, the Anatolian small commercial bourgeoisie, and factions of the *ulama* and local religious constituents alongside intelligentsia and the petty bourgeoisie, especially lawyers and doctors. On the other hand, they mobilised and gained the support of peasants, smallholders, and workers by calling for national independence in response to the invasion. The fact that this revolutionary alliance rested on the dominant classes constituted the basis of the contradictions and limitations of the 1923 Revolution under the dynamics of unevenness and dependency.

The War of Independence further took the form of a civil war pursued against counter-revolutionary forces consisting of precapitalist remnants and comprador elements represented by the Sublime Porte. Local resistance groups, called the Defence of Rights Societies (*Müdâfaa-i Hukuk Cemiyetleri*), brought together the modernised civil-military bureaucracy, landlords, the Anatolian commercial bourgeoisie, local religious constituents, the petty bourgeoisie, and intelligentsia.[15] In April 1920, the Defence of Rights Societies were

---

15   The possibility of a foreign mandate, particularly that of the United States, which impressed the factions of intelligentsia with Woodrow Wilson's liberalism (Zürcher

unified under the Grand National Assembly (*Büyük Millet Meclisi*) in Ankara through the Constitutional Act of 1921, which unconditionally claimed sovereignty over territories in the name of the nation. The National Pact (*Misak-ı Milli*) confirmed the territories inhabited by an Ottoman Muslim majority— "united in religion, race and aim" (Zürcher 2007: 138)—as an indivisible entity, and demanded economic, financial, and judicial independence. In this way, the Assembly emerged as the de facto representative of an emerging modern nation-state, fostering the dissolution of the *ancien régime* and consolidating national sovereignty and economic integration. The War of Independence indeed contributed to the integration of the national economy as the Assembly reclaimed the authority to collect taxes by legislating for duties on import, customs, and income. The war further enabled the Assembly to mobilise substitutive mechanisms in the form of extraordinary taxes on and confiscations of food, clothing, wax and kerosene, and carriages and horses (Müderrisoğlu 1994: 37–41), all of which contributed to the financing of the war and the unification of the national economy.

The War of Independence mainly took place on four fronts, namely, the southern, eastern, and western fronts, and the internal front. The southern, eastern, and western fronts, which assumed the form of a war of national liberation, were respectively fought against France, Armenia, and Greece supported by Britain. These fronts enabled the emergence of the Ankara government as the legitimate representative of Turkey and the creation of modern Turkey as a politically independent country. Significantly, the Ankara government signed the Treaty of Moscow (Treaty of Friendship, 1921) and Treaty of Kars (1921) with the Soviet Union (Allen and Muratoff 2011: 500), and the Treaty of Ankara (Franklin-Bouillon Accord, 1921) with France (Hurewitz 1956: 97–100). The internal front assumed the form of a civil war fought against *Kuva-yı İnzibatiye* (Forces of Order/Caliphate Army) established by the Sublime Porte upon *Şeyhülislam*'s *fatwa* (Islamic legal ruling) calling for the suppression of the nationalist uprising, separationists, and revolts of certain nationalist forces which refused to join the regular army. This front enabled the Assembly to purge counter-revolutionary forces and establish the modern Turkey. Following the unanimous abolition of the Sultanate by the Assembly in October 1922 (TBMM 30 October 1922), the Ankara government signed the Treaty of Lausanne (1923) (Hurewitz 1956: 119–127), which recognised Turkey as an independent country. The treaty established the borders of Turkey, abolished capitulations and a

---

2007: 146), was soon rejected by the small but pioneering cadre of modernised civil-military bureaucracy at the Defence of Rights Congresses.

considerable amount of war reparations for the First World War, and split the Ottoman debt among states declared independent from the Empire.

3.2 The Political Economy of the Republican Modernisation

In October 1923, the Assembly established the Republic (TBMM 29 October 1923), which concretised the abolition of the Ottoman *ancien régime* and the political independence of Turkey. The establishment of the Republic was followed by a profound process of modernisation aiming at the consolidation of capitalist relations and construction of a secular modern society and state apparatus. The revolutionary civil-military bureaucracy, which regarded secular modernity as a progressive path to purge counter-revolutionary forces and achieve a Western level of material and intellectual development (see CHP 1935), remained the dominant social force behind the Republican modernisation. This was because the interests of the dominant classes on which the revolutionary alliance rested, particularly landlords and the Anatolian small commercial bourgeoisie, were resistant to secular social and political transformation. This brought about cleavages within the revolutionary alliance through which the radical fraction soon organised itself as a political party, *Cumhuriyet Halk Partisi* (Republican People's Party, CHP). The establishment of the CHP government in October 1923 indicated that the power bloc was constituted by the modern civil-military bureaucracy and factions of landlords and the Anatolian small commercial bourgeoisie who were not willing to challenge secular modernisation (TBMM 30 October 1923). The fragile and provisional structure of the revolutionary alliance constituted the basis of progress and its limitations, as well as the rise of the military as the subject and object of secular modernisation.

Between 1923 and 1929, the CHP fostered Turkey's integration with the world capitalist system by advancing market-oriented agricultural production, which was in accordance with the Decisions of the Izmir Economic Congress, convened between February and March 1923 with the participation of farmers, merchants, industrialists, and workers. By further adhering to the Decisions, the CHP welcomed foreign investment that complied with domestic law so that the capitulations regime could be avoided (Ökçün 1968: 59–99). Nonetheless, the CHP remained radical enough to confiscate and nationalise the railways and the tobacco industry and to grant the cabotage rights to Turkish-flagged vessels (Boratav 2014: 46–47). In addition, partnerships between national and foreign capital remained insufficient for meaningful industrialisation. Such insufficiency compelled the CHP to resort to certain incentives. Most significantly, the Law on Industrial Promotion (1927) was enacted to provide tax exemptions and subsidies, including land grants, and cheap raw material and energy. The CHP also enabled the state apparatus to actively participate in capital accumulation in order to promote the growth of the national bourgeoisie. Significantly, İş Bank was established 1924 in co-operation with the commercial bourgeoisie to finance state-led infrastructure investments, and Sanayii ve Maadin Bank—transferred to Sümerbank in 1933—was established in 1925 to provide credits and technical advice to the industrial bourgeoisie (Marois 2012: 47).

The 1929 crash of the New York Stock Exchange was followed by a major depression, manifested by collapsing production, declining stock markets, and unemployment and falling wages around the world (Dunn 2009: 129–130). The Great Depression of 1929 coincided with the commencement of the payment of the Ottoman debt, both of which contributed to declining foreign trade and highlighted the urgency of industrialisation. The industrialisation of the Soviet Union, which already supported the Turkish War of Independence with a notable amount of financial and military aid (Müderrisoğlu 1990: 512–520),[16] remained a significant example of a planned economy that Turkey soon borrowed. In this regard, the CHP adopted two principles, namely, protectionism/a closed economy and statism, both of which enabled the state to dominate the national economy by acting as an investor, an administrator, and an auditor (Boratav 2014: 68). The CHP launched import-substitution industrialisation, whereby industrialisation was limited to the production of basic consumer goods for the domestic market. Remarkable progress was achieved regarding industrialisation in the textile, paper, mining, porcelain, and chemical industries (Timur 2013: 152). Meanwhile, the CHP established the Central Bank in 1931 to manage currency and monetary policy, Etibank in 1935 to finance mining and mineral marketing, and Halkbank in 1938 to provide small trade credits (Marois 2012: 48).

The period between 1923 and 1929 enhanced the overall accumulation of commercial capital and agricultural production, and thus benefited landlords and the Anatolian small commercial bourgeoisie. The prolonged agrarian nature of the Republic complicated the CHP's ability to respond to the agrarian question. On the one hand, the CHP further significantly consolidated capitalist relations by abolishing customary (*örfi*) and *sharia*-mandated taxes, particularly tithes (*öşür/aşar*) (TBMM 17 February 1925), which in return eradicated precapitalist land property and tax farming. On the other hand, the period between 1930 and 1939 fostered the accumulation of industrial capital,

---

16   The Third International (Communist International, Comintern) regarded the Turkish War of Independence as having the potential to trigger future revolutions in the East (see Riddell 2012, 2015).

and thus enabled the radical civil-military cadres within the CHP to implement land reform to enhance social transformation in rural areas. Nonetheless, the cadres could only provide peasants with uninhabited lands of the Treasury and promote agricultural credits and co-operatives (Avcıoğlu 1996: 355). All of these practices inevitably benefited landlords as resettled lands were transferred to landlords by indebting peasants and smallholders. Furthermore, the state apparatus developed a paternalistic relationship with the emerging industrial bourgeoisie while suppressing the working classes. Most significantly, the Labour Law (1936) forbade strikes, unionisation, and collective bargaining and foresaw reconciliation and arbitration in cases of labour disputes, even though it provided regulations regarding health and safety. For this reason, social transformation in rural and urban areas remained limited.

Limited social transformation combined with the dominant role of landlords and the bourgeoisie compelled the radical civil-military cadres within the CHP to pioneer secular modernisation. Most significantly, secular modernisation was consolidated through the enactment of the Civil Code (1926), accepting the equality of citizens before the law,[17] and was followed by the Penalty Code (1926) and the Code of Obligations (1926), all of which eradicated *sharia* law. The inclusion of the principle of secularism in the Constitution completed the abolition of the recognition of an official religion in 1928 (TBMM 9 April 1928; TBMM 5 February 1937). Certain other reforms, such as the national unification of education under the Republican state's authority (TBMM 3 March 1924), the transition from the Rumi to the Gregorian calendar (Law on the Change of the Calendar 1926), the introduction of surnames (TBMM 24 November 1934), and the abolition of titles and appellations (Law on the Abolition of Titles and Appellations 1934), further consolidated secular modernisation.

The radical civil-military cadres within the CHP further aimed to purge counter-revolutionary forces through secular modernisation. Most significantly, the abolition of the Caliphate eradicated the state's spiritual authority as well as purging an important reactionary element, since social forces opposing the Republic considered the Caliphate to be "the government, whose rights and competences could not be abolished by any parliament" (TBMM 3 March 1924). The abolition of the office of *Şeyhülislam* and the Ministry of Religious Affairs and Pious Foundations (TBMM 3 March 1924) and the submission of foundations under the Directorate-General of Foundations,

---

17 Marx (1980: 72) argued that "to introduce a new civil code in Turkey, a code altogether abstracted from religion, and based on a complete separation of State and Church" was to undertake "such a gigantic task, involving a perfect social revolution". The Civil Code of 1926 achieved 'such a gigantic task' and hence 'a perfect social revolution'.

which had competence to sell landed property, also consolidated the purge of counter-revolutionary forces (Foundations Law 1935). In 1931, People's Homes (*Halkevleri*) were introduced to familiarise peasants with "language and literature, fine arts, drama, sports, village development, and history" and provide them with "classes and courses, libraries and publications, and museums" (Karpat 1963: 60) in order to foster modern social transformation. Beginning in 1937, the CHP's radical cadres fostered experimental studies on which the Village Institutes (*Köy Enstitüleri*), established in 1940, were founded. The Village Institutes focused on the development of rural areas through the modernisation of social relations, the education of peasants about the agricultural economy and industrialisation, increases in agricultural productivity, and the termination of poverty (Karaömerlioğlu 1998: 47–48).

Nevertheless, the dominant role of landlords and the bourgeoisie soon hindered or caused deviation from the main goals of the reforms and restricted the depth and breadth of modern social transformation. Most significantly, the consolidation of private property through the sale and purchase of *vakıf* lands consequently benefited landlords, as only they could afford to buy (Erdost 2005: 292). This advanced the exploitation and domination of peasants and smallholders by landlords. Moreover, beginning in 1946, the Village Institutes were "adjusted" to curtail revolutionary radicalism and preserve rural social structures in the service of notables (Kirby 1962: 457–484). Furthermore, certain reforms remained formalistic and lacked any substance to foster social transformation. To illustrate, the Hat Law (1925) forbade wearing of the *fez*, turban, and quilted turban, and required the personnel of public and private local and provincial administrations to wear Western-style hats. Similarly, the Law on Prohibition of Certain Garments (1934) prevented Muslim and non-Muslim clergy from wearing their religious symbols and clothing outside of their temples and rituals, except in cases where the government could authorise a provisional permission for ritual purposes. The limited social transformation inevitably hampered the purge of counter-revolutionary forces, whose members soon resorted to violence in order to challenge the Republic and secular modernisation. This compelled the radical military cadres to safeguard the Republican modernisation. This will be discussed further.

Beginning in the late 1930s, the CHP consolidated its single-party state. This state-party regime rule took place under President Atatürk until his death in 1938, and later President İsmet İnönü until the end of the Second World War. As confirmed by then-Prime Minister İnönü in a speech at the Assembly, "the CHP [was] not a political organisation separated from executive power; it [had] been entangled with executive power and united with the state and nation" (Şener 2015: 271). This book accepts the state apparatus under the state-party regime as an exceptional form of state.[18] The integrated place of the CHP's bureaucratic cadres within the state apparatus and the imminence of war at Turkey's borders enabled the cadres of the civil-military bureaucracy in the CHP to grasp power, as opposed to the rising bourgeoisie. Even though the enhanced relative autonomy of this exceptional state enabled the CHP's radical factions to favour the working classes, peasants, and smallholders, the state continued to represent the interests of the bourgeoisie and landlords to maintain capital accumulation. In the words of Marx (1979: 186), "the state seem[ed] to have made itself completely independent ... and yet the state power [was] not suspended in mid-air".

In this regard, Kemalism, named after Kemal Atatürk, was adopted as the state's official ideology of modernisation, which was manifested through the CHP's six principles, namely, republicanism, nationalism, secularism, populism, statism, and revolutionism (CHP 1935: 3). Republicanism constituted the fundamental element that purged the precapitalist political, juridical, and ideological superstructure as well as its main ruling class, the dynasty. Despite the limited achievement of popular participation, as the short-lived *Terakkiperver Cumhuriyet Fırkası* (Progressive Republican Party, TCF) between 1924 and 1925 and *Serbest Cumhuriyet Fırkası* (Liberal Republican Party, SCF) in 1930 demonstrated (Zürcher 2007: 168, 178),[19] it constituted the basis of democratisation with its achievement of popular rule. Republicanism was further closely related to populism as the idea of general will in a capitalist state obscured antagonistic class relations.

---

18 This book acknowledges a number of critical scholars' understanding of the Republican state as a Bonapartist state (see Cengiz 2020), which is an exceptional form of state that emerges as a result of an "'equilibrium' between the two main forces" (Poulantzas 1979: 84), particularly between the bourgeoisie and the proletariat (Jessop 1985: 69). This book underlines that the urban working classes remained quantitatively and qualitatively weak in the 1930s and 1940s (Şener 2015: 217–221), and thus relates such equilibrium or the "'exceptional'" moment of "'frozen'" class struggle to the bourgeoisie's weakness to rule (see Carnoy 1984: 53–55).

19 The TCF was co-founded by Ali Fuat (Cebesoy), Cafer Tayyar (Eğilmez), Refet (Bele), Kazım (Karabekir), and Rauf (Orbay). The SCF was co-founded by Ali Fethi (Okyar). All were prominent military officers who had fought on the side of the Ankara government during the War of Independence. Nevertheless, both the TCF and the SCF soon represented the interests and demands of counter-revolutionary forces. The Istanbul bourgeoisie and media, and local religious constituents especially in eastern Anatolia, supported the TCF, whereas landlords and the commercial bourgeoisie supported the SCF to oppose the secular modernisation pursued by the civil-military bureaucracy. While the TCF was closed by the court, Okyar himself abolished the SCF (see Şener 2015: 234–245).

Populism, on the one hand, purged the precapitalist superstructure by enforcing equality before the law and abolishing social privilege. On the other hand, populism veiled antagonistic class relations as it understood the people as diverse but unified, comprising the totality of the nation. In the face of limited social transformation, Kemalist populism embraced the motto of "'for the people, despite the people'" (Çelik 2009: 76). Nationalism, the constituent idea constructing a modern secular Turkish nation and state, maintained an anti-imperialist and anti-colonial element. Nonetheless, it served as a tool to veil class struggles and contradictions as its idea of one unitary, coherent nation rejected class antagonisms. Nationalism was further related to secularism as Kemalism defined the "Turkish nation" in terms of secular citizenship. Secularism, which indicated the separation of religion from the affairs of the world and of the state and the treatment of religion as a matter of conscience (see Uysal 2019a), constituted the social and political basis of the 1923 Revolution.

Secularism aimed to emancipate the people from the domination of religious determination of social relations and safeguard freedom of thought and conscience, and thus contributed to the radicalisation of subordinate classes. Nonetheless, the principle of freedom of conscience permitted religious freedom limited to the private sphere and brought about a negotiation between religion and capitalism in which the former was domesticated and remained compatible with the latter. The establishment of the Directorate of Religious Affairs (*Diyanet*), whose duty was to implement provisions concerning the faith and worship aspects of Islam and the administration of religious institutions and their personnel (TBMM 3 March 1924), demonstrated the submission of the domesticated interpretation of religion under the Republican state's control.

Statism, a state's interventionism aimed at economic, social, and cultural development, remained the provisional pillar of Kemalism that was contingent to the post-1929 era. Revolutionism, organisation and mobilisation of the people for the creation of a modern secular nation soon lost its progressive dynamism and turned into the safeguarding of the existing social order. In this sense, Kemalism represented the contradictions of the radicalism of the CHP's bureaucratic factions and their alliance with dominant classes curtailing such radicalism. The military's role as the guardian of Kemalist principles, all of which were to be subjected to transformation in the course of the development of capitalist relations, was to manifest class contradictions in the historical context.

3.3 The Military as the Pioneer and Guardian of the 1923 Revolution

The role of the modern military and its officers as the dominant social force pioneering, carrying out, and safeguarding the 1923 Revolution granted the military its guardianship role. Between 1919 and 1922, the War of Independence significantly contributed to the emergence of a modern military through the national unification of regular and irregular forces. As has already been argued, the Armistice of Mudros required the "immediate demobilisation of the Turkish army except for such troops as [were] required for surveillance of frontiers and for the maintenance of internal order" and granted the Allies the competence to decide on the number and disposition of effectives (Hurewitz 1956: 36–37). Nevertheless, the Ottoman military preserved its chain of command particularly through the 3rd Corps, 12th Corps, 15th Corps, and 20th Corps. These regular forces constituted the backbone of the modern military. In addition, the majority of *Kuva-yı Milliye* (National Forces), which were irregular resistance forces, joined the military with the Constitutional Act of 1921 (Shaw and Shaw 1977: 350). Similarly, the intelligence services, namely *Teşkilat-ı Mahsusa* and *Karakol Cemiyeti* (Guards' Society), both of which were formed by the ITC as guerrilla bands, contributed to the formation of the modern military (Erickson 2021: 43–45).[20]

Most significantly, the Internal Service Act defined the mission of the Republican military as the safeguarding and preservation of the Republic and its principles, and of its territories, as determined by the Constitution against internal and external threats (TBMM 10 June 1935). The CHP further considered the Republican military as "the description of Turkish unity, power, and ability … and the guarantee of the systematised efforts to realise Turkish territories and Turkey's *raison d'étre*" (Atatürk 2006: 410). This identification of the Republican military with modern Turkey and the nation corresponded with the military's role of safeguarding secular modernisation against counter-revolutionary forces. Significantly, between February and March 1925, the Sheikh Said revolt erupted against the Republican regime in southeastern Turkey with Islamic symbols and slogans. The sheiks of the Nakşibendi order, providing an organisational framework, declared the rebellion to be a *"jihad* [holy war] in which whoever was killed would be a martyr and go straight to paradise". In this so-called *jihad*, Sheikh Said was the chief of the *jihadists* (Ahmad 2008b: 310).[21]

---

20 Even though *Teşkilat-ı Mahsusa* was known to have undertaken black operations during the First World War, its role regarding the atrocities committed against non-Muslims, particularly Armenians, has been debated in academia (Salt 2019: 245–246; Shaw 2006: 353–456; cf. Bloxham 2005: 69–71).

21 There is an emerging body of literature which considers the Sheikh Said rebellion as a Kurdish-nationalist rebellion (see Olson 1989). Nonetheless, this book agrees with

The Law for the Maintenance of Order was rushed through the Assembly, declaring martial law and mobilising the military (TBMM 4 March 1925).

Similarly, a revolt broke out in Menemen, Izmir, demanding the restoration of *sharia* and the Caliphate; the ringleader Dervish Mehmed, belonging to the Nakşibendi order, decapitated a reserve officer in the local gendarmerie who was sent to suppress the riot (Ahmad 2003: 60). On the one hand, the Menemen incident succeeding the Sheikh Said rebellion demonstrated that outlawing religious brotherhoods remained an important but limited attempt to purge counter-revolutionary forces and eradicate the social significance of religion (see the Law on the Closure of Dervish Convents and Tombs, and Abolition and Prohibition of the Office of Keeper of Tombs and Certain Titles 1925). On the other hand, the Menemen incident crucially brought about the rise of lower- and middle-ranking military officers as the vanguard of secular modernisation. Conscription was already thought to function as the "school of the nation" (see Hale 1994: 328).[22] In cases when conscription was insufficient, the lower and middle ranks were to use force if necessary to foster secular modernisation.

Civil–military relations in the early Republican era demonstrated the legitimisation of the guardianship role of the military on the one hand, and the submission of the military under civilian authority on the other. Despite the prominence of military cadres within the CHP, it mainly consisted of civilian representatives. In addition, the military cadres within the CHP, particularly Kemal, who dropped his Pasha title and adopted Atatürk as his surname, had an uneasy relationship with the military's role in politics. To illustrate, Kemal, leading the Action Army until Mahmud Şevket Pasha took over the command in 1909, supported the separation of the army and daily politics at the ITC's Congress of 1909 (Zürcher 1984: 51–52). According to him, the military's interference in politics prevented officers from tackling their military duties adequately and hampered the ITC's ability to reach subordinate classes, compelling the ITC to rely on military force (Atay 2009: 67–68). More importantly, the CHP's civilian authority in the 1920s and the 1930s rested on the relatively stable

---

Ahmad's (2008b: 310) assertion that "the terms in which the rebellion was launched and sustained were entirely religious. Not only was the authority of these sheikhs religious in nature but the peasants who joined the movement responded only to religious symbols and slogans".

Similarly, the Marxist-Kurdish movement of the Revolutionary Cultural Eastern Hearths (*Devrimci Doğu Kültür Ocakları*) further underlined the "reactionary and feudal" character of the Sheikh Said rebellion (Yeğen 1996: 224).

22 The Law on Military Service (1927) reinforced conscription for every male Turkish citizen between the age of twenty-two and forty-six.

hegemony of landlords and the commercial bourgeoisie. In this regard, civilian supremacy over the military was maintained under the CHP government.

The CHP's attempt to separate the military from politics and to submit it to civilian authority was manifested and sustained through the legal and institutional frameworks. Most significantly, the competences and duties of the Ministry of War in Istanbul were assumed by the Ministry of General Staff (*Erkân-ı Harbiye-i Umûmiye Vekâleti*) and the Ministry of National Defence (*Müdâfaa-i Milliye Vekâleti*, later *Milli Savunma Bakanlığı*) in Ankara during the War of Independence. Following the proclamation of the Republic, the Ministry of War was abolished and replaced by the General Staff (*Genelkurmay Başkanlığı*), whose place in the Cabinet was also abolished (TBMM 3 March 1924). Nonetheless, Chief of the General Staff Fevzi (Çakmak), who previously served as the Minister of National Defence during the War of Independence, continued to enjoy great autonomy in his conduct of military affairs (Rustow 1959: 549), such as attending Cabinet meetings (see also Chapter 3). Çakmak's autonomy was related to his continued close relations with Atatürk and İnönü, who previously served as the western front commander during the War of Independence.

Moreover, civilian supremacy over the military was maintained since the chief of the General Staff was to be appointed by the president upon the proposal of the prime minister (TBMM 3 March 1924). The chief of the General Staff was granted the competence to command the military during peacetime, and the person who was to be appointed by the president upon the proposal of the Cabinet was to command the military during wartime (Constitutional Act 1924). Civilian supremacy over the military was strengthened through civilian supervision of military expenditure as the Ministry of Defence was given the responsibility of presenting the military budget to the Assembly (TBMM 3 March 1924). However, the separation of the General Staff from the Ministry of Defence made it unclear to whom the General Staff was responsible.

Certain institutions and practices continued to grant the military a certain level of autonomy. These have constituted the basis of fields of struggle between the military and the civilian authority in times of hegemonic crises. Significantly, the Supreme Defence Assembly (*Yüksek Müdafaa Meclisi*) was established in April 1933 to consist of the chief of the General Staff and members of the Cabinet, and to be chaired by the prime minister as well as the president, if required. The Supreme Defence Assembly was competent to determine necessary principles and tasks of the ministries in the case of national mobilisation, and to assemble annually and hold extraordinary meetings if required (MGK 2013). Nevertheless, the establishment of the Supreme Defence Assembly coincided with the rise of the threat of fascist Italy in the

Mediterranean in the 1930s. Significantly, Benito Mussolini, the prime minister of Italy, dropped the idea of launching an expeditionary force from Naples to Asia Minor in the face of Turkey's partial military mobilisation in 1926, and signed a Treaty of Neutrality, Mediation and Judicial Settlement with Turkey in 1928 to counter France's influence (Hale 2013: 45). Following Adolf Hitler's triumph in 1933 and his appointment as the chancellor of Germany, fascism truly became "a *universal* movement" (Hobsbawm 1995: 116). Such a revisionist policy of territorial expansionism compelled Turkey to prepare for a coming war in the Mediterranean and Balkans.[23] The conclusion of the Balkan Pact between Turkey, Greece, Romania, and Yugoslavia in February 1934, which guaranteed the frontiers of the signatory states in the event of an aggression and necessitated consultation in the event of any threat to peace in the region, illustrates Turkey's anticipation (Hale 2013: 46). Therefore, the competence of the Supreme Defence Assembly to make decisions on issues pertaining to national mobilisation and defence of the country was arguably related to Turkey's preparation for the coming world war.[24]

In addition, the Supreme Military Council (*Şurayı Askeri*, later *Yüksek Askeri Şura*) was established in April 1925 to give opinions on promotions and retirements of the military cadres, military budget, military law, the training and equipping of officers, and issues pertaining to national defence. The Supreme Military Council was also competent to give opinions regarding the construction of military factories and roads for the transfer of officers and armaments during peacetime, and to co-ordinate with the General Staff about national mobilisation during wartime. The Supreme Military Council consisted of the minister of defence, the chief of the General Staff, the commander of the navy, the generals of the army and the navy, and the military inspectors. The Supreme Military Council was to assemble annually as well as when either the president or the chief of the General Staff recognised the necessity of a meeting (TBMM 22 April 1925). The president was entitled to chair Supreme Military Council meetings and to invite the prime minister and other MPs. In case of the absence of the president, the chief of the General Staff was to chair the meetings. If the prime minister or an MP was invited during the president's absence, the prime minister or the minister of defence was to chair the meeting (TBMM 30 May 1926). Since the Supreme Military Council's role was limited

---

23   According to Hobsbawm (1995: 104), "[t]he gates to the Second World War were opened in 1931".
24   The Supreme Defence Assembly's decisions could not be *sua sponte* adopted due to legal, fiscal, and administrative regulations (Sezen 2000: 67).

to giving expert opinion on military matters under the chairing of the civilian authority, civilian control over the military was still ensured.

Finally, the role and place of paramilitary forces remained one of the most important issues that complicated and reinforced the military's role in politics. In the Ottoman Empire, the provincial military police forces (*asakir-i zabtiye*), which were organised on ad hoc basis during the 1840s, were reformed into a uniform and centralised organisation in the form of a gendarmerie (*jandarma*) beginning in 1879 to advance and extend the state's authority over rural areas. The Gendarmerie Department was placed under the jurisdiction and command of the chief of the General Staff (Özbek 2008: 53). In the Republic, the gendarmerie was reformed into the Gendarmerie Command. The gendarmerie was simultaneously placed under the Ministry of the Interior regarding administration and duties pertaining to the safeguarding of security and public order, under the General Staff regarding training, and under the Ministry of Defence in case of national mobilisation (Law on Gendarmerie 1930). The location of the gendarmerie under the civilian executive power enhanced civilian supremacy over the military. Nevertheless, the paramilitary nature of the gendarmerie, which made it rather "auxiliary units to the army but separately organised" (Janowitz 1977: 114), enhanced the military's role in politics.

CHAPTER 3

The Coup of 1960 and the Guardianship of the Military

> Best adapted to the capitalist stage of development is the army built on universal military service which, though an army constituted by the people, is not an army of the people, but an army against the people, or becomes increasingly converted into such a one.
> KARL LIEBKNECHT (1917 [1906])

∴

This chapter discusses the institutionalisation of the guardianship role of the military following the coup of 1960. The coup of 1960 established and legitimised the military's guardianship role by overthrowing *Demokrat Parti* (Democratic Party, DP), which previously maintained hegemony in the 1950s by denouncing the influential role of the civil-military bureaucracy in politics. Nonetheless, the coup was only possible after the DP had suffered from a prolonged hegemonic crisis in the late 1950s and the military remained the only social force that could safeguard the bourgeois social order. This chapter discusses the prominence of the civil-military bureaucracy in the 1940s, the rise of the DP and its hegemonic project in the 1950s, and the coup of 1960 in accordance with the reorganisation of patterns of capital accumulation and class relations under the dynamics of unevenness and dependency.

1 Classes and the State in the Post-Second World War Order

1.1 *The Political Economy of the Legacy of the War*

During the Second World War, Turkey remained a de facto neutral state despite pressure from the Allies and Germany to join the war on their side. Turkey, in fact, managed to stay out of the war through nonaggression and alliance agreements with the Allies and the Axis powers by pursuing a policy of balance of power under the changing circumstances of wartime. In October 1939, Turkey signed the Treaty of Mutual Assistance with Britain and France. The Treaty can be considered as a tripartite alliance since it expected Turkey to join the war on the Allied side if the Axis powers invaded the Balkans or started a war in the Mediterranean (Hurewitz 1956: 226–228). Nonetheless, Turkey sought to appease Germany against this agreement, and continued its economic and political relations with Germany, which dominated Turkey's foreign trade (Schick and Tonak 1987: 337). Most importantly, Turkey signed the Treaty of Nonaggression with Germany in June 1941 (Hurewitz 1956: 231). This was followed by the "'Clodius agreement'" between Turkey and Germany in October 1941, which foresaw the import of German armaments in 1944 in exchange for the export of Turkish chromite in 1943 (İnanç 2006: 910). Turkey eventually declared war on Germany in February 1945, following the restriction of membership of the proposed United Nations to those states that had joined the war on the Allied side (Hale 2013: 75).

The war, inevitably, had an immense impact on Turkey's economic and political landscape. It compelled the CHP government to strengthen the military and mobilise the national economy for war production while curtailing agricultural production and imports and advancing food shortages (Boratav 2014: 81–83). The decline in agricultural production negatively affected the questions of food supplies and shortages, which advanced black-marketing, profiteering, and corruption (Aydın 2005: 27). In response, the CHP enhanced state intervention mainly through the Law on National Protection, the Wealth Tax, and the Land Crops Tax. The Law on National Protection (1940) enabled the CHP to regulate the labour force by increasing workloads, lengthening the workday, and curbing wages. It further enabled the CHP to oversee production and commerce by temporarily confiscating private enterprises, determining prices for import, export, and domestic trade, and rationing basic goods. The failure of the CHP's bureaucratic factions to ally with the subordinate classes nevertheless resulted in the coercion of the working classes and the favouring of the commercial bourgeoisie. Moreover, the Law on the Wealth Tax (1942) foresaw the collection of a one-time extraordinary tax mainly from the commercial bourgeoisie as well as landlords and artisans. However, the Wealth Tax was mainly applied to non-Muslims, who paid more than half of the tax revenue. Therefore, it functioned to transfer wealth from the non-Muslim bourgeoisie to the Muslim bourgeoisie.[1] Furthermore, the Law on the Land Crops Tax (1943), an extraordinary tax-in-kind, sought to prevent landlords from

---

1   Non-Muslims who could not pay the extraordinary tax within a month, as required by law, were transported to the labour camp in Aşkale, a province of Erzurum, in 1943 (Boratav 2014: 85). Therefore, the Wealth Tax remained one of the most controversial issues in the history of modern nation-building in Turkey.

selling agricultural products to merchants at higher prices. However, the alliance between the CHP and the dominant classes put peasants and smallholders under the tax burden.

The CHP's bureaucratic factions remained radical to a certain extent as they sought to implement land reforms. Land reforms were not only required for social transformation in rural areas but also to restrain landlords' resistance against price controls and taxes in the face of the devastating impact of the war. Following the end of the war, the CHP promulgated the Land Reform Law (1945), which foresaw the redistribution of lands that exceeded five hectares (roughly twelve acres) to peasants and smallholders. However, the land reform was overwhelmingly resisted by landlords, and the resettlement of private lands remained vastly limited. The land reform was already resisted by landlords in the Assembly, and this was to bring about the fragmentation of the CHP and the emergence of the DP as the representative of landlords.

1.2 The Reconfiguration of Class Relations in the Aftermath of the Second World War

The end of the Second World War staged the reconfiguration of global political economy, founded on the Bretton Woods Agreement of 1944. Global capitalism was restructured through the selective advancement of free trade, the regulation of international finance, and the introduction of new international economic institutions, mainly the International Monetary Fund (IMF), the International Bank for Reconstruction and Development (IBRD, the World Bank's most important section), and the General Agreement on Tariffs and Trade (GATT) (Kiely 2010: 100–101). The IMF was to oversee exchange rate arrangements among countries; the IBRD was to provide loans and concessional assistance; and the GATT was to provide a multilateral platform co-ordinating and facilitating international trade (Krueger 2020: 7–8). The Bretton Woods system further foresaw a transfer of reserves from capital-surplus to capital-deficit countries through an international currency, which could promote international trade by avoiding competitive devaluations. However, the United States, as the global hegemonic power, led the introduction of "'the dollar-gold standard'", which fixed the prices of national currencies against the price of the US dollar and the price of the dollar against gold, thereby rendering the dollar the international means of payment (Kiely 2007: 43).

The reorganisation of the global political economy coincided with the geopolitical division of the world into two main blocs, namely, the capitalist bloc under the leadership of the United States, and the socialist bloc under the leadership of the Soviet Union.[2] In March 1947, US President Harry S. Truman (1947) promised financial and material aid, including military equipment and personnel, to Greece and Turkey against "communists" and the Soviet Union, both of which were presented as "threats" against "free and independent nations". This constituted the basis of the Truman Doctrine, which granted the United States the role "to restore peace, stability, and freedom to the world", and thus signified the beginning of the Cold War (Truman 1949).[3] As a result of the uneven and dependent integration of Turkey into the world capitalist economy under Western hegemony, particularly that of the United States, Turkey was assigned the role of bulwark against socialism and the Soviet Union in the Middle East and eastern Mediterranean. In this regard, Turkey soon allied with the United States by revisiting the 1945 Communication of Vyacheslav Molotov, Soviet commissar for foreign affairs, which demanded the introduction of Soviet military bases in the Straits—the Dardanelles and the Bosphorus—to enable "joint defence" during the Second World War (Coş and Bilgin 2010: 43).[4] It should be noted that the United States previously proposed the internationalisation of the Straits, which were placed under Turkish sovereignty by the Montreux Convention of 1936 (Hasanli 2011: 99–100). Furthermore, the Turkish officials did not expect the Soviet Union to apply military force throughout late 1945 and 1946, despite alarming US reports (Leffler 1985: 810–811). Therefore, the class interests of the Turkish power bloc lay at the heart of Turkey's alliance with the United States.

The implementation of the Truman Doctrine in the Mediterranean was complemented by the European Recovery Plan of 1947, also known as the

---

2 The United States arguably already considered the Soviet Union to be "a past and a future problem ... even at the height of the War" between 1942 and 1943, when the Soviet Union "was carrying more than its share of the fighting" (Dowd 2004: 283).
3 The declared US aim of advancing and preserving expanding markets under the guise of liberal democratic ideals, by military means if necessary, resulted in the fragmentation of and political cleavages among late-developing countries. The Third World emerged as a bloc of peripheral countries which had already completed or were undergoing the process of decolonisation and sought an independent path between the capitalist and socialist blocs (McMichael 2017: 44). Nonetheless, certain late-developing countries, significantly Turkey, soon converged with the Third World economies in accordance with the global division of labour even though they allied with the capitalist bloc. In this regard, this book underlines the similarities regarding the patterns of capital accumulation between Turkey and the Third World, both of which were characterised by late development.
4 The Soviet Union identified certain passages of German and Italian warships and auxiliary crafts in 1941 and 1944 through the Straits as having caused the need to "establish a new regime of the Straits" under "the competence of Turkey and other Black Sea powers" (Orekhov 1946: 48–49).

Marshall Plan, named after the US Secretary of State George C. Marshall. The Marshall Plan was to restore the multilateral trading system, maintain global price stability, and revive industrial production particularly in Europe while financing the US export surplus through aid and suppressing rising left-wing movements, significantly through an intervention in labour movements (Block 1977: 82–92). The Marshall Plan was to incorporate Turkey as a supplier of food and raw materials in order to rebuild Europe (Aydın 2005: 29), thus peripheralising the Turkish economy. The commercial bourgeoisie and landlords, the constituents of the power bloc under the CHP, were eager to accumulate wealth through the liberalisation of the economy and foreign trade, which was complemented by the inflow of foreign aid and credit that promoted agricultural production. This could be illustrated by Turkey's request for a 500-million-USD loan from the US Export-Import Bank following the visit of the US battleship *Missouri* in Istanbul in April 1946, with its aim of displaying US power to the Soviet Union (Yılmaz 2012: 482–483).[5] Moreover, at the Economic Congress of 1948, the national economy was liberalised, and statism was narrowed to the railways, ports, communication, radio, energy, forests, state financial institutions, and industrialisation in the fields in which private capital did not suffice (Toprak 1982). After having joined the IMF, the World Bank, and the Organisation for European Economic Co-operation (later the Organisation for Economic Cooperation and Development, OECD) between 1947 and 1948 in the same vein, Turkey began to receive loans from the IMF in 1947 (IMF 1947) and from the IBRD in 1950 (TCHMB 2009). These international organisations, as the representatives of Western capital, were to determine the way Turkey was incorporated into the world capitalist economy.

In the domestic political arena, landlords and the bourgeoisie, the same dominant class fractions as within the CHP, formed an opposition within the CHP when the law on land reforms passed in the Assembly. This opposition declared the Memorandum of the Four (*Dörtlü Takrir*) in June 1945, demanding democratisation. Following the CHP's rejection of the Memorandum, the opposition split off and established a new political party, the DP, in January 1946 (Zürcher 2007: 210 –211). The role of Celal Bayar, Adnan Menderes, Refik Koraltan, and Fuat Köprülü as the main cofounders of the DP demonstrated that landlords and the bourgeoisie became strong enough to dismiss the civil-military bureaucracy and rule the country with the help of the petty bourgeoisie and the intelligentsia. Bayar represented the big bourgeoisie, having

---

5 The United States refused Turkey's request and informed that Turkey could receive "a maximum of 25 million USD" (Yılmaz 2012: 483).

previously cofounded İş Bank, the major private commercial bank, which also financed state-led infrastructure investments (Marois 2012: 47). Menderes was a prominent landlord from Aydın province,[6] and an ardent opposer of land reforms (Aydemir 1993: 116). Koraltan was a lawyer, representing the petty bourgeoisie, and Köprülü was a historian, representing the intelligentsia (Yerasimos 1989: 169). The transition to multiparty politics in Turkey, manifesting the reorganisation of class relations in the aftermath of the Second World War, corresponded to Turkey's integration with global capitalism under the hegemony of the Western capitalist bloc, supposedly representing liberal democracy. Consequently, the CHP was compelled to abolish the state-party regime, which was concretised with President İnönü's "national chiefdom" (*milli şef*) (Aydemir 1991: 37–39), in May 1946 (CHP 1946).

2 The State and Classes under *Demokrat Parti*

2.1 The National Economy between 1950 and 1958

In May 1950, the DP formed a majority government (TBMM 29 May 1950), creating a power bloc under the hegemony of landlords and the commercial bourgeoisie. The national economy under the DP, therefore, manifested the characteristics and contradictions of the power bloc. Between 1950 and 1953, the DP fostered Turkish integration with the world capitalist system through capital accumulation based on agricultural production and exports. In this sense, the DP advanced the CHP's economic policies of the late 1940s aimed at the liberalisation of the economy, particularly foreign trade. Even though the Turkish lira was devalued in 1946 to limit imports and promote exports, free trade stimulated imports of machinery and equipment, raw material, construction materials, and consumer goods in comparison to agricultural exports (Kepenek and Yentürk 2001: 118–120). This brought about a persistent external deficit, which soon turned into a chronic element of the Turkish economy, characterising it as dependent on foreign aid and credit. The DP managed to postpone the impact of a payments deficit until 1953 owing to substantial aid inflows, growing wheat exports, and favourable world prices for Turkey's exports (Krueger 1974: 20). Meanwhile, the DP promoted mechanisation in agriculture by importing tractors and encouraged the establishment of public and private banks, such as Şekerbank and Doğubank (Atılgan 2015a: 393), to

---

6 Menderes declared that his lands diminished from around 5,000–6,000 hectares to 350 hectares during the land reform trials between 1944 and 1945 (Aydemir 1993: 62).

provide credits for agricultural production and the marketisation of agriculture. The DP also undertook investments in infrastructure and construction to respond to the growth of urban areas and to connect urban areas to rural areas, maintaining the flow of agricultural products to the domestic and international markets. Nonetheless, under the pressure of US aid, the DP promoted the construction of highways and roads instead of railways (Kazgan 2006: 83).

The massive crop failure in 1954 as a result of bad weather conditions coincided with the end of favourable international conditions for agricultural exports. Economic stagnation combined with inflation arising due to the obstruction of agricultural production and exports compelled the DP to regulate foreign trade and imports beginning in 1954 (Krueger 1974: 8–9). The conjunction of the control over the import of consumer goods and the rapid growth of urban areas beginning in the 1950s brought about a growing need for industrialisation in consumer goods. In the face of the weakness of national industrial capital, the DP promoted the establishment of state-owned enterprises (SOEs), particularly in the fields of fertilisers, meat, and fish; cement and nitrogen; cellulose and paper; iron and steel; and coal (Cengiz 2020: 31). The DP further encouraged public-private partnerships between the SOEs and national and foreign capital, in order to transfer the majority of surplus value to national and foreign capital. The transfer of surplus was through the distribution of profits according to private capital's liabilities rather than actual payments[7] and the undertaking of commercial activities almost only by private capital (Kepenek and Yentürk 2001: 99). Meanwhile, the emerging industrial capital became active in the production of nondurable goods, such as textiles, food and beverages, and tobacco (Boratav 2014: 112).

The liberalisation of the economy was founded on the inflow of foreign aid and credit, and foreign capital, which was already encouraged by the DP. Significantly, the Law on Foreign Capital Incentives (1954) broadened the expansion of foreign capital in industry, energy, mining, infrastructure, transport, and tourism by abolishing limitations regarding the transfer of profits and the diffusion of foreign capital in agriculture and commerce. Foreign capital was allowed to install oil refineries in 1957, broadening the abolition of the state monopoly over oil exploration in 1954 (Kazgan 2006: 83). Furthermore, the process of industrialisation in consumer goods took the form of import-substitution industrialisation (ISI), however unplanned and limited it remained under the DP. This book discusses the application of ISI in detail

---

7 The Commercial Code required private capital to pay one fourth of their liabilities, whereas SOEs were required to undertake all their stipulations (Kepenek and Yentürk 2001: 99).

following the coup of 1960. Nonetheless, it is important to briefly underline that the import of investment goods and raw materials to manufacture consumer goods brought about dependence on foreign capital under the DP. The Turkish industries significantly became dependent on American capital in the fields of oil excavation and leasing, vessels and motor vehicles, intermediate goods, and industrial plants in the 1950s (Atılgan 2015a: 397).

Combined with the liberalisation of capital flows, foreign credit further increased foreign debt and turned it into one of the most significant elements of Turkey's dependency on foreign capital. The conditions attached to foreign credit demonstrated the dependent nature of credit and debt that reproduced the primacy of Western capital over Turkish capital. Most significantly, the DP used US credit to fund the government budget and the SOEs, while a certain amount of credit was lent to private capital that was in partnership with American companies (Kepenek and Yentürk 2001: 100). While the DP heavily resorted to foreign credit for economic growth until 1953 and to compensate for economic stagnation beginning in 1954, it eventually had an obstructive impact on economic development. To illustrate, the total foreign debt increased by 750 per cent in the Turkish lira (TRY) and 410 per cent in the US dollar (USD), and the share of foreign debt in the national income remained greater than economic growth between 1950 and 1960 (Kepenek and Yentürk 2001: 100). Nevertheless, Turkish national capital was eager to accumulate wealth through such an uneven relationship. Significantly, in 1953, the DP broadened the liability of the Treasury regarding the payments of debts of private capital, and enabled private commercial banks to provide credits for imports without the liability of transferring foreign currencies to the Treasury (Kazgan 2005: 102). Meanwhile, the foreign trade deficit also turned into foreign debt as a result of payment difficulties. To illustrate, the foreign trade deficit of 22.3 million USD in 1950 rose to 193 million USD in 1952, and became 256 million USD by 1958 (Aydın 2005: 32).

The DP's success at maintaining economic growth between 1950 and 1953 favoured the urban working classes and rural peasants and smallholders by improving living standards and income, even though the DP rested on and favoured the dominant classes. The income of the rural classes increased in comparison to the urban working classes, and the income of the civil-military bureaucracy remained stable during this period. Economic growth based on agricultural production and exports benefited the commercial bourgeoisie in comparison to the emerging industrial bourgeoisie (Boratav 2014: 103–104). In the face of economic stagnation beginning in 1954, the DP resisted devaluation and deflation, which aimed to stimulate export and reduce aggregate demand in line with the IMF's prescriptions for the stabilisation and liberalisation of trade. While the Law on National Protection (1956) granted the DP wide interventionist competences, including the determination of prices of goods and services (Atılgan 2015a: 399), the DP pursued populist and inflationary policies to favour the rural classes. In this way, the income of the rural classes, including peasants and smallholders, continued to increase between 1954 and 1958. As a result of capital accumulation through the ISI, however unplanned and limited it remained, the income of the urban classes, including workers, also increased during this period (Boratav 2014: 114).

2.2 Demokrat Parti's *Hegemonic Project*

Beginning in the late 1940s, the integration of Turkey with the world capitalist system through agrarian capitalism brought about rapid social transformation in rural and urban areas. Regarding rural areas, the uneven development of geographies brought about remarkable capitalist transformation in western Anatolia and the Mediterranean, whereas capitalist transformation remained slow in central and very limited in southeast Anatolia (Atılgan 2015a: 404). The advancement of mechanisation in agricultural production paved the way for industrialisation in agriculture and the subsequent proletarianisation and displacement of masses of landless peasants, who either became agricultural workers in rural areas or formal and informal economy workers in urban areas (Gürel 2015a: 327). While contributing to social transformation, this process consolidated the dominant role of landlords in rural areas. Rapid proletarianisation combined with the DP's lack of a planned economy further brought about the growth of irregular urbanisation and squat (*gecekondu*) settlements where burgeoning formal and informal economy workers maintained their bonds with rural areas (Boratav 2014: 108).

The DP rested on landlords and the commercial bourgeoisie and obtained the consent of the petty bourgeoisie and the liberal-conservative intelligentsia, as these social strata benefited from and supported the liberalisation of the economy under Western hegemony. The DP also managed to obtain the consent of the working classes and peasants by improving their economic conditions and employing populist redistributive mechanisms, including favourable credits and pricing in agriculture (Sunar 1983: 2082). The DP's identification of the CHP with the civil-military bureaucracy and its attempt at discrediting both the CHP and the civil-military bureaucracy further resonated with the subordinate classes regarding the economic burden of the Second World War. This will be further discussed in relation to civil–military relations under the DP. The DP further incorporated populism, which differed from the CHP's populism of the 1930s. The DP's populism fostered relations of patronage and clientelism, which determined relations of distribution on the basis of political support.

Such relations of patronage and clientelism included the direction and supply of government subventions and investments; the allocation of economic rent; public employment policies (Sunar 1983: 2083); and the recruitment of rural notables into the party ranks and the use of local personal patronage in exchange for votes (Toprak 1981: 72).

The DP's promotion of clientelism was combined with its merging of liberalism and conservatism. The DP articulated liberalism in connection with democracy and populism, where democracy was identified with the national will and the ballot box, and populism indicated social harmony. Even though the DP's discourse on democracy underlined fundamental rights and freedoms and equality before the law, it necessitated limitations in the case of any social movement that threatened territorial integrity and freedoms (DP 1946: 2). In accordance with the DP's populism that obscured class antagonisms, the DP's discourse on democracy manifested the contradictions of the uneven and dependent integration of Turkey under Western hegemony. On the one hand, the DP sought to keep election promises that guaranteed the votes of the growing working classes in urban areas. The DP broadened labour rights by introducing paid weekly rest days, holiday pay for workers according to their seniority, and lunch breaks for workplaces in cities and towns with populations of over 10,000, and by incorporating an increasing number of workers into social security (Atılgan 2015a: 409). On the other hand, the DP opposed the organisation of the working classes and discouraged union rights. The DP closed the Federation of Istanbul Labour Unions (*Istanbul İşçi Sendikaları Birliği*) and put its members on trial (Özçelik 2010: 174), and did not recognise the right to strike or to freedom of peaceful assembly. Similarly, the DP maintained its firm opposition to land reforms. For instance, it amended the land registry law to prevent land occupations by peasants in certain regions, particularly Denizli and Bursa provinces, and to preserve the private land rights of landlords (Timur 2003: 105). Therefore, the DP's attempt to benefit peasants and smallholders remained limited to favourable prices. Combined with the Western portrayal of socialist and left-wing movements as threatening freedom and independence, the DP's discourse on democracy foreshadowed its future of resorting to authoritarianism and repressive and coercive measures against the rise of socialist and left-wing movements and organised subordinate classes. In fact, the DP aggravated the penal code against the left-wing movements by introducing imprisonment for individuals and organisations seeking to and/or propagandising to "establish domination of a certain social class over other classes, or eliminate a certain social class, or overthrow the current social order" (Act on the Amendment of the Turkish Penal Code 1951).

The DP's discourse on conservatism similarly represented Turkey's uneven and dependent integration with the world capitalist system, which articulated precapitalist remnants into the social structure. The combination between Turkey's aim to undertake its role of bulwark against socialist movements and the Soviet Union and the dominant role of landlords and the bourgeoisie brought about the incorporation of Islamic elements and symbols by the state apparatus to obscure class antagonisms and struggles. This process can be dated back to the CHP government of the late 1940s; the CHP's Congress of 1947 considered Islam a "national bastion" against "the threat of red seeds" of socialism by bringing about "spiritual, patriotic, and disciplined generations equipped with morality and solidarity" (CHP 1948: 451–458). The DP fostered this incorporation of Islam into the state's ideology by incorporating conservatism in its hegemonic project. While the DP portrayed Islam as a tool with which to integrate the nation and the state (DP 1946: 4), the DP's instrumental understanding of Islam functioned to mobilise the support of the subordinate classes and sought to obscure class antagonisms and prevent the emergence of left-wing movements.

The DP's incorporation of religion and conservativism was combined with the state's control over religion. This combination resulted in the articulation of Islamic symbols and references in the public sphere and the increase in the public visibility of Islam, a process which can also be dated back to the late 1940s. For instance, in 1949, the CHP proposed the introduction of religious instruction on a voluntary basis, and this proposal was rejected (TBMM 17 January 1949). The DP, by bypassing the modernist civil-military bureaucracy, moved beyond the CHP's timid steps. In November 1950, the DP included religious instruction in the primary-school syllabus (Sevim 2007: 67), while changing the voluntary character from *opting in* to *opting out*. Similarly, the CHP opened ten-week *imam-hatip* (prayer leader and preacher) schools in ten cities in December 1948, which the DP replaced with four-year *imam-hatip* schools in the form of secondary schools in seven cities in October 1951 (Sevim 2007: 67). The DP further strengthened the competences and influence of the *Diyanet* by transferring the management of mosques, worship places, and religious personnel from the Directorate-General of Foundations back to the *Diyanet* (Act on the Amendment of Duties of the Directorate of Religious Affairs 1950).

The DP's instrumental understanding of Islam also aimed to control the organisation of Islamist movements which considered the victory of the DP to be an opportunity for the accumulation of wealth and power. Unlike its attempts to outlaw religious brotherhoods in the 1930s, the CHP already sought to legitimise political Islam and religious brotherhoods beginning in the late 1940s. Most significantly, Ahmed Hamdi Akseki, a prominent writer of the Islamist newspaper *Sebilürreşâd*, served as the director of religious affairs between 1947 and 1951 (Azak 2010: 188). The CHP further allowed the reintroduction of tombs of a number of the Ottoman sultans and other significant historical religious and political figures in March 1950 (TBMM 1 March 1950). Nevertheless, the DP's hesitant but supportive position vis-à-vis the Islamist movements encouraged religious brotherhoods, whose factions soon developed into Islamist movements. On the one hand, the Law on Protection of Freedom of Conscience and Assembly (1953) facilitated the punishment of assembly, propaganda, and indoctrination on a religious basis to gain political or individual benefit with imprisonment and/or abolition of the association. On the other hand, the DP represented local religious constituents and developed clientelist relations with religious brotherhoods. Most significantly, Said-i Nursi, a Sunni-Kurdish theologian publicly opposed to Atatürk and the Republican understanding of modernity and who led the Nurcu congregation with his religious teachings, called Epistles of Light (*Risale-i Nur*) (Yavuz 2009a: 264–268), actively supported the DP during the elections of 1954 and 1957 (Pelt 2008: 95).

2.3 The Political Economy of the Transformation of the Military

The military underwent a remarkable transformation in the aftermath of the Second World War and the uneven and dependent integration of Turkey with the world capitalist system. Turkey's role of containing the Soviet Union brought about the modernisation of the Turkish military under the hegemony of the United States, a process which can be dated back to the late 1940s under the CHP, within the frameworks of the Marshall Plan and the Truman Doctrine. The modernisation of the Turkish military during this period took place mainly through military aid. The American Mission for Aid to Turkey (AMAT) was formed in August 1947, which was later transformed into the American Military Mission for Aid to Turkey (JAMMAT) in November 1949 (Uyar and Güvenç 2022: 94–95). This military aid mostly assumed the form of impact training programmes and the purchase of armaments and equipment, manifesting the expansion of American capital in Turkey. To illustrate, US aid received by Turkey in 1948 totalling 100 million USD was used for the purchase of heavy artillery, vehicles, army equipment, aircraft, and naval supplies from the United States. Almost half of this aid—48.5 million USD—was utilised by the armed forces, with the Air Force and Navy utilising almost the remaining half—26.8 million USD and 14.8 million USD respectively. The United States further provided 182 personnel, including 51 civilians, 71 army, 34 air force, and 13 navy personnel, as well as training in the fields of supply, communications, artillery, aircraft flight and maintenance, machine operation and maintenance, highway construction, and medical care (McGhee 1990: 43–44).

The modernisation of the Turkish military brought about institutional restructuring to maintain civilian supremacy over the military to conform to liberal democracy on the one hand, and to enhance the role of the military as a means of coercion and repression to contain socialism and the Soviet Union on the other. Most significantly, the power of the General Staff was curbed through its submission to the authority of the Ministry of Defence in June 1949 (Law on the Establishment and Duties of the Ministry of Defence 1949). The chief of the General Staff was to be appointed by the Cabinet upon the proposal of the minister of defence. All other generals, admirals, and inspectors were also to be appointed by the Cabinet upon the minister's proposal after having consulted the chief of the General Staff.

Moreover, the Supreme Defence Assembly was transformed into the Supreme Council of National Defence (*Milli Savunma Yüksek Kurulu*) in June 1949 (Law on the Supreme Council of National Defence 1949). The Supreme Council was to determine the principles of defence policies implemented by the government, identify the duties and responsibilities related to the defence of public institutions and citizens, supervise the implementation of measures, prepare national mobilisation plans, and express opinions after having examined the prime minister's proposals. The Supreme Council was to convene at least once a month. If its decisions were to be implemented directly, it required the prime minister's notification; otherwise, the decisions were submitted to the Cabinet. The Supreme Council was headed by the prime minister and composed of the minister of defence, the chief of the General Staff, and ministers, including the ministers of the interior, foreign affairs, finance, civil works, the economy, trade, transport, and agriculture (Decree No. 3/9548 1949). During wartime, the commander of the army was also a member of the Supreme Council. When deemed necessary, the Supreme Council could call the members of the Supreme Military Council and other relevant experts for consultations.

Furthermore, the Supreme Military Council was restructured in May 1949 to comprise fifteen permanent members, including the minister of defence, the chief of the General Staff, the commanders of the army, navy, and air force, the secretary-general of the Supreme Council of National Defence, the military inspectors, and certain generals ranked according to their achievements (Act on the Amendment of the Law on the Establishment and Duties of the Supreme Military Council 1949). The minister of defence was to chair the Council, and the chief of the General Staff could chair ordinary meetings in the absence of the minister. The prime minister could also chair the meetings and invite other ministers to attend if necessary.

The restructuring of the military under US hegemony further brought about the need to purge high-ranking military officers who were still moved by the previous German/Prussian influence. This process can be dated back to the mid-1940s, during the Second World War. Most significantly, Marshal Fevzi Çakmak, the chief of the General Staff, was forced to retire in January 1944 with the reason that he had reached the age of retirement after having served for more than twenty years. During his term in office, Çakmak held immense authority and wide military and political autonomy (see Chapter 2). Under Çakmak's authority, the army, navy, and air force had not been able to maintain separate institutional identities. Similarly, the gendarmerie, the coast guard, and the customs and border guards, which were located under the Ministry of Interior, de facto functioned under the General Staff (Uyar and Güvenç 2022: 100). Çakmak also attended Cabinet meetings and reported directly to the prime minister (Hale 1994: 78). Çakmak's retirement coincided with the termination of British-American aid in February 1944 as a result of Turkey's neutrality against Nazi Germany (Ahmad 2010: 94).

Çakmak's purge was also consistent with the strict adherence of high-ranking military officers to İnönü and the CHP. Significantly, Asım Tınaztepe, the commander of the First Army in Istanbul, and a number of senior commanders were reported to be concerned about the transition to multiparty politics. İnönü persuaded them of the necessity of the liberalisation of politics and convinced military officers to stay out of politics before the election of 1950. In June 1950, the DP government undertook a comprehensive purge at the top of the military, removing the chief of the General Staff, the commanders of the army, navy, and air force, and a number of other generals, including Tınaztepe (Hale 1994: 92–93). In this way, the DP guaranteed the compliance of the higher ranks. To illustrate, in January 1958, nine military officers were arrested and tried for forming secret cells to overthrow the DP government. Nonetheless, the officer who leaked the information was found guilty of slander due to a lack of evidence. Menderes remained convinced that the higher ranks' support of the government indicated the loyalty of the military as a whole to the DP government, and decided not to extend the investigation of the conspiracy (Ahmad 1977: 58–59). The coup was eventually to be undertaken by the lower and middle ranks only two years later, in May 1960.

In addition, the process of Turkey's membership of NATO, which had a great impact on the military's political role, reinforced US hegemony over Turkey. When NATO was established by the United States, Canada, and Western European countries as a military alliance to "unite efforts for collective defence and preservation of peace and security" in 1949 (NATO 1949), its first and foremost target remained the Soviet Union. Turkey's immediate application for membership was denied in 1949 as most NATO members were reluctant to extend geographical commitments and increase the rearmament burden. When Turkey reapplied for membership in May 1950, the DP considered an alliance with the United States, which supported South Korea against North Korea, backed by the Soviet Union, as an opportunity to join NATO. The DP's Cabinet violated the Constitution of 1924 in bypassing the Assembly and deciding to deploy a brigade in South Korea during the Korean War under the command of the US 25th Infantry Division (Atılgan 2015a: 497–498). Meanwhile, the United States regarded the strengthening of Turkey, Iran, and Iraq as a strategy to safeguard the security of the Middle East from the Soviet Union, which was "vital" for US security. Turkey was indeed considered "the Middle Eastern anchor" to the security of Europe and the establishment of a regional organisation for the security of the Middle East (McGhee 1990: 52–54). In February 1952, Turkey was formally admitted to NATO as a full member, and Turkey's membership was approved unanimously by the Turkish Assembly (Karaosmanoğlu 1988: 296), unifying dominant classes and their representatives, the DP and the CHP. Consequently, the Turkish ground forces, including the First, Second, and Third Armies, were put under NATO's Southern Command (Hale 2013: 86).

Following Turkey's application for admission to NATO in 1949, the United States and Turkey signed several bilateral military and economic agreements. Nonetheless, a number of these bilateral agreements were never discussed at the Assembly and remain classified today. These bilateral agreements granted the United States rights to introduce military bases and deploy American military personnel and tactical nuclear weapons in Turkey.[8] NATO members had clandestine networks through which the military secret services operated an "anti-communist army within the state in close collaboration with the CIA or the MI6 unknown to parliaments and populations" (Ganser 2004: 1). These clandestine networks were known by the executive, represented by the prime minister, the president, and the ministers of defence and the interior. In Turkey, this anti-communist army, called the Turkish *gladio* or the counter-guerrilla (*kontrgerilla*), was formed as a stay-behind army to be directed by the Special Forces Command (*Özel Kuvvetler Komutanlığı*; later *Özel Harp Dairesi*). The Special Forces Command was originally called the Tactical Mobilisation

---

8 According to Atılgan (2015a: 498–499), the United States established more than ninety military bases in Turkey, whose locations were determined by the United States, and which were exempt from bills of electricity, gas, petroleum, and postal services, as well as taxes on alcoholic drinks and tobacco.

Group and was later renamed the Special Warfare Department in 1965. The headquarters of the Special Forces Command was located in the building of the American Aid Delegation (the Joint US Military Mission for Aid to Turkey). The counter-guerrilla, whose task was to "organise resistance in the case of a communist occupation" (Ganser 2005: 73), represented a right-wing paramilitary group consisting of Turkish nationalists and Islamists (Örnek and Üngör 2013: 10). By being utilised against the organisation of the working classes and left-wing movements, the counter-guerrilla was to play a significant role in paving the way to coups d'états.

2.4 Demokrat Parti's *Hegemonic Crisis and the Military*

Beginning in the mid-1950s, the United States and international organisations reduced the foreign aid and credits received by Turkey to compel the DP to comply with the IMF's prescription for devaluation and deflation. The relatively closed economy, combined with the unplanned ISI pursued by the DP beginning in 1956, reached an impasse by 1958. The slowdown in agricultural growth (4 per cent per year) beginning in 1954 already hampered the economic growth rate (5.1 per cent per year), despite the rapid advancement in industrialisation (9.3 per cent per year). The DP's resort to import restrictions, barter, and export dividends could not solve the payment difficulties. Meanwhile, the increase in inflation (15 per cent) disrupted the fixed exchange rate and exports (Kazgan 2005: 105). By 1958, total outstanding foreign debt constituted 12 per cent of the GNI and was close to the total value of exports, while foreign debt constituted 10 per cent of the GNI (Kepenek and Yentürk 2001: 122). Consequently, the DP declared a debt moratorium and began to pursue an IMF-led stabilisation programme in August 1958. The programme mainly aimed to curb inflation through restrictive monetary and fiscal policies and the lifting of government price controls, and stimulate exports through the devaluation of the Turkish lira and the liberalisation of foreign trade (Kazgan 2005: 116–117). While the liberalisation of foreign trade combined with devaluation stimulated imports and increased foreign debt, the DP prioritised the import of intermediate goods and raw materials to encourage industrialisation (Kepenek and Yentürk 2001: 122). In the meantime, increases in the prices of SOE goods and the regulation of bank credits brought about an economic recession (Kazgan 2005: 117).

The economic and currency crisis of 1958 concretised the hegemonic crisis of the DP, which began following the economic stagnation of the mid-1950s. The discourse on democracy articulated within the DP's hegemonic project rested on the premise that the DP received the majority of votes and hence represented the national will. This premise constituted the basis of the DP's attempt at legitimisation of its authoritarianism. The DP's resort to authoritarianism had already begun—however hesitantly—in the early 1950s. To illustrate, the DP utilised the Constitution of 1924, which lacked constitutional checks and balances, to strengthen executive power despite its declared goal of amending the Constitution prior to the election of 1950 (Karpat 1988: 138). Similarly, the DP launched a carrot-and-stick strategy against the media with the Decree on Official Announcements and Advertisements (1953), and strengthened the government's position vis-à-vis freedom of speech, which was further curtailed with the tightening of the Press Law in March 1954 (Ahmad 1977: 53). The DP's efforts to hamper the organisation of the subordinate classes, as discussed above, demonstrate that the DP's authoritarianism was in accordance with its representation of the dominant classes.

The hegemonic crisis of the mid-1950s brought about a fragmentation within the power bloc whereby the DP remained the representative of the commercial bourgeoisie and landlords, mainly the rural dominant classes. The interests of the industrial bourgeoisie were in contradiction with those of landlords and the commercial bourgeoisie, which accumulated its wealth through agricultural production and exports. The industrial bourgeoisie demanded planned ISI policies, which the DP lacked the class basis to provide. The urban social strata, including workers, the intelligentsia, the media, and the universities, joined the industrial bourgeoisie regarding their opposition to the DP, demanding the broadening of democratic rights and freedoms.

The hegemonic crisis of the mid-1950s was further complicated by domestic and international ruptures. The Istanbul pogrom of 1955, also known as the Events of 6–7 September, was one of the most severe social and political ruptures. During the negotiations between Turkey, Greece, and Britain over the future of Cyprus in September 1955, Menderes and Foreign Minister Fatin Rüştü Zorlu planned "a limited 'spontaneous' demonstration" to express public opinion regarding the issue (Zürcher 2007: 231). The demonstration soon descended into demolition, sabotage, and the pillaging and looting of shops, houses, churches, schools, and graveyards of non-Muslims, especially Greeks, in several Istanbul districts, including Karaköy, Eminönü, Kumkapı, Fener, and Kuzguncuk, on 6 and 7 September 1955. The DP later covered up its role in the events and appeased the public by forcing Minister of the Interior Namık Gedik and three generals to resign (Atılgan 2015a: 436–438).

In the international arena, the DP sought to pursue regional relations in the Middle East that confirmed Western hegemony. Significantly, Turkey joined the Baghdad Pact, which was created among Iran, Iraq, and Pakistan in 1955 and later became the Central Eastern Nations Treaty Organization (CENTO) in 1958 (Yerasimos 1989: 217). Both the Baghdad Pact and CENTO were opposed by

Egypt and Syria. Thus, both of these organisations complicated Turkey's relations regionally and with the Non-Aligned Movement, whose members were in the process of decolonisation and pursued anti-colonial and anti-imperialist policies against the Western capitalist bloc. The DP's enthusiasm to undertake the role of "devotee" of Western imperialism often brought Turkey to the brink of war in the Middle East (Gerger 1999: 68), deepening the DP's hegemonic crisis. To illustrate, Turkey deployed troops and ammunition on the border following Syria's declaration of American diplomats as *persona non grata* in 1957, planned a military intervention against the coup that overthrew the monarchy in Iraq in 1958, and permitted the United States to use the Incirlik base in Adana in support of the US military intervention in Lebanon (Atılgan 2015a: 502).[9]

When the DP intensified its turn to authoritarianism as a response to the hegemonic crisis, the CHP emerged as the representative of the urban dominant and subordinate classes. For this reason, the DP's authoritarianism most vividly targeted the CHP to overrule the political opposition in the Assembly. The DP's aim to quash the CHP could already be dated back to the early 1950s. In December 1953, five months before the election, the DP legislated a bill to transfer the CHP's properties to the Treasury, claiming that the CHP had an unfair advantage in electoral campaigns due to its state-party background (TBMM 14 December 1953). This position against the CHP was in line with the DP's representation of the rural dominant classes, since such a transfer further resulted in purges of the People's Homes (Akşin 2001: 78) and hampered modern social transformation in rural areas. The DP's attempt to reinforce authoritarianism aggravated its aim to eliminate the CHP in the late 1950s. In October 1958, the DP called for the creation of "a fatherland front" as a means of national solidarity against the CHP, which the DP accused of conspiring a coup against the government (*Milliyet* 1958).

The formation of the fatherland front marked the extension of the DP's utilisation of the state apparatus to quash the CHP. For instance, the office of the governor prohibited the CHP's Congress in Karşıyaka, Izmir, in May 1959. More dramatically, in April 1960, İnönü was cordoned off by army troops in Kayseri following the governor's interdiction of the CHP's Congress on the basis of "provocation and conspiracy" (Atılgan 2015a: 450). The breaking point was the decision of DP MPs to establish a committee of inquest with wide powers to investigate the CHP's activities (Zürcher 2007: 240). During the parliamentary debate on the establishment of the committee, İnönü declared: "If you

---

9 The mission of the Incirlik base has been the protection of "NATO [and] the US interests in the southern region" (Bölme 2007: 87).

continue ... to deviate from democracy and foster an authoritarian regime ... even *I* cannot save you" (TBMM 18 April 1960).

It is still debatable to what extent İnönü knew about the dissidence among the military ranks. However, the changing position of the military vis-à-vis the DP between 1950 and 1960 demonstrates that the combination of the hegemonic crisis and the DP's authoritarianism made the lower and middle ranks, who undertook the coup of 1960, increasingly discontent.

The fragmentation within the power bloc as a result of the hegemonic crisis was further reproduced within the state apparatus, particularly the military. In this regard, the military was divided into two main factions: the upper ranks, and the middle and lower ranks. The formation of a power bloc under the hegemony of landlords and the commercial bourgeoisie had already resulted in the marginalisation of the civil-military bureaucracy beginning in 1950. The DP further discredited the civil-military bureaucracy by identifying it with the CHP, the main opposition, and portraying it as an oppressor (DP 1951: 47). More importantly, the DP strengthened the executive against the bureaucracy by empowering the government "to suspend, and after a period of suspension, to retire employees of the state" (Ahmad 1977: 53). The DP also publicly belittled the military to degrade its social significance. To illustrate, Menderes stated that he could "command the armed forces with reserved officers" (Atılgan 2015a: 401). Nonetheless, the lower and middle ranks remained content with the DP and its efforts at the modernisation of the military in the early 1950s. The most urgent issue for the lower and middle ranks was the restructuring of the military to prevent the ossification of the upper ranks. The appointment of Seyfi Kurtbek, who reorganised the military to pursue modernisation and the creation of flexible opportunities for promotion, as the minister of defence in November 1952 impressed the lower and middle ranks (Ahmad 2003: 123).

Nonetheless, the majority of lower- and middle-ranking military officers came from smallholder and peasant families and still suffered from material backwardness in the military compared to Western NATO members (Ahmad 1977: 154). This made the lower and middle ranks more susceptible to the impact of the crisis of 1958. Moreover, the establishment of the committee of inquest was followed by several demonstrations in Ankara and Istanbul. Most significantly, huge university student demonstrations took place against the DP in April 1960, later known as the 28 April Events. During the demonstrations, the dean of Istanbul University was manhandled by the police while being detained and taken to the police station. Forty students were injured, and one was shot dead by the police. When police forces proved insufficient, army troops were called upon to suppress the demonstrations. However, the military officers and conscripts did not intervene after they were welcomed by students (Akşin 2001: 135–136). On the following day, martial law was proclaimed (TBMM 29 April 1960). This demonstrated that the DP's attempt to use the military against the protests of students and professors backfired. In May 1960, students of the Ankara War College marched in Ankara against the DP government. The DP responded by introducing martial law and declaring the city in a state of siege (Ahmad 1977: 66). The protests of future military officers clearly demonstrated the opposition of the lower ranks to the DP's authoritarianism.

The lower and middle ranks had already been radicalised beginning in the mid-1940s as they had opposed the CHP and the upper ranks prior to the DP government. This radicalisation facilitated the formation of secret cells among the lower and middle ranks beginning in the mid-1950s. Nonetheless, these cells retained their disagreements regarding the extent of a military intervention and its aftermath. Even though these cells initially agreed on the aim of military reform rather than a military takeover, the idea of overthrowing the DP became the most appealing action by the late 1950s. The radical group advocated a long-lasting military rule to solve the socioeconomic problems in the country, whereas the moderate group rejected this idea for its possibility to turn into a totalitarian and autocratic military dictatorship. Certain members of the moderate group argued in favour of handing power to the CHP, whereas others argued for an interim period of military rule to prepare a new constitution and hold an election so that the military could transfer power back to the civilians (Hale 1994: 100–104). The latter faction of the moderate group was to succeed when the DP was overthrown by the coup in May 1960.

3   The Coup of 1960 and Its Aftermath

3.1   *The Coup of 1960 and the Social Classes*

On 27 May 1960, a coup was broadcasted by military officers whose declared purpose was "to extricate 'the parties from the irreconcilable situation', to set up an above-party administration, hold free elections, and hand back political power to the winning party" (Ahmad 1977: 161). The military officers' statement also gave references to the Internal Service Act (Hale 1994: 102–103; see also Chapter 2). The coup faced hardly any resistance from the loyalist troops, demonstrating that it had obtained the consent of various social classes. The self-proclaimed *Milli Birlik Komitesi* (National Unity Committee, MBK) soon began to rule in the interim period between the military takeover and the enactment of the Constitution of 1961, which was followed by the transition to multiparty politics and the election in October 1961.

The coup of 1960 represented a modern-bourgeois reaction of radical lower- and middle-ranking military officers in alliance with the intelligentsia to overcome the hegemonic crisis of landlords and the commercial bourgeoisie. The greatest manifestation of the coup's modern-bourgeois—and hence relatively progressive—characteristic was the enactment of the Constitution of 1961. The Constitution of 1961 consolidated the normal state, encompassing institutionalised mechanisms for national-popular representation within a relatively stable bourgeois democratic framework (Poulantzas 1978: 294–295). In fact, it remains today the most democratic constitution Turkey has ever had. It introduced the principles of constitutional supremacy on the basis of the protection of social democracy, as well as the separation of powers and constitutional checks and balances on executive and legislative powers. Further, it established the principle of the rule of law and provided a strong regime of fundamental rights and freedoms with its emphasis on the protection of citizens against the state (Tanör 1994: 19–28).

The coup of 1960 further focused on secularism to force the reversal of the conservative shift in the state's ideology. The Constitution of 1961 (1961: 4644) prohibited the political use of religion by any individual or organisation. It enabled the Constitutional Court (*Anayasa Mahkemesi*) to close the political parties that called for the determination of social, economic, political, and legal foundations of the state on a religious basis. Similarly, the Constitution of 1961 (1961: 4653) protected the laws pertaining to secularisation enacted in the 1920s and the 1930s under a constitutional umbrella. While the *Diyanet* was recognised as a constitutional state institution (Constitution 1961: 4653), it was considered a tool to control the political use of religion, particularly by religious brotherhoods.

The lower- and middle-ranking military officers undertook and legitimised the coup of 1960 and subsequent social, economic, and political reforms in alliance with the intelligentsia and university youth, as already illustrated through the protests of students and professors supported by the military cadets. Law professors, who were given the task of preparing a new constitution, also legitimised the coup on the grounds that the DP had breached the Constitution of 1924. This, nevertheless, conflicted with the MBK's initial declaration regarding the impartiality of the military and the nonpartisan character of the coup (Zürcher 2007: 242). The lower and middle ranks also received the support of the judiciary. Significantly, the Supreme Court of Justice was set up in Yassıada, an island in the Sea of Marmara, and a number of DP MPs, state officials, police officers, and businessmen were tried for corruption, criminality, and violation of the Constitution. During the Yassıada trials, the DP was officially closed down in September 1960 (Hale 1994: 127).[10]

The coup of 1960 further rested on the industrial bourgeoisie. This was manifested by Article 41 of the Constitution of 1961 (1961: 4644), which underlined social and economic development based on "full employment" and "democratic means", including "increasing national savings, directing investments to benefit society, and planning". This article, complemented by subsequent reformation of the national economy, demonstrated that the coup restructured the pattern of capital accumulation and achieved the transition to ISI through a planned economy. Such restructuring indicated that the coup paved the way for the formation of a power bloc under the hegemony of the industrial bourgeoisie. These points will be further discussed below.

The position of the coup of 1960 vis-à-vis the subordinate classes, nevertheless, remained ambivalent. On the one hand, it broadened democratic rights and freedoms that paved the way for the radicalisation and organisation of the urban and rural subordinate classes. Most significantly, the Constitution of 1961 (1961: 4643–4644) granted freedoms of peaceful assembly, demonstration, and association, and rights to strikes and collective bargaining. The Constitution further fostered social transformation particularly in rural areas by promoting land reforms. Significantly, it facilitated the state redistribution of land to landless peasants and the ownership of the means of production by smallholders and peasants (Constitution 1961: 4643). On the other hand, the coup reproduced the uneven and dependent relations between Turkey and Western countries, particularly the United States, and Western international organisations. Significantly, the MBK confirmed Turkey's commitment to NATO and CENTO (*Milliyet* 1960). Western hegemony was to be reproduced in economic and political relations, particularly through the contradictions of planned ISI and the restructuring of the state apparatus, including the military.

3.2 The Transition to Import-Substitution Industrialisation, the State, and Class Relations

Import-substitution industrialisation (ISI) emerged as a form of development strategy of late industrialisation in the peripheries of world capitalism following the end of the Second World War. ISI was based on the advancement of a domestic industrial base in the service of the home market, the curtailment of dependence on the import of expensive manufactured goods and the export

---

10   Bayar, Menderes, Zorlu, and Hasan Polatkan, the former minister of finance, were unanimously sentenced to death. Bayar's death sentence was commuted, whereas Menderes, Zorlu, and Polatkan were executed (Zürcher 2007: 248).

of cheap unprocessed goods, and the protection of the domestic industries through tariffs and import controls. The state was to play a central role by protecting domestic industry through high tariffs and import controls, and certain incentives and state subsidies (Kiely 2005a: 79). ISI consisted of three main stages: the first stage of manufacturing consumer goods through the import of investment goods and raw materials; the second stage of producing relatively simple industrial machinery and intermediate goods; and the third stage of producing capital goods (Gereffi 1990: 17).[11] ISI corresponded to the needs of foreign productive capital, which was in the process of internationalisation, since the integration of late-developing countries into a unified international network of capitalist production and exchange facilitated the internationalisation of productive capital (Yaghmaian 1990: 180).

Turkey's statism of the 1930s can be regarded as a hesitant attempt of ISI aimed at the production of nondurable goods. This production process was completed through unplanned ISI under the DP beginning in the mid-1950s. The coup of 1960 paved the way for planned ISI policies, which responded to the needs of the industrial bourgeoisie to complete the primary stage, especially the production of durable goods, and the secondary stage of ISI. Planned ISI also conformed to the interests of the civil-military bureaucracy which sought to play a central role in the national economy and politics. Nonetheless, class antagonisms and contradictions inherent in ISI brought about the crisis of ISI beginning in the late 1960s (see Chapter 4).

Regarding planned ISI beginning in the 1960s, the State Planning Organisation (*Devlet Planlama Teşkilatı*, DPT) was established under the Office of the Prime Minister in October 1960. The DPT's major duty was to determine and supervise short-, medium-, and long-term plans in accordance with economic and social policies of the government as well as the advancement and regulation of objectives of the private sector (Law on the Establishment of the State Planning Organisation 1960). The DPT's initial draft of the Five-Year Development Plan (1963–1967) encompassed reforms on land ownership, taxation, public administration, and entrepreneurship in a way designed to prevent the use of public resources by the private sector. In this sense, it demonstrated the left-wing bureaucrats' quest for progress and development

---

11   Intermediate goods refer to products which are bought for current use in other industries, especially if they are used to produce consumer goods (sector C), investment goods for consumer goods (sector I), and intermediate goods and raw materials (sector R) (Raj and Sen 1961: 45). Borrowing from Raj and Sen's (1961: 46) classification of investment goods, this book utilises the term capital goods (sector M) to indicate investment goods used for the sectors I, R, and M.

within the limits of capitalist relations. Following the government's rejection of the initial draft, the DPT proposed a second draft which conformed to the expectations of the industrial bourgeoisie, such as the advancement of foreign debts and credits, and the curbing of certain aspects of public goods and services (Küçük 1985: 295–297).

The welfare state emerged in the advanced capitalist Western countries in the aftermath of the Second World War, characterised by the Fordist mass-production systems based on capital-intensive machinery and (semi-)skilled labour, and a strict division of labour and specialisation in the workplace, bringing about rapid economic growth (Kiely 2007: 48). The welfare state remained a particular form of state that represented a social compromise between capital and labour. It simultaneously fulfilled two main contradictory roles; on the one hand, the welfare state supported the reproduction of capital through nationalised and socialised welfare functions, such as education and healthcare, that enhanced social reproduction and the pacification of the working classes; on the other hand, the welfare state weakened the reproduction of capital as further concessions acquired by the organised working classes eventually increased costs to capital and squeezed profits, leading to an accumulation crisis, and hence threatening social reproduction (Ankarloo 2012: 380–382).

In Turkey, a particular sociohistorical form of welfare state emerged in relation to the reorganisation of the state apparatus as a result of the transition to industrial capital accumulation based on import-substitution and a planned economy beginning in 1960. The welfare state in Turkey was equipped with labour rights, welfare provisions, and social security. In this regard, the welfare state was sometimes referred to as a "social state", to be differentiated from its counterparts in Western Europe (Buğra and Candaş 2011: 516). The coup of 1960 paved the way for the introduction of a law-based welfare system and social security policies since the Constitution of 1961 (1961: 4644) regarded social security as a right for every citizen and charged the state with the duty to institutionalise social security and social assistance. The employment-based welfare system significantly broadened social security beyond blue-collar workers in the public and private sectors and civil servants to include farmers, artisans, and the remaining self-employed in the 1960s (see Elveren 2008). On the one hand, the increasing mass of surplus product based on industrial capital accumulation in the 1960s enabled the welfare/social state to compromise the short-term interests of the dominant classes. On the other hand, the modern-bourgeois alliance's aim at the broadening and deepening of social democracy attached the law-based welfare system to the strengthening of labour rights and the organised working classes (see Chapter 4).

3.3 The Institutionalisation of the Military's Guardianship Role

The coup of 1960 institutionalised the military's guardianship role, defined and legitimised by the Internal Service Act and institutionalised through economic, political, and judicial autonomies granted through the establishment of the Military Personnel Assistance Fund (*Ordu Yardımlaşma Kurumu*) and the National Security Council (*Milli Güvenlik Kurulu*), and the reorganisation of the General Staff and the military courts. The institutionalisation of the military's guardianship role remained in line with the protection of the capitalist social order under the dynamics of unevenness and dependency.

Most significantly, in March 1961, the Military Personnel Assistance Fund (OYAK) was established as an autonomous organisation subject to the Commercial Code, even though it was placed under the authority of the Ministry of Defence (Law on the Military Personnel Assistance Fund 1961). OYAK's mission was to provide social security to military personnel and their dependants, such as economic assistance in case of retirement, death, and disability, and other social services. However, OYAK soon accumulated contributions of its members and channelled its funds to accumulate commercial, financial, and industrial capital in the automotive, cement, transport, food, insurance, and banking sectors (Uzgel 2003: 183). In this sense, the military's economic autonomy constituted the material basis of the military's role in politics. More importantly, the military rapidly developed objective capitalist interests and organic relations with various foreign and domestic capital through its economic autonomy. In this way, the military was gradually integrated into the capitalist system by functioning as a capitalist fraction. This was to bring about a reactionary alliance of the military with the dominant classes beginning in the 1970s.

Regarding the military's political autonomy, the Supreme Defence Assembly was transformed into the National Security Council (NSC) in December 1962 (Law on the National Security Council 1962).[12] The NSC was granted the mission of assisting the Cabinet regarding the determination of social, economic, and political policies pertaining to national security. In this sense, the military's authority was reinforced through, first, the subjection of civilian governments to the NSC's views, and second, the broadening of the NSC's agenda to include nonmilitary issues arising from the reproduction of capitalist relations. Moreover, the NSC was composed of the prime minister and deputy prime minister; the ministers of defence, the interior, foreign affairs, finance,

---

[12] The emphasis on national security was in line with the formation of the National Security Council under President Truman's premiership in 1947 (National Security Act 1947), corresponding to the US hegemony over Turkey.

transportation, and labour; the chief of the General Staff; and the commanders of the army, navy, air force, and gendarmerie. The NSC was chaired by the president; however, the prime minister could also chair the Council in the absence of the president, as well as being able to invite Ministers and experts from various institutions for consultation depending on the NSC's agenda. This shifted the balance between the military and civilian government in favour of the former, institutionalising the military's behind-the-scenes influence regarding the decisions on what constituted matters of security for the safeguarding of the capitalist social order.

The reorganisation of the General Staff further corresponded to the military's political autonomy. The Cabinet was charged with the responsibility of safeguarding national security and preparing the military for a war (Constitution 1961: 4649). The Assembly was to supervise the Cabinet while the Cabinet was undertaking such a responsibility. The chief of the General Staff was to be appointed by the president upon the proposal of the Cabinet. The General Staff was submitted under the authority of the prime minister, broadening the military's political autonomy.

The military's judicial autonomy was institutionalised through the restructuring of military courts. In December 1962, the Military Court of Appeal (*Askeri Yargıtay*) was established to review the decisions of lower military courts (Law on the Establishment of the Military Court of Appeal 1962). In October 1963, the minister of defence was charged with the competence to establish the military courts (Law on the Establishment of Military Courts and Proceedings 1963). The military courts composed of two military judges and one associate military judge, whose rank had to be higher than that of the defendant. However, if a military court was established before the General Staff where generals and admirals were tried, it composed of three military judges and two generals/admirals. The military courts were competent to try military officers and conscripts whose crimes affected their military duty. Since the decisions of military courts could only be appealed to the Military Court of Appeal, the lack of civilian judicial review granted judicial autonomy to the military and institutionalised its guardianship role.

The pioneering role of the lower and middle ranks within the military regarding the coup of 1960 demonstrated cleavages between them and the upper ranks. The coup's plotters originally asked Cemal Gürsel, the commander of the army, to lead the coup to maintain the chain of command. Gürsel not only commanded the coup, but also the MBK and the military as the president and the chief of the General Staff (*Milliyet* 1960). The purge of the radicals, who demanded comprehensive political reforms under the junta before the transfer of power to a civilian government, in October 1960 further aimed to resolve the division within the MBK and maintain the military hierarchy (Özdemir 1990: 196–197). Nonetheless, the cleavages between the upper ranks and the middle and lower ranks could not be solved as the middle and lower ranks remained radical in the 1960s.

In 1962, the military forced the CHP to form a coalition government under İnönü's premiership, since the military did not support *Adalet Partisi* (Justice Party, AP), heir to the DP, which gained the majority of votes in the election of October 1961. The coalition government could not implement social and economic reforms to tackle growing unemployment, and thus failed to maintain social and political stability to favour the industrial bourgeoisie. Meanwhile, the AP's demands to enact an amnesty for the DP officials deepened the hegemonic crisis (Atılgan 2015b: 558–559). Talat Aydemir, the colonel who organised the lower and middle ranks in Ankara and broadened the grassroots of the coup of 1960 (Atılgan 2015a: 489), pioneered two abortive coup attempts in 1962 and 1963. As a radical, Aydemir represented the left wing as opposed to the right-wing radical Alparslan Türkeş, the colonel who broadcasted the coup and was later purged from the MBK in 1960 (Ahmad 2003: 144). Therefore, Aydemir's failed coup attempts demonstrated the deepening cleavages within the military between the left and the right, which were to be solved through future military interventions in 1971 and 1980.

CHAPTER 4

The Coup of 1980 and the Reorganisation of the Military

> The tradition of all the dead generations weighs like a nightmare on the brain of the living.
>
> KARL MARX (1979 [1852])

∴

This chapter discusses the transformation of the military's guardianship role following the coup of 1980 in accordance with political and economic relations between and among the dominant and subordinate classes. Import-substitution industrialisation (ISI) was inherently constituted with labour-capital and intra-capital contradictions, which were augmented under the impacts of the rise of the working classes and the Third World in the 1960s, and of the economic crisis of the mid-1970s. As the Turkish military emerged as a mediator that reorganised patterns of capital accumulation, the hegemonic crises of the late 1960s and the late 1970s in Turkey brought about two military interventions, namely, the memorandum of 1971 and the coup of 1980. This chapter focuses on the coup of 1980 as a key military intervention that responded to the prolonged hegemonic crises of the late 1960s, which could not be solved by the memorandum of 1971, and of the late 1970s to enable the transition to neoliberalism to take place.

1 The Crisis of the Late 1960s and the Memorandum of 1971

1.1 Class Relations in the 1960s

The enactment of the Constitution of 1961 was followed by the transition to social democracy, however limited it remained. Social democracy indicated a compromise between capital and labour that sought to respond to the destructiveness of the capitalist market through the redistribution of wealth in a more equalitarian and efficient way, such as through public goods, social security and provisions, and broadened labour rights (Uysal 2018: 40; see also Przeworski

1985: 37–42). The sharp contrast between the authoritarian populism of the 1950s and the social democracy of the 1960s fundamentally manifested different class configurations arising from different patterns of capital accumulation: agricultural production in the 1950s and industrial production in the 1960s. The implementation of three consecutive Five-Year Development Plans (1963–1967, 1968–1972, and 1973–1977) maintained rapid and steady economic growth, which was illustrated by the average growth rate of 6.6 per cent for the GNP (Kazgan 2006: 93). This economic growth was based on protectionist economic policies aimed at production for the domestic market and the replacement of imported manufactured goods with domestically produced goods. The state continued to play an important role in industrialisation, especially by favouring the industrial bourgeoisie. To illustrate, the goods produced by the SOEs were sold at below-cost prices to the private sector (Kepenek and Yentürk 2001: 157).

On the one hand, the industries of consumer durable goods, which initially assembled imported goods into finished goods and were dependent on the participation of foreign capital, developed into modern industries with the growing contribution of national capital and blooming subindustries beginning in the 1960s. Meanwhile, industrial capital accumulation further advanced the agricultural sector and commerce by broadening agricultural credits and the use of tractors, chemicals, and fertilisers (Kepenek and Yentürk 2001: 158). On the other hand, these industries remained dependent on the import of technology, and capital and intermediate goods. These industries further lagged behind the advanced Western industries in terms of scale of production, unit costs, and quality (Boratav 2014: 119). The remarkable place of foreign capital in the fields of food and beverages and tobacco demonstrated that the interest of foreign capital was to make higher profits through the production of consumer nondurable goods (Atılgan 2015b: 522). Foreign capital that invested in consumer durable goods, particularly rubber, chemicals, and electrical machines, quickly monopolised (Kepenek and Yentürk 2001: 169–170). The primacy of foreign capital was further enhanced through the transfer of state enterprises to private companies, particularly in the fields of mining, iron and steel, manufacturing, and raw material processing. For instance, 80 per cent of rubber production was transferred to three foreign companies, namely, Goodyear, Pirelli, and Royal Tire. Similarly, three foreign oil companies, namely, Mobil Oil, Shell, and British Petroleum, continued to exert monopolistic control over the Turkish oil industry, despite the challenge of the state-owned Turkish Petroleum Corporation (Berberoglu 1982: 95). Furthermore, the industrial bourgeoisie relied on foreign aid and credit to finance the import of technology, raw materials and intermediate goods, and energy (Schick and Tonak

1981: 66). This negatively affected the persisting question of foreign debt and the balance of payments.

Industrial capital accumulation brought about the rise of the bourgeoisie as a class-conscious and organised social stratum. Significantly, in 1962, *Türkiye İşveren Sendikaları Konfederasyonu* (Turkish Confederation of Employer Associations, TISK) was formed to enable the capitalists to directly engage with governments and trade unions during collective bargaining and strikes (Yalman 2002: 37). Industrial capital accumulation further brought about a remarkable increase in the industrial proletariat in urban areas, and thus the organisation and radicalisation of the urban working classes against the bourgeoisie.[1] The radicalisation of the working classes brought about a series of workers' demonstrations and strikes between 1960 and 1963, including the march of Sümerbank workers in 1961, the Saraçhane demonstration of 1961, the protests of Ereğli iron and steel workers in 1962, and the *Kavel* strike in 1963 (Çelik 2021: 288). These demonstrations and strikes resulted in the codification of rights to strike, collective bargaining, and unionisation as recognised by the Constitution of 1961. In 1967, *Türkiye Devrimci İşçi Sendikaları Konfederasyonu* (Confederation of Progressive Trade Unions of Turkey, DISK), which played an important role regarding the formation of class consciousness with the help of the socialist intelligentsia, was established (Akkaya, 2002b: 75–82). The establishment of *Türkiye İşçi Sendikaları Konfederasyonu* (Confederation of Turkish Trade Unions, *Türk-İş*) in 1951 was funded through the Marshall Plan to prevent the radicalisation of the working classes (Akkaya 2002a: 147–164). Therefore, the establishment of DISK manifested a significant leap forward, expanding the limits of social democracy.

The organisation and radicalisation of the urban working classes coincided with the radicalisation of the rural subordinate classes. Landless peasants and smallholders undertook widespread land occupations and demonstrations, particularly in the fields of tobacco, hazelnuts, garlic, potatoes, beet, and chickpeas (Atılgan 2015b: 536), demanding lands from landlords and equal exchange from the commercial and financial bourgeoisie. The land occupations of peasants and smallholders in Çukurova and in the eastern and southeastern regions were suppressed through state violence to maintain private property (Gürel 2015a: 330–331), manifesting the limits of social democracy.

---

1 This coincided with the rise of peoples of the Third World, and of subordinate classes and university youth in the advanced capitalist Western countries. In this regard, the rise of the organised and radicalised working classes in Turkey arguably proves "the law of the transformation of quantity into quality and *vice versa*" (Engels 1987: 356).

1.2   The Hegemonic Crisis of the Late 1960s

The rapid social transformation in urban and rural areas was manifested on the political stage in the form of the proliferation of political parties and movements, giving different responses to labour-capital and intra-capital antagonisms. The AP, the heir of the DP, mainly represented landlords and the commercial bourgeoisie, and maintained close and organic ties with religious brotherhoods (see AP 1969). Even though the AP represented some of its fractions, the CHP became the main representative of the industrial bourgeoisie. With its discourse on social democracy (CHP 1965), the CHP managed to represent urban and rural subordinate classes, including the industrial proletariat, civil servants, peasants, and smallholders. The AP also obtained consent of fractions of the urban and rural subordinate classes with its conservative discourse. The AP and the CHP published a protocol of "good relationship" (Millet Meclisi 27 November 1961). The protocol identified socialism with totalitarianism to comply with the interests of the dominant classes and recognised the military as the custodian of national independence—the custodian of the capitalist social order.

In addition to the centre-left CHP and centre-right AP, the escalating class antagonisms broadened the political stage to encompass socialist, Islamist, and ultranationalist political movements and parties. The CHP's inadequacy to respond to the demands of the working classes brought about the rise of *Türkiye İşçi Partisi* (Turkey Workers' Party, TIP), a socialist party established by workers, and which remained influential among the intelligentsia. The left was further radicalised with the emergence of various socialist/Marxist movements mainly consisting of the intelligentsia and university youth, including the journal *Yön* (*Direction*), students' debating societies (*Fikir Kulüpleri Federasyonu*, Federation of Debating Societies), and the organisation *Dev-Genç* (Revolutionary Youth).

Class antagonisms crystallised in the heart of the AP resulted in the emergence of *Milli Görüş* as an Islamist movement and *Milli Nizam Partisi* (National Order Party, MNP) as an Islamist party, and of *Milliyetçi Hareket Partisi* (Nationalist Action Party, MHP) as an ultranationalist party. Both *Milli Görüş* and the MHP represented the fractions of landlords, small- and medium-scale capitalists, and urban and rural working classes. The radical right was further broadened with the emergence of various Islamist and ultranationalist movements mainly consisting of the intelligentsia and university youth, including *Komünizmle Mücadele Derneği* (Association for Fighting Communism), *Ülkü Ocakları* (Grey Wolves), and *Milli Türk Talebe Birliği* (National Union of Turkish Students, MTTB).

Beginning in the mid-1960s, the political arena was polarised between the left and the right, manifesting escalating class antagonisms and contradictions of social democracy. The election of 1965 demonstrated a major threshold that signalled the aim of the dominant classes and their representative political parties to defeat the working classes and left-wing movements, and hence the hegemonic crisis of the late 1960s. In October 1965, the AP formed a majority government under Süleyman Demirel's premiership (TBMM 22 October 1965), representing the alliance of the dominant classes under the hegemony of industrial capital. Fifteen TIP MPs also entered the Assembly, demanding the renouncement of bilateral agreements with the United States and the closure of American military bases, the nationalisation of banks and petroleum, the adoption of land reforms and statism in favour of public goods, and the broadening of freedom of speech (Özdemir 1990: 222). The TIP's legitimate place and representation in the Assembly demonstrated the rise of socialism in the 1960s.

The rise of socialism was combined with the organisation and radicalisation of students and the working classes in urban and rural areas. Beginning in the mid-1960s, Turkey saw the students' protests against the US Sixth Fleet in Istanbul, representing NATO and the United States; university boycotts and occupations demanding reforms in education and administration; and protests against Turkey's association with the European Economic Community (EEC, later the European Union) (Atılgan 2015b: 607–611). There was a close connection between the rise of students' protests and socialist movements and the radicalisation of the urban and rural subordinate classes. To illustrate, peasants undertook land occupations and demonstrations against landlords and usurers, and protested minimum prices for tobacco, chickpeas, opium poppies, garlic, cotton, potatoes, and beet in central Anatolia, Marmara, the western and southern Mediterranean, eastern and southeastern Anatolia, and the Black Sea region (Gürel 2015a: 331–333). Similarly, workers and civil servants undertook strikes, boycotts, and occupations, such as the occupations of the Derby tire factory in 1968 and the Singer sewing machine factory in in 1969, the strike in the Sümerbank weaving factories in 1969, and the strike in and occupation of the Ereğli steel and iron factory in 1969 (Atılgan 2015b: 616–617).

In response to the rise of socialism and the subordinate classes, the right increasingly resorted to the use of Islamist and ultranationalist symbols and references. This brought about overlaps among Islamist and ultranationalist organisations, and religious brotherhoods. Significantly, Fethullah Gülen, the founder of the branch of the Nurcu congregation named after him, and many prominent disciples of the Nurcu congregation were involved with the Association for Fighting Communism in the 1960s (Yavuz 2013: 34). Similarly, the MTTB, receiving funding from Saudi Arabia in the 1970s (Köni 2012: 106), replaced its nationalist discourse with Islamic symbols and references in the fight against socialism. Meanwhile, a number of prominent members of *Milli Görüş* had their background in the MTTB (Okutan 2004: 175–179). The same *Milli Görüş* established the MNP and its heirs, *Milli Selamet Partisi* (National Salvation Party, MSP) and *Refah Partisi* (Welfare Party, RP), with the Nakşibendi order's "encouragement, support, and acceptance" (Çakır 1991: 22–23; see also Chapter 5).

The state apparatus not only consented to but also actively supported the advancement of Islamist and ultranationalist organisations in accordance with the role of Turkey as a bulwark against the Soviet Union and socialism. Most significantly, President Gürsel remained the honorary secretary-general of the Association for Fighting Communism until his resignation following İnönü's call for legal action against the Association for its provocations against the left, including the CHP (Atılgan 2015b: 591). The state's support for the radicalisation of the right corresponded to Western hegemony over Turkey. To illustrate, the Grey Wolves were young militants of the MHP, which was established by Alparslan Türkeş with a pan-Turkist and fascist agenda. Türkeş previously served in the Turkish military mission to NATO in Washington, DC between 1955 and 1958, and allegedly remained a CIA liaison officer, recruiting among the Grey Wolves to staff the counter-guerrilla beginning in the late 1960s (Ganser 2005: 225–229).

The right further engaged in acts of violence against the left beginning in the mid-1960s. Significantly, during the parliamentary debate for the annual budget on security in 1968, AP MPs attacked TIP MPs before the eyes of the general director of security, who remained unresponsive (*Milliyet* 1968a). Furthermore, the MTTB and the Association for Fighting Communism called for the "crushing" of the left-wing protests against the visit of the US Sixth Fleet in Istanbul in 1969. The lynching attempt against protesting students and workers before the eyes of constabulary forces, known as Bloody Sunday, resulted in the death of two people and the wounding of more than 200 (Bora 2020: 148–149). The right's public show of force, combined with verbal and physical assaults targeting the left at the Assembly, demonstrated the legitimisation of right-wing violence at the state level. The factions of the state apparatus further supported and committed violence against the left. Significantly, the counter-guerrilla undertook "'assassinations, bombings, armed robbery, torture, attacks, kidnap, threats, provocation, militia training, hostage-taking, arson, sabotage, propaganda, disinformation, violence, and extortion'" (Ganser 2005: 230).

In the late-1960s, Turkey suffered from import shortages, which had an impact on ISI due to the dependence on the import of capital and intermediate goods. In the face of the appreciation of the Turkish lira, the IMF began to apply pressure for devaluation (Kazgan 2006: 97). Meanwhile, foreign debt continued to increase, reaching 1.77 billion USD in 1967, 2.03 billion USD in 1968, and 2.33 billion USD in 1969 (Schick and Tonak 1981: 68). The industrial bourgeoisie, nonetheless, were opposed to the possibility of devaluation as it would further deteriorate imports. Even though the AP formed a majority government in 1969 (Millet Meclisi 22 October 1969), the AP was already split up in the late 1960s with the emergence of the MNP in accordance with intra-capital rivalries. In August 1970, the AP government decided on a stabilisation package, which foresaw devaluation of the Turkish lira in exchange for foreign credit, the reduction of import restrictions, and additional export incentives for nontraditional exports (Tekin 2006: 147).

Even though the AP's decision on devaluation encouraged the IMF to grant aid totalling 50 million USD, imports increased more than exports and the foreign trade deficit tripled from 1969 to 1972 (Schick and Tonak 1981: 68–69). Moreover, the AP's attempt at manipulating exports to favour the commercial bourgeoisie and landlords against the industrial bourgeoisie constituted the basis of its failure to maintain hegemony. The AP further failed to obtain the consent of the urban and rural subordinate classes by not addressing their democratic demands and consenting to the recruitment of radical-right factions as paramilitary forces to fight against the left and the organised working classes. To illustrate, the AP responded to the students' boycotts and occupations in universities and violent clashes during political protests, which turned into murders and unsolved bomb attacks, with reluctance and contempt (*Milliyet* 1968b). The hegemonic crisis of the late 1960s was to bring the military to the political stage.

1.3   *The Memorandum of 1971*

On 12 March 1971, the military issued a memorandum to President Cevdet Sunay and the presidents of the Assembly and the Senate[2] calling for the formation of a new "strong" government to implement democratic reforms and signalling the possibility of a military takeover in case of the "failure to implement such reforms" (Cumhuriyet Senatosu 13 March 1971). Following the memorandum, the AP and Demirel resigned from the government and the premiership respectively, and a technocratic government was established under the premiership of Nihat Erim, a CHP MP (Millet Meclisi 31 March 1971).

---

2 The Constitution of 1961 introduced bicameralism, whereby the Republican Senate (*Cumhuriyet Senatosu*) was the upper house of the National Assembly (*Millet Meclisi*) (Tanör 1994: 12).

Even though the memorandum of 1971 resulted in Demirel's resignation, the AP was not the actual target of the memorandum. The AP already maintained good relations with the higher ranks of the military. Demirel previously proposed Sunay, the former chief of the General Staff, as the presidential candidate, and Sunay was elected as the president by the Assembly in March 1966 (TBMM 28 March 1966). The memorandum in fact aimed to curtail the rise of the left and suppress the organised urban and rural subordinate classes dominating the political arena in the late 1960s. An important illustration of this remained the Demonstrations of 15–16 June 1970, which were the pinnacle of the rising militancy of the working classes, paving the way for a military intervention. In June 1970, the AP amended the Law on Trade Unions to prevent DISK from being active in workplaces and to strengthen the place of *Türk-İş*. DISK responded to this amendment by rallying between 70,000 and 100,0000 workers, including members of *Türk-İş*, throughout Istanbul and Kocaeli on 15 and 16 June 1970. The AP could only proclaim martial law to enable the military alongside the police to violently suppress the demonstrations (Berberoglu 1981: 280; Küçük 1985: 335). The amendment was annulled by the Constitutional Court (Savran 2004: 25), displaying the strength of the working classes. The proclamation of martial law by the AP highlighted the guardianship role of the military as the custodian of capitalist relations in the face of the inability of a civilian government to respond to the advancing working classes.

Furthermore, the memorandum of 1971 could be regarded as a pre-emptive action of the higher-ranking military officers to maintain the chain of command and strangle the influence of left-wing ideas among the lower and middle ranks. The polarisation between the left and the right in the 1960s was reproduced through cleavages between the upper ranks and the middle and lower ranks within the military. On the one hand, the upper ranks became a natural ally of the dominant classes as a result of the growing organic relations between the military and fractions of capital. In the 1960s, OYAK advanced subsidiary operations including merchandise and retail sales of consumer goods through supermarket chains; the construction, sale, and renting of apartments and offices through real estate development; the trading of stocks and bonds; and insurance operations. OYAK further developed organic relations with foreign capital through joint ventures, such as partnerships with Renault in the automobile industry and Goodyear in tire industry (Sönmez 1987: 87). In this way, OYAK turned the military into "a merchant, industrialist, financier, and rentier" by 1971 (Parla 1998: 29). For this reason, the higher ranks of the military were determined to eliminate the threat of socialism. Significantly, the chief of the General Staff included the *Handbook on the Fight against Communism* in the training programme of all headquarters, units, and institutions within the military. The *Handbook* ordered the "quashing of communism wherever possible [as] communism remained the biggest enemy of the Turkish public" (TSK 1966: 7). The counter-guerrilla was restructured as the Special Warfare Department in 1965 and began to work in collaboration with the National Intelligence Agency (*Milli İstihbarat Teşkilatı*, MIT) (Ganser 2005: 230).

On the other hand, left-wing cleavages emerged among the lower and the middle ranks in the military in line with the radicalisation of the left. By the late 1960s, a faction within *Yön* formulated an idea of National Democratic Revolution (*Milli Demokratik Devrim*, MDD), which aimed at land reforms to eliminate precapitalist remnants, the nationalisation of big industries and banks, and an anti-imperialist foreign policy. According to the MDD, such a revolution could only be undertaken by a national front in which the civil-military bureaucracy remained the major pioneer, supported by the intelligentsia (Şener 2010: 175–180). The MDD was welcomed by cleavages among the lower and middle ranks within the military, who were disillusioned by parliamentary democracy and sought fundamental socioeconomic and sociopolitical reforms that would foster social transformation and challenge Western hegemony (Akyaz 2002: 278–283). The slogans of "'Army and Workers, Hand in Hand'" shouted by workers during the Demonstrations of 15–16 June 1970 further alarmed the higher ranks (Koelle 2000: 47), who were already troubled by the possibility of a left-wing uprising in the military (Özdemir 1990: 212–214). The signing of the memorandum of 1971 by the chief of the General Staff and the commanders of the land forces, air force and navy demonstrated the urge of the higher ranks to maintain the military hierarchy and purge the left-wing officers.

The aftermath of the memorandum of 1971 demonstrated that the real mission of the military was to suppress the subordinate classes and the left wing while advancing Turkey's integration with the world capitalist system. Most significantly, the technocratic government under Erim's premiership selected Cabinet members from political parties represented at the Assembly and individuals outside the Assembly to amend the Five-Year Development Plan. The new Plan was to comply with the Additional Protocol signed between Turkey and the EEC in 1970, which foresaw the establishment of a customs union between Turkey and the EEC (Additional Protocol and Financial Protocol 1970). In this regard, the Plan sought to catch up with the EEC's "levels of national income and economic structures" by implementing "reforms" aimed at increasing GNI and economic growth rates, and transition to the production of intermediate and capital goods. Such "reforms" included "sacrificing" certain rights and freedoms (Kepenek and Yentürk 2001: 151), implying the curtailing of labour rights. Erim's government in fact could only rule the country through short periods of martial law declared between 1971 and 1972, which suppressed the subordinate classes and left-wing movements through mass arrests, tortures, and censorship. While the right to unionise was denied for civil servants and judicial review over the executive branch was narrowed,[3] workers' rights to strikes and collective bargaining were in effect suspended (Tanör 1994: 54–60).

The aftermath of the memorandum of 1971 further demonstrated that the dominant classes were unified against the rise of the subordinate classes and the left. The AP government's stabilisation package of 1970 partly resolved the industrial bourgeoisie's financial needs and expanded the domestic market by amending financial law and land tax, even though the package overall benefited landlords and the commercial bourgeoisie. The high pricing in agriculture following the memorandum of 1971 demonstrated that landlords and the commercial bourgeoisie continued to obtain relative gains, a process which was consented to by the industrial bourgeoisie (Küçük 1980: 496–500). The memorandum, nevertheless, favoured the industrial bourgeoisie by curbing real wages, increasing the prices of industrial goods, and turning on the Central Bank's credit taps (Küçük 1985: 345–359).

The memorandum of 1971 reinforced the military's guardianship role by broadening the duties of the Supreme Military Council in July 1972. The new duties included giving opinions on the definition and revision of the National Military Strategic Concept (*Milli Askeri Stratejik Konsept*), which was prepared by the General Staff; the goals and legal structure of the military; and any other issues asked by the prime minister, the chief of the General Staff, and the minister of defence. The Supreme Council's decisions were to be taken with a simple majority. In the case of a tied vote, the side on which the chair voted was to prevail (Law on the Establishment of the Supreme Military Council 1972). The Supreme Council was broadened in May 1979 to consist of the prime minister; the chief of the General Staff; the minister of defence; the commanders of the army, navy, air force, and gendarmerie; and the generals and admirals. The prime minister was entitled to chair the Supreme Council, and in case of their absence the chief of the General Staff was the chair. The deputy-chief of the

---

3 Judicial review over the executive branch in the 1960s mostly functioned to the detriment of the dominant and ruling classes as a result of the rise of the working classes and the left. To illustrate, the Constitutional Court annulled the Law on the Fundamentals of Implementation of the Development Plan in 1969, which was enacted by the AP in 1967 and enabled executive power to remove customs duties and tariffs and increase discount rates for investments (Küçük 1985: 356).

General Staff was appointed as the secretary-general of the Supreme Council (Cumhuriyet Senatosu 17 May 1979).

Moreover, in July 1972, the Military Court of Appeal was restructured as an independent supreme court (Law on the Military Court of Appeal 1972). Similarly, the Military Supreme Court of Administration (*Askeri Yüksek İdare Mahkemesi*) was established as an independent supreme court charged with acting as the court of first and last instance and supervising the military's decisions regarding officers and military service (Law on the Military High Court of Administration 1972). In addition, in 1971 and 1973, the amendments to the Constitution of 1961 abolished the Court of Accounts' (*Sayıştay*) competence to audit the military (Özbudun 2000: 111). This reinforced the military's economic autonomy.

The military's role as the custodian of the capitalist social order was reinforced. Significantly, the State Security Courts (*Devlet Güvenlik Mahkemeleri*, SSCS), consisting of civilian and military judges, were introduced in June 1973 to deal with crimes against the security of the state (Law on Establishment and Proceedings of the State Security Courts 1973). The decisions of the SSCS could be reviewed by the Court of Appeal (*Yargıtay*) to ensure civilian supervision. However, the trial of civilians in military courts during peacetime demonstrated that the dominant classes correctly understood the nature of class war and interpreted the advancement of the organised working classes and left wing as a declaration of war on the capitalist system. In fact, the crimes tried at the SSCS encompassed the crimes listed in the Law on Freedom of Assembly and Demonstration and the Law on Collective Bargaining, Strike, and Lockout. DISK's organisation of demonstrations and protests against the SSCS beginning in 1975 turned into a general strike in September 1976, and the SSCS were abolished in October 1976 (Ozan 2015: 669–670).

2   The State and Classes in the 1970s

2.1   *The Political Landscape and Class Relations in the 1970s*

The memorandum of 1971 sought to respond to the core and common need of the dominant classes: a solution to the crisis of capital accumulation of the late 1960s. The memorandum achieved this goal to a great extent. Significantly, the GNP growth rates were 6.4 per cent between 1963 and 1967, 6.7 per cent between 1968 and 1972, and 7.2 per cent between 1973 and 1977 (Çeçen, Doğruel, and Doğruel 1994: 38). However, the memorandum constituted an insufficient response to the inherent contradictions of ISI, which were to constitute the basis of the crisis of capital accumulation beginning in the mid-1970s. The memorandum further responded to a certain extent to the need of the dominant classes regarding the suppression of the organised subordinate classes and the left wing. To illustrate, the TIP, which highlighted the urgency of a socialist revolution and called for a fight against fascism in the early months of 1971, was closed by the Constitutional Court in July 1971 (Şener 2010: 267). Nevertheless, the power bloc under the hegemony of industrial bourgeoisie formed under Erim's technocratic government remained provisional and unstable. In fact, Erim formed two short-lived technocratic governments between 1971 and 1972, which were followed by two short-lived technocratic governments formed by Ferit Melen and Naim Talu, both of whom were Cabinet members under Erim's premiership, between 1972 and 1974. The cleavages among the dominant classes were soon complemented by the advance of working-class militancy beginning in the mid-1970s. In this regard, the memorandum remained insufficient regarding the reorganisation of class relations to maintain hegemony.

Class composition in the 1970s manifested the rise of a new fraction of capital, finance capital, which was to fundamentally reorganise class relations and restructure the state apparatus. In April 1971, *Türk Sanayicileri ve İş İnsanları Derneği* (Turkish Industry and Business Association, TUSIAD) was established, demonstrating the formation of finance capital. This first generation of finance capital was formed through conglomerations of large-scale industrial capital in the form of holding companies, each having its own bank, mainly in Istanbul and Izmir (Oğuz 2008: 8). This monopolist unification retained its roots in the commercial capital accumulation that began in the 1920s, and the transition from commercial to industrial capital that began in the 1950s (Yılmaz 2005: 228). This first generation further developed organic relations mainly with Western capital, represented in particular by American and European companies. Nevertheless, such organic relations often assumed dependent relations, bastardising the first generation as subordinate to/a subcontractor of Western capital (Öztürk 2011: 130). Furthermore, OYAK completed its transformation into an organ of finance capital in the 1970s and became a dominant group within TUSIAD. Partnerships engaged in by OYAK demonstrated the alliance between the military and finance capital on the one hand, and its dependent relations with Western capital on the other. To illustrate, OYAK and Koç Holding, the largest conglomerate in Turkey and one of the dominant members of TUSIAD, formed a partnership with Goodyear, which was to become the second-biggest tire firm in the Turkish market in the 1980s. OYAK and Koç Holding's shares remained 12 per cent and 17 per cent respectively (Sönmez 1987: 53).

The 1970s further saw the emergence of Islamic capital, manifested by the emergence of political Islam, even though the impact of Islamic capital in economic relations remained limited until the 1980s. In 1969, Necmettin Erbakan, the representative of the religious cleavage within the AP and the founding leader of *Milli Görüş*, was elected as the Chair of *Türkiye Odalar ve Borsalar Birliği* (Turkish Union of Chambers and Commodity Exchanges, TOBB) with the support of small- and medium-scale capitalists in Anatolia. TOBB was a business organisation of the commercial and industrial bourgeoisie formed under the hegemony of the former and favoured by former in the 1950s. In the 1960s, rivalries emerged among the commercial bourgeoisie and smaller capitalists, and the industrial bourgeoisie and bigger capitalists, as a result of ISI. In this regard, Erbakan's election as the chair of TOBB in 1969 demonstrated the victory of small- and medium-scale capitalists, whose fractions included Islamic and conservative capital, against large-scale capitalists (Öztürk 2015: 124–125). Erbakan's breakaway from the AP and establishment of the MNP in 1970 also demonstrated the formation of Islamic capital (see also Chapter 5).

Intra-capital contradictions were eased in the early 1970s as the industrial bourgeoisie negotiated and allied with the commercial bourgeoisie and landlords against the subordinate classes. To illustrate, the industrial bourgeoisie consented to the legislation of *ad valorem* tax and moves towards the advancement of export, the liberalisation of trade, and accession to the EEC (Ozan 2015: 668). Nonetheless, ISI deepened labour-capital contradictions, bringing about the rise of organisation and unionisation and the broadening of practices of resistance, such as workplace occupation, manufacture of faulty products, negligence of machinery and equipment, walkouts, slowdowns, and lunch boycotts (Akkaya 2010: 210–215). The growing class antagonisms were reflected in the political sphere, particularly by the CHP. In May 1972, Bülent Ecevit, the mastermind of the social democratic project that aimed to turn the CHP into a mass party through organic relations with peasants and trade unions (Ecevit 1966), dethroned İnönü and won the chairpersonship election. Ecevit owed his victory to his interpretation of the memorandum of 1971 as a military intervention against the CHP and the left (Uysal 2018: 42). Moreover, the CHP formed a coalition government with the MSP under Ecevit's premiership in January 1974 (Millet Meclisi 29 January 1974), despite the tension between the CHP's secularism and the MSP's political Islam. The coalition government mainly represented the urban and rural working classes, especially workers living in squats; small- and medium-scale capitalists; and the petty bourgeoisie, including artisans and shopkeepers.

2.2 The Prolonged Hegemonic Crisis of the Late 1970s

The early 1970s foreshadowed the beginning of the dissolution of the Bretton Woods system and the restructuring of world capitalism. In the early 1970s, the United States suffered from balance-of-payments and trade deficits and an unfavourable position in its economic rivalry against Germany and Japan. This compelled US President Richard Nixon to devalue the US dollar in 1971 and 1973 (Dowd 2004: 160), thereby replacing the system of fixed exchange rates with a regulated floating system. The devaluation of the US dollar brought about the fall of the relative price of oil, since the trade of oil took place in dollars and at prices fixed in dollars (Beaud 1984: 202). Between 1973 and 1974, OPEC (Organization of Arab Petroleum Exporting Countries) imposed an oil embargo against countries supporting Israel during the Arab-Israeli War of 1973, and as a result the price of oil quadrupled (Kiely 2010: 135). The oil crisis of 1973–1974 "catalyse[d]" a major recession (Dunn 2014: 104), which essentially broke out as a result of the fall in productivity and profit rates in capital-intensive sectors in the advanced capitalist Western countries as capital accumulation in mass production depended on the availability of low-cost oil (Kiely 2007: 63). This recession of 1974–1975, which manifested in severe slowdowns in economic growth and increases in inflation and unemployment, was the forerunner of the transition to neoliberalism of the late 1970s, which aimed to overcome the obstruction of capital accumulation.

Turkey was inevitably impacted by the oil crisis of 1974–1975. To illustrate, between 1972 and 1977, Turkey's imports increased by 4.2 billion USD, of which 90 million USD was spent on the increased oil prices and 2.5 billion USD was spent on the increased prices of items other than oil (Kazgan 2005: 177). When the Turkish workers' remittances remained insufficient to offset the foreign trade deficit, the coalition government of the AP, MSP, and MHP—called the Nationalist Front (*Milliyetçi Cephe*)—overwhelmingly resorted to foreign credit. In the international sphere, the oil-exporting countries already deposited their windfall profits in international banks, which in return loaned petrodollars to peripheries. While private bank lending—rather than from the IMF and World Bank—became a major source of capital for late developers, such private loans were provided in "a competitive and 'unregulated' climate, often commit[ting] enormous sums" (Kiely 2010: 136). The Nationalist Front mainly loaned petrodollars from these banks in order to respond to the deficit. This move only postponed the impact of the oil crisis of 1973–1974 to the late 1970s, and caused the deterioration of the major economic and currency crisis the country faced beginning in 1978. Significantly, Turkey's total foreign debt increased from 2.2. billion USD to 3.5 billion USD between 1970 and 1975, reaching 12.5 billion USD by the end of 1977 (Berberoglu 1982: 110).

The memorandum of 1971 previously sought but failed to respond to the inherent contradictions of ISI; first, the limitations of the domestic market; and second, the foreign exchange bottleneck in the face of dependency on foreign capital and growing foreign debt. These two fundamental contradictions were combined with the postponed impact of the oil crisis of 1973–1974 and resulted in the crisis of ISI by the late 1970s. The crisis of ISI was common in most of the late developers, since ISI failed to solve the balance-of-payments problems and the question of foreign exchange shortages as a result of reductions in imports. ISI generated a relatively larger demand for the import of foreign capital, especially in the form of intermediate and capital goods and credit, and thus negatively affected balance-of-payments difficulties (Bina and Yaghmaian 1990: 90).

ISI, therefore, brought about a complex picture in Turkey in the late 1970s. On the one hand, the transition to the production of intermediate and capital goods was achieved to a certain extent. Between 1971 and 1981, the share of the food and beverages, tobacco, textiles and clothing, and leather industries as a proportion of total industry decreased from 49 per cent to 29 per cent. During this period, the share of chemicals, petroleum, coal, rubber, metal works, and machinery increased from 16 per cent to 51 per cent (Yılmaz 2005: 230). This was accompanied by rapid economic growth. Between 1974 and 1976, the growth rate of GDP was 8.6 per cent, and the share of investments in the GNP increased from 19.8 per cent to 25.2 per cent by 1977 (Kazgan 2005: 185). On the other hand, industrialisation remained predominantly in labour-intensive sectors and retained its dependency on foreign capital. The majority of foreign capital—84 per cent—was invested in manufacturing (Yılmaz 2005: 230). Industrialisation also continued to resemble an assembly industry, considering its dependency on the import of intermediate and capital goods. In 1978, Turkish exports mainly consisted of livestock, fruits, grain and cereals, seeds, bagasse, tobacco, metals (copper and chrome), wool, and cotton in exchange for the import of fuel oil, chemicals and paint, textiles, iron and steel, machinery, vehicles, plastics and rubber, and fertilisers (TCMB 1979: 103). This dependency worsened the foreign trade deficit, aggravating the foreign exchange bottleneck. Significantly, Turkey's foreign trade deficit increased from 494 million USD (8.7 billion TRY) to 2.25 billion USD (31.9 billion TRY) between 1971 and 1974, and reached 4 billion USD (73.6 billion TRY) in 1977 (TCMB 1979: 102).[4]

---

4 The Turkish lira suffered from devaluation against the US dollar in the late 1970s. In 1979, Turkey's foreign trade deficit reached 102.8 billion TRY, which was equivalent to 2.8 billion USD (TCMB 1979: 152).

Meanwhile, the growth rate of the GNP per capita decreased from 5 per cent to 1.4 per cent between 1976 and 1977 (Schick and Tonak 1981: 72).

The deteriorating national economy was accompanied by a deepening hegemonic crisis in the political sphere. The first Nationalist Front government formed under Demirel's premiership in March 1975 failed to form a power bloc as the MSP attacked large-scale capital for being a member of the Western club, thereby damaging relations with the IMF (Millet Meclisi 6 April 1975). The AP's close alliance with landlords and the commercial bourgeoisie further resulted in its failure to address the interests of large-scale capital, such as the reduction of support prices of agricultural products (Taylan 1984: 33). In the election of January 1977, the CHP obtained the plurality of the popular vote, but not a parliamentary majority. The second Nationalist Front government, established in July 1977, could not stand up to opposition from the working classes and the big industrial bourgeoisie. The CHP's minority government, which was established under Ecevit's premiership in January 1978, sought to respond to the IMF's demands for a drastic devaluation and austerity measures with a mild devaluation and price controls aimed at the stimulation of exports (Boratav 2014: 141). The IMF's demands corresponded with TUSIAD's interests, since TUSIAD called for the promotion of exports of manufactured products, reorganisation of the SOEs, curtailing of wages, liberalisation of exchange rates, and combatting the balance-of-payments deficit (Oğuz 2008: 101). As result of the CHP's failure to form a power bloc, the CHP's minority government was overthrown and replaced by the third Nationalist Front government in ten months.

3   The Political Economy of the Coup of 1980 and Its Aftermath

3.1   *The Coup of 1980 and Social Classes*

On 24 January 1980, Demirel announced an economic stabilisation programme that conformed to the IMF and World Bank's frameworks as well as the demands of Turkish finance capital (*Cumhuriyet* 26 January 1980). The Decisions of 24 January aimed to solve the crisis of ISI through the transition to export-oriented industrialisation (EOI) by adopting three main measures (Taylan 1984: 31). First, the Decisions sought to maintain severe deflation of the domestic market through restrictive monetary and credit policies. With this aim, the Decisions targeted state subsidies, including agricultural subsidies, and the public deficit, especially the welfare state and the wages of civil servants. Second, the Decisions sought to encourage the integration of Turkish capital with the global market through incentives and subsidies for exports and continuous devaluation of the Turkish lira. With this aim, the Decisions also prescribed liberalisation of the exchange regime, the reduction of customs, the liberalisation of foreign trade, and the establishment of free-trade and production zones. Third, the Decisions sought to reorganise the state's interventions in economics by abolishing price controls over the private sector, reorganising public enterprises, and advancing public investment in manufacturing.

Between the late 1970s and early 1980s, it was clear that the organised working classes were determined to struggle against the bourgeoisie and the bourgeoisie aimed to solve the crisis in its own favour. Between 1977 and 1978, metal and mine workers organised one of the biggest and longest mass strikes of the 1970s in the country. The strike fundamentally targeted *Türkiye Metal Sanayicileri Sendikası* (Turkish Employers' Association of Metal Industries, MESS) as well as the Nationalist Front government. During the demonstrations, workers' major slogan was that "[workers] defeated the State Security Courts, now [they] will defeat MESS" (Öztürk 2009: 348). The unresolved dispute between workers and capitalists during this strike was to incite a series of strikes in 1980, during which Kemal Türkler, the former chair of DISK, was assassinated (Ozan 2015: 726). Türkler's assassination was an important manifestation of the rising political violence that was directed against the left and labour movements. The intensified political violence was a result of "protection [and] indeed encouragement" of the far-right and fascist movements by the Nationalist Front governments (Schick and Tonak 1981: 71), representing the dominant classes.[5] The far-right, involving the counter-guerrilla, engaged in assassinations of significant political figures and massacres, thus fragmenting the social fabric and bringing it to the verge of total collapse in the late 1970s. The most notorious examples included the Taksim Square (Istanbul) massacre on 1 May 1977, the Bahçelievler/Ankara massacre on 8 October 1978, and the massacres of Alevis in Kahramanmaraş in December 1978 and Çorum in July 1980.

A series of martial law periods were declared between 1978 and 1980 to suppress the left and the working classes. The Nationalist Front declared martial law in thirteen provinces, including Istanbul and Ankara, following the Kahramanmaraş massacre in 1978. In April 1979, the CHP government increased the number of provinces under martial law to nineteen, and enhanced the authority of the martial law commanders. For instance, the commanders could undertake daily searches at universities, schools, dormitories, homes,

---

[5] The dominant classes not only consented to but also supported the rise of the far-right in Turkey as "'fascism [was] the choice of finance capital'" (Berberoglu 1982: 119).

and factories. The Labour Day demonstrations on 1 May 1979, which brought together thousands of workers in cities and towns, were followed by an array of student protests, strikes, factory occupations, and demonstrations between 1979 and 1980. These demonstrations and protests took place despite arrests and clashes with the police and the military under martial law (Berberoglu 1982: 119–121).

In this regard, it became clear that the Decisions of 24 January could not be implemented under civilian authority and without extraordinary measures. The need for the use of repressive state apparatuses was explicitly accepted and voiced by the United States and NATO, both of which already required a politically stable Turkey against the Islamic Revolution in Iran and the Soviet Union's invasion of Afghanistan. During a conference in 1980, Admiral Harold E. Shear, commander-in-chief of NATO's Allied Forces Southern Europe command, addressed the Turkish military, calling for a military intervention by asking, "in the face of anarchy and uncertainty, what are you doing?" (Özdemir 2002: 130).

On 12 September 1980, the military undertook a coup by abolishing the National Assembly, the Senate, and the government, and by overtaking the NSC. Under the junta of 1980, the NSC was fundamentally restructured to act as an extraordinary legislative and executive power, granted with competences to intervene in politics, the economy, and intelligence (Karpat 2013: 280). This book refers to the junta as the MGK (*Milli Güvenlik Konseyi*, National Security Committee) in this chapter to distinguish it from the NSC, which is a state institution.[6] The MGK ruled the country until the election of November 1983 under the premiership of the retired admiral Bülent Ulusu and the presidency of Kenan Evren, the former chief of the General Staff.

The MGK underlined its goal to "protect the unity of the country and the nation, prevent a possible civil war and fratricide, … and eradicate obstructions in the democratic order" (Communique No. 1 1980). Nevertheless, the main goal of the coup of 1980 was to safeguard the capitalist social order by curbing the power of the organised subordinate classes and the left. In this regard, its mission was similar to that of the memorandum of 1971. Most significantly, the MGK complied with the advice of TOBB and TISK, suspending unionist activities and forbidding the right to strike, replacing collective bargaining with the Supreme Council of Arbitrators (*Yüksek Hakem Kurulu*), and repressing agricultural subsidies and the wages and pensions of civil servants (Boratav 2014: 150).

---

6 This book uses the term MGK (*Milli Güvenlik Kurulu*) to refer to the National Security Council in the bibliography and citations.

The coup of 1980 further completed what the memorandum of 1971 sought to achieve: the reinforcement of the chain of command. The MGK was composed of the chief of the General Staff and the commanders of the land and air forces, the navy, and the gendarmerie to fortify the military's hierarchy (Communique No. 4 1980). The coup of 1980, nevertheless, went beyond the memorandum of 1971 regarding its aims and scope, which were related to the restructuring of the global economy and pattern of capital accumulation in Turkey.

3.2 The Transition to Neoliberalism and Export-Led Industrialisation

The global economic crisis of the mid-1970s, which brought about growing unemployment and rising inflation, was to be resolved through the transition to neoliberalism. Neoliberalism can be regarded as the latest phase of capitalism and a project for the restoration of the class power of the bourgeoisie, which has characterised world capitalism until today (Duménil and Lévy 2012). Neoliberalism aimed at solving the crisis of profitability and capital accumulation mainly through the advancement of marketisation, deregulation, and the precarisation of the labour force. The dissolution of the social compromise between labour and capital in favour of the latter required the control over and suppression of any potential opposing social force so that mobility of capital could be maintained. The process of neoliberalisation brought about the eradication of the welfare state and the rise of the neoliberal state as an authoritarian form of state (Boukalas 2014: 124–125; see also Chapters 6 and 7).

The process of neoliberalisation coincided with the transition to export-oriented industrialisation (EOI), indicating the restructured pattern of capital accumulation that aimed to solve the crisis of ISI in late developers. The outward-oriented strategy of export-oriented industrialisation sought to eradicate foreign exchange constraints through the export of manufactured goods. More importantly, EOI corresponded to a higher phase of internationalisation of production and circulation, and hence addressed the interests of foreign productive capital, which was in the process of internationalisation, in an absolutely integrated network of global production and circulation (Bina and Yaghmaian 1990: 90). In this sense, EOI reproduced dependency on foreign capital since industrialisation in late developers continued to rely on foreign credits and loans (money capital) and imports of intermediate and capital goods and foreign direct investments (productive capital). The transition to neoliberalism in late developers was supervised by the Washington, DC-based international organisations, particularly the IMF and World Bank, in the 1980s. This early stage of neoliberalism, often referred to as the Washington Consensus, remained consistent with EOI. The Washington Consensus involved fiscal and monetary discipline; public expenditure priorities reordered towards pro-growth; tax reform based on broad tax bases and marginal rates; liberalisation of interest rates and prices; a competitive exchange rate; liberalisation of trade; liberalisation of inward foreign direct investment; privatisation of state-owned enterprises; deregulation of industries to ease barriers to entry and exit; and protection of property rights (to enable the informal sector to obtain property rights) (Morrison 2018: 75; Williamson 2008: 16–17).

The transition to EOI in the 1980s also corresponded to the interests of Turkish finance capital to internationalise and expand on a global scale. By the end of the 1970s, large-scale capital gained control over the domestic circuit of capital to a certain degree and consumed the potential profits of inward-oriented capital accumulation. Since the country was specialised in the labour-intensive and low-value-added industries, including consumer durable and nondurable goods, large-scale capital sought to shift its production to high-value-added intermediate and capital goods. The inability of domestic industries to compete in international markets and the shift towards the production of capital-intensive goods increased the need for foreign currency to import technology and other necessary inputs (Oğuz 2008: 103–104). The foreign exchange crisis was already intensified by the country's increasing reliance on foreign debt, which reached 13.8 billion USD in 1978 and was mainly constituted by short-term loans, which made up almost 60 per cent. The major share of the total foreign debt belonged to the private sector, at 74 per cent (Kazgan 2005: 189). For this reason, the transition to EOI aimed to enable Turkish finance capital to "reproduce itself as a fraction of world capital" through export promotion (Taylan 1984: 30).

The transition to neoliberalism in the face of the organised subordinate classes would not be a peaceful process, and required the intensified use of means of coercion and repression. Especially in peripheries, including Chile and Argentina, neoliberal policies were implemented mainly through military takeovers and under military juntas (Harvey 2007: 15–16). In this regard, the major mission of the junta of 1980 was to implement the Decisions of 24 January, and hence neoliberal policies. Significantly, following the military takeover in September 1980, the secretary-general of TISK publicly stated, "workers were happy until now, but from now on, we [will] be happy" (Özçelik 2011: 91).

The neoliberal policies implemented in the 1980s mainly focused on the liberalisation of the economy, particularly liberalisation of the pricing of goods and services, deregulation of the labour force and capital markets, and liberalisation of the value of the Turkish lira (Kepenek and Yentürk 2001: 198–203). Regarding the promotion of industrialisation, the manufacturing export industries were particularly encouraged through credits and tax subsidies, investment incentives, and the establishment of specialised foreign trade companies and free-trade zones (Eres 2007: 120–121). Foreign investments were further encouraged through the Decree on Foreign Capital (1980), which mainly targeted the expansion of Turkish capital by requiring the export of a certain percentage of goods produced through foreign investments. The Decree, in this sense, reproduced the dependency of Turkish industry since it targeted labour-intensive and low-value-added sectors. The limitation of foreign investments to 2–50 million USD demonstrated that the Decree also mainly targeted the growth of small and medium-sized enterprises (SMEs) and foresaw the promotion of exports in durable and nondurable goods, including food, textiles, forest products, buses, lorries, and metal products (Kepenek and Yentürk 2001: 205). The Decree, nonetheless, remained in line with the diminishing place of the welfare state and the primacy of market dynamics as it sought to reduce bureaucratic rules and regulations for foreign investments, bypassing the protection of the public interest by the bureaucracy.

Moreover, the value of the Turkish lira was repressed through a continuous policy of devaluation. This created a discrepancy among industrialists by favouring exporting industrialists over those producing for the domestic market. It also impacted on industrialists whose production depended on the import of inputs, increasing the cost of imports. Therefore, the reduction of the price of agricultural products and the repression of revenues in agriculture, combined with the deregulation of the labour market and the repression of wages in the industries and agriculture, constituted the major policies of EOI (Yılmaz 2011: 101). To illustrate, between 1977 and 1987, real wages overall lost 55 per cent of their value, with real wages in manufacturing losing 20 per cent of their value. Such a decline in real wages also took place in the civil service and agriculture (Kazgan 2006: 130–131).

The re-regulation of relations of distribution between labour and capital to the detriment of the former required the defeat of the radical urban and rural subordinate classes. The left and labour and peasant movements were suppressed through mass arrests, trials, and torture. The MGK further supervised the preparation of the Constitution of 1982, which aimed to institute a neoliberal authoritarian state as the guardian of a free-market economy. The fact that the secretary-general of TISK was a member of the Consultative Assembly (*Danışma Meclisi*) charged with the preparation of the new Constitution and contributed to the sections on the regulation of labour rights and labour markets demonstrated the true nature of the Constitution of 1982 (Tanör 1994: 109), which sought to discipline and curtail social democracy by emphasising restrictions on fundamental rights and freedoms, and enabling the state to deny its responsibility regarding human rights violations. It strengthened executive against legislative power by reinforcing decrees, abolishing the relative autonomy of certain state institutions, and broadening the competences of the president as the arbitrator. This enabled the executive to bypass the class struggle that characterised the legislative. Further, it strengthened executive against judicial power by curbing the independence and supervisory role of the judicial branch over the executive branch and the private sector, further enabling the executive to comply with and safeguard market mechanisms.

3.3 *The State and Classes under* Anavatan Partisi

Following the election of November 1983, *Anavatan Partisi* (Motherland Party, ANAP) formed a majority government under Turgut Özal's premiership in December 1983 (TBMM 19 December 1983). Even though the formation of a civilian government demonstrated the transfer of power from the military junta to civilian authority, Özal and the ANAP rather represented the civilian face of the neoliberal transition and the authoritarian transformation of the state apparatus. The mission of the junta to destroy class belongings and homogenise the political grassroots by purging the political parties of the 1970s had already enabled the rise of the ANAP as an umbrella political party representing various social classes. While Evren publicly but indirectly discredited the ANAP a few days before the election to favour other political parties established under the MGK's direct guidance (Heper and Criss 2009: 214–218), nonetheless this perceived unfavourable position against the ANAP did not manifest a fundamental antagonism between Evren/the junta and Özal/the ANAP. Rather, it signified the junta's tendency to pursue direct influence over the political sphere. Özal was the former chair of MESS and the main architect of the Decisions of 24 January (Öztürk 2009: 338–339) and served as the deputy prime minister during Ulusu's premiership (Tanör 2011: 60). Özal's policy to liberalise interest rates resulted in the bankruptcy of many bankers and brokers in 1982, whose majority engaged in fraudulent investing schemes and subsequently fled abroad. The junta swept the "bankers' scandal" under the rug by contenting itself with Özal's resignation from his role in the Cabinet (Boratav 2014: 151–152).

The ANAP enhanced the transition to neoliberalism, most significantly by advancing privatisations, such as privatising mines and lifting the state's monopoly on tobacco (Haspolat 2012: 96), thereby enabling huge transfers of wealth from the public to the private sector. The ANAP promoted such transfers of wealth also by selling bonds and stocks to private banks, and hence increasing public debt (Saraçoğlu 2015: 752–753), to finance massive public investment in urban and rural infrastructure, including communication, energy, and motorways. The ANAP further promoted EOI based on export promotion and wage suppression.

EOI between 1980 and 1989 constituted the first phase of outward-oriented capital accumulation. During this phase, export promotion based on the liberalisation of foreign trade facilitated the internationalisation of commercial capital. EOI particularly promoted the growth of the labour-intensive and low-value-added industries dependent on foreign capital, reproducing the peripheralisation of the Turkish economy. To illustrate, total exports increased from 2.91 billion USD to 5.73 billion USD between 1980 and 1983, reaching 11.63 billion USD in 1989. Total imports increased from 7.91 billion USD to 9.24 billion USD between 1980 and 1983, reaching 15.79 billion USD in 1989. Exports mainly constituted food, cement, textiles, iron and metals, and leather products, whereas imports mainly constituted rubber and plastics, iron and steel, machinery, automotive parts, and industrial chemicals, including fertilisers, drugs, and paint (TCMB 1990: 199–201). Exports also included machinery and automotive parts to a certain extent, demonstrating that large-scale capital had achieved a shift towards the production and export of intermediate and capital goods. Between 1984 and 1987, the ANAP achieved an annual economic growth rate of 7 per cent, equal to the economic growth rate in 1977 (Kazgan 2006: 141).

The ANAP formed a power bloc under the hegemony of commercial fractions of finance capital, and hence consolidated its hegemony. This book considers the ANAP's hegemonic project as "the New Right" (Tünay 1993), which had parallels with Ronald Reagan's presidency in the United States and Margaret Thatcher's prime ministership in the United Kingdom (see Fine and Harris 1987). In this regard, the ANAP's hegemonic project merged neoliberalism and conservatism in an authoritarian manner. The element of neoliberalism emphasised a free-market economy and the withdrawal of the state apparatus from relations of distribution, including the implementation of anti-welfare policies to the detriment of the proletariat, the unemployed, the disabled, and retirees. The element of conservatism emphasised religious morality and anti-leftism to coerce and obtain the consent of the subordinate classes. The ANAP indeed presented itself as the representative of the "silent [Muslim] majority" in urban and rural areas (Bora and Taşkın 2009: 541), with its amalgamation of Islamic symbols and references and the principle of *laissez-faire*, which articulated religious piety as a "need for individual life" and a "cement to unify the society and harmonise the society and the state" (ANAP 1983: 21–22). For instance, Özal stated that "Islam and the Western market resemble[d] each other since they [were] both liberal ... [The] Islamic market [was] perfect ... encompass[ing] alms and charity to overcome problems of competition"

(Cemal 1989: 155). In this sense, the New Right aimed to veil class antagonisms in the face of the capitalist attack on labour.

The ANAP's use of populism, in combination with conservatism and neoliberalism, was pivotal to pacify the urban and rural subordinate classes. Populism, in the neoliberal era, remains in line with economic policies aimed at economic efficiency and the decline in state intervention in the economy to the detriment of labour. In the face of the increase in social costs and the decline in the participation of organised political forces, the implementation of neoliberal populist policies assumes an authoritarian form, eroding democratic representation and representative institutions, and personalising politics and legitimising the image of a powerful political leader (Öniş 2004: 126). Neoliberal populism seeks to exclude the subordinate classes from democratic mechanisms through depoliticisation and the isolation of state benefits from civil rights. In this way, the subordinate classes are transformed into consumer masses, which lack class-consciousness and obey neoliberal economic policies without opposition (Uysal 2019b: 21). Significantly, the ANAP implemented the Social Aid and Solidarity Promotion Fund in 1986 to provide irregular in-kind and cash benefits, solving socioeconomic problems outside the labour market, and hence reproducing poverty and personalised political relations (Şenses 1999).

The ANAP's use of Islamic symbols and references was further related to the expansion of Gulf capital in Turkey. This process was already in accordance with the Green Belt project of the United States, which aimed to contain the Soviet Union and radical Islamist movements through a buffer zone of "moderate" Islamic countries, including Turkey, Pakistan, and Afghanistan (Uzgel 2009: 37). The outward-oriented capital accumulation and the liberalisation of the economy had already enabled the MGK and the ANAP to advance the expansion of foreign Islamic capital, particularly Gulf capital. To illustrate, the Islamic Development Bank based in Saudi Arabia was exempt from the condition of the Decree on Foreign Capital requiring the export of a certain percentage of goods produced through foreign investments. Similarly, the investments of the Gulf countries were exempt from limitations regarding the amount and percentage of foreign investments determined by the Decree (Kepenek and Yentürk 2001: 205). The advancement of economic relations promoted political relations between Turkey and Islamic countries, thus advancing the diffusion of Islamic elements in Turkey. For instance, the Turkish clergy serving the Turkish migrant workers in Belgium and West Germany received their monthly salaries from *Rabitat* in the 1980s. *Rabitat*, which was under the Muslim World League and was mainly funded by Saudi Arabia, was known for its dissemination of a strict religious fundamentalism based on *sharia* (Eligür 2010: 115).

Both the junta of 1980 and the ANAP supported and developed organic—and rather nepotist and corrupt—relations with foreign and domestic Islamic capital and religious brotherhoods.[7] To illustrate, Evren established close relations with the Nakşibendi order and Mehmet Kırkıncı, a prominent leader of the Nurcu congregation. Evren, as president, allowed the corpse of Mehmet Zahid Kotku, a prominent leader of the İskenderpaşa congregation under the Nakşibendi order, to be buried in the Süleymaniye Mosque in Istanbul, alongside religious seminaries of the Süleymancı order (Yavuz 2003: 70–73). Özal had a background in the Nakşibendi order (Çakır 1991: 277) and continued to co-operate with and promote religious brotherhoods. The ANAP's legislation of a decree in 1988 to ensure that Özal's mother, who was a disciple of the Nakşibendi order, was buried near Kotku's grave serves to illustrate this point (Cemal 1989: 158).

The organic relations between the junta of 1980 and the ANAP and religious brotherhoods were related to the organic relations between foreign and domestic Islamic capital, religious brotherhoods, and the executive branch. Significantly, the Nurcu congregation supported the establishment of Faisal Finance, and Özal's brother, a prominent leader of the Nakşibendi order, established Al-Baraka Turk Finance. Both Faisal and Al-Baraka were integrated with Gulf capital. These financial institutions constituted only 3 per cent of Turkish lira deposits and 3–4 per cent of foreign deposits (Ergüneş 2009: 139); nevertheless, they still enabled Islamic capital to flourish by providing loans, assisting investments and deposits, and raising future managers who were to act as agents of capital in Islamic companies. The rise of a precarious and flexible labour force and cleavages between the relatively secure and insecure working classes as a result of the deregulation of the labour market also benefited Islamic capital in urban areas.

The support of the junta of 1980 and the ANAP for the religious brotherhoods was related to the neoliberal transformation of the state apparatus and the quest to pacify the urban and rural subordinate classes. Significantly, Vehbi Dinçerler, a prominent disciple of the Nakşibendi order, was appointed as the minister of education and the new curriculum prepared during his term of office focused on "rewriting the presentation of national history and culture" with religious symbols and references (Yavuz 2003: 75). Moreover, the junta of 1980 and the ANAP legitimised and promoted the growth of Islamic

---

7 The transition to neoliberalism under the ANAP became a "direct legacy" of corruption that had been on the rise in the 1990s since Özal's principle of "'economic punishments for economic crimes'", particularly regarding the misuse of export subsidies in the 1980s, had nullified the rule of law (Öniş 2004: 118).

foundations, which constituted the basis of the accumulation of wealth for the religious brotherhoods and Islamic capital. The revenue of these foundations depended on donations from Islamic capital and the Gulf states, ranging from the collection of sacrificed animals during Eid to a diverse array of favours. Certain foundations—not their businesses—were exempted from taxes upon the approval of the Cabinet in 1985 (Notice No. 28 on Corporate Tax 1985). This enabled religious brotherhoods to mainly establish foundation schools and preparatory schools (*dershane*), student dormitories, and funds for students coming from working-class and peasant backgrounds. In this sense, the rising role of Islamic foundations corresponded to the withdrawal of the state from relations of distribution and the general erosion of the welfare state.

3.4 *The Military's Guardianship Role and Authoritarian Statism*

The coup of 1980 complemented the memorandum of 1971 by completing the transformation of the military into an umpire that responded to hegemonic crises by serving the interests of capital. In this transition, the military abandoned "its historical mission of the modernisation of society" (Laçiner 2004: 22–23). This was clear with the institutionalisation of the Turkish-Islamic Synthesis (*Türk-İslam Sentezi*, TIS) as the state's ideology by the junta of 1980 and the ANAP.[8] The TIS was intellectually formulated by *Aydınlar Ocağı* (Intellectuals' Hearth) in the 1970s (Bora and Can 2004: 159), which merged repressive nationalism and Islamic conservatism to suppress the left.[9] The TIS was built on four institutions to produce a unified and disciplined society, namely, school, family, mosque, and conscription (Yavuz 2003: 73), and thus enable the implementation of *laissez-faire* policies in a stable domestic environment without class struggle.

The military became the subject and the object of the institutionalisation of the TIS at the state and societal levels. Significantly, the Constitution of 1982,

---

8 The junta of 1980 officially replaced Kemalism with Atatürkism as the state's ideology. Beginning in the 1960s, the conservative and nationalist movements already utilised Atatürkism, which blended Atatürk's cult with Islamic symbols and references, in opposition to the left, which borrowed its references from Kemalism (see Köker 2009). Atatürkism, therefore, corresponded to the Turkish-Islamic Synthesis.

9 This book underlines the adoption of repressive nationalism as a response to suppress the rise of the Kurdish movement, which achieved ideological, cultural, and political mobilisation by the 1980s. The Kurdish movement exhibited "important dynamics from the class point of view", such as the struggle of "the poor peasantry freed from the shackles of tribal ties" and "explosive" potential giving "the ruling classes the scare". However, such dynamics "never developed in a positive direction" (Öngen 2002: 68). The political economy of the military's guardianship role vis-à-vis the Kurdish movement is beyond the scope of this book.

enacted under the junta of 1980, articulated the importance of the element of morality based on Islam when it referred to freedom of conscience and religion and worship (Constitution 1982: 6–7). The Constitution (1982: 39) further charged *Diyanet* with the duty to maintain "national solidarity and unity". Furthermore, the junta of 1980 institutionalised the public visibility of Islamic symbols and references. For instance, Evren often referred to the importance of fasting during Ramadan (*Milliyet* 1982). Free public *iftar* (breaking of the fast) dinners during Ramadan soon became common charity practices that Islamic capital engaged in to obtain the approval of the working classes, and as symbols of prestige for conservative fractions of the dominant and ruling classes.

The coup of 1980 advanced the guardianship role of the military within the framework of authoritarian statism. In this sense, the guardianship role of the military was reinforced as an interim structure that enabled the military to directly oversee and exert power over society and civilian authority, and hence to directly act on the part of the ruling classes. This was consolidated through judicial, economic, and political mechanisms. To begin with the advancement of martial law under the junta of 1980, the Act on the Amendment to the Law on the State of Siege (1980) abolished judicial appeals before administrative or civil courts against the decisions of commanders of martial law. Commanders were allowed to try any case committed outside martial law regions if such cases were connected to a case under trial before the martial law court. Commanders were also allowed to broaden the scope of criminal offences to be tried. The Constitution of 1982 (1982: 34) replaced the prime minister with the General Staff as the competent authority to oversee the commanders of martial law, abolishing the supervisory role of civilian authority. The Constitution also abolished the burden of compliance of martial law with the principle of the rule of law, eliminating the judicial review of martial law practices (Özçelik 2011: 91).

Moreover, the NSC was restructured in November 1983 (Law on the National Security Council and the Secretary-General of the NSC 1983). The national security of the country was defined as the protection of the state's constitutional regime, national existence and unity, and the political, social, cultural, economic, and legal interests of the country in the international arena against external and internal threats. In this way, the duties of the NSC were broadened to include setting the framework of political, social, economic, cultural, and technological agendas pertaining to the domestic sphere. The NSC's views constituted the basis of the Cabinet's policy on national security. The NSC's agenda was to be prepared by the president upon the opinions of the prime minister and the chief of the General Staff. The Cabinet's actions regarding the NSC's decisions were to be monitored by the secretary-general of the NSC, and in return the secretary-general was entitled to inform the president, the prime minister, and the NSC about the Cabinet's implementation of the NSC's decisions. Moreover, the president played a further crucial role regarding the advancement of the NSC's role. In accordance with the empowerment of the executive branch against the legislative and judicial branches, the competences of the president, as the head of executive power, were broadened. The president was enabled to restructure the state apparatus by appointing the heads of state institutions, calling Cabinet and NSC meetings, and legislating bylaws. Similarly, decisions signed *ex officio* by the president could not be appealed to the court (Constitution 1982: 26–28). Under Evren's presidency, the NSC soon turned into a kind of superior Cabinet, which held control mechanisms over the Assembly and supervised legislative and executive powers without an actual military intervention.

Regarding the Supreme Military Council, the Constitution of 1982 (1982: 34–35) outlawed the appeal of the Council's decisions to the court despite the constitutional right to appeal actions and procedures of the administration regarding their compliance with law. The Council was further restructured in November 1983 to assemble biannually (Milli Güvenlik Konseyi 1 November 1983). One of the meetings was set for August, with the second meeting to be decided by the chief of the General Staff. The Council could further assemble upon the request of the chief of the General Staff.

Regarding military courts, the junta of 1980 reintroduced the State Security Courts (SSCs) as courts of aggravated felony, which were not located within the general judicial framework and had their own specific rules of procedure. The structure and practices of the SSCs contradicted with international standards and violated the fundamental right to a fair trial (see Ankara Barosu 1999). Significantly, the decisions of the SSCs could not be appealed to the court, abolishing a constitutional right. In accordance with the broadening of the definition of national security to include internal and external threats, the SSCs functioned to eradicate the organised labour movement and the left that threatened the capitalist social order.[10] In this regard, the SSCs remained reminiscent of extraordinary circumstances, especially the junta rule, and hence legitimised and normalised the military's role as the custodian of the rule of capital.

The ANAP enhanced the military's economic autonomy since the guardianship role of the military was to preserve the capitalist social order and the

---

10   For examples of cases tried at the SSCs, see *DGM'lere Karşı Özgürlük Girişimi* (1998).

military had already begun to function as a capital fraction. Significantly, the Turkish Armed Forces Foundation (*Türk Silahlı Kuvvetlerini Güçlendirme Vakfı*, TSKGV) was established in 1987. The main mission of the TSKGV was to enable the military to "develop the national armaments industry of Turkey, establish new branches of the armaments industry, and purchase weapons, vehicles and equipment" (Law on Turkish Armed Forces Foundation 1987: 16). TSKGV merged and restructured funds that were to support the army, navy, and air force so that the military could operate in the defence and war industries. The TSKGV was exempt from corporate tax—except for financial enterprises—as well as inheritance tax, death duty for donations and grants, and stamp duty on any kind of transaction. The TSKGV facilitated the rise of OYAK as a significant capital fraction operating in the defence and war industry in the 1990s, reinforcing the military's guardianship role in line with authoritarian statism.

CHAPTER 5

The "Postmodern Coup" of 1997 and Political Islam

> [I]n order to save its purse, [the bourgeoisie] must forfeit the crown, and the sword that is to safeguard it must at the same time be hung over its own head as a sword of Damocles.
>
> KARL MARX (1979 [1852])

∴

This chapter discusses the memorandum of 28 February 1997 as a response to the prolonged hegemonic crisis of the 1990s and a restoration project to moderate rising political Islam/Islamism. Financial liberalisation characterised the Turkish economy with boom-bust cycles in the 1990s under the dynamics of unevenness and dependency, eroding the bonds between the centre-left and centre-right political parties and various social classes. In this milieu of the prolonged hegemonic crisis, *Milli Görüş* mobilised large segments of social strata. The revival of political Islam in Turkey, in this regard, was a result of the rise of Islamic capital and the Islamisation of the state apparatus and social order beginning in the 1980s, and a response to the political, economic, and social crisis of the 1990s. Nonetheless, *Milli Görüş* and its Islamist project not only challenged the principle of secularism, but more importantly it challenged the primacy of Western capital and fractions of finance capital that maintained organic relations with Western capital. For this reason, the memorandum of 28 February 1997 aimed to fine-tune and domesticate political Islam.

1 The Political Economy of the Rise of Political Islam

1.1 *The Composition of Islamic Capital*

This book argues that Islamic capital—the Islamist bourgeoisie—has been an important social force that has transformed the state apparatus and social structure since the 1980s. In this regard, it defines Islamic capital as a capital fraction that utilises Islam as a system of norms and values to regulate relations between labour and capital, and intra-capital relations (Hoşgör 2015a). Nevertheless, it rejects the dominant literature on Turkey that understands rivalries between first-generation finance capital, which it accepts as Westernised/Western-oriented or secular/secularist capital, and Islamic capital in terms of cultural references (see Buğra 1998; Tanyılmaz 2015). So-called Westernised-secular capital consented to, if not supported, the rise in the public visibility of Islam beginning in the late 1940s, and the religionisation/Islamisation of the state apparatus and social structure beginning in the 1980s. Meanwhile, Islamic capital received the support of the state apparatus either under the junta of 1980 and the ANAP in the 1980s or under the AKP, beginning in 2002. In addition, Islamic capital has operated in collaboration with so-called Westernised-secular capital. For example, the Anadolu Group started to produce beer beginning in the late 1960s. Even though Islam prohibits alcoholic beverages, the Ülker and Topbaş Groups, prominent members of large-scale Islamic capital, co-operated with the Anadolu Group to set up a joint aluminium factory in 1973 (Öztürk 2015: 127).

The term Islamic capital does not indicate a homogeneous mass but a fragmented composition. Certain fractions of the Islamist bourgeoisie were thus subjected to varying degrees of pressure from the military following the memorandum of 28 February, as will be discussed further. Islamic capital broadly consists of two fractions, depending on their scale and the scopes of the fields they are operating in. The first fraction consists of the complex and extensive networks of religious brotherhoods involving small- and medium-scale as well as large-scale capitals. While religious brotherhoods have retained significant control, various firms have often been organised under holding companies, reinforcing the dominance of large-scale capital. To illustrate, Server Holding, consisting of firms operating in a wide range of sectors from publishing to health, is under the command of the İskenderpaşa congregation (Bulut 1997: 284). Certain Islamic businesses, often referred to as the "Anatolian holding companies" (Özcan and Çokgezen 2003), relied on religious affiliations and a nepotistic relationship with *Milli Görüş*, ruling either at the municipality or government level, to raise capital outside the legal framework in the 1990s. Therefore, these Islamic businesses, including Kombassan, Yimpaş, and Jetpa, further acted as coalitions of religious brotherhoods (Bulut 1997: 225). For example, Kombassan and Yimpaş emerged as "'entrepreneurial preachers'" or "'missionary merchants'" which collected money from their members in the form of charity, providing not only religious and educational services but also capital and customer bases (Hoşgör 2015a: 147). Therefore, these Anatolian holding companies can be regarded as part of the first fraction.

The second fraction consists of "'individual' Islamic firms" that do not belong to a religious order (Öztürk 2015: 120). This fraction mainly involves SMEs, often operating in the low-value-added and labour-intensive sectors, including textiles, construction, and services, and mainly located in inner Anatolia, such as in Denizli, Gaziantep, Kayseri, and Konya. This fraction also involves large-scale capital, which underplays religious affiliations and often develops connections with TUSIAD on the one hand and preserves organic relations with religious brotherhoods and the Islamic capital fractions on the other. Some fractions of Islamic finance capital further became members of TUSIAD beginning in the 2000s (see Chapter 6).

1.2   Financial Liberalisation and the Formation of Islamic Finance Capital

By the 1980s, Islamic capital emerged as an important social, economic, and political force (see Chapter 4). The economic liberalisation and outward-oriented capital accumulation that began in the 1980s provided Islamic capital with opportunities for accumulation, and thus advanced the impact of Islamic capital in economic relations. EOI pursued in the 1980s mainly benefited large-scale capital. It also benefited several SMEs located in inner Anatolia and operating in labour-intensive industries, especially textiles, construction, and services, through subcontracting under large-scale internal and foreign capital. To illustrate, by 1990, SMEs accounted for almost 90 per cent of manufacturing firms in Turkey, employing more than one third of all workers in the manufacturing sector (Hoşgör 2015a: 145). The term "Anatolian tigers" became a popular analogy to liken the burgeoning capitalists of Anatolia to the "Asian tigers" (Gürel 2015b: 33).[1]

By the late 1980s, EOI, based on substantial subsidies for export and wage suppression, reached its limits. This was manifested by the decline in the impetus of exports and an upsurge in labour movements and protests. To illustrate, the Turkish economy entered a period of stagflation between 1988 and 1989, manifested by the sharp drop in the growth rate of the GNP, at 1.5 per cent. This was combined with increasing interest rates and indirect taxes, the declining real effective exchange rate of the Turkish lira, and deteriorating wages of the working classes and agricultural revenues (Kazgan 2006: 147). Meanwhile, the aim of industrialisation in manufacturing through export promotion was not realised to a significant extent, demonstrating an important discrepancy between the perceived goal of EOI and what it brought about in reality. For example, the rate of growth of private manufacturing investments remained at 7.7 per cent between 1983 and 1987, and could reach its pre-1980 levels in

---

1   This presents EOI as a success story regarding industrialisation in East Asia, including Hong Kong, Singapore, South Korea, and Taiwan (see Kiely 2005a: 93–109).

real terms only by 1989 (Boratav and Yeldan 2006: 419). This reinforced and demonstrated the peripheralisation of the Turkish economy, including its dependence on certain labour-intensive industries, its failure to diversify its manufactured exports, and the increase in fictitious exports based on "illegal transactions [taking] advantage of incentives" and subsidies (Oğuz 2008: 109).

The exhaustion of EOI brought about a transition to the second phase of outward-oriented capital accumulation, which was based on the liberalisation of finance and the inflow of foreign money capital between 1989 and the late 1990s. This transition corresponded to the interests of foreign finance capital to generate profits through the expansion of a circuit of money capital that headed for "'financial expropriation'" (Lapavitsas 2013: 794). This process remained in harmony with the main premise of the Washington Consensus that capital would flow from rich to poor countries and hence stimulate development through the opening of domestic markets to international capital markets.[2] In Turkey, the financial liberalisation was initiated with the liberalisation of the value of the Turkish lira (Decree No. 32 on the Protection of the Value of Turkish Currency 1989). This removed foreign exchange controls on capital outflows and liberalised both current and capital accounts of the balance of payments.[3] This transition restructured capital accumulation and initiated financialisation that increased the scope and prevalence of fictitious capital.[4]

Financial liberalisation facilitated the state's ability to finance the public deficit by using the inflows of money capital. It also facilitated the state's ability to transfer wealth to the private sector, particularly by providing resources to the financial fractions of finance capital as holding banks became the major mediators for the external borrowing of the state. In this regard, financial liberalisation facilitated the ability of finance capital to control money capital and integrate with the global circuit of capital (Oğuz 2008: 110–111). The holding banks provided the state with high-interest loans that they received as low-interest credits in the international markets. This accumulated wealth enabled financial capital to internationalise through the establishment of financial institutions abroad in the 1990s. For instance, the number of financial institutions established by Turkish capital increased from fourteen to seventy-one

---

2 The Washington Consensus policies dictated to late developers can be summarised as "'stabilise, liberalise, and privatise'" (Öniş and Şenses 2022: 203).
3 According to Yeldan (2022: 233), the liberalisation of capital accounts in 1989 was even more extreme than in the economies of advanced capitalist Western countries at the time.
4 This book's understanding of financialisation is borrowed from Fine (2014). This contrasts with certain critical/radical political economists working on financialisation in Turkey (Akçay and Güngen 2022; Karaçimen 2014). See also Chapter 1.

in the 1990s (Öztürk 2011: 120). However, financial liberalisation brought about a vicious boom-and-bust cycle, where domestic deposits were dollarised and the government was compelled to issue government debt instruments when faced with the expansion of budget deficits. This further urged the banking sector to acquire higher volumes of foreign credit and hence aggravated the indebtedness of the private sector. During the next round of the cycle, the government had to face higher rates of interest, which were a result of the growing trade deficit combined with the risks and uncertainties of speculation (Yeldan 2022: 243). The liberalisation of capital accounts, therefore, deprived the Turkish state apparatus of its control over monetary policy and the foreign exchange regime. This fostered dependency on international capital markets and inflows of money capital in the form of foreign exchange, constraining the national economy to generate speculation-led growth based on increasing real interest rates and monetary deflation.

The financial liberalisation of the 1980s and the 1990s further provided Islamic capital with opportunities for accumulation, and thus contributed to the formation of Islamic finance capital and the subsequent rise of Islamic capital. Significantly, the introduction of interest-free banks (IFBs, later called participation banks) advanced the growth of Islamic capital. While providing the basis for investment through the initial mobilisation and concentration of small sums of capital into larger amounts, IFBs continuously transferred capital required for the expansion of Islamic capital. IFBs further functioned as "unofficial channels" or "informal linkages" based on religious affiliations to direct the savings of migrant workers in Europe and the Gulf countries to investments in Turkey (Hoşgör 2015a: 145–146). They also diversified financial institutions in the domestic market. In the 1980s, IFBs operated to attract inflows of foreign money capital, particularly from the Gulf. For instance, Al-Baraka Turk Finance, Faisal Finance, and Kuwait-Turk Finance were founded in the 1980s through partnerships between Turkish Islamic and Gulf capital. By the 1990s, Turkish Islamic capital became strong enough to establish Anadolu Finance, Ihlas Finance, and Asya Finance (Tanyılmaz 2015: 107–108).

In 1990, *Müstakil Sanayici ve İşadamları Derneği* (Independent Industrialists' and Businessmen's Association, MUSIAD) was established (Savran 2015: 62). This manifested the formation of the second generation of finance capital, Islamic finance capital. MUSIAD represented a limited group of large-scale capital in the form of holding companies in Anatolia, whose fractions operated mainly in labour-intensive and low value-added sectors—the same sectors often ignored by first-generation finance capital. To illustrate, the leading members operated in textiles, food, metal casting, iron and steel, and construction (Tanyılmaz 2015: 111). MUSIAD, nevertheless, predominantly represented

SMEs that operated primarily in labour-intensive and low-value-added sectors. Islamic banking in the form of IFBs established by holding companies enabled capital accumulation by MUSIAD-affiliated businesses, including SMEs. For example, the Istikbal Group, a leading furniture manufacturer, owned Anadolu Finance. Faisal Finance was sold to Kombassan Holding in 1998 and then to the Ülker Group, a prominent food producer, in 2001 (Hoşgör 2015a: 146). In this regard, MUSIAD, as a representative of Islamic finance capital, manifested a power bloc (Öztürk 2015: 129).

The financial liberalisation of the 1990s also corresponded to the internationalisation of financial capital. Since TUSIAD-affiliated financial capital pioneered the process of internationalisation, MUSIAD-affiliated financial capital engaged in competition with TUSIAD to find new regions to expand to, or to focus on new sectors in regions where TUSIAD-affiliated companies had already expanded. Such competition brought about the prominence of MUSIAD-affiliated businesses in low-value-added and labour-intensive sectors often ignored by TUSIAD, including textiles, food, metal casting, construction, and iron and steel. It further compelled MUSIAD-affiliated commercial and financial capital to expand soon after the formation of finance capital in the early 1990s. This temporal pressure was reproduced in spatial terms. MUSIAD-affiliated businesses mainly targeted Middle Eastern and Central Asian markets since the dissolution of the Soviet Union opened Central Asia and the Caucasus for the expansion of capitalist relations, and TUSIAD-affiliated businesses had already mainly expanded in the EU market. The competition between the first and second generations of finance capital also compelled MUSIAD-affiliated businesses to pursue an alternative model of integration into the world economy based on the "'Islamic Common Market'" (Avcı 2019: 174), thereby challenging Western hegemony.

1.3 The Rise of Milli Görüş

This book accepts political Islam/Islamism as a religio-political framework that "provides political responses to today's societal challenges by imagining a future, the foundations for which rest on reappropriated, reinvented concepts borrowed from the Islamic tradition" (Denoeux 2002: 61). While acknowledging the fact that Islam posited a political and juridical system since its inception (Achcar 2013: 16), this book focuses on Islamists and Islamist movements as political actors who have reinterpreted the Islamic religion in different ways to pursue certain economic, political, and cultural objectives. Political Islam inevitably manifests the contradictory nature of Islam as a religion, which remains a pristine form of structuration of social consciousness and social relations (Marx 1975: 297). This contradictory nature arises from the function of religion to mediate and turn "upside-down" the concrete reality of relations of exploitation, domination, and competition in class-based societies (Marx and Engels 1998: 41). On the one hand, religion hampers the ability of subordinate classes to control material relations by legitimising property relations and veiling class antagonisms (Ollman 1996: 223). In the case of Islam, the Quran accepts private property by setting rules for inheritance and protects it by advising against challenging inequalities and praising the pursuit for profit and trade (Rodinson 1973: 14–16). On the other hand, religion represents and reproduces material interests of not only the dominant classes but also subordinate classes. By acting as "the heart of a heartless world" (Marx 1992b: 244), religion assumes the form of "the protest of the disinherited against the frustrations forced upon them by the luxury and oppression of the rich and powerful" (Rodinson 1973: 25). In this regard, political Islam expresses "a violent revolt against the destructive effects of really existing capitalism" on the one hand, and rejects "the right for society to construct its own future", especially "the right of the working classes and progressive forces to organise and act", on the other (Amin 2009: 71–78).

The rise of political Islam beginning in the 1970s manifested the contradictions of world capitalism in general and of late development in particular. The rise of political Islam was the product of the amalgamation of two main dynamics. The first dynamic was imperialist support—particularly that of the United States—for political Islam as a bulwark against socialism. The second dynamic was the internal contradictions of the development of capitalism under secular nationalism, which were already exacerbated by the failure of secular nationalism to respond to economic crises (Kumar 2011a). In the 1990s, the Islamist movements were quick to fill the ideological vacuum created through the collapse of the Soviet Union, which disoriented and paralysed the left by symbolising the victory of the advanced capitalist Western countries, especially the United States. In response to the drastic impact of crises of capitalism, the Islamist movements "[grew] on the decomposing corpse of the progressive movement[s]" (Achcar 2013: 17) and managed to recruit from the urban classes. These urban classes included the educated youth as the cadre base; the petty bourgeoisie, such as artisans, shopkeepers, lawyers, and doctors; and "the very poor", such as slum dwellers (Kumar 2011b). Nonetheless, the Islamist movements mobilised the subordinate classes under the hegemony of the dominant classes, particularly in Turkey, where Islamic capital sought to establish hegemony over the working classes.

The case of *Milli Görüş* confirmed this general pattern of the revival of political Islam. *Milli Görüş* emerged as an Islamist movement representing small- and medium-scale capitalists, artisans and shopkeepers, the urban and rural working classes, the intelligentsia, and the university youth. Erbakan, the leader of *Milli Görüş*, was a mechanical engineer. Following the closure of the MSP, *Refah Partisi* (Welfare Party, RP) was established in 1983. The RP paradoxically represented a continuity and a discontinuity in the tradition of *Milli Görüş* with its hegemonic project of just order (*adil düzen*) (RP 1985). The just order called for welfare for the poor and the rich, manifesting the contradictions of harmonisation between political Islam and capitalism, and hence a continuity in the doctrine of *Milli Görüş*. Welfare, alongside felicity and salvation, could only be achieved through "the force of morality and virtue that already existed in the natural disposition (*fıtrat*)" (MNP 1970: 5). Therefore, it was the RP's common cause (*dava*) to pursue the just order as representative of the oppressed and marginalised Muslim majority against coercive secularism.[5] Nevertheless, the just order replaced state interventionism as a developmental strategy with an emphasis on the regulatory state that governs and supervises markets. This corresponded to outward-oriented capital accumulation and manifested a discontinuity in the tradition of *Milli Görüş*. To illustrate, the RP presented itself as "the one and only supporter of the private sector [and] free market economy" (Akpınar and Araman 2011: 96).

In the 1990s, the RP advanced its social and political influence as a result of the "gradual Islamisation of society" (Yavuz 2003: 38). The rise of the RP was also a result of the political paralysis of the left, suppressed by the junta of 1980 and the New Right, and disoriented following the collapse of the Soviet Union. In this regard, the RP managed to obtain the approval of large fractions of urban classes. The RP represented not only Islamist workers and civil servants, the petty bourgeoisie, and small- and medium-scale capitalists—like its predecessors, the MNP and the MSP—but also large-scale Islamic capital and larger segments of the proletariat. This was because the RP targeted the material interests of TUSIAD by challenging the hegemonic role of Western capital, particularly that of the United States and the European Union. The RP also mobilised the fractions of blue-collar workers in the formal sector as well as precarious workers and the urban poor working in flexible and insecure jobs and mostly living in squats (Gürel 2015b: 20; Gürgen 2012: 15). These fractions were subjected to the destructive impacts of economic crises and exploitation in labour-intensive sectors, operated mainly by small- and medium-scale Islamic capital. The decline of the left compelled these fractions to vote for the

---

5 *Dava* could be alternatively interpreted in relation to the Islamic term *dawah*, which indicates the duty to call people unto Allah's path. Since *Milli Görüş* employed the tradition of Islamic propagation (*tebliğ*) (Çakır 2009: 550), the RP's *dava* can be understood as the basis of Islamist propagation.

RP since the same fraction used to vote for the left-wing political parties in the pre-1980 coup era (Eligür 2010: 76). Further related to this, the RP represented the socially disadvantaged Islamist women, who engaged in activist practices such as introducing the RP to and recruiting other women during electoral door-to-door campaigns (Arat 2005: 76).

2 Classes, Crises, and *Milli Görüş*

2.1 *The Crises of Financialisation in the Early 1990s*

The memorandum of 28 February was a result of and a response to the "'lost decade'" of the 1990s (Öniş and Şenses 2022: 210). The economic aspect of the hegemonic crisis arose from the financial liberalisation of the 1990s, which can be divided into four main episodes of "growth, crisis, and adjustment" (Yeldan 2006: 199). The first episode took place between 1989 and 1993, which corresponded to economic growth through uncontrolled financial liberalisation. During this episode, short-term foreign capital, often referred to as "hot money", was attracted through the overvaluation of the Turkish lira and high interest rates (Erdem 2007: 132). This brought about an increase in the real rate of growth of GDP, which reached 4.8 per cent between 1989 and 1993, demonstrating an upturn from 2.1 per cent in 1988 (Boratav and Yeldan 2006: 419). This economic policy brought about a high level of trade, undermining exports but encouraging imports, and hence dramatically increasing the current account deficit. In fact, the foreign trade deficit increased from 4.17 billion USD to 14.08 billion USD between 1989 and 1993 (TCMB 1994: 187). While the private sector replaced the public sector regarding direct borrowing from the international markets, capital inflows were instrumental to compensate the current account deficit between 1989 and 1994. The fiscal balance also deteriorated because of high interest payments, which further enabled the transfer of wealth to the private sector. To illustrate, the ratio of securities issued by the state—in the form of government bonds and Treasury bills—to GNP increased from 7.7 per cent to 16.8 per cent between 1989 and 1993 (Boratav and Yeldan 2006: 423).

By the end of 1993, it became clear that the rapid economic growth of 1989–1993 took place through the overexpansion of public expenditure in exchange for insufficient increases in public revenue. For instance, the high-interest earnings of the financial sector brought about realised annual returns of 47 per cent in 1989, 25 per cent in 1990, and 18 per cent in 1992 and 1993 (Öniş and Aysan 2000: 129). To illustrate the severe deterioration of current account deficits and fiscal balances, the ratio of current account deficit to GNP increased from 1.7 per cent in 1990 to 3.6 per cent in 1993. Similarly, the ratio of the public-sector borrowing requirement to GNP increased from 7.4 per cent in 1990 to 12.1 per cent in 1993 (Yeldan 2006: 199). At the end of 1993, the government implemented the policy of a low interest rate, resorting to the Central Bank's resources with an aim to break domestic borrowing at high interest rates. Nevertheless, the government's aim of channelling money capital to the Turkish stock exchange market by selling foreign currency reserves and thereby decreasing the demand for foreign exchange backfired. In fact, the exchange rate of the USD increased from 19,000 TRY to 38,000 TRY between January and April 1994, and the Central Bank's foreign currency reserves decreased from 7 billion USD to 3 billion USD (Kepenek and Yentürk 2001: 485). Meanwhile, the two main credit rating institutions, namely, Moody's and Standard and Poor's, reduced Turkey's credit rating in response to this new economic policy (Öniş 1996: 11). The economic and financial crisis of 1994 broke following a major outflow of short-term capital, precisely 5.91 billion USD (Boratav and Yeldan 2006: 424). Between January and April 1994, the GDP declined by more than 5 per cent, whereas the stock of domestic debt reached 20 per cent of GDP, after having been at 2.4 per cent in 1990 (Yeldan 1998: 397).

An economic and financial crisis followed by a major outflow of short-term capital demonstrated Turkish dependency on foreign finance capital, characterising the Turkish economy with macroeconomic instability and a vicious boom-and-bust cycle beginning in the 1990s. This cycle indicated a dependent economic policy based on high interest rates offered by state securities and cheap foreign currency—against an overvalued Turkish lira—that aimed to prevent capital flight. In this vicious cycle, real interest rates could not decline below a certain floor, and further upward adjustment in domestic interest rates became the only mechanism to avoid a major devaluation and capital flight in the face of a destabilised current account balance (Boratav and Yeldan 2006: 424).

In April 1994, the government implemented a stabilisation package in association with the IMF. The package involved a major devaluation; an expansion in the supply of debt securities that increased interest rates; the privatisation of SOEs, including ERDEMIR iron and steel, the TÜPRAŞ oil refinery, PETKIM petrochemicals, Turkish Airlines, and DITAŞ maritime operations; and a reduction of agricultural subsidies for grain, tobacco, and beet (Kepenek and Yentürk 2001: 485–488). The stabilisation package, in this regard, sought to restructure relations of distribution between the financial and industrial sectors in favour of the former, and to transfer wealth from wage labour to financial capital and export-led commercial capital. In the aftermath of 1994, real wages in manufacturing declined by 30.1 per cent in the private sector and 19.1 per cent in the public sector, whereas the average mark-up rate in private manufacturing peaked, reaching its highest value in the era of post-1980 economic liberalisation (Yeldan 2006: 199). Following the implementation of the stabilisation package, the inflows of short-term capital recovered, and the Turkish economy experienced reinvigorated growth between 1995 and 1997. This episode of growth lasted until the contagion of the Asian financial crisis of 1997 (Boratav and Yeldan 2006: 419–420).

2.2 The Hegemonic Crisis of the Early 1990s

The early 1990s and the aftermath of the 1994 crisis, similarly to the post-1980 restructuring, demonstrated the reorganisation of class relations to the detriment of the urban and rural subordinate classes. This eroded the bond between the subordinate classes and the centre-left and centre-right political parties, fuelling the support of the working classes for Islamist movements. The macroeconomic instability of the 1990s also eroded the bond between the dominant classes and the centre-left and centre-right political parties, resulting in the failure to form a power bloc to establish hegemony. The hegemony of the New Right had already collapsed by the early 1990s, which was manifested by the rise of workers' protests and demonstrations beginning in the late 1980s. The political arena staged a wave of widespread strikes and protests in the private and public sectors beginning in the spring of 1989 (Saraçoğlu 2015: 776), which coincided with Özal's election to the presidency and Yıldırım Akbulut's takeover of the premiership in November 1989 (TBMM 15 November 1989). The ANAP government under Akbulut was rather submitted to Özal's control through broadened presidential competences. In fact, Özal often pioneered several decisions pertaining to the economy, security, and foreign policy (Tanör 2011: 84–85). Meanwhile, the ANAP could not obtain the consent of Western capital, particularly Western European capital, as Turkey's application for membership to the European Community in 1987 was rejected by the European Commission (1989).

The hegemonic crisis of the 1990s manifested itself most significantly on the political and social stages. The affirmative result of the referendum on the lifting of the political ban on politicians who dominated the pre-1980 era allowed these politicians to return to the political stage in 1987 (Decision of the Supreme Election Council 1987). Demirel was elected as the chair of *Doğru Yol Partisi* (True Path Party, DYP); Ecevit was elected as the chair of *Demokratik Sol Parti* (Democratic Left Party, DSP);[6] and Erbakan was elected as the chair of

---

6 Ecevit renounced the CHP, which was closed—alongside other political parties—by the junta of 1980.

the RP. The ANAP government under Akbulut's premiership could only resist until its dissolution in June 1991 in the face of the growing political demands of various social classes. Beginning in the early 1990s, the Turkish political arena staged a number of short-lived coalition governments (TBMM 2015), manifesting and deepening the hegemonic crisis.

Radicalised elements of political Islam began to come to the fore, revealing and reinforcing the hegemonic crisis of the 1990s. Such radical Islamist movements included the Sunni-Kurdish *Hezbollah* (Party of God) and *Islami Büyükdoğu Akıncılar Cephesi* (Islamic Great Orient Fighters Front, IBDA-C), both of which sought to establish the rule of *sharia* in the country by resorting to violence and terrorism. While *Hezbollah* became famous for its inhumane acts of torture (Eligür 2014: 172–173),[7] the IBDA-C often used firebombing to target "mainstream mosques, religious minorities, media and communications infrastructure, symbols of the [secular] state, secular banks, restaurants, and bars ... serving alcohol" (Rabasa et al. 2004: 193–194). Moreover, several assassinations and massacres took place in the 1990s either utilising Islamic symbols and references or paving the way for the prominence of Islamist movements. A number of prominent left-wing, secular, and Alevi intellectuals, journalists, and artists who were publicly opposed to Islamisation and Islamist movements were assassinated, and their cases remained unsolved until today (Eligür 2010: 4).

These Islamist terrorist attacks unveiled the paralysis—and arguably the complicity—of the state apparatus vis-à-vis Islamist violence. This was not only related to the hegemonic crisis of the 1990s but the Islamisation of the state apparatus. The case of the Sivas/Madımak massacre illustrates this point. In July 1993, thirty-five Alevi and left-wing intellectuals and artists were massacred by a crowd shouting "Allahu Akbar" ("God is the greatest") during a convention at the Madımak Hotel in Sivas (Tanör 2011: 104).[8] Neither the mayor nor the constabulary forces, including the police and gendarmerie, intervened in the crowd's siege of the hotel and arson attack, but "'simply looked as the hotel caught fire'" (Jongerden 2003: 85). While Prime Minister Tansu Çiller celebrated that the crowd launching the attack remained unaffected by the fire, President Demirel regarded the massacre as an isolated case and underlined

---

7 The most significant method of torture used by *Hezbollah* was hogtie (Uludağ 2023).
8 A number of lawyers who defended suspects of the massacre later became AKP MPs. The case was abated overall in 2012 due to the lapse of time (SOL 2013).

the prior provocation caused by the Turkish translation of Salman Rushdie's *The Satanic Verses*.[9]

2.3 Milli Görüş *and Social Classes*

In the local elections of 1994, the RP captured twenty-eight out of seventy-six provincial municipalities, including six major metropolitan municipalities, and leadership of 327 local governments, while receiving 19.1 per cent of the overall vote (Eligür 2010: 78). This demonstrated that an Islamist movement became the main political candidate and could claim the hegemony. The RP captured the metropolitan municipalities, including Istanbul and Ankara, and the municipalities of rural and poor provinces in central, southeastern, and eastern Anatolia, ousting the centre-left *Sosyaldemokrat Halkçı Parti* (Social Democratic Populist Party, SHP). The SHP, which was established by the rank-and-file members of the CHP,[10] had already distanced itself from state interventionism in relations of distribution and come to terms with neoliberalism by 1993. The SHP, which previously promoted the sale of food at cheaper prices and the expansion of food and housing co-operatives, advocated for outsourcing and privatisation, and engaged in nepotism and corruption (Doğan 2011: 60–61).

The RP's just order, in this regard, offered a viable negotiation between free-market capitalism and populist redistribution through social assistance and basic infrastructure. Significantly, the RP provided a wide range of free social services, including food banks, elderly houses, dormitories, medical services, cemetery services, rehabilitation centres, financial assistance, nursing homes, social housing, and subsidised food and public transport (Eligür 2010: 172 –173). Besides these populist redistributional mechanisms, religious brotherhoods played an important role in mobilising the support of the working classes for the RP. For instance, the İsmailağa congregation, a branch of the Nakşibendi order that was formed in Istanbul, called upon its disciples to vote for the RP, declaring that the RP was "the representative of a system based on the word of God" and that those who did not support the RP were "sinful" (*Milli Gazete* 1991).

Moreover, the fragmentation and disintegration of global production in the era of globalisation reinforced outsourcing and subcontracting, which benefited medium- and small-scale as well as large-scale Islamic capital. In this sense, the RP further offered a compromise for different fractions of Islamist capital

---

9 Aziz Nesin, who translated *The Satanic Verses* prior to his attendance at the convention, was later found guilty by the Ankara State Security Court for inciting anti-Islamic sentiments and thereby provoking the crowd (BBC Türkçe 2018).
10 The CHP and the SHP were later merged in 1995 (Güneş-Ayata 2002: 106).

at the local level, and thus obtained the consent, significantly, of MUSIAD. To illustrate, the RP dismissed hundreds of workers in Gebze and Kağıthane in Istanbul to improve the municipality budget. As a result, the budget was utilised for privatisations and construction biddings to transfer wealth to the members not only of MUSIAD but also of TUSIAD, particularly Sabancı Holding (Doğan 2011: 61–64). In this way, the RP's just order, "designed to form a broad coalition of political support" (Öniş 1997: 754), managed to obtain the approval of comprehensive fractions of capital, however temporarily.

In the general election of 1995, the RP gained the highest vote share, at 21.4 per cent, and the DYP and the ANAP formed a minority coalition government with the DSP's support to prevent the RP from coming to power. However, the coalition government was dissolved in June 1996 due to corruption allegations against the DYP (Akşin 2011: 169). These allegations did not prevent the RP from allying with the DYP to form a coalition government in June 1996 (TBMM 3 July 1996). In this way, the RP–DYP coalition, often called the *RefahYol* government, was established under Erbakan's premiership. The *RefahYol* government worsened the hegemonic crisis of the 1990s because of the RP's failure to obtain the consent of prominent fractions of the dominant classes, which was finance capital in the process of internationalisation.

The RP never challenged neoliberalism. On the contrary, it benefited from neoliberalism by favouring Islamic capital at the local and national levels. In an alliance with MUSIAD to balance the collaboration between the DYP and TOBB, the RP favoured large-scale and medium- and small-scale capital within MUSIAD through privatisations of SOEs and state subsidies. For instance, the large-scale capital firm Kombassan benefited from privatisations in the war and defence industries, particularly the privatisation of PETLAS, which produced military aircraft tires (Yankaya 2012: 32). The smaller fractions of Islamic capital sought to participate in bidding for the privatisation of Turkish Airlines, ISDEMIR iron and steel, Sümer Holding, TEDAŞ electricity, and PETKIM petrochemicals by forming a consortium called Yatırım Holding (*Sabah* 1997).

The RP, nonetheless, challenged the dominant role of Western capital and finance capital that had organic links with Western capital, particularly TUSIAD. The RP's position against Western capital was apparent in its anti-Western discourse, which presented the advanced capitalist Western countries as imperialist actors (Öniş 1997: 753). The RP further proposed an Islamic common market composed of Muslim countries and a unified Islamic currency to replace the primacy of the Western markets and the US dollar (Erbakan 1991: 12). The RP also initiated an organisation, the Developing Eight (D-8), as an alternative to the Group of Eight (G8) industrialised nations. The D-8 comprised the Muslim countries of Bangladesh, Egypt, Indonesia, Iran, Malaysia,

Nigeria, Pakistan, and Turkey (Dalay and Friedman 2013: 125). The RP's anti-Western discourse, which sought to advance integration with the Islamic markets, was in harmony with the interests of MUSIAD-affiliated capital in the process of internationalisation. To illustrate, MUSIAD-affiliated businesses agreed on contracts worth almost 800 million USD while accompanying Erbakan during his official visits to Muslim-majority countries (Yankaya 2012: 31).

Nevertheless, the RP's promotion of Islamic capital did not often conform to the rules and norms of the bourgeois social and economic order. In precise terms, the RP favoured certain fractions of Islamic capital that operated outside the legal framework. Most significantly, Kombassan and Yimpaş collected millions of US dollars from thousands of Turkish citizens and Turkish guest workers in Germany and other European countries through personal and informal relations with its religious symbols and references (Buğra 1998: 532). Moreover, the fractions of Islamic capital that operated as coalitions of religious brotherhoods resorted to extra-economic means when faced with extreme situations, such as severe competition in a particular sector or bankruptcy. For instance, certain businesses utilised the issuing of *fatwas* to call their followers to boycott other products and pool private resources and savings (Hoşgör 2011: 347).[11] In combination with the RP's anti-Western discourse, the RP's favouring of fractions of Islamic capital operating outside the legal framework threatened the interests of TUSIAD-affiliated businesses, which were integrated into the global markets in accordance with the formal and impersonal rules of capitalism. The RP's favouritism further threatened the interests of certain fractions of Islamic capital that maintained organic relations with Western capital. Significantly, *Hür Sanayici ve İşadamları Derneği* (Free Industrialists and Businessmen's Association, HURSIAD), which maintained organic relations with the Gülen congregation (Yavuz 2003: 192), did not support the RP. This was because the Gülen congregation, with which HURSIAD maintained organic relations, was supported by the United States and American capital to access the Central Asian markets after the dissolution of the Soviet Union (Bulut 1999: 382–384). Similarly, certain fractions of industrial and commercial capital affiliated with MUSIAD, particularly SMEs operating in the organised industrial zones, were in the process of internationalisation while competing with other fractions of

---

11 *Fatwas* were already being utilised to legitimise certain activities that did not conform to the Islamic principles. To illustrate, Ihlas Holding established an advisory board with the participation of prominent Islamic scholars to gain Islamic credibility and avoid criticism when it decided to join the Istanbul Stock Exchange. This decision was necessary to enter privatisation bids and secure capital for expansion into sectors requiring huge investments (Hoşgör 2011: 347).

Islamic capital that were favoured by the RP-ruled municipalities in Ankara and Istanbul (Doğan 2013: 289).

Furthermore, the RP's anti-Western discourse caused a number of international scandals, which led to further inflammation of the hegemonic crisis. One of the most significant examples remained Erbakan's visit to Libya in October 1996. During a joint press conference, Muammar Gaddafi, the prime minister of Libya, stated that he met Erbakan not as "the prime minister of Turkey" but as "a member of the International Islamic Popular Command", whose leader was Gaddafi himself (*Hürriyet Daily News* 1996). Gaddafi continued with "a public dressing-down over Turkey's developing links with Israel and openly called for the establishment of an independent Kurdish state" (Hale 2013: 228). Erbakan's silence in response to Gaddafi's statements caused public outrage and pushback from the military. During an NSC meeting in April 1997, Erbakan "managed to successfully dodge queries" from Güven Erkaya, the commander of the navy, regarding Erbakan's role in the International Islamic Popular Command (Gunter 1998b: 3). Nevertheless, when Lieutenant-General Çetin Doğan, representing the General Staff, was asked about this, he declared that the chief of the General Staff was the commander-in-chief during peacetime, and the president was the commander-in-chief during wartime (*Milliyet* 1997d). Doğan's statement reinforced the idea that the military did not recognise the *RefahYol* government as the civilian authority under which the military served.

The military's position against the *RefahYol* government's foreign policy mainly targeted RP's anti-Westernism—especially anti-Americanism—and the RP's search for regional alternatives. Significantly, the *RefahYol* government signed an agreement in August 1996, worth 23 billion USD, to import natural gas from Iran which directly disregarded the US-imposed sanctions on Libya and Iran, also known as the D'Amato Law (Gunter 1998b: 3). During the signing of the gas agreement, Erbakan further called for a summit meeting among Turkey, Iran, Iraq, and Syria to discuss the prospects of regional co-operation. Erbakan's call was followed by the visit of Şevket Kazan, the minister of justice, to Iraq (Jenkins 2008a: 160). In this way, the RP antagonised the United States. The RP's anti-Westernism was further merged with an anti-Israel rhetoric, which antagonised the United States and the EU, since both supported Israel's settler-colonialist claims to Palestine (Timur 2014: 17). The RP's anti-Israel rhetoric further clashed with the interests of the Turkish military regarding co-operation with Israel. The military had already pioneered the signing of a renewable five-year military training co-operation agreement between Turkey and Israel in February 1996 and was eager to strengthen co-operation in the war and defence industry. The *RefahYol* government had subsequently signed a defence industry co-operation agreement and approved a

632.5-million-USD contract for Israel Aircraft Industries to upgrade fifty-four Turkish F-4 Phantoms (Jenkins 2008a: 160–161).

The *RefahYol* government was further involved with domestic scandals despite the RP's claim that it would bring "an end to nepotism and corruption" (Yavuz 1997: 73). Most significantly, a November 1996 car accident in Susurluk province of Balıkesir caused the eruption of one of the biggest scandals in Turkish history. The occupants of the car included Abdullah Çatlı,[12] a prominent member of the mafia and the Grey Wolves; Hüseyin Kocadağ, former vice-chief of police for Istanbul; Sedat Bucak, a DYP MP and a tribal chieftain; and Gonca Us, a celebrity. Mehmet Ağar, another former chief of police for Istanbul and the minister of the interior under the *RefahYol* government, claimed that Kocadağ "had probably 'arrested' Çatlı and was bringing him into custody". Ağar was forced to resign when it became clear that all four occupants of the car had stayed in the same hotel together the previous three nights, where Ağar himself had "'coincidentally'" stayed (Gunter 1998a: 121). The MIT provided the *RefahYol* government with an investigation report which confirmed the existence of a deep state whose members belonged to the military, police, and mafia (*Hürriyet* 2011). However, Minister of Justice Şevket Kazan prevented a further investigation and the trial of Ağar by annulling the public prosecutor's suspension of Ağar's parliamentary immunity (*Milliyet* 1996b). As a response to the government's inaction against the deep state, mass public protests in the form of civil disobedience, such as switching off lights every night at 9 pm, were organised to call the *RefahYol* government to resign (*Milliyet* 1997c). This demonstrated the RP's failure to obtain the approval of the urban classes.

2.4 Milli Görüş *and Secularism*

The targeting of secularism as a founding principle by *Milli Görüş* constituted the political aspect of the hegemonic crisis under the *RefahYol* government. For *Milli Görüş*, Islam was not only a means for political mobilisation but a constitutive principle that aimed to replace secularism and religionise the state apparatus and social structure. *Milli Görüş* considered the Republican state to be an imitation of the West that caused the underdevelopment of Turkey and supported the custodianship role of the military (RP 1995: 19–24). While presenting a duality between the Republican state and the "true" Muslim majority, *Milli Görüş* claimed to pioneer the promotion of Islam, which was a symbol

---

12 Çatlı was the mastermind behind and one of the main assailants in the assassination of seven left-wing students, members of the TIP, in the Bahçelievler district of Ankara in October 1978. Çatlı, known as "the chieftain", later became the "official" contract killer of the Turkish deep state (see Yalçın and Yurdakul 2003).

of "'intense sacrifice and commitment'" for believers. In this way, supporting *Milli Görüş* became "'a special mission undertaken for God's sake'" without any expectation for material gains (Arat 2005: 36–37). In this regard, *Milli Görüş* turned into a religious brotherhood whose supporters were portrayed as true believers, seeking to "gain the greatest will of God (*sevap*)" by converting people to Islam "until there [were] no longer any unfaithful (*batıl*) left in the world" (Eligür 2010: 189).

Milli Görüş opposed the military's guardianship role with references to democracy (RP 1995: 24), which it interpreted with an emphasis on freedom of speech, freedom of faith, and human rights (RP 1991). In this regard, *Milli Görüş* instrumentalised democracy, which it degraded for being a worldly ideology, as opposed to Islam, which was based on divine rule, to accommodate Islamist demands and practices. For example, in July 1996, Recep Tayyip Erdoğan, the RP's then-mayor of Istanbul, presented the RP as a subject of God and not a subject of mortal man, and discredited democratic and Republican regimes for being man-made and mortal regimes. Erdoğan further presented democracy as a tool to establish just order (*Milliyet* 1996a). Moreover, *Milli Görüş*'s interpretation of democracy in majoritarian terms on the basis of Sunni Islam brought about an understanding of a polarised and hierarchical society divided between believers and unbelievers. Therefore, any citizen, social group, or social movement that did not embrace the Sunni interpretation could be denied human rights and freedoms. This interpretation also legitimised the RP's hostility against seculars and other Islamic sects, particularly Alevis. Significantly, Kazan, as a leading member of *Milli Görüş*, volunteered to defend those involved with the Sivas massacre in 1993 and even continued to visit the convicted in prison after his appointment as the minister of justice in 1996 under the *RefahYol* government (Jenkins 2008a: 253). Similarly, during the mass protests against the *RefahYol* government's role in the Susurluk scandal, Kazan publicly committed a hate crime against Alevis by comparing the light-switching protests with "burning out candles" (*Milliyet* 1997c).[13]

Milli Görüş's instrumentalisation of democracy aimed to replace the Republican state and its secular regime, which it understood as a "'spurious'" and "'fraudulent regime'" (Sayarı 1996: 38), with an Islamic state and regime. Significantly, Erbakan called for the introduction of a plurality of legal systems based on diverse religions of different communities so that Muslims could live "in a manner compatible with their beliefs" and prevent the "repression"

---

13   The phrase "burning out candles" (*mum söndü*) is a hate speech as it suggests that Alevis convene to commit incest instead of praying on religious days.

of a secular "single code of law" (ECHR 2003). This call, which was based on the reinterpretation of the seventh-century Charter of Medina (*Dustur al-Madinah*) (Bulaç 2009: 503), fundamentally sought to incorporate *sharia* law by introducing legal and social autonomy to religious communities. *Milli Görüş* further legitimised any resort to violence to dismantle the secular regime. In April 1994, Erbakan publicly stated that: "The RP will come to power and the just order will be established. What is the problem? Will the transition period be severe or soft, will it be harmonious or bloody?" (*Milliyet* 1994). Similarly, during a ceremony to commemorate the anniversary of Atatürk's death in November 1996, the mayor of Kayseri declared that: "This [secular Republican] system should change. We have waited. We will wait a little longer. And let Muslims keep alive the resentment, rancour, and hatred they feel in their hearts" (Jenkins 2008a: 161). More importantly, in December 1997, Erdoğan started a speech with a poem: "The minarets are our bayonets, the domes our helmets, the mosques our barracks, and the faithful our soldiers, this divine military waits for religion, *Allah-u Akbar*" (*Milliyet* 1997g).[14] Contrary to several liberal-conservative scholars who underplayed the significance of these speeches and the poem (see Gunter and Yavuz 2007; Heper and Toktaş 2003), this book underlines the importance of the sociohistorical and sociopolitical context in which these speeches were made and in which the—distorted and manipulated—poem was cited.[15]

When in power, the RP sought to Islamise the state apparatus and social order. In January 1997, the Cabinet passed a decree to reorganise working hours in state institutions in a way that would allow fasting during Ramadan. The decree was later annulled by the Council of State (*Danıştay*) on the basis that it violated the secular Constitution (Jenkins 2008a: 161). The RP further focused on certain state institutions which were considered to be bastions of secularism. For example, the RP planned to change the internal regulations of the Ministry of Foreign Affairs to employ personnel among those who knew Arabic; set up *masjids* in the Turkish embassies; and charge diplomats with the

---

14 In the aftermath of the memorandum of 28 February, Erdoğan was to be convicted for "'inciting religious hatred'" and would spend four months in prison (Park 2012: 26).
15 The poem was originally written by Ziya Gökalp, a Turkish-nationalist sociologist and writer, during the Balkan Wars in the 1910s. The original poem was as follows
    The rifle in my hand and faith in my heart,
    I have two wishes: religion and fatherland,
    The hearth is the military and respected is the Sultan,
    May God help the Sultan ...
    May God make Islam eternal.
        Bardakçı 2002

duty to act as Islamic missionaries (Heper and Güney 2000: 641). At the social level, the RP considered religious brotherhoods to be pillars of civil society through which to implement its Islamist project. In January 1997, Erbakan, as the prime minister, invited the director of religious affairs and leaders of various religious brotherhoods to an *iftar* dinner at his official residence (Güney 2002: 168). By hosting religious leaders at the level of the premiership, the RP legitimised religious brotherhoods, which it already equated with *Diyanet*, both at the state and societal levels.

3 The Political Economy of the Process of 28 February

3.1 *The Memorandum of 1997*

The military sought to reinforce its guardianship role while targeting the rise of Islamist movements. In this regard, the establishment of the Prime Ministerial Crisis Management Centre (*Başbakanlık Kriz Yönetim Merkezi*) and the Western Working Group (*Batı Çalışma Grubu*) were significant. In January 1997, the *RefahYol* government passed a regulation to broaden co-operation and co-ordination between the General Staff and relevant ministries (Bylaw on the Prime Ministerial Crisis Management Centre 1997). The regulation established the Prime Ministerial Crisis Management Centre within the structure of the Secretary-General of the NSC (SGNSC). The Centre had the competence to decide on and control measures regarding the prevention and removal of crises and threats, including hostile attitudes and activities against the national interest and the constitutional democracy, disasters and plagues, radiation and pollution, and economic depression. The SGNSC was authorised to co-ordinate activities in the name of the prime minister, regulate the operation of the Centre, and inform relevant departments. The SGNSC, resorting to its expanded competences, established the Western Working Group, consisting of military officers, and charged them with the duty to gather information about "the political orientations of civil society groups, mayors, governors, government employees, political party cadres, and media" (Cizre-Sakallıoğlu 2002: 196). Both the Centre and the Group were to function as the headquarters of the process of 28 February by monitoring the implementation of the NSC's decisions, collecting information against the Islamist movements, including *Milli Görüş*, and enabling the military to shape public opinion.

The Jerusalem Night, organised in January 1997 by the RP mayor of Sincan, a province of Ankara, with the support of Iranian diplomats, pulled the trigger of the process of 28 February. The audience displayed slogans and banners demanding the application of *sharia*. While the Iranian ambassador called for adherence to the Islamic canon, the mayor stated that he would "'infuse the *sharia*'" into the secular segments of society (Eligür 2010: 219). In response, tanks rolled through the streets of Sincan in February 1997 (*Milliyet* 1997a). Even though the military at the time officially declared that the passage was in accordance with the plan of action drills within NATO's framework (Habertürk 2014), the public regarded the incident as a show of force by the military against the RP. Çevik Bir, the vice-chief of the General Staff, later described the incident as "'fine tuning in democracy'" (Eligür 2010: 219). Despite Erbakan's attempt at downplaying the Sincan incident, the CHP and the DSP prepared an interpellation against the *Refahyol* government regarding the government's "insensitivity" about "the reactionary threat of Islamism" (*Milliyet* 1997b). While the Iranian ambassador was recalled, the mayor of Sincan was convicted for inciting religious hatred and was paid a visit by Kazan during his imprisonment (*Hürriyet* 1997a).

On 28 February 1997, the NSC held its ordinary meeting, chaired by President Demirel. The General Staff emphasised the rise of Islamism as a reactionary threat seeking to establish the *sharia* and trigger sectarian and religious polarisation (MGK 1997). The General Staff further proposed a set of measures, including:

> reinforcement of laws to prevent and punish the radical Islamist movements; reorganisation of the licensing procedures for weapons to prevent the armament of radical Islamist movements; monitoring of financial activities of Islamic capital and forecasting activities of the Islamist media; supervision of private educational institutions; extension of compulsory primary education for eight continuous years; abolition of religious brotherhoods; purge of Islamists from state institutions, universities, and judiciary; implementation of necessary actions against Iran's support for radical Islamist activities without damaging economic relations; reinforcement of the secular dress code in the public sphere; and supervision over collection of skins of sacrificed animals to cut the revenue of Islamist movements.
> TBMM INQUIRY COMMITTEE 2012: 165–167

Erbakan signed the NSC plan, despite his unwillingness, at the end of the nine-hour meeting. The SGNSC published a press release, which was rather a warning letter, accepting the NSC as the competent authority to decide on necessary measures against radical Islamism and to inform the Cabinet about the NSC's measures against it. This overruled civilian supremacy over the military. Moreover, the press release declared the prime minister, the president, and the

NSC competent entities to be informed about the implementation of measures in the short and long term. This legitimised the role of the NSC as an equal partner to the government. Last, but not least, the press release underlined that "if the government [did] not act in conformity with the NSC's plan, this [would] jeopardise social peace and security, create new clashes, and result in new sanctions" (MGK 1997). In April 1997, the General Staff announced the amended National Military Defence Concept which identified Islamist reactionism (*irtica*) alongside Kurdish separatism as the primary internal threat (Cizre 2003: 222). Combined with the amendment of the National Military Defence Concept, the emphasis on the prospects of sanctions in the NSC's press release implied the possibility of a coup, and thus turned the press release into a memorandum.[16]

The *RefahYol* government reinforced certain measures to a limited extent, such as regulations on clothing at the state level. Certain other measures to be undertaken at the state level, especially the purging of Islamists from state institutions and the extension of compulsory primary education, clashed with the RP's *raison d'être*. Regarding the purging of Islamists from state institutions, the military sought to expel Islamists from its own chain of command, owing to its institutional autonomy. In May 1997, before the extraordinary meeting of the Supreme Military Council, Erbakan criticised the generals' proposal to dismiss more than a hundred military officers based on their involvement in Islamist activities. Erbakan further tried to delay the purge by proposing a commission consisting of the ministers of justice and defence to investigate the officers. Nonetheless, Erbakan had no choice but to sign the proposal of dismissals during the Council's meeting (*Milliyet* 1997f).

Regarding the implementation of compulsory primary education for eight consecutive years, the RP rejected any discussion on the prospect of a bill at a parliamentary debate in May 1997. Such education reform would mean the closure of the secondary levels of *imam-hatip* schools,[17] and thus the loss of

---

16 The secretary of the General Staff defined the process of 28 February as "a postmodern coup ... with the participation of the people ... within the democratic framework ... to prevent Turkey from becoming a Republic of *mullahs* [Islamic clergy]" (Cevizoğlu 2001: 56). However, the succeeding commander of the navy presented the NSC's decisions as advice, not imposition, and argued that the NSC's decisions were taken jointly with civilian politicians (Cevizoğlu 2001: 20).

17 The *imam-hatip* schools (IHSs) were originally established to educate prospective clergy to be employed by *Diyanet*. Beginning in the 1970s, the IHSs were considered to be a tool to moderate political Islam and prevent the rise of socialism, and hence they were encouraged to flourish. Meanwhile, female students became eligible to study at the IHSs in 1976, even if they could not become clerics. In 1983, graduates of the IHSs became eligible to study in any department of any university (Sevim 2007: 69). Furthermore, the IHSs

support for the Islamist movements, particularly *Milli Görüş*. Hundreds of thousands of people, including graduates of *imam-hatip* schools and various Islamist foundations, such as *İlim Yayma Cemiyeti* (Society to Disseminate Science) and *Ensar Vakfı* (Ensar Foundation), joined the protests against the bill. Certain speeches called for the abolition of secularism. The Constitutional Court later considered such statements to be attempts at inciting religious hatred. These statements included an RP MP's declaration that "blood would flood", the İsmailağa congregation's call for a *jihad*, and several protestors' call for *sharia* (*Milliyet* 1997e).

3.2 Social Classes and the Process of 28 February

The RP's reluctance and resistance to the implementation of the NSC's decisions transformed the military's guardianship role into acting as "a pressure group" in the 1990s (Güney 2002: 170). The memorandum of 28 February indicated a process during which the military shaped public opinion and engaged in a psychological war against Islamist movements to compel the RP to resign and enable the implementation of a restoration project.[18] This transformation was mainly related to the impact of globalisation beginning in the 1990s, which regarded liberal democracy as a path for and indicator of development, and hence a "solution to the crisis in the Third World" (Kiely 2005b: 40). In the context of Turkey, EU membership became a key determinant for democratisation and conformity with democratic norms and institutions. In fact, Turkey had already advanced its relations with the EU by signing the Customs Union agreement in December 1995 (Öniş and Şenses 2022: 212). The compelling of the military to seek consent of particularly the EU ruled out any military intervention through the overthrow a government.

Furthermore, strong civil society remained one of the key pillars of democratisation praised particularly by the EU. This further compelled the military to pay special attention to constructing public opinion. Most significantly, the military launched a series of briefings to shape public opinion significantly against the RP, thus obtaining the support of various social classes.

---

attracted students from working-class and peasant families as the institutions functioned as free-of-charge boarding schools and the graduates were employed by state institutions and/or Islamic companies (Akşin 2011: 172). In this way, the IHSs offered Islamic education as an alternative to the secular education system and cultivated the grassroots of Islamist movements. Significantly, a "large portion of deputies, mayors, and grassroots activists of the RP" were IHS graduates (Coşkun and Şentürk 2012: 167).

18 The memorandum of 28 February was sometimes referred to as a "postmodern coup" (see Cevizoğlu 2001).

These briefings were generally called "briefings on reactionism" (Çolak and Aydın 2004: 215). High-ranking military officers gave briefings to the media in April 1997, civil society organisations and universities in May 1997, and judges and public prosecutors in June 1997 (Güney 2002: 170). For the military, civil society organisations played the most important role in obtaining support. Significantly, Erkaya stated:

> Everybody thought if things went wrong, the military would solve it ... However you should not expect the military to solve political problems ... First, commanders should make people realise that reactionary activities constitute a threat, and second, this problem should be solved not by armed forces but by civil society organisations, and MPs and the Assembly ... It should be solved by the unarmed forces.
> *HÜRRIYET* 1997b

A number of nongovernmental organisations (NGOs), including *Atatürkçü Düşünce Derneği* (Atatürkist Thought Association) and *Çağdaş Yaşamı Destekleme Derneği* (Association for Supporting Modern Life), indeed rallied against the RP (Rutz 1999: 96–97), as did the centre-left and centre-right political parties in the opposition. Mesut Yılmaz, the chair of the ANAP, blamed the RP for aiming to establish a totalitarian regime and supporting terrorists abroad. Similarly, Ecevit accused the RP of raising a militant cadre and having a relationship with militants in Muslim countries, and thereby posing a threat not only in Turkey but also in the Middle East (*Cumhuriyet* 1997).

The process of 28 February was fundamentally related to the military's precise aim to reorganise relations among fractions of capital in order to form a power bloc. In this process, the major targets of the military were the fractions of Islamic capital that operated outside the legal framework and pursued an Islamist-hegemonic alternative. Since the military further received the support of the judiciary, the vast range of methods and strategies included "criminalisation of capital accumulation processes through legal actions, police and financial investigations, systematic public display of unlawful acts by Islamic companies" alongside "boycotts and campaigns supported via the media" (Hoşgör 2011: 352). Islamic companies that operated outside the legal framework and/or called for Islamist alternatives, including Jetpa, Kombassan, and Yimpaş (Tanyılmaz 2015: 114), were put under close scrutiny by the Capital Markets Board (*Sermaye Piyasası Kurulu*) and their assets were frozen. These companies were later subjected to legal action. The military called for an embargo to protest against Islamic businesses by not entering into exchanges with them at the societal level and not inviting them for bids and tenders at the state level. The donation of animal skins to religious brotherhoods and foundations, which constituted an important means of capital generation, was also banned (Hoşgör 2011: 352). Moreover, Erol Yarar, the chair of MUSIAD, was put on trial for inciting religious hatred because of his statements on a public broadcast that considered the extension of compulsory primary education to be "an attempt of infidels [*kafir*]" (Yankaya 2012: 29).

The military did manage to obtain the consent of various fractions of the urban dominant and subordinate classes. In May 1997, MESS, TISK, TOBB, and *Türkiye Esnaf ve Sanatkarlar Konfederasyonu* (Turkish Confederation of Tradesmen and Craftsmen)—as the representatives of the bourgeoisie— and *Türk-İş* and DISK—as the representatives of the proletariat—launched "a civilian initiative" to support the military (Öztürk 2009: 356). The initiative underlined that "the political parties and the Assembly could not respond to the public demands [and] our secular Republic faces the threat of *sharia*-mongers and the mafia seeking to capture the state" (Doğan 2013: 296). Certain fractions of Islamic capital also supported the military, in competition with other fractions of Islamic capital targeted by the military. Significantly, the Gülen congregation publicly called for the implementation of the NSC's decisions. In return, the disciples of the Gülen congregation were given amnesty by the military, which was in the process of blacklisting religious brotherhoods that staffed the military. The disciples of the Gülen congregation were either not completely purged or they reclaimed their positions in state institutions, including the military, beginning in 1999 (Şık 2011: 4–6).

However, large-scale Islamic capital operating within the legal framework continued to accumulate wealth since the military did not fundamentally oppose the process of neoliberalisation. In this regard, private foundations and schools affiliated with the Islamist movements were not transferred to the Ministry of Education; the religious brotherhoods were not abolished; and the financial activities of Islamic capital remained largely unmonitored (Eligür 2010: 222). The process of 28 February, nevertheless, compelled Erbakan to resign from the office of prime minister, leaving the seat to Çiller, the chair of the DYP, in June 1997. Demirel charged Yılmaz with the duty of forming a new government. Consequently, the ANAP, the DSP, and *Demokrat Türkiye Partisi* (Democratic Turkey Party) formed a new coalition government, often referred to as the *AnaSol-D* government, in July 1997 (TBMM 7 July 1997).

3.3 Classes, the State, and the Military in the Aftermath of the Process of 28 February

The aftermath of the process of 28 February coincided with the effects of the 1997 Asian financial crisis on the Turkish economy, which was already characterised by "hot-money driven and speculation-led growth" (Yeldan 2022: 235). Under the dynamics of unevenness and dependency, the growth rate of GDP decreased from 7.2 per cent to 3.1 per cent between 1997 and 1998, further contracting by 5 per cent in 1999. The manufacturing sector suffered immensely; the growth rate of manufacturing decreased from 10.2 per cent to 1.2 per cent between 1997 and 1998, and manufacturing further shrank by 5.7 per cent in 1999. The investments of the private sector contracted by 13.7 per cent between 1997 and 1998, and by 11 per cent in 1999. Nonetheless, the dependency on imports continued since the rate of imports and exports steadily decreased from 23.2 per cent to 21.7 per cent and from 15.8 per cent to 14.2 per cent respectively between 1997 and 1999 (Yeldan 2001: 41). The crisis further manifested the reorganisation of the state apparatus to facilitate financial capital accumulation. Significantly, the interest costs on servicing the debt rose to 1,010 per cent of public investments, demonstrating the state's withdrawal from social infrastructure development and long-term economic growth (Balkan and Yeldan 2002: 46).

In 1998, Turkey and the IMF, whose "dogma on *austerity* at all expense, everywhere and under every condition" drastically failed, resulting in severe deflation in Asia (Yeldan 2022: 245), reached an agreement, according to which Turkey was to pursue disinflation and stabilisation based on exchange rates.[19] In July 1998, the *AnaSol-D* government adopted an extensive disinflation programme under the guidance and supervision of the IMF through the Staff Monitoring Programme (SMP) in Ankara, which enabled the IMF to closely follow the Turkish economy. The SMP required the government to replace the Treasury with an autonomous institution as the regulator and supervisor; restructure social security to make retirement more difficult; amend the Constitution to allow arbitration; sell the public shares in POAŞ petroleum, ERDEMIR, and Turkish Airlines; sell the distribution rights of TEDAŞ electricity; and sell 49 per cent of public shares in TURKTELEKOM telecommunication (BSB 2007: 18–19). Nonetheless, the *AnaSol-D* government could not fully pursue the SMP due to the hegemonic crisis having deepened with general elections and two earthquakes, both of which increased public expenditure. This increase in public expenditure led to further deteriorated fiscal balances (Yeldan 2022: 246). In December 1999, the coalition government of DSP-ANAP-MHP under Ecevit's prime ministership, often referred to as the fifty-seventh government (TBMM 4 June 1999), implemented another disinflation

---

19 The same economic policy was previously pursued and had failed in Latin America (Yeldan 2022: 245).

programme under the supervision of the IMF. The new economic programme was to result in the economic crisis of 2001, which was the biggest economic crisis Turkey had faced to that point (see Chapter 6).

The process of 28 February, in this regard, could not respond to the hegemonic crisis of the 1990s. It rather became a Pyrrhic victory of the military, since the military completely lost its legitimacy as an intermediate structure to respond to hegemonic crises in the eyes of various social classes. The scope of the process of 28 February remained limited to the implementation of a restoration project that aimed to moderate and bring the Islamist movements to the centre-right. The restoration project also included the narrowing of public visibility of Islam and the strengthening of secular symbols and references in the public sphere. Significantly, the RP was closed by the Constitutional Court in January 1998 (Eligür 2010: 214). The process of 28 February further sought to eliminate the duality between the *imam-hatip* schools and secular state schools. Despite Prime Minister Yılmaz's resistance to the pressure of the military during the NSC meeting of March 1998 (*Hürriyet* 1998a), the *AnaSol-D* government implemented a reform bill to reinforce compulsory primary education for eight consecutive years (TBMM 16 August 1997).[20]

Moreover, the *AnaSol-D* government reinforced certain secular regulations on the public visibility of Islam, especially the ban on the wearing of headscarves (*tesettür, türban, başörtüsü*) in state institutions and universities (*Hürriyet* 1998b). The headscarf remained the most visible and politicised symbol of Sunni-Islamic identity, constituting the roles and subject positions of Islamist women as political actors (see Göle 1997; Kalaycıoğlu 2006). The issue of headscarves, therefore, constituted the main site of contest regarding the state's control over religion as well as civil rights and freedoms in the modern secular Republic. Most significantly, Merve Kavakçı, an MP from *Fazilet Partisi* (Virtue Party, FP), the heir of the RP, sought to take the oath with her headscarf in May 1999. Prime Minister Ecevit presented Kavakçı's attempt as "a challenge to the secular state" (TBMM 2 May 1999), and subsequently Kavakçı's status as an MP was stripped.[21]

---

20   Primary education in Turkey had legally been for eight consecutive years since January 1961 (Law on Primary Education 1961). In 1983, a temporary article considered only the first five consecutive years compulsory so that a sufficient number of secondary schools for the last three consecutive years could be established (Milli Güvenlik Konseyi 12 October 1983). In this sense, the *AnaSol-D* government only abolished the temporary article in the law to reinforce the extension of compulsory primary education.

21   Kavakçı later called for the omission of the principle of secularism from the Constitution (*Yeni Akit* 2016). When Kavakçı applied to the European Court of Human Rights, the Court

The process of 28 February further reinforced the military's guardianship role behind the scenes by broadening the incorporation of political, economic, social, and cultural issues into the NSC's agenda. In this way, the military could resort to the use of extraordinary and emergency measures outside the political framework and overrule any political discussion that clashed with what the military considered a matter of national security. Beginning in 1999, the NSC discussed economic policies such as reports published by the State Planning Organisation (MGK 2000), plans on the construction of dams (MGK 1999a), and health and education policies in southeast Anatolia (MGK 1999b).

---

found Turkey's decision against Kavakçı disproportionate but underlined the legitimacy of the state's enforcement of the secular public sphere (ECHR 2007).

CHAPTER 6

Adalet ve Kalkınma Partisi and the "New Era in Civil–Military Relations"

> [T]he first time as a great tragedy, the second as a miserable farce.
> KARL MARX (1979 [1852])

∴

This chapter discusses the transformation of the state and the reorganisation of class relations under *Adalet ve Kalkınma Partisi* (Justice and Development Party, AKP) in order to explore the curtailment of the military's guardianship role and the arguable submission of the military to civilian authority. In this regard, it examines the consolidation of authoritarian statism within the framework of neoliberal Islamism, which constituted the basis of the AKP's hegemonic project of conservative democracy (*muhafazakar demokrasi*). This chapter divides the consolidation of hegemony under the AKP into two periods, namely, the period between 2002 and 2007, and the period between 2008 and 2013. The period between 2002 and 2007 corresponds to the AKP's reorganisation of class relations and capital accumulation to maintain capital-intensive and relative surplus value production under the supervision of the IMF. The period between 2008 and 2013 corresponds to the coincidence between the end of the IMF standby agreement and the global financial crisis of 2007–2008, after which the AKP soon failed to reform the pattern of capital accumulation and resorted to measures to postpone crisis dynamics. Nevertheless, the period between 2002 and 2013 corresponds to the consolidation of the ruling de facto coalition between the AKP and the Gülen congregation, reinforcing the authoritarian transformation of the state apparatus in which the military was submitted to civilian authority.

1   The Political Economy of the Rise of the AKP

1.1   *The Economic Crisis of 2001*

Following its establishment in May 1999, the fifty-seventh government—the DSP-ANAP-MHP coalition government—sought to maintain high growth rates in a low-inflation environment. With this aim, the fifty-seventh government continued to implement an extensive disinflation programme under the guidance and supervision of the IMF. In this process, the EU played a key "anchor" role by assisting the IMF in countering the resilience against the IMF discipline, since Turkey formally became a candidate country for EU membership in December 1999 (Öniş and Şenses 2009: 4). The IMF programme, originally adopted in 1998, has been discussed in Chapter 5.

The IMF programme soon turned into a standby agreement that was implemented between 2000 and 2002. The programme consisted of three main pillars, namely, fiscal adjustment based on increased privatisation revenues, structural reforms aimed at reducing public-sector debt, and firm exchange rates supported by consistent income policies (IMF 1999). The programme, therefore, aimed to foster neoliberal transformation of the national economy and the state apparatus through the privatisation of large-scale SOEs, downward pressure on wages, reduction of agricultural subsidies, curtailment of social security and pensions, regulation of the banking system through autonomous supervision, and refraining from trade restrictions. Moreover, the programme targeted nominal exchange rates and directly linked monetary expansion and tightening to money capital flows. Therefore, it reinforced Turkey's dependency on international capital markets and inflows of hot money. The programme sought to use the exchange rate as a nominal anchor and basis of price stability. It also sought to restrict monetary expansion to increases in the Central Bank's net foreign assets and decrease interest rates through capital inflows that effectively determined the growth of the domestic money supply (Yeldan 2006: 199–200).

Nevertheless, the programme destabilised the national economy and paved the way for an economic crisis in 2001. Following its contraction by 3.3 per cent in 1999, when the standby agreement was signed, GDP grew by 6.9 per cent in 2000, contracted again by 5.8 per cent in 2001, and grew again by 6.4 per cent in 2002 (World Bank 2023a). By mid-2000, the fifty-seventh government, the IMF, and international financial analysts praised the programme, declaring that every target except inflation and price increases had been met (IMF 2000a, 2000b). However, the Turkish economy was characterised by the high volatility of short-term interest rates, a remarkable increase in the ratio of short-term foreign debt to foreign exchange reserves of the Central Bank, and a constant increase in the ratio of the current account deficit to the GDP and foreign exchange reserves (Orhangazi 2002: 338). In November 2000, the outflow of 5.3 billion USD, which was a result of short-term speculative operations, brought about a rapid and massive increase in interest rates. Even though the IMF's additional 7.5-billion-USD loan temporarily halted capital outflows and devaluation, the outflow of 5 billion USD in February 2001 threatened to deplete the foreign exchange reserves of the Central Bank and cause a rapid increase in interest rates (Dufour and Orhangazi 2009: 105). The devaluation of the Turkish lira by 27 per cent against the US dollar was followed by the bankruptcies of 14,540 firms (*Cumhuriyet* 2001; *The Guardian* 2001), and 1.5 million workers losing their jobs (Akşin 2011: 180).

The huge magnitude of the economic crisis substantially destabilised and inflamed the hegemonic crisis the fifty-seventh government was facing. In response to the crisis, the government adopted a new standby agreement with the IMF, which focused on fiscal, monetary, and structural policies, including privatisations and reforms on agriculture, social security, and banking and finance (IMF 2001). The standby agreement was implemented under the close supervision and surveillance of the IMF. Prime Minister Ecevit appointed Kemal Derviş, the former vice-president of the World Bank for Poverty Reduction and Economic Management, as the minister of state responsible for economic affairs to adopt a new programme called the Transition to a Strong Economy (Boratav 2014: 194). Nonetheless, the fifty-seventh government was a coalition representing centre-right, nationalist, and centre-left elements whose support base consisted mainly of the urban and rural working classes, arguably the "losers" of the neoliberal transition. The IMF programme required not a "lukewarm" coalition government facing a hegemonic crisis (Öniş 2009: 414), but an assertive political actor that could address the interests of foreign and internal capital while coercing and obtaining the consent of the subordinate classes. This political actor was the AKP.

1.2   *The Emergence of the AKP*

Chapter 5 discussed how the main goal of the process of 28 February was to fine-tune and moderate political Islam. Beginning in the late 1990s, two main cleavages emerged within *Milli Görüş*, namely, the reformists and the traditionalists (Eligür 2010: 198). The main difference between the reformists and the traditionalists was not ideological but methodical in the sense that the former adopted liberal practices, whereas the latter preferred traditional methods (Çakır 2009: 550–552). The reformists offered a reconciliation between economic liberalism and Islamism while retaining their position against secular modernisation. The reformists' adoption of economic liberalism essentially signified the demands of certain fractions of Islamic capital, stemming from the harmonisation of interests of large-scale Islamic and foreign capital through market mechanisms. By the late 1990s, large-scale Islamic capital was in the process of transformation into transnational capital through deeper integration with the global economy and reinforced links with foreign capital. Therefore, the reformists became "much more 'globalist' and business-friendly in their outlook" (Öztürk 2015: 132). This transition also corresponded to the rise of global conservatism beginning in the 1980s, especially the alliance between big businesses and conservative Christians supported by the neoconservatives in the United States (see Harvey 2007: 50–51).

Following the closure of the FP in June 2001, the reformists, led by Recep Tayyip Erdoğan, Abdullah Gül, and Bülent Arınç, established the AKP in August 2001 (*Milliyet* 2001). The AKP declared a break from *Milli Görüş* and claimed to represent "the sole force of the centre-right" (*Milliyet* 2003a), presenting a merger between a free-market economy and political Islam. The AKP formulated a hegemonic project of conservative democracy articulating the neoliberal elements of a competitive market, economic welfare, and political stability under the rule of a majority government; the democratic elements of diversity and peace; the conservative element of religious piety; and the populist element of service to the people (AKP 2006). In this way, the AKP managed to diversify its voter base and obtain the consent of liberals, liberal-leftists, and the marginalised sections of society. The AKP also obtained the consent of the EU and received the support of the United States, with American diplomats paying special attention to Erdoğan (Timur 2014: 19).

1.3 The Rise of the Gülen Congregation

The AKP developed organic and clientelist relations with various religious brotherhoods to Islamise the state apparatus and social structure. In this regard, the Gülen congregation requires particular attention as it operated as the de facto ruling coalition partner of the AKP until the mid-2010s. Beginning in the mid-2010s, the Gülen congregation further engaged in a power struggle against the AKP, which brought about an abortive coup against the AKP in 2016 (see Chapter 7).

Beginning in 1994, the Gülen congregation brought together journalists, academics, and public intellectuals in workshops in the Abant province of Bolu. The workshops were later known as the Abant platform, which enabled the Gülen congregation to gain legitimacy through close relations with centre-right and centre-left politicians in Turkey as well as international religious leaders, including the pope and the Armenian patriarch (Hendrick 2015: 239). The reformists within *Milli Görüş* joined the Abant platform in 1998 following the memorandum of 28 February (Park 2008), where the AKP and the Gülen congregation agreed on a "search for a new social contract in Turkey" called an "interfaith dialogue" (Kuru 2007: 146–147). This agreement demonstrated that the AKP had allied with the Gülen congregation to maintain good relations with the United States and the EU, since the Gülen congregation had developed organic and dependent relations with the United States (see Chapter 5).

The rise of the Gülen congregation as a political actor was intertwined with its advanced economic power in the late 1990s and early 2000s. Gülen-affiliated businesses were originally organised under MUSIAD (Çavdar 2014: 11), which mainly represented nationally and internationally oriented SMEs alongside large-scale transnational capital by the 2000s. In the 2000s, Gülen-affiliated finance capital emerged through organic relations between the Gülen congregation and American companies, municipalities under Islamist political parties, and the state, through staffing (Doğan 2013: 291). Gülen-affiliated finance capital further benefited from Islamic banking through Bank Asya, operated by the Gülen congregation, and the participation of banks established by Gülen-affiliated holding companies (Avcı 2019: 220). In 2005, *Türkiye İşadamları ve Sanayicileri Konfederasyonu* (Turkish Confederation of Businessmen and Industrialists, TUSKON) was established, representing the formation of the third generation of finance capital in the form of a power bloc. TUSKON represented an umbrella organisation which involved seven regional federations, including those of Marmara, the Aegean and western Mediterranean, central Anatolia, the Black Sea, and eastern Anatolia, and combining more than 180 local businesses (Buğra and Savaşkan 2014: 123). TUSKON-affiliated businesses operated in a vast range of sectors, including education, such as private schools, preparatory schools, and dormitories; banking and finance; and media, such as news agencies, TV stations, daily newspapers, and journals (Özel 2010: 153). Nevertheless, TUSKON mostly involved nationally and internationally oriented SMEs operating mainly in labour-intensive sectors and a number of transnational holding companies, similarly to MUSIAD.

The upper echelons of the bureaucracy as well as the right-wing political parties and dominant classes already supported the Gülen congregation beginning in the 1960s owing to Gülen and his disciples' involvement in the Association for Fighting Communism at that time (Meşe 2016: 125–126). The Gülen congregation aimed to educate the "'golden generation'" of bureaucrats (Yavuz 2003: 192–198), assisted by other disciples in the public and private sectors organised against the left-wing and socialist movements (Başkan 2005: 853). Beginning in the 1980s, the Gülen congregation staffed the military by infiltrating the Maltepe Military High School (Ankara Devlet Güvenlik Mahkemesi Cumhuriyet Başsavcılığı 1999) and was put on a trial by the Ankara

State Security Court in 2000 for subverting the secular regime in staffing the state apparatus with its disciples. However, the military gave amnesty to the congregation by not completely purging Gülenist disciples or even enabling them to reclaim their positions in the state apparatus in the aftermath of the process of 28 February (see Chapter 5). Further, the Gülen congregation was acquitted by the Court of Appeal in 2008 during the AKP's term of office (Gözaydın 2009: 1220).[1]

Nonetheless, hundreds of military officers were dismissed based on their Gülenist affiliations between 1983 and 2003. After 2003, officers were no longer dismissed based on their affiliation with a religious brotherhood, arguably due to the alliance between the AKP, the religious brotherhoods, and higher-ranking military officers. This alliance will be further discussed in relation to the Dolmabahçe agreement in the aftermath of the military's press release in 2007. Beginning in the early 2000s, the Gülen congregation staffed especially military high schools and academies, military human resources, and the Military Court of Appeal to maintain its strategic infiltration (Demirağ 2015: 56–69). By the mid-2010s, the congregation was most heavily organised in the military, police, intelligence, and judiciary. More importantly, the congregation became "a state-like organisation", the parallel state, as the AKP has called it, with "an income and an authority that decide[d] how people should be organised and who should be appointed to which position within the Turkish state bureaucracy" (Şık and Çakırer 2019: 83).

2   The State, Classes, and the Military under the AKP (2002–2007)

2.1   Classes and the AKP

Following the election of November 2002, the AKP formed a majority government by receiving 34 per cent of the overall votes (TBMM 23 November 2002).[2] The ability to form a majority government enabled the AKP to establish its hegemony, which was to be consented to by the civil-military bureaucracy, however reluctantly. To illustrate, Erdoğan emerged as the AKP's leader; however, he was prevented from gaining a seat in the Assembly due to a court case (see Chapter 5), and Gül therefore became prime minister. In December 2002,

---

[1] The acquittal of the Gülen congregation was related to the amendment of the Law on Counterterrorism in May 2006 in accordance with the EU reforms (Taş 2018: 397–398).

[2] The CHP received 20 per cent of the vote and gained seats in the Assembly. However, the remaining 46 per cent of the vote remained unrepresented because other political parties could not pass the nationwide threshold of a minimum of 10 per cent (Çarkoğlu 2002: 30).

the Assembly passed an Act changing the Constitution in order to lift Erdoğan's ban. President Ahmet Necdet Sezer, former president of the Constitutional Court, vetoed the Act, criticising its subjective character; however, Sezer implemented the Act without calling for a referendum when the Assembly returned it to the presidency. In this way, Erdoğan managed to enter the Assembly to become prime minister following Gül's resignation in March 2003 (TBMM 15 March 2003).

The AKP completely committed to the IMF programme, which had already increased Turkey's external debt to multilateral institutions from 8 billion USD to 31 billion USD between 2000 and 2002 (Dufour and Orhangazi 2009: 117). The AKP further agreed on a standby agreement with the IMF in 2005 (IMF 2004). In this regard, the AKP continued fiscal and monetary policies, privatisations, and structural reforms regarding social security, agriculture, and banking and finance, all of which were borrowed from the fifty-seventh government. Since the programme the AKP pursued aimed to maintain the primary surplus of the consolidated budget, it mainly focused on debt rollover and the payment of interests (BSB 2007: 76). Moreover, EU membership was instrumental to the AKP's hegemony and its implementation of the IMF programme. The EU's accession criteria, also known as the Copenhagen criteria, included "a functioning market economy and the capacity to cope with competition and market forces" (EU 2022a). The EU's convergence criteria, also known as the Maastricht criteria, included "price stability, sound and sustainable public finances, exchange-rate stability, and long-term interest rates" (EU 2022b).

The AKP maintained an average real GDP growth of 7.2 per cent between 2002 and 2006.[3] This economic growth was further combined with falling inflation and a reduction in external debt. In fact, the ratio of external debt to GNP was falling steadily (Öniş and Şenses 2009: 5–6). This domestic situation was mainly related to the international economic conjuncture, which underwent a major boom beginning in 2003, boosting economic growth in all emerging economies.[4] Emerging market economies, indicating those late developers with better prospects of economic growth through deeper and broader integration with global markets, attracted voluminous global liquidity by offering

---

3 Despite the economic growth, the unemployment rate rose above 10 per cent following the economic crisis of 2001 and did not fall below pre-2001 levels in the 2000s or 2010s. Orhangazi and Yeldan (2021: 481) consider this characteristic of the national economy to be '"jobless growth"'.
4 The term emerging economies/emerging markets/emerging market economies was mainly utilised to refer to Brazil, Russia, India, and China in 2001. In 2005, Turkey was considered to be an emerging economy (Looney 2014: 3).

relatively higher yields, significantly for speculative fictitious capital. Turkey attracted remarkable levels of short-term capital inflows and foreign direct investment (FDI) through a combination of high real interest rates under a monetary policy targeting inflation and an extensive privatisation programme (Taymaz and Voyvoda 2022: 259). In 2005, the AKP privatised three large-scale and highly profitable SOEs, namely, TURKTELEKOM, a fixed-line telecommunications monopoly, TÜPRAŞ, the country's largest industrial enterprise with four oil refineries, and ERDEMIR, which owned 80 per cent of the iron ore reserves in the country (Angın and Bedirhanoğlu 2012: 140).

Between 2002 and 2010, the AKP maintained productive capital accumulation by adopting policies aimed at the internationalisation of capital through increased relative surplus value production and the restructuring of state economic apparatuses (Ercan and Oğuz 2020: 98).[5] In this regard, the AKP implemented administrative and institutional reforms to advance productive investments, shift productive investments from labour-intensive to capital-intensive sectors, and strengthen global competitiveness through regional policies and incentives (Oğuz 2011: 6). The AKP further implemented reforms in the banking sector to terminate accumulation through state borrowing and encourage productive investments (Gültekin-Karakaş 2009: 101–102). In this way, the AKP reorganised relations among capital fractions to enable the circuit of productive capital of finance capital to preserve its primacy and engage in internationalisation, and hence stabilise the hegemony of the power bloc by increasing the mass of surplus product in the national economy.

The AKP reorganised relations among and favoured capital fractions by facilitating market mechanisms. To illustrate, the AKP reformed the public procurement law, which regulated the governmental purchase of goods and services from the private sector, with references to its fight against corruption. This reform was supported by World Bank, the IMF, the World Trade Organization (WTO), and the EU because public-sector reform could secure the repayment of external debt and open national procurement to global competition, especially encouraging the participation of large-scale Western corporations (Oğuz 2008: 222). The reform enabled the AKP to favour and maintain control over SMEs, particularly Islamist SMEs, through bidding at the local government levels, such as on infrastructure and construction projects

---

5 This book argues that the accumulation of productive capital constituted the basis of the AKP's hegemony between 2002 and 2008. This argument contrasts with the proponents of radical/critical political economy who underline the prominence of financialisation and the accumulation of financial capital under the AKP (see Akçay 2021; Akçay and Güngen 2022; Bedirhanoğlu 2020).

(Buğra and Savaşkan 2014: 78–81). This in turn benefited MUSIAD and TUSKON as they developed subcontracting relations with Islamist SMEs. This also partly benefited TUSIAD, which developed connections with SMEs through subcontractor, supplier, and vendor relations (Öztürk 2015: 119),[6] even though TUSIAD became the major representative of large-scale transnational capital alongside large-scale national and international capital fractions.[7] The AKP favoured the fractions of finance capital and foreign capital through bidding at the state level and privatisation. Significantly, a 51-per-cent share of TÜPRAŞ was sold to the joint venture of Koç Holding, a prominent member of TUSIAD, and Shell, a UK-based transnational corporation (Angın and Bedirhanoğlu 2012: 157). Further AKP reforms aimed at financialisation, such as the introduction of general health insurance (Koç 2012: 16), benefited financial fractions of finance capital.

The AKP also continued to benefit the fractions of Islamic finance capital through crony relations and favouritism. To illustrate, the AKP developed organic relations with MUSIAD and TUSKON. Between 2002 and 2007, the AKP had eleven MUSIAD-affiliated MPs and three TUSKON-affiliated MPs. Between 2007 and 2011, the AKP had seven MUSIAD-affiliated MPs and three TUSKON-affiliated MPs (Çeviker-Gürakar 2016: 18).[8] The AKP also enhanced the transfer of wealth from the public sector to Islamic capital. Significantly, two state-owned banks, namely, Halkbank and Vakıfbank, provided 750 million USD in loans to Çalık Holding, whose CEO was Erdoğan's son-in-law Berat Albayrak and whose chairman Ahmet Çalık was Erdoğan's close personal associate. These loans enabled Çalık Holding to buy ATV-*Sabah*, the second-largest media group, in 2007 (Jenkins 2008b: 10–11). While Ali Koç, the vice-chairman of Koç Holding, publicly protested that TUSIAD was losing its influence, Çalık Holding joined TUSIAD in 2014 (Avcı 2019: 150). The AKP further utilised the state apparatus to favour the internationalisation and expansion of Islamic capital on a regional scale. The relationship between TUSKON and the Foreign Economic Relations Board (*Dış Ekonomik İlişkiler Kurulu*) illustrates this. Until the restructuring of the Board in 2014, TUSKON and the Board co-established

---

6 Significantly, TUSIAD supported SMEs to organise and establish *Türk Girişim ve İş Dünyası Konfederasyonu* (Turkish Enterprise and Business Confederation, TURKONFED) in 2005 (Öztürk 2015: 119).
7 TUSIAD is indeed "the club of big business" (Öztürk 2015: 119).
8 TUSIAD could arguably *afford* not to allow the membership of MPs or bureaucrats on its board of directors to avoid the possibility of a corruption scandal. Nevertheless, the AKP had two TURKONFED-affiliated MPs between 2002 and 2007, and four TURKONFED-affiliated MPs between 2007 and 2011 (Çeviker-Gürakar 2016: 18).

business councils in foreign countries to "'conduct'" the foreign economic relations of Turkish companies (Uysal 2021: 449). In this way, TUSKON organised trade summits with Asia-Pacific, African, and Eurasian countries (Atlı 2011: 118).

The AKP further favoured capital fractions by reorganising relations between the dominant and subordinate classes and restructuring the state apparatus. Most significantly, the AKP coerced the urban working classes by deregulating the labour market through de-unionisation, privatisation, and precarisation, such as outsourcing and subcontracting (Çelik 2015a). The AKP also coerced the rural working classes by reducing agricultural subsidies and seizing the properties of peasants and smallholders through privatisations (İslamoğlu 2017). This further advanced proletarianisation by forcing dispossessed peasants and smallholders to become part of the precarious workforce in the service and construction sectors while keeping their rural connections, or by forcing them to become contracted agricultural workers of agribusiness companies (BSB 2015: 104–105). Meanwhile, the AKP enhanced means of coercion and repression, such as the restructuring of constabulary forces and the law on terror, and privatising security. The AKP indeed encouraged a boom in the number of private security companies (Bedirhanoğlu 2013: 61).

Nevertheless, the AKP obtained the consent of conservative fractions of the urban and rural subordinate classes, including workers, civil servants, peasants, and artisans and shopkeepers. This was mainly possible because economic growth based on capital inflows and the increasing mass of surplus product enabled the AKP to increase the level of employment between 2002 and 2007. To illustrate, the total unemployment rate dropped from 10.8 per cent in 2004 to 8.7 per cent in 2006 (World Bank 2023b). The economic growth further enabled the AKP to merge its neoliberal policies with populist redistribution mechanisms to govern poverty and the working classes. This will be further discussed in relation to the AKP's hegemonic project of conservative democracy. Moreover, the AKP presented advanced integration with the international markets as having offered future opportunities for employment and the amelioration of the labour law (Hoşgör 2015b: 210). In addition, the AKP claimed to represent the "silent Muslim masses" against the marginalising impact of the secular Republican state (AKP 2006: 116). This claim disoriented and paralysed the poor in rural areas and squats as well as the working classes organised in the Islamist trade unions. Significantly, *Hak İşçi Sendikaları Konfederasyonu* (Confederation of Righteous Trade Unions, *Hak-İş*) supported the AKP's neoliberal policies, particularly privatisation, which *Hak-İş* considered to be a means to demolish the Republican state's interventions in the public sphere (Gürgen 2012: 16). The AKP further developed symbiotic relations with certain trade unions, including *Hak-İş* and *Memur Sendikaları Konfederasyonu*

(Confederation of Public Servants Trade Unions) since these trade unions increased the number of their members as a direct result of the support they provided to the AKP (Çelik and Altındiş 2019: 143).

However, there were a number of remarkable cases of workers' resistance against the AKP's neoliberal policies. Significantly, the workers of the SEKA paper factory resisted the AKP's policy of privatising the pulp and paper industry by occupying the factory in 2005.[9] Resistance ended when the workers were contracted by the Izmit municipality (BSB 2015: 83–84). Nonetheless, widespread resistance of the working classes to the AKP was to begin following the Great Recession of 2008–2009 (see Chapter 7).

2.2 The Hegemonic Project of Conservative Democracy

The AKP's hegemonic project of conservative democracy was essentially built on global conservatism, especially the merging of neoliberalism and neoconservatism in the United States. Even though the AKP often refused to be called "Muslim democrats" (Yavuz 2009b: 602), the AKP's commitment to the IMF framework enabled the AKP to pursue good relations with the United States. The AKP's hegemonic project aimed to reinforce Turkey's integration with the world capitalist system under Western hegemony, particularly that of the United States and the EU. Significantly, the AKP publicly declared its active support for the United States' hegemonic project of the Greater Middle East (Oran 2013: 31), which fundamentally aimed to eliminate any obstacle against the mobility of American capital through various means, including military interventions (Uysal 2019c: 151).[10] Moreover, the AKP implemented a series of EU reform packages, also called harmonisation packages, to respond to economic and political criteria of accession to the EU (Müftüler-Baç 2005; Öniş and Bakır 2007).[11] The same economic reforms already remained in line with the IMF framework, which will be discussed further.

---

9   The slogan of the workers' resistance was "if the *firman* (edict, order) belongs to the IMF, the factory belongs to us" (BSB 2015: 83).
10 The AKP's commitment to the Greater Middle East project caused public dissidence against the AKP. In February 2003, during the Iraq War, the AKP proposed a bill to permit the deployment of Turkish troops in Iraq and the deployment of American troops in Turkey. The bill was overwhelmingly unpopular due to the presence of a Muslim majority in Iraq and the strength of public opposition to US imperialism. Therefore, the bill was rejected in the Assembly (TBMM 1 March 2003). Nevertheless, the AKP allowed the United States to use the Incirlik Air Base for transit rotation in November 2003 (Bölme 2007: 86).
11 The relationship between the AKP and the EU was never smooth, despite the AKP's commitment to the implementation of the EU's economic reforms. This was because the EU accepted the state's intervention in the public sphere on the basis of secularism, and this was in tension with the Islamist agenda the AKP followed that required state intervention

The AKP's hegemonic project of conservative democracy was based on an amalgamation of neoliberalism, populism, and Islamism. To begin with, neoliberalism fundamentally brought about the transformation of the state apparatus. Since neoliberalism was a "class project" that sought to restore capitalist class power through global commodification, marketisation, deregulation, and depoliticisation (Harvey 2010: 10; see also Apeldoorn and Overbeek 2012), neoliberalisation brought about the transition to an authoritarian form of state, which can be considered as a type of normal state that maintained institutionalised mechanisms for national-popular representation within a relatively stable bourgeois democratic framework (Poulantzas 1978: 294–295). The authoritarian neoliberal state is characterised by the transfer of power from the political scene to the state apparatus and the centralisation of power within the executive branch, which overall curtails formal liberties and democratic institutions and escalates state control over socioeconomic life (Poulantzas 2000: 203–204). In the case of Turkey, the authoritarian neoliberal state is characterised by the technocratisation of social and economic issues, the centralisation of decision-making processes, and the domination of executive power over the legislative and judicial branches (Özden, Akça, and Bekmen 2017: 190).

Even though the transition to the authoritarian neoliberal state began in the 1980s, much of this transition remained limited to the decisions and choices of the Cabinet and the prime minister. This transition became more comprehensive and systematic through the transformation of institutional and legal structures of the state apparatus beginning in the late 1990s. Significantly, the Constitution was amended to promote privatisations and the internationalisation of capital through the introduction of international arbitration. This was followed by the establishment of independent regulatory agencies, including the Capital Markets Board, the Competition Agency (*Rekabet Kurumu*), the Banking Regulation and Supervision Agency (*Bankacılık Düzenleme ve Denetleme Kurumu*), and the Public Procurement Agency (*Kamu İhale Kurumu*) (Oğuz 2008: 176–181). The AKP, in this regard, fostered the consolidation of the authoritarian neoliberal state by reforming the administration within the frameworks of the IMF, the World Bank, and the EU. The Public Administration Law in 2004 sought to privatise public services at the central and local administration levels by enabling the private sector to provide services, and transferring powers of central administration, such as health,

---

for religionisation. To illustrate, the European Court of Human Rights decided the ban on women's headscarves in universities did not violate human rights and freedoms in November 2005 (ECHR 2005). Since the Court's decision reinforced the process of 28 February, the AKP began to fall out with the EU following the decision.

tourism, construction, and transportation, to local administrations (Oğuz 2008: 196). Furthermore, the AKP adopted a new Labour Law in 2003, which legitimised flexible and temporary work by recognising part-time and contract labour and enabling employers to discharge workers collectively "'in times of crisis'" (Oğuz 2009: 12).

The neoliberal restructuring under the AKP was already in accordance with the post-Washington Consensus, which prescribed an active role of the state as a regulator and a provider of social protection and benefits, privatisation, liberalisation, and macro-stability through price stability (see Stiglitz 2008). Regarding the provision of social protection and benefits, the AKP articulated populism as the basis of redistribution mechanisms in the face of the withdrawal of the neoliberal state from many areas of social provisions, the curtailment of labour rights and social security, and the rise of poverty and unemployment. The merging of neoliberalism and populism is distinct from classical populism because of its social and economic content and its meaning for class relations. As a hegemonic project, neoliberal populism aims to mobilise the subordinate classes as the masses under the leadership of finance capital in the face of the attack on organised labour, the aggravated exploitation of labour, and insecure working conditions (Yıldırım 2013: 78). Neoliberal populism is not defined in terms of relations of production through wage policies, but as relations of social reproduction through social assistance programmes that address specific areas, including education and health (Bozkurt 2013: 378). This indicates the transformation from employment-based social security policies to income-based social assistance policies beginning in the 1980s (Yörük 2022: 187–188). Significantly, the AKP utilised the Social Aid and Solidarity Promotion, originally introduced by the ANAP (see Chapter 4), to solve socio-economic problems outside of the labour market and to govern poverty in a way to coerce the poorest sections of society (Çelik 2010: 69).

The AKP further merged neoliberal populism with Islamism, which functioned as the constitutive principle that aimed to religionise and Islamise the state apparatus and its regime as well as the social structure. The process of incorporating Islamic symbols and references into the state's ideology had already begun in the 1980s (see Chapters 4 and 5). Nevertheless, the AKP sought to replace the secular modern understanding of the sovereign nation with the model of the *ummah* (community of believers) that would submit to executive power, the representative of capital (Uysal 2019b: 21–22). In this regard, the AKP articulated the element of democracy, whose meaning was reduced to the primacy of the ballot box (TBMM 15 March 2003), to legitimise its Islamism as long as such democracy remained compatible with *sharia*: "Islam and democracy are compatible … sovereignty belongs to Allah; however, the divine will is represented by Islamic society in the world ... through voting and submission as declaration of free will of society" (Akdoğan 2004: 81–84).

The combination of neoliberalism, populism, and Islamism aimed to depoliticise the people and "transform subordinate classes into consumer masses who lacked class-consciousness and would submit to the neoliberal economic programmes without any opposition" (Uysal 2019b: 21). The AKP utilised the ideological state apparatuses to diffuse conservatism and piety combined with charity.[12] *Diyanet*, which developed objective capitalist interests through the Diyanet Foundation (*Diyanet Vakfı*) beginning in the 1970s (Peköz 2009: 228–239), played a remarkable role. In the field of education, the Foundation opened dormitories for undergraduate and postgraduate students, and offered scholarships to students in Turkey and abroad (Çitak 2020: 175). The AKP further allied with religious brotherhoods, which the AKP presented as civil society organisations, to respond to socioeconomic needs following the neoliberal state's withdrawal from relations of distribution. Religious brotherhoods undertook charity practices in urban and rural areas, such as providing cash and in-kind donations (Çelik 2010: 74–79). Religious brotherhoods significantly functioned in the field of education by opening private schools, preparatory schools, dormitories, and providing scholarships to low-income families (Peköz 2009: 99–100). The AKP also allied with and developed organic relations with religious brotherhoods to staff the state apparatus. The Gülen community played a key role in this regard, which will be discussed further.

2.3   The Military and the AKP

By the mid-2000s, the military remained one of the biggest social, economic, and political forces. The military's budget share did not fall below 2.2 per cent of GDP in the 2000s (SIPRI 2023) and OYAK became strong enough to buy ERDEMIR iron and steel in 2005 (Angın and Bedirhanoğlu 2012: 159). In fact, OYAK completed its transformation to finance capital by the late 2000s by conglomerating and turning into one of the country's biggest holding companies. By the late 2000s, OYAK operated in the automotive, cement, steel and iron, construction, finance and banking, food, domestic and foreign trade,

---

12   There is a growing literature on the thriving redistributive mechanisms institutionalised and utilised by the AKP as an indicator of state capitalism and the new welfare regime (Akçay 2018; Altınörs and Akçay 2022; Öniş and Kutlay 2021). This book argues that neoliberalism transformed the state's role regarding relations of distribution. In this regard, the transition from law-based social compromise to governance of poverty outside the labour market transformed the character of social policy and replaced welfare with charity (see Uysal 2019b).

agricultural chemistry, technology and informatics, tourism, logistics, defence and security fields. OYAK also developed organic relations with foreign and domestic capital through partnerships, joint ventures, mergers and acquisitions, and licence agreements (Akça 2010: 18–19). Combined with its economic power, the military further sought to reinforce its guardianship role by making references to secularism, which remained in tension with the AKP's Islamism. Significantly, the General Staff allegedly scrutinised the AKP's election campaign, which was based on the introduction of a new constitution, during the NSC meeting of November 2002. Then-Prime Minister Gül allegedly reassured the military about the AKP's respect for the fundamental Republican principles (*Milliyet* 2002).

Nevertheless, the AKP implemented a series of reform packages within the EU framework to civilianise the political sphere and submit the military to civilian authority. Regarding the process of civilianisation, the second reform package abolished the temporary mandate of the gendarmerie as the deputy of civilian authority (ABGS 2007: 231). The third and seventh reform packages abolished the requirement for the NSC's opinion on the teaching of different languages and dialects before the Cabinet's legislation (ABGS 2007: 228). The eighth reform package abolished the place of the members appointed by the NSC in the Council for Protection of Minors from Harmful Publications and the High Council of Radio and Television. It also abolished the place of the members appointed by the General Staff in the High Council of Education (ABGS 2007: 236, 237, 243). Nonetheless, the AKP's understanding of civilian supremacy over the military indicated strengthened executive power (*Hürriyet* 2003), which remained in line with the neoliberal authoritarian statism. With its aim to maintain civilian supremacy over the military, the AKP restructured the NSC, the State Security Courts, and the Supreme Military Council, and reshaped the relationship between the military and the Court of Accounts.

To begin with the military's political autonomy, the NSC was restructured as an advisory council that expressed an opinion when asked. The prime minister was authorised to appoint the deputy prime minister to distribute and monitor NSC decisions. This abolished the competence of the Secretary-General of the NSC (SGNSC) to pursue the Council's decisions by monitoring both state institutions and private corporations. The NSC's advice was also to be sent to the Cabinet for evaluation by the government. While the NSC's monthly meetings were replaced by bimonthly meetings, the prime minister was authorised to propose NSC meetings, and the president was authorised to call them. Furthermore, the SGNSC was to be appointed based upon the prime minister's proposal and the president's consent. If the proposed SGNSC belonged to the

Turkish armed forces, the chief of the General Staff was to be asked for an opinion. This abolished the competence of the chief of the General Staff to propose the SGNSC. Finally, the number of civilians in the NSC was increased through the inclusion of the deputies of the prime minister and the minister of justice (ABGS 2007: 232–236). However, the Interior Security Group (*İç Güvenlik Grubu*), whose duty was to report on terror and extremism, was transferred from the NSC to the Department of Planning of National Mobilisation and War Preparations (*Seferberlik ve Savaş Hazırlıkları Planlama Dairesi Başkanlığı*), which remained under the military's control (Akça 2013: 68). This reinforced the military's role in the supervision of domestic security.

Regarding the military's judicial autonomy, the State Security Courts were replaced with the Special Aggravated Felony Courts (*Özel Yetkili Ağır Ceza Mahkemeleri*) in June 2004 (Act on the Amendment to the Law on Penal Proceeding and the Abolition of State Security Courts 2004). Although unlike the State Security Courts the Special Aggravated Felony Courts did not have military judges, these courts were granted with the latter's competences and duties to deal with crimes against the security of the state. In this regard, the AKP maintained the role of the military as the custodian of the capitalist social order, reinforced by the junta of 1980.

Regarding the military's economic autonomy, the AKP curtailed the military budget. Between 2002 and 2008, the military budget was reduced from 3.8 per cent to 2.2. per cent of GDP (SIPRI 2023). Moreover, the AKP introduced an amendment whereby public properties owned by the military were to be reviewed by the Court of Accounts (*Sayıştay*) in accordance with the confidentiality of the national defence. The pillars of auditing were to be prepared by the minister of defence after the opinions of the General Staff and the Court of Accounts were taken. These pillars were to be confirmed by the Cabinet with a classified regulation (ABGS 2007: 243–244). This amendment can be regarded as a significant attempt to curb the military's economic autonomy in accordance with the liberal democratic principles of accountability and transparency. However, since the regulations were to be classified, political leverage was given to executive power represented by the Cabinet rather than legislative power represented by the Assembly. In this regard, the amendment was in line with authoritarian statism.

2.4 The "E-Memorandum" of 2007

The reluctant consent of the civil-military bureaucracy for the AKP government remained fragile in the 2000s. The secular factions within the civil-military bureaucracy accused the AKP of committing *taqiyya* (a form of religious dissimulation),[13] biding its time to consolidate its power in order to implement its agenda of Islamisation of the state apparatus and social structure. In April 2007, Sezer stated that political Islam could not coexist with democracy because of its tendency to easily radicalise, and portrayed political Islam as a "threat" that sought to abolish secularism and turn Turkey into an Islamic country under "the disguise of democratisation" (*Milliyet* 2007b).

Sezer gave his abovementioned speech before the termination of his term of office and the election of a new president by the Assembly. During his term, Sezer used his presidential veto to block certain legislative changes and prevented the appointment of hundreds of AKP nominees to key positions in the bureaucracy (Jenkins 2008b: 6). Owing to its majority in the Assembly, the AKP could elect any candidate as president. Therefore, the presidency became the site of the contest between the AKP and the Islamists, and the secular factions of society and the civil-military bureaucracy. On 12 April 2007, Chief of the General Staff Yaşar Büyükanıt underlined the need for the future president's commitment to the foundational principles of the Republic, including secularism, while highlighting the role of the Assembly as the decision-maker (*Milliyet* 2007a). Two days later, various nongovernmental organisations, including the Atatürkist Thought Association, the Association for Supporting Modern Life, and *Çağdaş Eğitim Vakfı* (Foundation for Modern Education), organised "Republican Protests" in several cities. Thousands attended the demonstrations, with the majority carrying banners that stated, "no *sharia*, no coup, democratic Turkey" (*Milliyet* 2007c). This demonstrated the call of the secular segments of society for the military not to intervene in politics, and for the election of a secular president by the Assembly. In response, the AKP declared that the president would be "civilian, pious, and democratic", highlighting the future Islamisation of the executive branch (*Milliyet* 2007d). Consequently, the AKP nominated Gül on 24 April 2007 (*Milliyet* 2007e).

On 27 April 2007, the first round of the presidential election took place in the Assembly. Deniz Baykal, the chair of the CHP, applied to the Constitutional Court to challenge the validity of the first round since the condition of a two-thirds majority of members of the Assembly required by the Constitution was not met (*Milliyet* 2007f). Later in the evening, a controversial press release was published on the website of the chief of the General Staff, underlining the

---

13 The notion of *taqiyya* does not exist in the Sunni interpretation of Islam as a concept. However, there are reported cases that debated the practice of disguising one's beliefs in situations threatening one's life or property. By committing *taqiyya* in these situations, the Sunnis could arguably be deemed blameless in accordance with the Quran (see Strothmann and Djebli 2000).

military's concern about Islamist-reactionary activities seeking "to reinterpret the foundational Republican values", "politically abuse religious feelings of the people", and "challenge the state's authority ... and national unity". It referred to certain events as evidence for such a threat.

> The competition to read the Quran was planned to coincide with the National Sovereignty Day [on 23 April] but cancelled due to the public pressure; headteachers were ordered to attend the festival to celebrate the Prophet Mohammad's birth in Altındağ province of Ankara; veiled young girls sang Islamic carols in an event organised by a political party and the *mufti* in Denizli; women were lectured about religion and preached in a primary school in Denizli despite the presence of four mosques nearby.
> MILLIYET 2007g

In response, the AKP presented a press release as an attempt to pressure the Constitutional Court and warned the military to obey civilian supremacy (*Milliyet* 2007h). On 1 May 2007, the Constitutional Court blocked the presidential election on the basis that the quorum had not been satisfied (*Milliyet* 2007i). On 5 May, Büyükanıt attended a meeting with Erdoğan at Dolmabahçe Palace in Istanbul and declared the military's co-operation with the civilian government, a meeting later dubbed "the Dolmabahçe agreement" (Yaşlı 2008). The content of the meeting was never revealed, even though meetings between the prime minister and the chief of the General Staff were a matter of state. The Dolmabahçe agreement, nevertheless, became a key moment in which the military turned away from direct confrontation and consented to the AKP's restructuring of the state apparatus, particularly the military. Following the CHP's boycott of the presidential election, which paralysed the Assembly, the AKP called for an early general election, which turned into a plebiscite for the AKP's legitimacy. Consequently, the AKP formed a majority government and Gül was elected president in August 2007 (TBMM 28 August 2007).

Since the press release concluded with references to the military's guardianship role, many commentators and scholars considered this to be an e-memorandum (Aydınlı 2011). Nevertheless, this book contests this interpretation, which emphasises the military's will to undertake a direct intervention in politics, since both the dominant and subordinate classes did not support a military intervention. This became very clear when the AKP was re-elected in July 2007 with an almost 48-per-cent majority (Bilgin 2008: 408).

The military also suffered from internal cleavages, preventing any military intervention. By the 2000s, the higher ranks of the military were divided between the critical and co-operative wings.[14] In May 2003, Mustafa Balbay, the journalist who was arrested and brought to the Ergenekon trial in March 2009, wrote an article titled "Young Officers are Worried" in which he suggested that the armed forces commanders had communicated with the chief of the General Staff regarding the concerns of the lower and middle ranks. Such concerns included the AKP's support for the schools of religious brotherhoods, the government's annotations to the decisions of the Supreme Military Council, the AKP's criticisms of celebrations of the National Days, and the issue of headscarves (Balbay 2003). While accepting the disagreements, then-Chief of the General Staff Hilmi Özkök denied the cleavages within the military ranks and highlighted the co-operation between the AKP and the military (*Milliyet* 2003b). However, during the handover ceremony in August 2003, Commander of the Fourth Army Hurşit Tolon underlined the military's awareness of the political use of Islam for deception (*Milliyet* 2003c). Similarly, Secretary-General of the NSC Tuncer Kılınç also highlighted the threat of Islamic fundamentalism posed by religious brotherhoods (*Cumhuriyet* 2003). In response, Özkök discredited the generals to reinforce the power of the co-operative wing over the chain of command (*Milliyet* 2003d).

The division between the co-operative and critical wings demonstrated a power struggle within the chain of command regarding the implementation of neoliberalism under Western hegemony. Most significantly, Özkök was presented as "more of an Atlanticist than any of his recent predecessors" by the United States (Pehlivan and Terkoğlu 2012: 165). In order to prevent Özkök from becoming the chief of the General Staff, the fifty-seventh government had wanted to extend Hüseyin Kıvrıkoğlu's term of office in 2002. Although Kıvrıkoğlu did not accept this offer, he appointed Şener Eruygur as the commander of the gendarmerie, in an attempt to isolate Özkök in the higher ranks. Özkök was replaced by Büyükanıt as the chief of the General Staff in 2006, ensuring that the higher ranks would co-operate with the AKP government (Yaşlı 2011). During the handover ceremony in August 2003, Commander of the First Army Çetin Doğan declared his disagreement with his successor Büyükanıt (*Milliyet* 2003c). Doğan was later arrested and brought to the Sledgehammer trial in February 2010, which will be discussed further. Büyükanıt was never arrested, even though the press release was published during his term of office.

---

14 These cleavages within the military are sometimes known as the status-quo and progressive wings (see Aydınlı 2009). Since this book understands the notion of progress in relation to the struggles of the subordinate classes, it refrains from using the adjective progressive for military officers who paved the way for the consolidation of neoliberal Islamism.

Therefore, this book considers the press release to be a direct confrontation between the military and the AKP government, which the latter won. The AKP's victory can be demonstrated with the aftermath of the press release, which brought about the restructuring of the military and the decline of the military's guardianship under the hegemony of the AKP. This will be discussed further.

3   The State, Classes, and the Military under the AKP (2007–2010)

The period between 2007 and 2013 saw the consolidation of the ruling de facto coalition of the AKP and the Gülen congregation. Beginning in 2013, the power struggle between the AKP and the Gülen congregation that took place in the state apparatus became publicly visible. Meanwhile, the standby agreement signed between the AKP and the IMF in 2005 terminated in 2008. This resulted in the continuous implementation of economic policies and corresponding social and political reforms under the supervision of the IMF between 1998 and 2008, also known as the "long decade with the IMF" (BSB 2007: 148). The termination of the standby agreement coincided with the Great Recession of 2008–2009, and the subsequent rise of social, economic, and political difficulties challenging the AKP's hegemony. For this reason, it is important to focus on the period between 2007 and 2010, in order to understand the reorganisation of class relations and the restructuring of the state apparatus.

The Great Recession of 2008–2009, which started with the crash of Wall Street in 2007 and spread to the City of London and later Europe, resulted in sharp falls in production, investment, and employment in the United States and Europe (Harvey 2011: 102–108). The impact of the Great Recession took the form of a short-term stagnation in Turkey, including a decline in the rate of growth of GDP, a decline in manufacturing, and an increase in unemployment, between 2008 and 2009 (BSB 2009: 96–97). The rapid economic recovery beginning in 2010 was in line with the rising role of the emerging economies in offering profitable investment opportunities and hence steering the world economy. Goldman Sachs, one of the largest global investment banking companies, identified Turkey as an emerging market economy with a potential to experience remarkable development (Kiely 2015: 12). To illustrate, after having contracted by almost 5 per cent in 2009, the Turkish economy grew by almost 8 per cent in 2010 (BSB 2011: 82). Nevertheless, such rapid recovery manifested the advanced dependency of the Turkish economy on foreign capital. This process almost permanently ensured the correlation between the growth rate and the current account deficit at higher thresholds. For instance,

GDP increased from 742.1 billion USD to 786.4 billion USD between 2008 and 2012. During this period, the net increase in external debt amounted to 55.8 billion USD, which was higher than the cumulative increase of 44.3 billion USD. While external borrowing continued to be characterised by its short-term structure, 37.3 billion USD of the net increase in external debt was contracted by the private sector, particularly by the financial institutions—98.4 per cent (Yeldan and Ünüvar 2016: 21–22).

The AKP, nevertheless, maintained the hegemony of its power bloc and fostered the implementation of neoliberal Islamism as the political regime of the authoritarian state. Most significantly, the AKP declared its intention to create "a new generation of civil servants" in December 2003 (Timur 2004: 166). The true nature of this new generation was to be explicitly declared almost ten years later, when Erdoğan stated that the AKP was bringing up "pious youth" in February 2012 (*Hürriyet* 2012). This new generation was to be shaped by various religious brotherhoods. This became apparent when the Office of the Prime Minister abolished all regulations against religious brotherhoods dating back to the process of 28 February in December 2010 (TBMM Araştırma Komisyonu 2012: 1137). In this regard, the Gülen congregation played a key role not only at the societal level through its charity practices, but more importantly at the state level by staffing the state apparatus with its disciples and developing organic relations with the AKP. Two key processes were instrumental regarding the rise and later fall of the Gülen congregation as the de facto coalition partner of the AKP, namely, the Ergenekon and the Sledgehammer trials, and the constitutional amendments of 2010.[15]

3.1   The Ergenekon and the Sledgehammer Trials

The Ergenekon trials were launched in June 2007 when a crate of hand grenades and explosives were discovered by police in a house in the Ümraniye district of Istanbul. In October 2007, Deputy Chief Public Prosecutor of Istanbul Zekeriya Öz, who was the primary actor undertaking the Ergenekon trials, asked the Police Headquarters in Istanbul for details of a series of "assassinations, racist murders, terrorist attacks … [and] protest marches" (Jenkins 2011: 3). The indictment accused "a single, centrally coordinated, hierarchical … armed terrorist organisation" of "inciting the people to an armed rebellion

---

15   The consolidation of the ruling de facto coalition between the AKP and the Gülen congregation could also be examined through the trials of *Kürdistan Topluluklar Birliği* (Kurdistan Communities Union, KCK) (Oğuz 2016: 95–96). Nonetheless, as previously discussed, the military's guardianship role vis-à-vis the Kurdish movement is beyond the scope of this book.

against the [AKP] government" (Jenkins 2011: 4). The Ergenekon trials soon became controversial as they were broadened by several waves of merged cases and the detention of 275 individuals, including retired military officers, members of organised crime, retired police officers, members of civil society organisations, academics, lawyers, journalists, authors, doctors, businessmen, and politicians. The indictment, consisting of 2,455 pages, contained contradictions, absurdities, and false documents that were accepted as evidence in court. The indictment significantly blamed the so-called Ergenekon organisation for "every act of political violence in Turkey" since the 1980s (Jenkins 2011: 4). To illustrate, Osman Yıldırım was tried for being both the instigator and the suspect of the armed attack against the Council of State. When his trial was merged with the Ergenekon trial, Yıldırım eventually became an instigator, a suspect, a secret witness, and a complainant in one single trial (Bolaç 2013). The Ergenekon's wide spectrum of alleged actions included meeting with the vice-president of the United States, intervening in elections in Cyprus, flying banners at Fenerbahçe football games, undertaking assassinations abroad, and attempting to produce chemical weapons (Timur 2014: 38).

The Sledgehammer (*Balyoz*) trials were launched following the publication of journalist Mehmet Baransu's article in *Taraf*, a Gülen-affiliated newspaper. In his article, Baransu alleged a coup plan based on a seminar at the First Army Headquarters in Istanbul between 5 and 7 March 2003. During the seminar, Doğan allegedly developed a strategy to overthrow the AKP government in case of a war in the Aegean against Greece and the eruption of Islamist violence (*Taraf* 2010). Doğan stated that it was a war-game scenario (*Milliyet* 2010).[16] The Sledgehammer trials became as controversial as the Ergenekon trials, with an indictment consisting of 968 pages and 365 suspects. The indictment also consisted of contradictions, absurdities, and false documents that were accepted as evidence in court (Jenkins 2011: 7). For instance, a document presented *Türkiye Gençlik Birliği* (Turkey Youth Union) as one of the NGOs that could support a coup in 2003. However, the Turkey Youth Union was only founded in 2006. Another document referred to NATO's Southern Command as CC MAR NAPLES. However, the Command's name had been HQ NAVSOUTH until July 2004 (Jenkins 2011: 7).

Public opinion was divided regarding the Ergenekon and Sledgehammer trials. One side regarded the trials as a confrontation with the deep state, consisting of counter-guerrilla and coup-plotters, whereas the other side considered

---

16   According to witnesses and recordings of the seminar, the scenario was called sovereign (*egemen*), not sledgehammer, even though the indictment included a document called "sledgehammer" as evidence of the coup plot (*Milliyet* 2010).

the trials to be a conspiracy of the coalition between the AKP and the Gülen congregation (Polat 2011: 213). Nevertheless, it was clear that both trials were political trials from the very beginning. Before any discussion on the indictment, Erdoğan stated that he would be the prosecutor of the Ergenekon trial in July 2008 (*Vatan* 2008). This demonstrated the primacy of executive power over judicial power, consolidating the merging of authoritarian statism and political Islam.

The relationship between the trials and the deep state further revealed the political nature of the trials. Within the framework of the Ergenekon trial, a number of important names involved with the counter-guerrilla were arrested. These names included Veli Küçük, a retired brigadier-general who was the alleged founder of the Gendarmerie Intelligence Organisation (*Jandarma İstihbarat Teşkilatı*, JITEM); Atilla Oğuz, a retired colonel who was involved with the JITEM; and İbrahim Şahin, a retired chief of police in the Special Warfare Unit who was involved with the Susurluk scandal. The Ergenekon trial neither questioned nor investigated the structure of the deep state since the trial was not based on the activities of the aforementioned individuals within the JITEM or the Special Warfare Unit. Rather, the trial sought to reveal the coup-plotting against the AKP government. For instance, the trial did not question the relationship between Şahin and the RP–DYP coalition government during the Susurluk scandal (Bolaç 2013). Therefore, this book argues that neither the Ergenekon nor the Sledgehammer trial aimed to bring justice to and dismantle the counter-guerrilla. Rather, they aimed to purge certain members of the deep state while locating the deep state under the authority of the executive branch.

The political nature of the trials revealed the Gülen congregation's place vis-à-vis the state apparatus. From the very beginning, there were significant accusations that staff in the judiciary and police who had initiated and conducted the trials were involved with the Gülen congregation. One of the most controversial incidents that proved such accusations was the arrest of journalist Ahmet Şık. In his book *İmamın Ordusu* (*The Imam's Army*), Şık documented the staffing of state institutions, especially the judiciary and police, with disciples of the Gülen congregation. Before his book was published, Şık was arrested and copies of the manuscript were retained for Öz's investigation of the Ergenekon (*Radikal* 2011a). Similarly, İlhan Cihaner, a public prosecutor in Erzincan who investigated the JITEM in the 1990s, began an investigation in 2007 against the crony relationship between local disciples of the Gülen congregation and the İsmailağa congregation, and the leading members of the AKP. When Cihaner refused to drop his investigation despite the pressure of the Ministry of Justice (*Adalet Bakanlığı*) in 2009, he was suspended for alleged abuse of office, and was arrested and tried for membership of the Ergenekon in 2010. The investigations into the religious brotherhoods were later quietly shelved (Jenkins 2011: 5).

The political nature of the trials further revealed the true nature of the restructuring of the military. In this regard, the trials aimed to purge the critical wing and maintain the chain of command under the leadership of the co-operative wing. Significantly, Büyükanıt and his successor, İlker Başbuğ, consented to the trials. In August 2009, Başbuğ visited Kenan Evren in hospital, even though public opinion was in favour of bringing Evren to trial as the leader of the junta of 1980 (*Radikal* 2009). Başbuğ's visit can be considered a gesture of co-operation with the extension of the junta regime under a civilian government. In January 2012, Başbuğ was arrested and brought to the Ergenekon trial following his opposition to the amendment of the military law that would enable the trying of military officers in civilian courts and his suggestion that the Gülen congregation was involved with the trials (BBC Türkçe 2010). Beginning in 2014, judges and public prosecutors who were involved with Başbuğ's trial were suspended from duty and arrested for the fabrication of false documents and malfeasance in office in collaboration with the Gülen congregation (*Sözcü* 2019).

The restructuring of the military to consolidate the primacy of the co-operative wing was further maintained through the reinforcement of civilian supremacy over the military. In July 2011, the AKP sought to intervene in the course of the military's internal promotion by putting pressure on the Supreme Military Council not to promote certain generals who had been tried in the Ergenekon or Sledgehammer trials. The AKP's intervention took place following the introduction of a judicial remedy in September 2010, which legislated the appeal against the Supreme Council's decision to the civilian court in cases of dismissal from the military other than resignation (TBMM 6 May 2010). As a response, the chief of the General Staff and the generals of the army, navy and air force resigned from their posts (*Milliyet* 2011). Consequently, Commander of the Gendarmerie Necdet Özel was promoted to the position of commander of the army, and then to chief of the General Staff (*Radikal* 2011b). In July 2013, the president was given competence to ratify the Supreme Military Council's decisions regarding promotions (Act on the Amendment of Certain Laws and the Law on Contracted Non-Commissioned Military Officers 2013). In March 2014, the Constitutional Court decided that there had been a violation of rights with regard to the hearing of testimonies of both defendants and witnesses. Such violation included the destruction of evidence and fabrication of false evidence in the Sledgehammer trials (*Hürriyet* 2014) and prolonged detention in the Ergenekon trials (NTVMSNBC

2014). However, the Supreme Military Council decided on the resignation of all higher- and middle-ranking military officers (Yıldız 2014), demonstrating the reorganisation of the military in accordance with the primacy of the cooperative wing under Özel's leadership.

The trials also sought to enable the staffing of the military with the disciples of religious brotherhoods. During the trials, 400 military officers were tried, including 72 generals and admirals, 125 colonels, 146 commissioned officers, and 54 non-commissioned officers (OdaTV 2012). Even though the Constitutional Court decided on the violation of rights of the detainees during the trials, the detainees could not seek judicial remedy due to the prolonged nature of the trials and the Supreme Military Council's decisions on resignations. Combined with the intervention of the AKP in the military's internal promotion, the amendment that offered judicial remedy to military officers was utilised by religious brotherhoods to staff the military with their disciples. The lower and middle ranks were staffed by Islamists either through the readmission of officers who had been dismissed for their Islamist links or through the prevention of future dismissals. The key role played by the Gülen congregation regarding the staffing of the military during his period of leadership was later accepted by Özel (*Sözcü* 2016).

3.2   The Constitutional Amendments of 2010

In May 2010, the Assembly voted for constitutional amendments proposed by the AKP that reshaped fundamental rights and freedoms, the judiciary, and the national economy (TBMM 6 May 2010). The constitutional amendments of 2010 essentially consolidated the regime of neoliberal Islamism within the framework of authoritarian statism and paved the way towards the transition to the exceptional form of state by the mid-2010s (see Chapter 7). Most significantly, the amendments placed the judiciary branch under the executive branch, corresponding to the consolidation of neoliberalism. The Constitution of 1982 limited jurisdiction to the review of compliance of administrative acts and processes with the law. Since the review of expediency was not outlawed, judges annulled or suspended a number of neoliberal regulations for conflicting with the public interest. The constitutional amendments of 2010, nonetheless, explicitly outlawed the review of expediency (Oğuz 2012: 12). This amendment sought to block any appeal to the Council of State against the neoliberal regulations legislated by the government. This amendment was reinforced by the strengthening of competences of executive power over judicial power. To illustrate, the composition and election procedure of the Supreme Council of Judges and Prosecutors (*Hakimler ve Savcılar Yüksek Kurulu*, HSYK) were restructured to increase the control of the executive over the judiciary (Alemdar 2020: 206). Similarly, the executive was enabled to determine the members of the Constitutional Court and intervene in the Court's mechanisms (Oğuz 2012: 12). The control of the executive over the judiciary also enabled the Gülen congregation, the AKP's de facto coalition partner, to staff the judiciary since such control enabled the AKP to revise the composition of judicial bodies and dismantle the secular judiciary (Taş 2018: 398).

The AKP and the liberal-conservative intelligentsia supported the constitutional amendments by presenting them as a means to "purge the tutelary custodianship regime" and strengthen parliamentary control over the civil-military bureaucracy (Yılmaz 2010: 4). Certain amendments indeed narrowed the military's judicial autonomy, such as the introduction of civilian judicial remedy for the Supreme Military Council's decisions regarding dismissals. However, a number of amendments curtailed especially labour rights and civil rights and freedoms, thereby undermining the liberal-conservative intelligentsia's emphasis on improvements of human rights and freedoms, such as freedom of movement and children's rights. Most significantly, the Supreme Council of Arbitrators was enabled to make final decisions regarding collective labour agreements of civil servants, and civil servants were denied the right to strike. Therefore, the constitutional amendments constituted an omnibus bill that included irrelevant and incompatible provisions. This clashed with the principle of *lex Caecilia Didia*, as confirmed by the Venice Commission, which banned the omnibus legislation to prevent political bribes and the enactment of undesired provisions which were included among desired ones (Özbek and Ertosun 2010: 9). Nevertheless, the AKP had already revealed the mission of the constitutional amendments, which was to weaken the judiciary and hence foster privatisations and inflows of foreign capital (AKP 2010: 40).

The CHP, the MHP, and *Barış ve Demokrasi Partisi* (Peace and Democracy Party) representing the Kurdish movement, and the judiciary represented by the HSYK and the Association of Judges and Prosecutors (*Yargıçlar ve Savcılar Birliği*), opposed the constitutional amendments (Memurlar.Net 2010). The AKP soon turned the referendum on the constitutional amendments into a plebiscite and delegitimised any criticism. Significantly, then-Prime Minister Erdoğan portrayed the opposition as coup-plotters (NTV 2010). The AKP further received the support of foreign capital. To illustrate, then-Minister of Foreign Affairs Ahmet Davutoğlu stated that the AKP could not "explain the failure in the referendum to the international community" (*Zaman* 2010). Moreover, the majority of religious brotherhoods, particularly the Gülen congregation, the Menzil order, the İsmailağa congregation, and the İskenderpaşa congregation, called their disciples to vote in favour of the referendum. Most significantly, Gülen stated that his congregation "would bring the dead back to life and make them vote if it could" (OdaTV 2010). Therefore, the constitutional amendments of 2010 consolidated authoritarian statism under the de facto coalition of the AKP and the Gülen congregation.

CHAPTER 7

The Failed Coup Attempt of 2016
Resistance, Crisis, and Restoration

> 'Order reigns in Berlin!' You stupid lackeys! Your 'order' is built on sand. The revolution will 'raise itself up again clashing,' and to your horror it will proclaim to the sound of trumpets: *I was, I am, I shall be.*
> ROSA LUXEMBURG (1971 [1919])

∴

This chapter explores the transition to the exceptional form of state, particularly the fascist state and regime, under the AKP between the early 2010s and 2018. It approaches the exceptional form of state as a response to the political crisis and the crisis of state that manifests a specific conjuncture of class conflict. For this reason, it examines the moments of organic crises and attempts at restoration in relation to capital accumulation, class relations, and state beginning in the 2010s. In this regard, it discusses the emergence of indications of an economic crisis, the rise of resistance against neoliberal Islamism, and the crisis of the ruling de facto coalition between the AKP and the Gülen congregation as processes that facilitated the transition to the exceptional state. It further discusses the suspension of the electoral principle in 2015, the state of emergency in the aftermath of the abortive coup in 2016, and the transition to presidentialism as processes that enabled the exceptional state to assume its fascist character. Therefore, it examines the restructuring of the military and the reorganisation of civil–military relations beginning in the 2010s in accordance with the consolidation of the fascist state and regime.

1 The State, Classes, and the Crisis under the AKP (2010–2015)

By the 2010s, the AKP had failed to maintain the transition from labour-intensive sectors to relative surplus production (see Chapter 6). In response, the AKP adopted various measures to postpone crisis dynamics and fostered the consolidation of authoritarian statism in the early 2010s. When the hegemonic crisis of neoliberal Islamism became clear with the rise of the working classes and resistance of various social forces, the AKP resorted to the transition to the exceptional form of state, which takes place when a hegemonic crisis—an organic crisis of capital accumulation that threatens capitalist relations—cannot be resolved through normal democratic channels where class struggle takes place. The exceptional state is a response to resolve the crisis through the institutionalisation of exceptional means. The term crisis, in this regard, indicates the political crisis and the crisis of the state, which result only from an economic crisis and manifest the condensation of class antagonisms in their political struggles with the state apparatus. The political crisis and the crisis of the state can lead to the transformation and adaptation of the state to "the new realities of class conflict" (Poulantzas 2008: 297), and thereby transformation of the state into an exceptional form. The emergence of indications of an economic crisis, the rise of resistance against neoliberal Islamism, and the crisis of the ruling de facto coalition between the AKP and the Gülen congregation presented specific conjunctures of configuration of class relations that enabled the transition to the exceptional state in Turkey.

1.1 The Emergence of Indications of an Economic Crisis

Beginning in 2010, the AKP failed to maintain the transition from labour-intensive sectors to relative surplus production. This failure was a result of insufficiencies of capital as well as the AKP's class basis. The dependency of productive capital accumulation on the import of capital goods and hence the growing current account deficit reinforced the dependency on foreign exchange. The need to secure the inflow of foreign exchange brought about the policy of the combination of the overvalued Turkish lira and high interest rates, which continued until 2015. While this policy ensured the inflow of money capital,[1] it negatively affected the SMEs that constituted the AKP's support base. In response, the AKP simultaneously fostered the import of capital goods on the one hand and sought to decrease interest rates on the other hand (Ercan and Oğuz 2020: 105). Beginning in 2013, it became clear that the Turkish economy demonstrated the indications of a belated economic crisis, including a decline in the economic growth rate and exports, and an increase in unemployment (Yeldan and Ünüvar 2016: 14, 18). Between 2012 and 2016, the

---

1 Despite their reduction in the 2010s, interest rates in Turkey remained remarkably higher than the prevalent interest rates in the world and in similar emerging economies in the aftermath of the financial crisis of 2007–2008. The crisis had already reduced interest rates in the advanced capitalist countries to nearly zero (Orhangazi and Yeldan 2021: 467).

economic growth rate decreased by an average of 3.4 per cent. The economic slowdown was mainly because of the capital outflows following the decision of the US Federal Reserve to raise interest rates (Akçay 2018: 19), illustrating the dependency of the Turkish economy on foreign capital. The indications of a belated economic crisis were worsened beginning in 2015 with the hikes in interest rates and the rapid depreciation of the Turkish lira, which accelerated inflation and affected the competitiveness of large-scale conglomerates as a result of the dependent national industrial and agricultural production. This process further reinforced the fragility of the national economy in the face of capital flows, emphasising the prominence of portfolio flows regarding the financing of the current account deficit (Akçay and Güngen 2022: 305).

On the one hand, the AKP continued to obtain the consent of the fractions of large-scale finance capital as well as small- and medium-scale capital fractions by implementing policies to postpone crisis dynamics. Such policies included the enhancement of control over labour by curbing labour rights; the advancement of labour-intensive sectors, including construction and services; the creation of new spheres of commodification, such as housing, energy, land, mining, and water; and the advancement of the internationalisation of capital, particularly financial capital (Ercan and Oğuz 2020: 106–107). On the other hand, the AKP began to lean on and favour Gulf capital, as well as SMEs and Islamic capital, particularly that affiliated with MUSIAD, above all in the fields of real estate, construction, and finance, and through the subterranean economy (Aykut and Yıldırım 2016: 150–151). The AKP's aim to restructure the power bloc under the hegemony of Islamic capital went in-hand-in with the AKP's favouring of Western capital and the first-generation finance capital that had developed organic relations with Western capital. Such favouring, which was a part of bargaining for social and political leverage, included privatisations and various incentives, including tax cuts, deregulation, and the broadening of credits (Güngen and Akçay 2016: 33–35).

The AKP's strategy to postpone crisis dynamics further enabled it to obtain the consent of the fractions of the urban and rural subordinate classes. In this regard, social assistance programmes enabled the AKP to transfer some of the newly created wealth to the poorest sections of society and mobilise them in support of neoliberal Islamism. To illustrate, the AKP's use of the so-called Green Card system in social security, the general health insurance system, and conditional cash transfers benefited workers in informal and agricultural sectors, the same segments of society that were previously not covered by social security (Akçay 2018: 10–12). Nonetheless, the AKP's support base began to narrow and the AKP began to fail to obtain the consent of larger segments of the urban and rural subordinate classes. This became clear with the rise of resistance beginning in the early 2010s.

1.2 Resistance against Neoliberal Islamism

This book examines the workers' strikes and the Gezi Park resistance in 2013 as key moments in the rise of the working classes and various social forces that challenged neoliberal Islamism, thereby compelling the AKP to consolidate the exceptional form of state. To begin with, the deregulation of the labour market, de-unionisation, and the repression of social opposition beginning in the 1980s had already curtailed labour movements. Nevertheless, several workers' strikes broke out in the SOEs against the AKP's policies of privatisation beginning in the early 2000s. These examples included the workers' strikes in the Şişecam glass factory in 2003, and in the TÜPRAŞ oil refinery and the SEKA paper mill in 2005. These strikes remained sporadic, with very limited public support, and the AKP consequently succeeded in its aim at privatisation of these SOEs. However, these strikes enabled workers to achieve a limited but significant progress. For instance, the SEKA resistance, which involved a fifty-one-day-long factory occupation joined by the families of striking workers, enabled the workers to maintain their employment and social security by earning their transfer to the closest municipality (Yalman and Topal 2019: 452). The labour movements in the SOEs were also followed by the workers' resistances in the private sector, including at Sinter metal in 2008, Çel-Mer steel in 2011, Greif industrial packaging in 2014, and Şişecam glass in 2014 (Saraçoğlu and Yeşilbağ 2015: 893).

The resistances in TEKEL tobacco, salt, and alcoholic beverages, Kazova textiles, and Soma mining particularly demonstrated the definite conjunctures of configuration of class relations that compelled the AKP to facilitate the transition to the exceptional state. The TEKEL workers' resistance, which took place between December 2009 and March 2010, essentially opposed to the AKP's attempt at deregulation of the labour market. The AKP sought to deprive the workers, who were made redundant as part of the privatisations of the SOEs, of job security and redundancy payments by providing them with temporary contracts (Yalman and Topal 2019: 452). The resistance took the form of a seventy-eight-day sit-in demonstration in front of *Türk-İş* headquarters in the Sakarya neighbourhood in central Ankara, turning the neighbourhood into the "'Sakarya Commune'" (Savran 2010). Even though the resistance endured the brutal attacks of the police, *Türk-İş*'s reluctance to defend the workers and the negotiation between *Türk-İş* and the AKP brought about the failure of the resistance (Saraçoğlu and Yeşilbağ 2015: 894). Nevertheless, the resistance remained one of the most important workers' resistances regarding its national scale, the public support it received, and its direct targeting of the AKP and its neoliberal policies.

Furthermore, in January 2013, the workers of the Kazova textile factory, producing woollen products for the domestic and international markets, occupied the factory to reclaim their salaries, which had not been paid for several months before the owner laid off workers and abandoned the workplace. While waiting for the lawsuits concerning their salaries and severance payments, a number of workers, supported by artists, academics, and journalists in an act of solidarity, relaunched production. In January 2015, the court officially granted the workers the ownership of textile machines in exchange for their unpaid salaries. The 'Free Kazova' initiative regularly paid the rent, bills, and salaries; introduced shops in Ankara, Balıkesir, Diyarbakır, Istanbul, and Izmir; and enabled workers to collectively make decisions during weekly and bimonthly meetings (Dinler 2017: 232–233). The Kazova resistance, which offered the first example of workers' self-management and self-governing in Turkey, directly threatened the AKP and its neoliberal policies. The resistance also influenced future labour movements, of which the Soma miners' resistance was an important example.

In May 2014, 301 workers died in a mining disaster in the underground coal mine in the Soma province of Manisa. The lignite mines had previously been owned by Turkish Coal Enterprises (*Türkiye Kömür İşletmeleri*), an SOE which was privatised in 2005 through outsourcing and royalty payment. In the royal payment system, which was applied to Soma coal, the state kept the property rights of the mines while transferring their operating rights to private companies, which in return sold their monopolistically priced products to the state-owned thermal power plants (Ercan and Oğuz 2015: 117). Soma Holding ignored safety concerns and allowed activities to continue even though the heat in the galleries increased to alarming levels before the disaster.[2] In response, then-Prime Minister Erdoğan emphasised fatalism by highlighting *fitrat* (Adaman,

---

2 There is a growing literature that considers the Turkish economy under the AKP as crony capitalism by focusing on organic relations among the Erdoğan family; a few businesses operating in the construction, energy, media, and war industries; and economic government departments, especially the Treasury (see Çeviker-Gürakar 2016). Soma Holding, in this regard, was already known as one of the "*enfants bien-aimés*" of the AKP (Adaman, Arsel, and Akbulut 2021: 155). Nonetheless, this book argues that the emphasis on crony capitalism interprets the development of organic relations between the executive branch and particular capital fractions as a deviation from an idealised understanding of capitalism. Such emphasis implies praise for the early years of the AKP's term in office, during which large-scale conglomerates, often represented by TUSIAD, were strong enough to benefit from the AKP's economic reforms (Uysal 2021: 449).

Arsel, and Akbulut 2021: 155), thereby suggesting that accidents and deaths were inherent in the nature of mining. However, the surviving miners occupied the headquarters of the company and the company union (Ercan and Oğuz 2015: 132), demonstrating their resistance against the AKP and the neoliberal Islamism that had brought about the largest work-related massacre in Turkish history.

Moreover, in May 2013, an intense period of protests, demonstrations, and civil disobedience erupted in the Taksim neighbourhood of Istanbul and soon expanded countrywide—excluding only two cities—with the participation of more than 2.5 million people (*Hürriyet Daily News* 2013).[3] The protests were named after Gezi Park, which was to be demolished by the municipal government of Istanbul for the reconstruction of military barracks either as a shopping mall or a hotel. The Gezi Park resistance was met with the police's abusive use of force across the country, leaving more than 8,000 people injured and five people dead (Amnesty International 2013: 18–34).

The resistance originally erupted as a reaction to the widespread environmental destruction and the AKP's Islamist interventions in the public and private spheres and brought together various social forces and segments of society (see Uysal 2013b). Even though the working classes did not join the resistance with their own organisations and programmes,[4] the class composition and political struggles and demands of the protesters revealed the class character of the resistance. The fractions of the wage-earning working classes took the lead in the resistance (Gürcan and Peker 2015b), politically struggling against the moments of capital accumulation, namely, production, realisation, and revalorisation. These struggles included protests against low wages, casualisation, and poor working conditions, all of which sought to intervene in production; against the commodification and commercialisation of public services, which sought to intervene in realisation; and against the commodification and commercialisation of nature (Ercan and Oğuz 2015: 116). In this sense, the Gezi Park resistance directly challenged the AKP and neoliberal Islamism.

In January 2015, almost 15,000 metal workers from twenty-two workplaces participated in a series of protests and strikes in the metal industry under

---

3 Taksim Square holds major symbolic importance in the late-Ottoman and Republican eras. Prior to the Gezi Park protests, trade unions were denied the right to march into the square for International Workers' Day on 1 May 2013. When a number of trade unions challenged the AKP's ban and proceeded to the Square, they were met by the police and their heavy-handed crowd control methods, resulting in several wounded (Uysal 2013a).
4 This book rejects the debates that either see no class content in the resistance (Göle 2013) or consider the resistance to have been an uprising of the "new" middle class (Keyder 2013).

the leadership of *Birleşik Metal-İş* (United Metal Workers' Union). When the AKP suspended these strikes and protests on the grounds of national security (*Evrensel* 2015), an intense "storm" of metal workers' "'wildcat'" strikes and protests erupted in the automotive industry, which had an overwhelming share in the metal industry, between May and June 2015 (Çelik 2015b: 21–22). These protests and strikes targeted foreign and domestic capital, affecting RENAULT, a partnership between the French Renault and OYAK; FORD, a partnership between the American Ford and Koç Holding; TOFAŞ, a partnership between the Italian Fiat and Koç Holding; and TÜRK TRAKTÖR, a partnership between Koç Holding and the Italian-American CNH Industrial.[5] The workers dictated their basic demands to RENAULT, negotiated their demands with TOFAŞ, and failed to sustain the unified action in TÜRK TRAKTÖR, where the strike was broken (Dölek 2016). Nevertheless, the strikes and protests threatened the AKP and neoliberal Islamism.

1.3 The Crisis of the Coalition between the AKP and the Gülen Congregation

The crisis of the ruling de facto coalition between the AKP and the Gülen congregation further facilitated the transition to the exceptional state so that the AKP could restore the hegemony of neoliberal Islamism. It is debatable when exactly the de facto coalition between the AKP and the Gülen congregation began to collapse.[6] However, the enactment of the constitutional amendments of 2010 combined with the Ergenekon and Sledgehammer trials brought about a crucial question: which actor was to dominate the state apparatus? The AKP and the Gülen congregation, therefore, engaged in a power struggle that took place in the state apparatus. This power struggle, which can be likened to "an ugly divorce with daggers drawn" (Gürsel 2013), is particularly important in

---

5 The 'wildcat' strikes and protests further targeted *Türk-İş* as well as MESS, the biggest employer association.
6 A number of scholars and commentators accept the *Mavi Marmara* incident in 2010 as the beginning of the power struggle between the AKP and the Gülen congregation. The attempt of the *Mavi Marmara* aid flotilla, which involved the members of the Islamist IHH (*İnsani Yardım Vakfı*, Foundation for Human Rights and Freedoms and Humanitarian Relief) to break the Israeli blockade of Gaza, was met with Israel's raid in 2010. While the AKP completely supported the flotilla and condemned Israel, the Gülen congregation, known for its support for strengthening ties with Israel, criticised the flotilla for undermining Israeli authority and breaking international law (Taş 2018: 398). This was consistent with pressure from the Gülen congregation to maintain Turkey's adherence to US hegemony, considering the fact that the Gülen congregation opposed the AKP's alliance with the Muslim Brotherhood following the Arab Spring in 2010 (Akçay 2018: 21). For a discussion on the alleged links between the IHH and the Muslim Brotherhood, see Ehrenfeld (2011: 76–77).

the examination of the failed coup attempt of 2016, as disciples of the Gülen congregation within the military and police allegedly emerged as the main coup-plotters.

The power struggle became publicly visible in February 2012,[7] when Hakan Fidan, undersecretary of the MIT, was subpoenaed by the Public Prosecutor in Ankara regarding his contact with the PKK (Kurdistan Workers' Party, *Partiya Karkeren Kurdistane*).[8] The Public Prosecutor was arguably "'pro-Gülen'", and Fidan was well known for being Erdoğan's "confidante" (Taş 2018: 399). Fidan's contact with the PKK, which involved secret talks in Oslo, Norway, stirred up the political opposition against the AKP since such contact suggested a secret negotiation process between the government and the state and the PKK, which Turkey recognised as a terrorist organisation. The AKP responded to this by providing the prime minister with the competence to determine the capacities, duties, and responsibilities of the MIT in order to immunise Fidan from a future investigation. Erdoğan condemned the Public Prosecutor and defended Fidan by explaining that he himself had instructed Fidan. Erdoğan further emphasised the signs of "a 'parallel state' operating illegitimately under the control of non-elected actors" (Demiralp 2016: 4), highlighting a rivalry between the AKP and the Gülen congregation within the state apparatus.

By fundamentally threatening the hegemony of neoliberal Islamism, the Gezi Park resistance targeted the Gülen congregation as much as it targeted the AKP. Therefore, the Gülen congregation continued its alliance with the AKP and explicitly dishonoured the protestors as "immoral deviant subjects devoid of compliance and belief" (Gürcan and Peker 2015a: 122).[9] Gülen publicly stated:

> If you are infested by a swarm of ants, you do not think they are only small ants. It is an infestation; ants invade and poison your space, so you must not underestimate them ... A generation that is rotten and in ruins must be restored ... rehabilitated ... and recovered with spirituality ... Otherwise such unruliness continues.
>
> *HÜRRIYET* 2013a

---

7 For a discussion on the AKP's response to the arrest of İlker Başbuğ within the framework of the Ergenekon trial in January 2012 by Gülen-affiliated staff in the judiciary and police, see Chapter 6.

8 For a historical discussion on the relationship between the Kurdish movement and the PKK and the conflict between the Turkish state and the PKK, see Bozarslan (2008).

9 Erdoğan adopted a similar but arguably more aggressive discourse, emphasising that "those who raise their hands against the police shall have their hands broken" (*Hürriyet* 2013b).

However, the power struggle between the AKP and the Gülen congregation resumed in the aftermath of the Gezi Park resistance. In November 2013, the AKP sought to shut down Gülen-affiliated preparatory schools, which were crucial for the mobilisation of new disciples and supporters. In response, in December 2013, the Gülen congregation mobilised public prosecutors to investigate a corruption case involving the upper echelons of the AKP, which provided links between Turkey's and Iran's subterranean economies (Akçay 2018: 22).[10] The public prosecutor who launched the investigation was Zekeriya Öz, the same deputy chief public prosecutor of Istanbul who had conducted the investigation in the Ergenekon trial. Meanwhile, the Gülen congregation leaked secret tape recordings of phone conversations among government officials, including Erdoğan and his family members, and businessmen, thereby exposing corruption. Between 2014 and 2015, the AKP responded by removing and reallocating hundreds of police officers and prosecutors who had Gülenist affiliations. The AKP also targeted Gülen-affiliated corporate media, such as the Samanyolu TV channel and *Zaman* newspaper, and Gülen-affiliated financial, commercial, and industrial capital, such as Bank Asya and Koza Holding (Demiralp 2016: 5–6).

2 The State, Classes, and the Crisis under the AKP (2015–2018)

By 2015, the AKP had consolidated the exceptional state, which it called "new Turkey" (AKP 2012). The exceptional state essentially indicates the transformation of the hierarchies among, and fundamental functions of, the ideological and repressive state apparatuses in relation to the specific conjunctures of organisation and configuration of class relations (Poulantzas 1978: 309; 1979: 11–14; 2000: 208–209). In this regard, the exceptional state extends its relative autonomy vis-à-vis the dominant classes. It further advances the relative autonomy of the repressive state apparatuses and intensifies repression and "conducts an 'open war'" against the subordinate classes (Jessop 2014). The exceptional state is characterised by the suspension of the electoral principle—but not plebiscites/referenda—and the plural party system, the interruption of the rule of law to amend the Constitution and administration, and the subordination of the ideological state apparatuses to the repressive state apparatuses and dominant classes (Jessop 2008: 129–130).

---

10   Erdoğan publicly accepted the coalition between the AKP and the Gülen congregation in December 2013 when he proclaimed that "whatever [the Gülenists] wanted, we [the AKP] provided them" (*Sözcü* 2014).

This book considers the form and regime of exceptional state the AKP consolidated as a fascist form of state and regime (see Uysal 2019b). Fascism can be regarded as "an exceptional set of relations to politics made feasible and compelling" (Eley 2016: 112), and "a particular response to capitalist crisis" (Robinson 2019: 156) thriving from the paralysis of the state apparatus. Fascism is an exceptional form of state and regime corresponding to political crisis and the crisis of the state in the particular conjuncture of class conflict (Poulantzas 1979: 57–59). The fascist state and regime assume different concrete forms and relations and processes in different social formations in different phases of capitalism (Poulantzas 2008: 319). In the context of neoliberalism, the current phase of capitalism, fascism emerges in "the triangulation of transnational capital with reactionary political power in the state and neo-fascist forces in civil society" (Robinson 2019: 157). Nonetheless, fascism can be only understood in relation not to what it replicates about the past, but what it assumes to be original in response to the current crisis of neoliberalism and within its domestic milieux of the political and ideological struggles and the conjuncture of class conflict (Ahmad 2016: 190).

In Turkey, the AKP consolidated fascism by forming a new power bloc, which rested on MUSIAD-affiliated Islamic capital and the fractions of Islamic capital that had developed organic relations with Gulf capital, and which was supported by TUSIAD-affiliated finance capital and the fractions of capital that had developed organic relations with Western capital. The fascist state and regime absorbed and transformed two reactionary moments and forces, namely, the Turkish-Islamic Synthesis (TIS) and the counter-guerrilla (Oğuz 2023: 110).[11] In this regard, the AKP's fascism merged and transformed the TIS articulated by the junta of 1980 to suppress the organised left wing and working classes, and the counter-guerrilla formed as an anti-communist army in the aftermath of the Second World War. The amalgamation between the TIS and the counter-guerrilla and neoliberal Islamism was crucial regarding the AKP's

---

11   According to Oğuz (2023: 110), the AKP's fascism further absorbed Turkish-Sunni nationalism articulated by Kemalism in the 1920s and the 1930s, since Kemalism marginalised the non-Turkish and non-Sunni minorities, including the Kurdish, Alevi, Armenian, Greek, and so on. This book agrees with Oğuz that Kemalism marginalised the non-Turkish and non-Sunni minorities. However, this book argues that Turkish nationalism in the AKP's discourse remains fragile and ambivalent, and the AKP's Islamism fundamentally contradicts the secular nationalism formulated by Kemalism. Turkish nationalism articulated by the AKP is essentially a part of the Turkish-Islamic Synthesis, in which the Islamic element remains prominent. This contradiction is also recognised by Oğuz (2023: 110), that the AKP's emphasis on "the glorious past" of the Ottoman era opposes the secular Turkish nation-building pursued by Kemalism during the consolidation of capitalist relations.

open war against the left wing and the working classes. This book examines the period between 2014 and 2018 as a spiral of consolidation (2015–2016) and crisis and restoration (2016–2018) of the fascist state and regime.

2.1 The Consolidation of Fascism (2015–2016)

The transition to the exceptional state in Turkey brought about the restructuring of executive, legislative, and judiciary powers. The AKP facilitated this transition mainly through the constitutional amendments of 2010 (see Chapter 6). The consolidation of the fascist state beginning in 2014 enabled the AKP to increase its relative autonomy vis-à-vis the fractions of capital, including large-scale finance capital that had developed organic relations with Western capital. This was particularly important with regard to the AKP's power struggle against the Gülen congregation. The AKP targeted Gülen-affiliated capital through the extended relative autonomy of the fascist state. This can be illustrated with the seizure of Bank Asya by the Savings Deposit Insurance Fund (*Tasarruf Mevduatı Sigorta Fonu*) and the appointment of a new trustee in May 2015. Similarly, the Criminal Court appointed a new trustee to Koza Holding and its subsidiaries, including gold mines and media channels, in October 2015 (Demiralp 2016: 5–6).

In the election of June 2015, the AKP received 40.9 per cent of the vote, a drop from 49.9 per cent in the election of 2011 which caused the AKP to lose its parliamentary majority (Yeşilada 2016: 21). Despite the public calls for negotiations for a coalition government, the AKP stayed in power and forced a snap election in November 2015. Prior to the election of June 2015, the AKP government had already assumed the legislative function and overruled the Assembly owing to its majority. The fact that the AKP stayed in power following its loss of majority in the Assembly in June 2015 demonstrated the suspension of the electoral principle and the submission of the legislative under the executive.[12]

Between June and November 2015, Turkey suffered a series of terrorist attacks. In July 2015, in the Suruç province of Şanlıurfa, an Islamic State of Iraq and the Levant (ISIS) suicide bomber attacked a rally in support of Kurdish forces fighting against ISIS in Syria. In October 2015, ISIS bombing attacks targeted an Ankara demonstration bringing together several left-wing trade unions, including DISK and *Kamu Emekçileri Sendikaları Konfederasyonu* (Confederation of Public Employees' Trade Unions); professional associations, including *Türk*

---

12 The suspension of the electoral principle can be further illustrated by the arrest of a large group of HDP MPs, including the co-presidents, Figen Yüksekdağ and Selahattin Demirtaş, for their political statements regarding the Kurdish question, despite their parliamentary immunity. As of May 2023, Yüksekdağ and Demirtaş are still in prison.

Mühendis ve Mimar Odaları Birliği (Union of Chambers of Turkish Engineers and Architects) and *Türk Tabipleri Birliği* (Turkish Medical Association); the pro-Kurdish *Halkların Demokratik Partisi* (Peoples' Democratic Party, HDP); and a number of civil society organisations. The election of November 2015 took place under the shadow of these bloody events, to which the AKP responded with a more nationalist and militarist agenda. While President Erdoğan called the voters to unite around "'one nation, one flag, one homeland, and one state'", the AKP presented its success in the snap general election as "the only way out of chaos" (Şahin 2021: 24–25). Consequently, the AKP won a majority with 49.5 per cent in November 2015 (Yeşilada 2016: 21).[13]

2.2 The Abortive Coup of 2016

On 15 July 2016, certain factions within the military attempted to overthrow the AKP and Erdoğan by flying military jets over Ankara and Istanbul; bombarding the headquarters of police special forces and the police air force; and forcing Turkish Radio and Television (TRT) to announce the military's seizure of power. The coup-plotters were also active in several cities and provinces, including Adana, Malatya, Mersin, Sakarya, and Marmaris province of Muğla, where Erdoğan was on a holiday. The failed coup attempt saw more than 300 killed, more than 1,000 wounded, and thousands detained. The AKP soon presented the Gülen congregation, which the AKP referred to as the Fethullahist Terror Organisation (FETO), as the main culprit of the abortive coup (Kasapoğlu 2016). As the cumulative evidence demonstrated, the coup was apparently planned and carried out by disciples of the Gülen congregation (Yavuz and Koç 2016: 142). Even though the coup-plotters did not manifest a monolithic body and possibly involved different affiliations and orientations (Rodrik 2016), the larger body of supposedly secular nationalist-Kemalist elements did not support, and actively resisted, the coup (Azeri 2016: 465).

The AKP explained the failure of the coup attempt by making references to the handful of protestors on the streets mobilised following Erdoğan's call and the larger body of military officers resisting the coup-plotters (*Yeni Şafak* 2023). Even though the resistance of the larger body of military officers remained the key decisive factor, it remained the *explanandum* rather than the *explanan*.

---

13 The AKP's failure to obtain enough votes to form a single-party government in June 2015 compelled it to form an alliance with the MHP (Altınörs and Akçay 2022: 1038). At the time of writing, the alliance between the AKP and the MHP continues. This alliance was in line with the collapse of the Kurdish Opening/Peace Process, which involved negotiations between the AKP and the PKK between 2009 and 2015 and terminated following the Suruç attack in July 2015 (Savran 2020: 788).

This book argues that the coup-plotters did not fundamentally pose an alternative hegemonic project that challenged neoliberalism or political Islam. In this regard, they could not convince the resisting military officers to side with them, since their attempt could not obtain the consent of the dominant and subordinate classes. The Gülenist affiliation already cut across various social classes. For example, TUSKON and the trade unions, namely, *Aksiyon-İş* representing workers and *Cihan-Sen* representing civil servants, adhered to the Gülen congregation (Turan 2016: 11). However, these segments remained too small for the coup-plotters to form a power bloc and consolidate hegemony despite the possible support of their members. Furthermore, the position of hegemonic Western capital remained ambiguous. On the one hand, Western leaders declared their support for the AKP as a democratically elected government. On the other hand, a false report claiming that Erdoğan sought asylum in Germany was leaked to the Western media during clashes (Soylu 2016). This ambiguity demonstrated that Western capital and hence the advanced capitalist Western countries were cautious about the possibility that the coup attempt might have succeeded.

In response to the abortive coup, the AKP declared a state of emergency, which was prolonged seven times after its initial inception and enabled the AKP to rule the country by decrees between July 2016 and July 2018.[14] During the state of emergency, more than 400,000 people were subjected to judicial inquiry, of which tens of thousands of people were detained, and more than 100,000 people in civil service were purged without fair trial. More than three-dozen decrees were promulgated to amend the present law (IHOP 2018). The state of emergency can be considered to be an interim regime during which the AKP restored the fascist state and regime. The state of emergency further manifested an open war against the working classes in terms of labour rights and movements. The purges in the civil service and the private sector meant thousands of workers laid off without any concrete evidence, any means of defence, or access to a fair trial, and thus torn away from work and social security. The purges further disregarded the right to work as those workers were socially declared guilty and hence subjected to obstacles regarding finding replacement jobs in the private sector (Çelik and Altındiş 2019: 144). The

---

14 In April 2011, just two months before the election, the Assembly granted authority to the executive to rule the country by decrees for a period of six months. During this period, the AKP legislated thirty-five decrees to reorganise the civil service, including public administration and institutions, and personnel (see TMMOB 2011: 9–11). The decrees enacted in 2011, nevertheless, consolidated the authoritarian neoliberal state that fostered commodification, marketisation, commercialisation, and privatisation of public goods.

state of emergency also enabled the AKP to effectively suspend the exercise of labour rights, especially the right to strike, by banning industrial action and other forms of protests and demonstrations with references to national security. During the meeting of TOBB and *Uluslararası Yatırımcılar Derneği* (International Investors' Association) in July 2017, Erdoğan highlighted that the purpose of the state of emergency was to safeguard the rule of capital.

> We declared a state of emergency so that the business world could work in a comfortable environment. Do you have any troubles in the business world? When we came to power, there was a state of emergency. However, all factories were under the threat of industrial actions. Remember those days? Today, we see the opposite. Now, we take the advantage of state of emergency to intervene in any industrial action. We say we do not allow any strike here because [workers] cannot upset the business world.
> EVRENSEL 2017

Following a referendum in April 2017, the system of presidentialism was enacted. In June 2018, presidentialism came into force and Erdoğan was re-elected as president. The transition to presidentialism resolved the question of the system of government, which was provisional and fragile since the AKP and Erdoğan began to eliminate the Assembly in November 2015. This transition manifested the consolidation of the state-party regime since the fascist political party dominates the fascist state (Poulantzas 1979: 332). Most significantly, the transition to presidentialism nullified the president's responsibility to cut ties with their associated political party, a responsibility required for the impartiality of the president (Act on the Amendment of the Constitution 2017).

Following this transition, which signalled the end of the state emergency, Erdoğan began to rule the country by presidential decrees. In this sense, this transition demonstrated the restructuring of the state apparatus and hierarchies among the executive, the legislative, and the judiciary in favour of the executive, particularly the president. Significantly, the president assumed all duties and competences of the Cabinet. The president further assumed duties and competences of the Assembly since presidential decrees could amend the present law. The president did not have to abide by the law while promulgating presidential decrees, which were only subjected to the judicial review of the Constitutional Court (Barın 2022: 293–295). Between 2018 and 2022, Erdoğan promulgated ninety-eight presidential decrees, of which twenty-seven were original and seventy-one were amendments (Barın 2022: 297). The president also assumed judicial power by appointing judges at the supreme courts (Ardıçoğlu 2017: 25). The transition to presidentialism was essentially related to the open war against the working classes. Significantly, the place of the Commission to Determine Minimum Wage (*Asgari Ücret Tespit Komisyonu*) in the Labour Law was abolished and the Commission was placed under the authority of the president. Similarly, the duties and responsibilities of the State Supervisory Council (*Devlet Denetleme Kurulu*), whose head was appointed by the president, were extended to include the supervision of all public institutions, associations, foundations, and trade unions, and the authority to discharge the administrators of all these organisations (Pınar 2021: 42).

The fascist state, characterised by the continuous mobilisation of the masses, is dominated by an anti-intellectual, obscurantist, and racist ideology that addresses the power-fetishism of the petty bourgeoisie, constructs a cult of personality, glorifies violence, and grants special functions for education and the family (Poulantzas 1979: 253–256). The transition to presidentialism was armoured by a myth of revival merged with populism, where Erdoğan's cult of personality played the most crucial role in mobilising the masses and addressing their power-fetishism. The abortive coup of 2016 functioned as the key moment for the fascist myth, in which the people killed during clashes became "martyrs" and the restoration of the AKP rule became "the 15 July saga" (TCCB 2016b). Building on his image as "the voice of the deprived 'real people' and the champion of their interests against the old elites" and "the man of the people" (Yılmaz and Bashirov 2018: 1821), Erdoğan already became the chieftain (*reis*) of the masses. To illustrate, in September 2016, Erdoğan brought together neighbourhood chiefs (*muhtar*), who remained the most influential figures in small towns and villages, and consulted them about the extension of the state of emergency (Diken 2016).

Erdoğan's cult of personality was further merged with the special functions of education and family that aimed to mobilise young supporters for the fascist regime. Two civil society organisations, namely, *Türkiye Gençlik ve Eğitime Hizmet Vakfı* (Service for Youth and Education Foundation of Turkey, TURGEV) and *Kadın ve Demokrasi Derneği* (Women and Democracy Association, KADEM), emerged as important entities. TURGEV, which was founded by Erdoğan in 1996 and has since been run by Erdoğan's family, has been instrumental in attracting children from poor families by offering educational opportunities free of charge. TURGEV has also been instrumental in fostering organic relations between the executive and capital fractions, since it acts as "a quasi-official charity" of the regime by collecting enormous sums of donations from foreign and domestic companies, and in return providing them with advantageous deals with the government (Yılmaz and Bashirov 2018: 1820). Following the purge of the Gülen congregation from the field of education, TURGEV further developed organic relations with the Ministry of Education, reinforcing the Islamisation of education (Mertcan 2021: 185). KADEM was founded in 2013 as a government-organised NGOs that narrowed the defence of women's rights to the promotion of Islamic familialistic policies. To illustrate, KADEM's platforms for divorced people and family advocated initiatives against the already enacted legal amendments for gender equality to the detriment of women (Coşar 2021: 154). In this way, KADEM has been instrumental in terms of Islamising social reproduction and hence the youth.

3   The Fascist State and Regime and the Military (2015–2018)

The state of emergency between 2016 and 2018 and the transition to presidentialism beginning in 2017 manifested the consolidation, crisis, and restoration of the fascist state and regime. The restructuring of the fascist state mainly took place through the submission of state institutions as well as legislative, executive, and judiciary powers to the "triangle" of the president, the Ministry of the Interior, and the Ministry of Justice (Adar and Seufert 2021: 18). To begin with, the fascist state is characterised by the loss of regulatory power of the rule of law and the reign of "arbitrariness" (Poulantzas 1979: 322). The transition to the exceptional state beginning in the early 2010s restructured the judiciary to safeguard the primacy of the executive.[15] To illustrate, in February 2014, the Ministry of Justice was authorised to appoint the chief inspector of the HSYK, enabling the executive to undertake judicial power to decide whether a judge or a prosecutor had committed a crime (Oğuz 2023: 116). The supremacy of the executive over the judiciary manifested and reproduced the rule of arbitrariness. Significantly, in February 2016, Erdoğan stated that he rejected the ruling of the Constitutional Court, the highest legal authority in the country, requiring the release of detained journalists (TCCB 2016a). The rule of arbitrariness further manifested and reproduced the dysfunctionality of the state apparatus. For instance, in January 2018, the Istanbul High Criminal Court (*Ağır Ceza Mahkemesi*) ignored the ruling of the Constitutional Court that required the release of detained writers and journalists (Adar and Seufert 2021: 18). The dysfunctionality of the state apparatus corresponded to the growing relative autonomy of the state-party regime, whose aim was to favour Islamic capital. While the president frequently restructured public administration and institutions through regulations, decrees, and communiques, such administrative

---

15   The transition to the neoliberal authoritarian state beginning in the 1980s curtailed judicial power in favour executive power. Most significantly, Turgut Özal often violated the Constitution to foster especially privatisations (see Soysal 2005).

and legal changes often targeted public procurement and the construction sector, where Islamic capital was prominent (World Bank 2019: 57).[16]

The restructuring of the fascist state further brought about the politicisation of the state economic apparatuses and their relocation under the executive, particularly the president. Most significantly, in 2018, the Central Bank was submitted under the Ministry of Treasury and Finance (*Hazine ve Maliye Bakanlığı*, TCHMB), which merged the Treasury and the Ministry of Public Finance.[17] The TCHMB and hence the Central Bank were further submitted under the authority of the president (Oğuz 2023: 110–111), which held competence to appoint the head of the Central Bank and the monetary policy board members (Kutun 2020: 141). Therefore, the president was enabled to control not only the finances of public administration, but also monetary policy. This was in line with the AKP's class basis and aim to maintain low interest rates that were crucial for capital accumulation in labour-intensive and low-value-added sectors which were dependent on credit expansion (Boratav and Orhangazi 2022: 305). The politicisation of the state economic apparatuses and their relocation under the executive corresponded to the politicisation of the class struggle in the fascist state, whose effects "extend the contradictions within the [power] bloc itself" (Poulantzas 1979: 71), and the extended relative autonomy of the state-party regime. To illustrate, the Wealth Fund (*Varlık Fonu*) was established in 2016 as a discretionary fund that encompassed Treasury shares in the SOEs, ranging from major banks and the postal service to petroleum and mining companies. By 2021, the Fund, chaired by President Erdoğan, managed resources worth around 33.5 billion USD and amounting to 40 per cent of the central budget (Adar and Seufert 2021: 18). This enabled the AKP to utilise the Fund as a trump card to favour or punish the fractions of foreign and domestic capital.

In the fascist state, the ideological role of religious institutions might become prominent (Poulantzas 1979: 317). This is particularly valid regarding the Islamist regime of the fascist state in Turkey. In this sense, *Diyanet* became the most significant ideological state apparatus, fostering relations among several state institutions and government agencies, municipalities, civil society organisations, universities, and the media. *Diyanet*, whose status in public administration was promoted from a general directorate to an

---

16 The pattern of capital accumulation in the 2010s was often considered to be a construction-centred growth model (Orhangazi and Yeldan 2021: 476–480).
17 The emerging cleavages within the power bloc beginning in the early 2010s compelled the AKP to reform the central administration through decrees to politically control the Central Bank (Kutun 2020: 141–143).

under-secretariat, was charged with involvement in "'outside mosque' activities". Such activities included "'developing educational programmes, planning and implementation through cooperation with relevant government agencies and institutions, organising and monitoring activities'" and "'enlightening and guiding various sections of society, such as family, women, youth and others, in religious matters'" (Çitak 2020: 174). By 2020, *Diyanet* accessed a wide range of institutions, including schools and dormitories, youth centres and camps, prisons, hospitals, and social services, and a broad array of social groups, including disabled people, people with addictions, and immigrants (Çitak 2020: 174–175). Similarly, *Diyanet* signed co-operation protocols with the Ministries of Family and Social Policies, Foreign Affairs, Health, Justice, Interior, Education, Youth and Sports; the TRT; *Türkiye Belediyeler Birliği* (Union of Municipalities of Turkey); the Disaster and Emergency Management Presidency (AFAD); and Istanbul Zaim University (Diyanet 2023). Furthermore, the fascist party acts as "a *link* for the centralised cohesion" of the ideological state apparatuses it dominates (Poulantzas 1979: 333). In July 2018, *Diyanet* was submitted under the authority of the president (Decree No. 703 2018), reinforcing the primary role of the executive within the state apparatus in line with the state-party regime.

The fascist state, in which the relative autonomy of the repressive state apparatuses is extended, is characterised by the significance of the political police, which might not have a dominant role (Poulantzas 1979: 332). In Turkey, the politicisation of police and intelligence to consolidate the primacy of the executive was important regarding the restructuring of the fascist state. Beginning in 2015, the police, which was located under the Ministry of the Interior, replaced the judiciary by putting pressure on public prosecutors regarding counter-terrorism cases, keeping hold of inquiry dossiers, and stationing special police forces in courts, especially in southeast Anatolia (Oğuz 2023: 116). The police were further granted an ideological role with the introduction of nightwatchmen, which rather functioned as moral police (Şahin 2017). The ideological role of the police was in line with the Islamisation of the state apparatus, as the graduates of *imam-hatip* schools were promised privileged access to police recruitment (Babacan 2021: 134). Similarly, the MIT replaced the judiciary by gaining extraordinary competences, including in the gathering of information, documents, and data from any public or private institution without a judicial decision, in April 2014 (Act on the Amendment of the Law on National Intelligence 2014). The MIT, which was submitted under presidential authority in 2017, was tasked with the gathering of information about the on-duty and off-duty activities of military personnel (Decree No. 694 2017).

Regarding the extended relative autonomy of the repressive state apparatuses, the fascist state is further characterised by its support for paramilitary forces (Poulantzas 1979: 126). Following the transition to the exceptional state beginning in the early 2010s, the AKP supported paramilitary forces, significantly *Osmanlı Ocakları* (Ottoman Hearths), *Esedullah Timi* (Esedullah Task Force), and SADAT (*Uluslararası Savunma Danışmanlık İnşaat Sanayi ve Ticaret*, International Defence Consulting Construction Industry and Trade Inc.) (Oğuz 2016: 111–112). Ottoman Hearths, which amalgamated the organisational structures of the Grey Wolves and *Milli Görüş*, was instrumental in suppressing the protests against the AKP and mobilising AKP supporters, including during the constitutional referendum on presidentialism in 2017 (Çubukçu 2018). The Esedullah Task Force emerged in southeastern Anatolia and operated in urban areas, undertaking "revenge attacks" during the curfews (Dinçer 2020). SADAT, which was established by Islamist officers dismissed from the military in the 1990s, operated as a private security company from 2012 without being subjected to legal regulations or judicial oversight. SADAT's operations involved consultancy and military training, including irregular warfare (Toker 2016). In 2016, Erdoğan appointed Adnan Tanrıverdi, the head of SADAT, as his personal advisor (Bashirov and Lancaster 2018: 1223). SADAT allegedly trained and organised the Esedullah paramilitary groups active in urban warfare in 2015 as well as the mercenary groups active in Syria and Libya (Işık 2021: 244). The rise of paramilitary forces was also in line with the dysfunctionality of judiciary. In 2017, the paramilitary groups were safeguarded through the introduction of immunity to civilians and officials on duty regarding their activities to "thwart the failed coup attempt of July 2016 and its subsequent insurrections" (Decree No. 696 2017)

3.1   *The Reorganisation of the Military*

During the transition to the exceptional state in the early 2010s, the AKP restructured the military to curtail its political and judicial autonomy and submit it under civilian authority. In 2010, the AKP submitted military personnel to the jurisdiction of civilian courts and limited the jurisdiction of military courts in times of war by introducing judicial remedy (see Chapter 6). In July 2013, the Internal Service Act was amended to restrict the duty of the military to safeguard the Republican state and the country only against external threats (Act on the Amendment of Certain Laws and the Law on Contracted Non-Commissioned Military Officers 2013). This amendment sought to curtail the military's political role and locate the military under civilian authority by delegitimising any future military intervention with references to domestic threats.

Beginning in the mid-2010s, the reorganisation of the military was in line with the restructuring of the repressive state apparatuses in the fascist state, which submitted the military under the authority of the executive. This process reinforced the place of the military as the repressive state apparatus, on the one hand, and paralysed the military and reinforced the rule of arbitrariness on the other. The failed coup attempt of 2016 remained one of the most significant thresholds regarding the dysfunctionality of the state apparatus and the reign of arbitrariness under the state-party regime. In the aftermath of the abortive coup, the AKP did not claim any responsibility for its de facto coalition with the Gülen congregation and the staffing of the military with Gülenists. The majority of higher-ranking military officers among the coup-plotters had been appointed during the term of office of then-Chief of the General Staff Özel, who was appointed following the military officers' *resign en masse* as a response to the AKP's interference in the internal promotions of the military in July 2011 (see Chapter 6). Then-Chief of the General Staff Hulusi Akar and force commanders did not claim any responsibility for their gross negligence since these commanders had been previously warned by Ahmet Zeki Üçok, the former air force prosecutor, about the Gülenist staffing in the military. In fact, the coup-plotters involved these commanders' batmen and Akar was taken hostage by his own batman (İlter 2016).[18] Nonetheless, Akar was not invited to give a testimony before the parliamentary commission investigating the coup attempt. Akar was further appointed as the minister of defence in July 2018 (*Hürriyet* 2018).

Following the declaration of the state of emergency in 2016, the military and the institutions through which the military maintained its autonomy were reorganised to reinforce the power of the executive, particularly the president and the minister of defence. Most significantly, the commands of the army, navy, and air force were removed from the General Staff and submitted to the authority of the Ministry of Defence. The president was authorised to receive direct information from and give direct orders to the force commanders and their subordinates, who were to carry out such orders without further approval of the chief of the General Staff (Decree No. 669 2016). The Ministry of Defence was authorised to command the armed forces in peacetime, and the chief of the General Staff was to command the armed forces only during times of war (Decree No. 671 2016). The commands of gendarmerie and coast guard were also removed from the armed forces and submitted to the Ministry of the Interior (Decree No. 668 2016), transforming them into constabulary forces and reinforcing the primary role of the Ministry of the Interior in the executive.

---

18 Üçok, whose status as the military judge was revoked by the Ministry of Defence, was one of the detainees of the Sledgehammer trial (İlter 2016).

Moreover, the internal promotion of the military was restructured to reinforce the primacy of the executive, particularly the president, the Ministry of Defence, and the Ministry of the Interior. First, the chief of the General Staff was to be appointed from among four-star generals upon the nomination of the Cabinet and with the approval of the president (Decree No. 671 2016). Second, the Ministry of Defence and the Ministry of the Interior were authorised to approve the promotions of sub-lieutenants and colonels in the gendarmerie and the coast guard, replacing the authority of force commanders. Similarly, the president was authorised to approve the promotions of brigadier-generals as well as generals and admirals proposed by the Ministry of Defence and the Ministry of Interior—for the gendarmerie and coast guard (Decree No. 681 2017).

Furthermore, the Supreme Military Council was reorganised to include the ministers of justice, foreign affairs, and the interior alongside the prime minister, deputy prime minister, minister of national defence, and force commanders. This resulted in the withdrawal of the commander of the gendarmerie and four-star generals and admirals from the Council. Similarly, the role of the chief of the General Staff as the secretary-general of the Council was replaced by the minister of defence (Decree No. 669 2016).

The transition to presidentialism reinforced the supremacy of the executive over the military, particularly that of the Ministry of Justice and the president. In April 2017, the Military Court of Appeal, the Military Supreme Court of Administration, and other military courts were closed down, and military personnel were subjected to the jurisdiction of civilian courts. Military courts could be established with jurisdiction over military personnel only during wartime (Act on the Amendment of the Constitution 2017). This transformation reinforced the primacy of the Ministry of Justice, which assumed the powers of the executive and judiciary. In July 2018, the chief of the General Staff was submitted to the authority of the president through a presidential decree (Kaynar 2022: 389). The president was further authorised to determine the promotions of brigadier-generals, generals and admirals, and the appointment of the commanders of the gendarmerie and coast guard (Presidential Decree No. 3 2018).

The reorganisation of the military fundamentally corresponded to the restoration of capital accumulation in the field of war and defence industry in accordance with neoliberal principles, including commodification, privatisation, and commercialisation. During the state of emergency in 2017, the AKP aimed to restructure military factories and navy shipyards to respond to the needs of domestic and foreign capital by reorganising production, promoting partnerships, and fostering research and development. With this aim, *Askeri Fabrika ve Tersane İşletme Anonim Şirketi* (Military Factory and Shipyard Management,

ASFAT) was established (Decree No. 696 2017). From 2017, ASFAT established good relations with the civilian bureaucracies and militaries of Burkina Faso, Iraq, Libya, Pakistan, and the Philippines; signed agreements with the government bodies and military companies of Georgia and Kazakhstan; and exported ammunition to Togo (ASFAT 2023).[19] However, the advancement of capital accumulation in the war and defence industry was in line with the AKP's aim to curtail the military's economic autonomy. To illustrate, in 2017, the Inspection Board (*Teftiş Kurulu Başkanlığı*) was established under the Ministry of Defence with a duty to examine, inspect, and investigate the activities of companies in which the command forces and the Ministry as well as TSKGV individually or jointly had at least 50 per cent of shares (Decree No. 694 2017).

The reorganisation of the military was also in accordance with the Islamist regime of the fascist state. Significantly, war academies, military high schools, and non-commissioned officer preparation schools were closed during the state of emergency in 2016. *Milli Savunma Üniversitesi* (National Defence University, MSU) and *Jandarma ve Sahil Güvenlik Akademisi* (Gendarmerie and Coast Guard Academy) were established. The president was authorised to appoint the rector of the MSU, who was to be nominated by the minister of defence; the minister of defence was further authorised to determine the university curriculum (Decree No. 669 2016). In this way, the AKP fostered the Islamisation of military education. This process can also be illustrated by the transfer of *Gülhane Askeri Tıp Akademisi* (Gülhane Military Medical Academy) and other military hospitals to the Ministry of Health (Decree No. 669 2016), which has been staffed with the disciples of the Menzil congregation (Terkoğlu 2020).

The reorganisation of the military process further demonstrated the dynamics of unevenness and dependency. On the one hand, the extended relative autonomy of the fascist state enabled the AKP to enhance the relative autonomy of Turkey vis-à-vis the advanced capitalist Western countries and challenge the hegemony of the United States and the EU. Significantly, Minister of the Interior Süleyman Soylu, who remained in Erdoğan's close circle and represented a key organ of the fascist state, accused the United States of "being behind" the abortive coup of 2016 (Reuters 2021). The AKP dismissed several military officers who were assigned to NATO for their alleged involvement in the coup plot, such as the ordering of aerial refuelling of the rebel jets (*BirGün* 2016). The AKP's dismissals were heavily criticised by the United States and the EU as the purged officers were technically NATO officers (RT 2016). On the

---

19 For a critical discussion on the advanced military relations between Turkey and the Middle East, North Africa, and sub-Saharan Africa, see Uysal (2019c, 2021, forthcoming).

other hand, the AKP reproduced Western hegemony over Turkey, particularly that of the United States and the EU. Most significantly, the AKP continued to allow the United States to use the Incirlik Air Base and (NATO 2016). The AKP also continued to prevent the Aegean Sea from becoming a migratory route (NATO 2016) and maintained its adherence to the migrant readmission agreement with the EU (Corrao 2016). In this way, the AKP safeguarded a process that turned the Turkish military into the guardian of Western interests in the peripheries of world capitalism.

CHAPTER 8

Conclusion

> History has gone on till now, but goes on no longer.
> VLADIMIR ILYICH LENIN (1977 [1899])

∴

This book has examined state–military–society relations and military interventions in Turkey, a late-developing country, by exploring state–class–capital relations. In this regard, it has offered a critical/radical rebuttal of the dominant literature on civil–military relations (CMR). The main assumption of the dominant CMR literature is that the state, of which the military is a part, is a political organisation addressing the needs and demands of civil society consisting of propertied and unpropertied social classes. This assumption significantly narrows the question of the military's role in politics to the question of civilian control over the military in the nexus of the relationship between the military, and the government and civil society. The dominant CMR literature understands discrepancies regarding state–military–society relations in the peripheries of world capitalism as inorganic deviations from social, economic, and political institutions and practices of the advanced capitalist Western countries, where capitalism is thought to have delivered development. Therefore, it discusses military interventions in peripheries in relation to praetorianism, characterising the military with an inherent tendency to intervene in politics in the assumed context of underdevelopment. While the dominant CMR literature has tended to legitimise military interventions in peripheries as precursors of capitalist modernisation in the context of the Cold War, it has promoted political and economic reforms towards the consolidation of market economies, where civilian control of the military is ensured, in the aftermath of the Cold War.

This book further refuses the dominant literature on CMR in Turkey, which has mainly borrowed from seemingly opposing but interconnected approaches, namely, modernisation theory and the conservative-liberal paradigm, and has suffered from similar theoretical and conceptual inadequacies. Modernisation theory and the conservative-liberal paradigm share a similar understanding of development and its relationship with capitalism and state–military–society relations. Both approaches understand the process of capitalist modernisation in the advanced capitalist Western countries as an organic process bringing about development, as opposed to the supposedly top-down consolidation of capitalist modernisation pursued inorganically by the state in Turkey. Furthermore, both approaches understand the state (and its military) as an abstract and ahistorical political entity that can aspire to certain interests and goals on its own merits owing to its location external to and above social classes. Such similar—and implicit—understanding of the relationship between development and capitalism paradoxically compels them to arrive at distinct but similar conclusions regarding the political role of the military in Turkey, all of which have been disproved by the concrete realities of class struggles.

Modernisation theory's perception of the military as the guardian of the secular Republic and its inclination to credit military interventions as transitional processes until the consolidation of modernity have been disproved by the institutionalisation of the military's role in politics. More importantly, modernisation theory's assumptions were disproved by the coup of 1980, which incorporated Islamic symbols and references in the state's ideology and paved the way towards the rise of political Islam in the 1990s. Nonetheless, the conservative-liberal paradigm criticises modernisation theory and considers this guardianship role as a tutelary regime through which the military maintained its control over socioeconomically and sociopolitically marginalised groups in urban and rural areas. The "dissident but hegemonic" approach of the conservative-liberal paradigm (Yalman 2002: 23)—since the AKP rose to power in a milieu in which the conservative-liberal paradigm dominated the CMR literature on Turkey under Western hegemony—has been significantly disproved with the authoritarian and later exceptional transformation of the state under the AKP.

This book has offered a critical/radical and coherent framework borrowing from historical materialism/Marxism to examine the military interventions in Turkey in the context of late development. Development essentially indicates the development of productive forces, including labour and means of production. Late development indicates the late development of capitalist relations in temporal terms and sociohistorical particularities pertaining to the late development of capitalist relations in a given social formation. Late development has been conceptualised in relation to the dynamics of uneven and combined development, articulation of modes of production, and dependency. This conceptualisation has provided a critical and comprehensive conceptual framework to discuss the military's role in politics in Turkey as a particular sociohistorical form arising from class relations and patterns of capital accumulation in the nexus of Turkey's peripheral integration with the world capitalist system. In this regard, late development absorbs and redefines the notions of articulation and dependency in relation to unevenness arising from contradictions of expansion of capital accumulation and integration of peripheries into the world capitalist system. The conceptualisation of the capitalist state and military in accordance with class relations in its historical context further critically/radically and coherently refuses the perception of the state and the military in the dominant literature on CMR in Turkey.

1 From Concrete to Abstract: Late Development, the State, and the Military

The expansion and transformation of capitalist relations across the globe and the integration of peripheries into the world capitalist system are inherently contradictory processes, characterising peripheries with uneven development. The tendency of capital to concentrate in some spaces and marginalise other spaces—a tendency that creates unevenness—arises from competition as an essential element of capital accumulation. Competition, in return, compels latecomers to benefit from "the privilege of historic backwardness" (Trotsky 2008: 4) by adopting the latest advances, skipping the intermediate stages, and "substituting" or mobilising replacement mechanisms (Anievas 2015: 846). In this sense, unevenness brings about combinedness, characterising latecomers with "an amalgam of archaic with more contemporary forms". Consequently, social formations in late-developing countries represent complex and contradictory combinations of 'backwardness and leaps forward in development'.

The backward and archaic forms in late-developing social formations indicate the articulation of precapitalist and capitalist modes of production under the domination of the capitalist mode of production—which can never be found in its pure form—where contradictions are resolved through class relations. The backward and archaic forms further indicate structures, relations, and processes arising from dependency. Dependency refers to the primacy of dominant foreign capital to determine patterns of capital accumulation and class relations in late-developing social formations through confrontation with and the harmonisation of interests of foreign and domestic capitals. Even though such confrontation and later harmonisation bring about the domination of foreign capital, these processes create symbiotic relations between domestic and foreign capital through which domestic capital retains its relative autonomy vis-à-vis foreign capital.

In order to discuss concrete manifestations of backward and archaic forms, this book has periodised the integration of peripheries into the world capitalist system and the development of capitalist relations in peripheries in relation to the expansion and internationalisation of different circuits of capital and different patterns of capital accumulation. In the nineteenth century, during which the development of capitalist relations reached the point of no return in Turkey, peripheries were characterised as suppliers of raw material and agricultural products and as buyers of manufactured commodities, corresponding to the internationalisation of commercial capital accumulation. Beginning in the late nineteenth century, the internationalisation of finance capital—formed as a power bloc integrating the circuits of money capital, productive capital, and commodity capital under the conditions of monopolisation and internationalisation of capital—resulted in the rise of infrastructural investments in peripheries through foreign credit. Even though the period beginning in the late nineteenth century demonstrated the internationalisation of productive capital and financial circuits of capital, the expansion of commercial capital still dominated this period.

The expansion of foreign productive capital in peripheries beginning in the aftermath of the Second World War can be periodised into two stages, namely, import-substitution industrialisation (ISI) between the late 1940s and the late 1970s and export-oriented industrialisation (EOI) between the 1980s and the 1990s. ISI brought about the rise of industrialisation in peripheries in consumer durable and nondurable goods, relatively simple industrial machinery, and intermediate goods produced for the domestic market. ISI took place through the implementation of import-substitution policies and the expansion of foreign productive capital in the forms of intermediate and capital goods (commodity capital) and foreign credit and aid (money capital). EOI, which emerged as a response to ISI and the transition to neoliberalism, brought about the internationalisation of the internal capital of latecomers in the form of the export of durable and nondurable goods. EOI took place through the expansion of foreign capital in the form of foreign credit and aid (money capital) and foreign direct investments (productive capital).

Financial liberalisation and financialisation in peripheries beginning in the 1990s maintained the intensive and extensive accumulation of fictitious capital, on the one hand, and accelerated the internationalisation of production on the other hand. This process advanced the internationalisation of internal capital through various mechanisms, including financial inflows and outflows, mergers and acquisitions, joint ventures, and licence agreements. By the late 2010s, capital in late-developing countries had assumed three main fractions given that the internal capital was formed and internationalised: national, international, and transnational capital. The categorisation of capital fractions according to the stages in capital accumulation at which each fraction is integrated is important to understand antagonistic class interests bringing about the consolidation of hegemony as well as hegemonic crisis.

The conceptualisation of the state as a field of relations and struggles among classes and class fractions is important to understand the capitalist state as a concrete entity that has been structured and restructured in a particular historical context. The state in late-developing countries further diverges from that of the advanced capitalist Western countries since it represents the interests of dominant capital within the national social formation in the process of the internationalisation of capital, and such dominant capital remains foreign capital in the context of dependency. Different class configurations arising from diverse patterns of capital accumulation manifest distinctive forms of state, which can be examined in combination with forms of political regime. Since the military is understood as a repressive and coercive state apparatus, the articulation of the military alongside other repressive and ideological state apparatuses manifests the relations within the power bloc and determines the form of state. The military's organisation and its relations with social classes and civilian governments become a response to and a result of the changes in social, economic, and political structures and processes determining and manifested by the forms of state and regimes.

The military, which is not a monolithic entity but is characterised by divisions among the upper ranks and the middle and lower ranks, remains a special social category and holds a provisional place in the class configuration. The military's central place in the state apparatus combined with its fragile place in the class configuration enable it to intervene in times of hegemonic crises, during which fierce class struggles prevent the restructuring of patterns of capital accumulation and the reorganisation of class relations in latecomers. This tendency of the military to intervene in politics as an intermediary is particularly valid for late-developing social formations, as the uneven nature of world capitalism subjects peripheries to the major impacts of economic and political crises. Any successful military intervention obtains the consent of particular social classes and class fractions, mainly including certain fractions of the bourgeoisie, and coerces the opposing classes and class fractions so that a new power bloc can be established on the basis of the new pattern of capital accumulation. This point is important to understand that the bourgeoisie is willing to accept the suspension of a rather liberal political order representing bourgeois domination so that the capitalist social order can be preserved. To put this differently, the bourgeoisie "forfeit[s] the crown, and the sword" to the military "in order to save its purse" (Marx 1979: 143).

2 From Abstract to Concrete: State–Military–Society Relations in Turkey

This book has accepted Turkey as a late-developing country characterised by a transition to capitalism between the seventeenth and eighteenth centuries, and a consolidation of capitalism at the point of no return in the nineteenth century. Therefore, this book has discussed the modernisation of the military in the late-Ottoman era in relation to the expansion of capitalist relations under the dynamics of unevenness and dependency. By the early twentieth century, Turkey had become rather a semi-colony of the advanced capitalist Western countries, particularly Britain and France. Nonetheless, the country was characterised by manufacturing and industrial production limited to certain regions, including Istanbul, western and southern Anatolia, and coastal areas in the eastern Black Sea, and market-oriented agricultural production in southern and western Anatolia and Thrace. This was complemented by railways, docks, and mines across Anatolia and Thrace. Therefore, the late Ottoman Empire suffered from the conflicting interests of foreign and domestic dominant classes as well as the urban and rural subordinate classes. In this regard, both the revolution of 1908 and the revolution of 1923, which were pioneered by modernist fractions of the military, rested on fractions of the urban and rural dominant and subordinate classes. By abolishing the Ottoman *ancien régime* and securing the political independence of the country, the revolution of 1923 granted the military a role as the guardian of the secular modern Republic.

The aftermath of the Second World War brought about a contradictory process under the conditions of unevenness and dependency. On the one hand, the transition to multiparty politics abolished the state-party regime of the CHP, which had ruled the country between the 1930s and the early 1940s. On the other hand, Turkey was submitted under the hegemony of the United States, corresponding to the interests of landlords and the commercial bourgeoisie, both of which benefited from market-oriented agricultural production. This was particularly illustrated by the rise of the DP to power in 1950. In the face of the crisis of capital accumulation based on agricultural production and exports by the late 1950s, the DP lacked the class-ability to maintain the planned economy and import-substitution required for industrial capital accumulation. The combination of this DP inability with the rise of its authoritarianism brought about the coup of 1960, undertaken by lower- and middle-ranking military officers. The coup of 1960 again resulted in a contradictory process under the conditions of unevenness and dependency. On the one hand, it brought about planned ISI policies and the Constitution of 1960, which institutionalised liberal democracy and the welfare state in the context of late development. On the other hand, it reinforced Western hegemony, particularly that of the United States. It further institutionalised the guardianship role of the military by broadening its political, economic, and judicial autonomy.

The crisis of ISI in the late 1960s under the conditions of dependency on foreign capital was deepened by the rise of the urban and rural working classes and trade unions. Neither the CHP, representing the urban and rural subordinate classes, nor the AP, representing landlords and the commercial bourgeoisie, managed to respond to the needs of the industrial bourgeoisie and form the power bloc. Meanwhile, the military suffered from the disruption of its chain of command by the coup of 1960 and rising cleavages between the lower and middle ranks and the upper ranks. In the face of the prolonged hegemonic crisis, higher-ranking military officers intervened in politics with a memorandum in 1971 to suppress the working classes and purge the left-oriented factions within the military. The chain of command could only be maintained with the coup of 1980, which was a result of and a response to the questions the memorandum of 1971 could not solve and prolonged in the 1970s. The junta of 1980 paved the way towards the transition to neoliberalism by curtailing the power of trade unions and the working classes and suppressing left-wing and socialist movements. In order to do so, the junta incorporated Islamic symbols and references to the state's ideology, which marked the military's withdrawal of its secular modernising role. Nonetheless, the coup broadened and deepened the military's role in politics by expanding its political, economic, and judicial autonomy.

Beginning in the 1990s, Turkey witnessed the rise of political Islam, which was related to the formation and advancement of Islamic capital in the 1970s, and the utilisation of Islamic symbols and the legitimisation of religious brotherhoods by the junta of 1980 and the ANAP in the 1980s. *Milli Görüş* reinforced its role as the representative of Islamic capital, consisting of some large-scale capital alongside SMEs operating in the low-value-added and labour-intensive sectors; artisans and shopkeepers; the urban and rural working classes; the Islamist intelligentsia; and the university youth. In the face of the economic crises of the 1990s under financial liberalisation, combined with the inability of centre-left and centre-right parties to obtain the consent of the popular masses, the RP managed to form a coalition government. Nevertheless, the RP failed to form a power bloc because it mainly rested on small- and medium-scale capitalists and the petty bourgeoisie, and divided finance capital on the basis of Islamism. The RP favoured second-generation finance capital represented by MUSIAD through privatisations, whereas it alienated first-generation finance capital represented by TUSIAD, which had developed organic relations with

Western capital, through its anti-Western discourse. The RP further favoured Islamic capital by violating the rules and norms of the bourgeois order, such as by allowing the informal networks maintained by religious brotherhoods. The RP also alienated the military by challenging Western hegemony, particularly that of the United States, under which the Turkish armed forces were restructured beginning in the aftermath of the Second World War, and by challenging the principle of secularism on which the Republic was founded. Thus, the military intervened in politics on 28 February 1997 with a memorandum. However, the main purpose of the process of 28 February was to moderate—not to eliminate—political Islam in line with the bourgeois social and economic order under Western hegemony.

The 'lost decade' of the 1990s ended with the economic crisis of 2001, which further eroded the bonds between social classes and centre-right and centre-left political parties as a result of its major economic, social, and political impact. The AKP rose to power with its claim to have broken its links with *Milli Görüş* and by receiving the support of conservatives, liberals, liberal leftists, and marginalised sections of society, as well as the United States and the EU. By forming a power bloc under the hegemony of finance capital, the AKP undertook its hegemonic project of conservative democracy based on neoliberalism and political Islam. While conforming to the IMF framework and favouring TUSIAD, MUSIAD, and TUSKON through privatisations, deregulation of the labour market, fostering productive capital accumulation, and enhancing financial markets, the AKP obtained the consent of the urban and rural subordinate classes through redistributive mechanisms enabled by economic growth. The consolidation of its hegemony further enabled the AKP to submit the military to civilian authority in a de facto coalition with the Gülen congregation. This move was consented to by the higher ranks of the military, who co-operated with the AKP following the so-called e-memorandum of 2007 that brought about the defeat of the military vis-à-vis the AKP government. The AKP submitted the military to civilian authority by purging the critical wing through the Ergenekon and Sledgehammer trials and restructuring the economic, political, and judicial autonomy of the military through the constitutional amendments of 2010. While doing so, the AKP paved the way towards the staffing of the military by disciples of the Gülen congregation in line with its aim to Islamise the state apparatus.

Turkey staged the transition from a normal form to an exceptional form of state beginning in the early 2010s. The transition to neoliberalism beginning in the 1980s had brought about the emergence of authoritarian statism which had been consolidated by the AKP by the 2010s. The AKP's failure to maintain the transition from labour-intensive sectors to relative surplus production and the emergence of indications of an economic crisis were combined with the rise of a power struggle between the AKP and the Gülen congregation beginning in the 2010s. These manifestations of economic and political crisis were further aggravated by the rise of the resistance of the working classes. All these moments compelled the AKP to facilitate the transition from authoritarian statism to an exceptional form of state, particularly fascism. The fascist form of state was consolidated following the abortive coup of 2016, allegedly undertaken by disciples of the Gülen congregation. The consolidation of the fascist state brought about the restructuring of the military in line with the submission of the armed forces to the authority of executive power, which remained the ruling core of the fascist regime.

3   Concluding Remarks on the Crisis of Fascism

In 2018, the Turkish economy entered a period of combined recession and rising inflation as a result of the global financial crisis as well as the contradictions of the economic growth model the AKP had pursued since the mid-2010s. The long period of capital inflows beginning in the early 2000s resulted in the overvaluation of the Turkish lira for a long period, which brought about an increase in the dependency on imports and a decline in the industrial base in export-oriented sectors. This, in return, curbed the ability of increases in exports to recover the sudden decline in the value of the Turkish lira (Orhangazi and Yeldan 2021: 491). Moreover, the liberalisation of borrowing in foreign-exchange-denominated loans in the aftermath of the Great Recession of 2008–2009 coincided with the accelerating dollarisation of Turkey's deposit. The AKP responded to the growing indebtedness of the private sector with interest rate hikes and depreciation of the Turkish lira between 2015 and 2018 (Akçay and Güngen 2022: 305). Beginning in 2016, the Central Bank's policy of lowering interest rates was complemented by various credit support mechanisms that increased the current account deficit and external debt (Boratav and Orhangazi 2022: 293). Meanwhile, Turkey experienced growing political uncertainties in the international and domestic spheres, including the abortive coup of 2016 and a prolonged period of states of emergency; growing tension with NATO, the United States, and the EU; an increasing role to play in Syria; and a rapprochement with Russia and China (see Öniş and Kutlay 2021).

The sudden capital outflows in 2018 triggered a debt and currency crisis beginning in August 2018,[1] during which the Turkish lira lost more than 30 per cent of its value against the US dollar, and the national economy faced the possibility of a balance-of-payments crisis by 2020. This crisis brought about a wave of bankruptcy for hundreds of firms and a record-high level of unemployment. In response, the Central Bank increased its de facto policy rate from 12.8 per cent in January 2019 to 24 per cent in September 2019 (Akçay and Güngen 2022: 305), while utilising Central Bank reserves to stabilise the exchange rate, resulting in the depletion of the official reserves (Öniş and Kutlay 2021: 521).[2] The shock of the COVID-19 pandemic in 2020 further subjected the national economy to rapid capital outflows and sudden decreases in demand and supply (Boratav and Orhangazi 2022: 293).

The crisis of 2018–2019 took the form of a shock in relations of distribution (Boratav 2023). On the one hand, the AKP aimed to safeguard economic growth, despite the decrease in the economic growth rate. In fact, the average annual economic growth rate remained at 2.6 per cent in 2019 (Akçay and Güngen 2019: 1) and 1.8 per cent in 2020 (Boratav 2022: 614). Such economic growth was centred on the dependency on capital inflows as well as debt and credit expansion that mainly favoured the labour-intensive and low-value-added sectors where SMEs dominated in terms of their production and export. TUSIAD consented to the AKP's economic policy since it remained indifferent to lower interest rates owing to its ability to get loans in the international markets and continued to dominate production in and exports from Turkey. In this way, the AKP pursued an economic policy of lowering interest rates, expanding credits, issuing tax amnesties for the private sector, and cheapening the cost of labour (Orhangazi 2022). Most significantly, the average real wage decreased by 15 to 25 per cent—depending on the statistics for the inflation rate—between 2016 and 2022 (Boratav 2023).

On the other hand, the safeguarding of economic growth was translated into an increase in employment. The number of people employed increased by 2.1 million between 2020 and 2021 (TUIK 2022a), and by almost 2 million between 2021 and 2022 (TUIK 2023). Similarly, the rate of employment increased by 2.5 percentage points between 2020 and 2021 (TUIK 2022a), and

---

1 Unlike previous economic crises, during which the government's budget deficits and public borrowing constituted the basis of economic fragilities, the excessive and rapid expansion of domestic credit for the private sector rendered the national economy more vulnerable to capital flows (Orhangazi and Yeldan 2021: 489).
2 According to the IMF, Turkey had a relatively low reserve adequacy ratio and high external financing requirements in 2020 (Öniş and Kutlay 2021: 521).

by 2.3 percentage points between 2021 and 2022 (TUIK 2023). Furthermore, the AKP fostered redistributive mechanisms to gain the support of and mobilise the poorest sections of society in urban and rural areas. Total spending on social benefits sharply increased beginning in 2015 (Özdemir 2020: 257), demonstrating the AKP's resort to redistributive mechanisms in the face of the deteriorating conditions of the working classes. Total spending on social benefits increased by almost 21 per cent between 2019 and 2020 (TUIK 2021), and by almost 20 per cent between 2020 and 2021 (TUIK 2022b).

In May 2023, Erdoğan won the presidential election by receiving 52.18 per cent of the overall vote in the second round of the presidential election (YSK 2023b), and the AKP obtained 45.22 per cent of the overall vote (YSK 2023a). On the one hand, Erdoğan was not an ordinary presidential candidate and the AKP was not just a political party running in the election. Erdoğan and the AKP were the main agents of the state-party regime that had maintained extensive control over the state apparatus as well as executive, legislative, and judicial powers, and comprehensive control over the popular masses through its links with Islamic capital and religious brotherhoods. In this sense, the race between Erdoğan and Kemal Kılıçdaroğlu, chair of the CHP and the presidential candidate of the Opposition Alliance—also called the Nation Alliance (*Millet İttifakı*)—did not take place between equals. Furthermore, the AKP won the electoral race by establishing a wider alliance—called the People's Alliance (*Cumhur İttifakı*)—that brought together ultranationalists and Islamists, including the MHP, *Milli Görüş*, and the Sunni-Kurdish Hezbollah.

On the other hand, the failure of Kılıçdaroğlu and the Opposition Alliance was attributed to the crucial deficiencies and inadequacies of their political agenda. The Opposition Alliance involved centre-left and centre-right parties and dissident nationalists and Islamists, including prominent names with backgrounds in the AKP, *Milli Görüş*, and the MHP.[3] Even though Kılıçdaroğlu received the support of the Kurdish movement and socialist parties, the Opposition Alliance remained an ambivalent and hesitant bloc, consisting of a coalition between Islamism and conservatism and neoliberalism. In this sense, the Opposition Alliance did not offer a real alternative to the neoliberal Islamism of the state-party regime under Erdoğan and the AKP. Moreover, the Opposition Alliance targeted a small clique of Islamic capital favoured by the AKP through crony relations, rather than first- and second-generation finance capital, which continued to benefit from the AKP's economic policies

---

3 These names included Ahmet Davutoğlu and Ali Babacan, both of whom resigned from the AKP; Temel Karamollaoğlu, whose background was in *Milli Görüş*; and Meral Akşener, who was involved with both the AKP and the MHP.

owing to its dominant place in the national economy. Related to this point, the Opposition Alliance did not mobilise the working classes and popular masses against the fascist state and state-party regime, as well as TUSIAD and MUSIAD, and narrowed the meaning of democracy to elections and ballot boxes.[4]

The rise of the People's Alliance to power demonstrated the establishment of the most reactionary alliance, whose power reached beyond the Nationalist Front of the 1970s. Unlike the Nationalist Front, which only captured executive power, the AKP represented the state-party regime and the People's Alliance was consolidated at the heart of the fascist state and regime. Erdoğan's victory speech in May 2023 signalled that the state-party regime was prepared to resort to coercion and to mobilise paramilitary forces against the social and political opposition (TCCB 2023). The military's support for the AKP during the electoral campaign further demonstrates the AKP's control over the coercive and repressive state apparatuses (Çelik 2023).[5]

The fascist state is a form of state that is "at the extreme 'limit' of the capitalist state" (Poulantzas 1979: 57). The fascist state remains a "'brittle'" form that cannot "secure the sort of flexible, organic regulation of social forces and the smooth circulation of hegemony" (Jessop 2014). In this regard, the fascist state and regime represents the intensified internal contradictions of the state apparatus as well as class conflict. Since the transition from a normal state to an exceptional state involves political crises, breaks, and ruptures, the transition from an exceptional state to a normal state involves a series of crises and breaks and does not follow a continuous and linear path. The internal contradictions of the fascist state and regime, which are "the decisive factor" paving the way towards crises and ruptures, provide the working classes and wider popular masses with opportunities to "intervene in the actual realisation of this break" (Poulantzas 1976b: 97). The class character of the normal state, nevertheless, is determined by the outcome of the class struggle.

In Turkey, the working classes' support for the AKP clearly eroded from the mid-2010s and the AKP could only compensate such erosion by establishing the People's Alliance. More importantly, Kılıçdaroğlu received 47.82 per cent of the overall vote (YSK 2023b). This demonstrates that Turkish society has

---

4 Kılıçdaroğlu often legitimised the AKP's attempt to criminalise and abolish the freedom of peaceful assembly and the right to protest by discouraging the popular masses from "marching in the streets" and encouraging them to "wait for the elections" (Sayın 2022).
5 The Ministry of Defence set up a stand next to the AKP's election stand in the Üsküdar district of Istanbul in May 2023, where it presented military aircraft, drones, tanks, and warships (CNN Türk 2023). Significantly, the TCG *Anadolu* warship has been the object of AKP propaganda and featured in its electoral campaign (NTV 2023).

been polarised and divided into two, and nearly half of the population, and the working classes, do not want the AKP and Erdoğan in power. This suggests that the crisis of the fascist state and regime can only be targeted and dissolved through a true secular and pro-labour alternative to neoliberal Islamism and the organisation and mobilisation of the working classes and popular masses by trade unions and socialist and left-wing movements. This is particularly important to understand the significance of the formation of social and political resistance whose aim reaches beyond the supposed duality between the military and civilian authority when it comes to responses to political crises and crises of the state.

References

Primary Sources

Official Gazette

Act on the Amendment of Certain Laws and the Law on Contracted Non-Commissioned Military Officers, No. 6496. Official Gazette (OG) [*Resmi Gazete*], 28724, 31 July 2013.

Act on the Amendment of the Constitution, No. 6771. OG, 29976, 11 February 2017.

Act on the Amendment of the Law on National Intelligence, No. 6532. OG, 28983, 26 April 2014.

Act on the Amendment of the Law on the Establishment and Duties of the Supreme Military Council, No. 5400. OG, 7223, 3 June 1949.

Act on the Amendment of the Law on the Establishment and Duties of the Directorate of Religious Affairs, No. 5634. OG, 18202, 29 March 1950.

Act on the Amendment of the Turkish Penal Code, No. 5844. OG, 7979, 11 December 1951.

Act on the Amendment to the Law on Penal Proceeding and the Abolition of State Security Courts, No. 5190. OG, 25508, 30 June 2004.

Act on the Amendment to the Law on the State of Siege, No. 2301. OG, 17112, 21 September 1980.

Bylaw on the Prime Ministerial Crisis Management Centre, No. 96/8716. OG, 22872, 9 January 1997.

Civil Code, No. 743. OG, 339, 4 April 1926.

Code of Obligations, No. 818. OG, 366, 8 May 1926.

Communique No. 1 of the National Security Committee. OG, 17103 bis, 12 September 1980.

Communique No. 4 of the National Security Committee. OG, 17103 bis, 12 September 1980.

Constitution of the Turkish Republic. OG, 10859, 20 July 1961.

Constitution of the Turkish Republic. OG, 17863 bis, 9 November 1982.

Constitutional Act, No. 491. OG, 71, 20 April 1924.

Constitutional Act, No. 85. OG, 3, 7 February 1921.

Decision of the Supreme Electoral Council, No. 398. OG, 19572, 12 September 1987.

Decree No. 3/9548. OG, 7261, 18 July 1949.

Decree No. 32 on the Protection of the Value of Turkish Currency. OG, 20249, 11 August 1989.

Decree No. 668. OG, 29783, 27 July 2016.

Decree No. 669. OG, 29787, 31 July 2016.

Decree No. 671. OG, 29804, 17 August 2016.

Decree No. 681. OG, 29940 bis, 6 January 2017.

Decree No. 694. OG, 30165, 25 August 2017.

Decree No. 696. OG, 30280, 24 December 2017.

Decree No. 703. OG, 30473 bis, 9 July 2018.
Decree on Foreign Capital, No. 8/168. OG, 16880 bis, 12 January 1980.
Decree on Official Announcements and Advertisements, No. 4/1696. OG, 8555, 12 November 1953.
Foundations Law, No. 2762. OG, 3027, 13 June 1935.
Hat Law, No. 671. OG, 230, 28 February 1925.
Labour Law, No. 3008. OG, 3330, 15 June 1936.
Land Reform Law, No. 4753. OG, 6032, 15 June 1945.
Law on Foreign Capital Incentives, Law No. 6224. OG, 8615, 23 January 1954.
Law on Gendarmerie, No. 1706. OG, 1526, 22 June 1930.
Law on Industrial Promotion, No. 1055. OG, 608, 15 June 1927.
Law on Land Crops Tax, No. 4429. OG, 5423, 7 June 1943.
Law on Military Service, No. 1111. OG, 635, 17 July 1927.
Law on National Protection, No. 3780. OG, 4417, 26 January 1940.
Law on Primary Education, No. 222. OG, 10705, 12 January 1961.
Law on Protection of Freedom of Conscience and Assembly, No. 6187. OG, 8470, 29 July 1953.
Law on the Abolition of Titles and Appellations, No. 2590. OG, 2867, 29 November 1934.
Law on the Change of the Calendar, No. 698. OG, 260, 2 January 1926.
Law on the Closure of Dervish Convents and Tombs, and Abolition and Prohibition of the Office of Keeper of Tombs and Certain Titles, No. 677. OG, 243, 13 December 1925.
Law on the Establishment and Duties of the Ministry of Defence, No. 5398. OG, 7223, 3 June 1949.
Law on the Establishment and Proceedings of the State Security Courts, No. 1773. OG, 14591, 11 July 1973.
Law on the Establishment of Military Courts and Proceedings, No. 353. OG, 11541 bis, 26 October 1963.
Law on the Establishment of the Military Court of Appeal, No. 127. OG, 11280, 12 December 1962.
Law on the Establishment of the State Planning Organisation, No. 91. OG, 10621, 5 October 1960.
Law on the Establishment of the Supreme Military Council, No. 1612. OG, 14257, 26 July 1972.
Law on the Military Court of Appeal, No. 1600. OG, 14239, 8 July 1972.
Law on the Military High Court of Administration, No. 1602. OG, 14251, 20 July 1972.
Law on the Military Personnel Assistance Fund, No. 205. OG, 10702, 9 January 1961.
Law on the National Security Council and Secretary-General of the NSC, No. 2945. OG, 18218, 11 November 1983.
Law on the National Security Council, No. 129. OG, 11286, 19 December 1962.
Law on the Prohibition of Certain Garments, No. 2596. OG, 2879, 13 December 1934.

REFERENCES

Law on the Supreme Council of National Defence, No. 5339. OG, 7223, 3 June 1949.
Law on the Turkish Armed Forces Foundation, No. 3388. OG, 19498, 25 June 1987.
Law on Wealth Tax, No. 4305. OG, 5255, 12 November 1942.
Notice No. 28 on Corporate Tax. OG, 18675, 23 February 1985.
Penalty Code, No. 765. OG, 320, 13 March 1926.
Presidential Decree No. 3. OG, 30474, 10 July 2018.

Turkish Grand National Assembly Proceedings

Cumhuriyet Senatosu, 10th, vol. 64, 13 March 1971.
Cumhuriyet Senatosu, 18th, vol. 43, 17 May 1979.
Millet Meclisi, 1st, vol. 1, 27 November 1961.
Millet Meclisi, 3rd, vol. 1, 22 October 1969.
Millet Meclisi, 3rd, vol. 12, 31 March 1971.
Millet Meclisi, 4th, vol. 1, 29 January 1974.
Millet Meclisi, 4th, vol. 11, 6 April 1975.
Milli Güvenlik Konseyi, vol. 10, 12 October 1983.
Milli Güvenlik Konseyi, vol. 11, 1 November 1983.
TBMM (*Türkiye Büyük Millet Meclisi*), Period 1, 3rd legislative year, vol. 24, 30 October 1922.
TBMM, 2, 1st, vol. 3, 29 October 1923.
TBMM, 2, 1st, vol. 3, 30 October 1923.
TBMM, 2, 1st, vol. 7, 3 March 1924.
TBMM, 2, 2nd, vol. 14, 17 February 1925.
TBMM, 2, 2nd, vol. 15, 4 March 1925.
TBMM, 2, 2nd, vol. 18, 22 April 1925.
TBMM, 2, 3rd, vol. 25, 30 May 1926.
TBMM, 3, 1st, vol. 3, 9 April 1928.
TBMM, 4, 4th, vol. 25, 24 November 1934.
TBMM, 5, 1st, vol. 4, 10 June 1935.
TBMM, 5, 2nd, vol. 16, 5 February 1937.
TBMM, 8, 4th, vol. 15, 17 January 1949.
TBMM, 8, 5th, vol. 25, 1 March 1950.
TBMM, 9, 1st, vol. 1, 29 May 1950.
TBMM, 9, 5th, vol. 26, 14 December 1953.
TBMM, 11, 3rd, vol. 13, 18 April 1960.
TBMM, 11, 3rd, vol. 13, 29 April 1960.
TBMM, 1st, vol. 1, 22 October 1965.
TBMM, 5th, vol. 5, 28 March 1966.
TBMM, 17, 1st, vol. 1, 19 December 1983.
TBMM, 18, 4th, vol. 34, 15 November 1989.
TBMM, 20, 1st, vol. 7, 3 July 1996.

TBMM, 20, 2nd, vol. 30, 7 July 1997.
TBMM, 20, 2nd, vol. 33, 16 August 1997.
TBMM, 21, 1st, vol. 1, 2 May 1999.
TBMM, 21, 1st, vol. 1, 4 June 1999.
TBMM, 22, 1st, vol. 1, 23 November 2002.
TBMM, 22, 1st, vol. 6, 1 March 2003.
TBMM, 22, 1st, vol. 7, 15 March 2003.
TBMM, 23, 1st, vol. 1, 28 August 2007.
TBMM, 23, 4th, vol. 69, 6 May 2010.

Treaties, Protocols, Acts, and Regulations

Additional Protocol and Financial Protocol signed on 23 November 1970, annexed to the Agreement establishing the Association between the European Economic Community and Turkey. OJ L 293, 29 December 1972.

National Security Act of 1947. Public Law 253, 80th Congress; Chapter 343, 1st Session; S. 758.

NATO. The North Atlantic Treaty. 4 April 1949, Washington DC.

Court Decisions

Kavakçı v. Turkey, Sılay v. Turkey and Ilıcak v. Turkey. 71907/01, 8691/02 and 15394/02. European Court of Human Rights (ECHR) 2007.

Leyla Şahin v. Turkey. 44774/98. ECHR 2005.

Refah Partisi and Others v. Turkey. 41340/98, 41342/98, 41343/98 and 41344/98. ECHR 2003.

Official Documents, Reports, Memoirs, and Speeches

ABGS (Secretariat General for European Union). 2007. *Avrupa Birliği Uyum Yasa Paketleri*. Ankara: Dumat.

AKP. 2006. *Adalet ve Kalkınma Partisi: Kalkınma ve Demokratikleşme Programı.* Ankara: AK Parti Yayınları.

AKP. 2010. *12 Eylül'de Referanduma Evet.* Ankara: AK Parti Tanıtım ve Medya Başkanlığı.

AKP. 2012. *AK Parti 2023 Siyasi Vizyonu: Siyaset, Toplum, Dünya*. Ankara: AK Parti Yayınları.

Amnesty International. 2013. *Gezi Park Protests: Brutal Denial of the Right to Peaceful Assembly in Turkey.* London: Amnesty International.

ANAP. 1983. *Anavatan Partisi Programı*. Ankara: Tisa.

Ankara Barosu (Ankara Bar Association). 1999. *Devlet Güvenlik Mahkemeleri.* Ankara: Ankara Barosu İnsan Hakları Komisyonu Yayınları.

Ankara Devlet Güvenlik Mahkemesi Cumhuriyet Başsavcılığı (Public Prosecutor of the Ankara State Security Court). 1999. *Fethullah Gülen Örgütü Hakkında İddianame,* edited by Public Prosecutor Nuh Mete Yüksel (1920l). Ankara: Ankara Devlet Mahkemesi.

AP. 1969. *Adalet Partisi Programı*. Ankara: Orijinal Matbaa.

ASFAT. 2023. "Haberler". Accessed 25 May 2023, www.asfat.com.tr.

Atatürk, Mustafa Kemal. 2006. *Atatürk'ün Söylev ve Demeçleri*, vol. 1. Istanbul: Divan.

CHP. 1935. *The Party Programme of The Republican Party of The People*. Ankara: TBMM Matbaası.

CHP. 1946. *CHP Büyük Kurultayının Olağanüstü Toplantısı 10 Mayıs 1946*. Ankara: Ulus Basımevi.

CHP. 1948. *CHP 7. Büyük Kurultayı Tutanakları, 17 Kasım-4 Aralık 1947*. Ankara: Ulus Basımevi.

CHP. 1965. *CHP Söz Veriyor*. Ankara: Güzel Sanatlar Matbaası.

Corrao, Ignazio. 2016. *EU-Turkey Statement and Action Plan*. Accessed 25 May 2023, www.europarl.europa.eu/legislative-train/theme-towards-a-new-policy-on-migration/file-eu-turkey-statement-action-plan.

DGM'lere Karşı Özgürlük Girişimi [Freedom Initiative against the SSCs]. 1998. *Devlet Güvenlik Mahkemelerine Hayır*. Ankara: ÇHD Ankara.

Diyanet. 2023. "Din Hizmetleri, Duyurular". Accessed 19 May 2023, https://dinhizmetleri.diyanet.gov.tr/icerikler/Duyurular.

DP. 1946. *Demokrat Parti Tüzük ve Programı*. Ankara: Güneş Matbaacılık.

DP. 1951. *Demokrat Parti Tüzük ve Programı*. Ankara: Güneş Matbaacılık.

Ecevit, Bülent. 1966. *Ortanın Solu*. Ankara: Kim Yayınları.

Erbakan, Necmettin. 1991. *Adil Ekonomik Düzen*. Ankara: Semih Ofset Matbaacılık.

European Commission. 1989. *Commission Opinion on Turkey's Request for Accession to the Community*. Brussels.

EU. 2022a. "Accession Criteria". Accessed 12 March 2023, https://neighbourhood-enlargement.ec.europa.eu/enlargement-policy/glossary/accession-criteria_en.

EU. 2022b. "Convergence Criteria for Joining". Accessed 12 March 2023, https://economy-finance.ec.europa.eu/euro/enlargement-euro-area/convergence-criteria-joining_en.

IHOP (Human Rights Joint Platform). 2018. *21 July 2016–20 March 2018: State of Emergency in Turkey, Updated Situation Report*. Accessed 15 May 2023, www.ihop.org.tr/en/wp-content/uploads/2018/04/SoE_17042018.pdf.

IMF. 1947. *Annual Report of the Executive Directors for the Fiscal Year Ending 30 June 1947*. Washington DC.

IMF. 1999. "Letter of Intent, Turkey". Accessed 10 March 2023, www.imf.org/external/np/loi/1999/120999.htm.

IMF. 2000a. "Letter of Intent, Turkey". Accessed 10 March 2023, www.imf.org/external/np/loi/2000/tur/01/index.htm.

IMF. 2000b. "Letter of Intent, Turkey". Accessed 10 March 2023, www.imf.org/exter nal/np/loi/2000/tur/02/index.htm.
IMF. 2001. "Letter of Intent, Turkey". Accessed 11 March 2023, www.imf.org/external/np /loi/2001/tur/02/.
IMF. 2004. "Letter of Intent, Turkey". Accessed 12 March 2023, www.imf.org/exter nal/np/loi/2004/tur/01/index.htm.
MGK. 1997. *Milli Güvenlik Kurulu Toplantılarının Basın Bildirileri, 28 Şubat 1997*. Ankara: MGK Basın Bildirileri Arşivi.
MGK. 1999a. *Milli Güvenlik Kurulu Toplantılarının Basın Bildirileri, 23 Temmuz 1999*. Ankara: MGK Basın Bildirileri Arşivi.
MGK. 1999b. *Milli Güvenlik Kurulu Toplantılarının Basın Bildirileri, 29 Aralık 1999*. Ankara: MGK Basın Bildirileri Arşivi.
MGK. 2000. *Milli Güvenlik Kurulu Toplantılarının Basın Bildirileri, 31 Ocak 2000*. Ankara: MGK Basın Bildirileri Arşivi.
MGK. 2013. "Milli Güvenlik Kurulu ve Milli Güvenlik Kurulu Genel Sekreterliği hakkında Genel Bilgi". Accessed 10 May 2013, www.mgk.gov.tr/index.php/kurum sal/hakkimizda.
MNP. 1970. *Milli Nizam Partisi Program ve Tüzük*. Istanbul: As Matbaası.
NATO. 2016. "NATO Secretary General Thanks Turkey for Long-Standing Contribution to the Alliance". Accessed 25 May 2023, www.nato.int/cps/en/natohq/news_130 164.htm?selectedLocale=en.
Orekhov, Fedor. 1946. "The Soviet Charge at Washington to the Acting Secretary of the State, 7 August 1946". In *The Problem of the Turkish Straits*, edited by the United States Department of State, 47–49. Washington, DC: US Government Printing Office.
RP. 1985. *Refah Partisi Tüzük ve Programı*. Ankara: Elif Matbaası.
RP. 1991. *Refah Partisi Seçim Beyannamesi*. Ankara: Milsan.
RP. 1995. *Refah Partisi Seçim Beyannamesi*. Ankara.
SIPRI. 2023. SIPRI Military Expenditure Database. Accessed 31 March 2023, https: //milex.sipri.org/sipri.
TBMM. 2015. "Hükümetler". Accessed 10 November 2022, www5.tbmm.gov.tr/kutuph ane/e_kaynaklar_kutuphane_hukumetler.html.
TBMM Araştırma Komisyonu (Turkish Grand National Assembly Inquiry Committee). 2012. *Ülkemizde Demokrasiye Müdahale Eden Tüm Darbe ve Muhtıralar ile Demokrasiyi İşlevsiz Kılan Diğer Tüm Girişim ve Süreçlerin Tüm Boyutları ile Araştırılarak Alınması Gereken Önlemlerin Belirlenmesi Amacıyla Kurulan Meclis Araştırması Komisyonu Raporu*. 376, vol. 1–2, Ankara.
TCCB (Presidency). 2016a. "Anayasa Mahkemesi'nin Kararına Uymuyorum, Saygı da Duymuyorum". Accessed 18 September 2023, www.tccb.gov.tr/haberler/410/39955 /anayasa-mahkemesinin-kararina-uymuyorum-saygi-da-duymuyorum.html.

TCCB. 2016b. "15 Temmuz'da Bu Millet Yeniden Çanakkale Destanı Yazdı". Accessed 23 May 2023, www.tccb.gov.tr/haberler/410/55781/15-temmuzda-bu-millet-yeniden-canakkale-destani-yazdi.

TCCB. 2023. "Seçimin Ardından Külliye'de Yaptıkları Konuşma". Accessed 20 June 2023, www.tccb.gov.tr/konusmalar/353/147335/secimin-ardindan-kulliye-de-yaptiklari-konusma.

TCHMB. 2009. "Relations with World Bank Group". Accessed 15 June 2022. https://ms.hmb.gov.tr/uploads/sites/2/2009/01/World-Bank-Group-Relations.pdf.

TCMB (Central Bank). 1979. *Yıllık Rapor, 1978*. Ankara: TCMB.

TCMB. 1990. *Yıllık Rapor, 1989*. Ankara: TCMB.

TCMB. 1994. *Yıllık Rapor, 1993*. Ankara: TCMB.

TMMOB (Union of Chambers of Turkish Engineers and Architects). 2011. *AKP'nin KHK'leri ve TMMOB*. Ankara: Mattek.

Truman, Harry S. 1947. "Special Message to the Congress on Greece and Turkey: The Truman Doctrine", 12 March. Accessed 15 June 2022, www.trumanlibrary.gov/library/public-papers/56/special-message-congress-greece-and-turkey-truman-doctrine.

Truman, Harry S. 1949. "Inaugural Address", 20 January. Accessed 6 May 2022, www.trumanlibrary.gov/library/public-papers/19/inaugural-address.

TSK (Turkish Armed Forces). 1966. *Komünizmle Mücadele El Kitabı*. Ankara: Genelkurmay Basımevi.

TUIK (Turkish Statistical Institute). 2021. "Sosyal Koruma İstatistikleri, 2020". Accessed 14 June 2023, https://data.tuik.gov.tr/Bulten/Index?p=Sosyal-Koruma-Istatistikleri-2020-37193.

TUIK. 2022a. "İşgücü İstatistikleri, 2021". Accessed 14 June 2023, https://data.tuik.gov.tr/Bulten/Index?p=Isgucu-Istatistikleri-2021-45645.

TUIK. 2022b. "Sosyal Koruma İstatistikleri, 2021". Accessed 14 June 2023, https://data.tuik.gov.tr/Bulten/Index?p=Sosyal-Koruma-Istatistikleri-2021-45744.

TUIK. 2023. "İşgücü İstatistikleri, 2022". Accessed 14 June 2023, https://data.tuik.gov.tr/Bulten/Index?p=Isgucu-Istatistikleri-2022-49390.

World Bank. 2019. *Turkey Economic Monitor*. Washington, DC.

World Bank. 2023a. "GDP Growth, Turkiye". Accessed 10 March 2023, https://data.worldbank.org/indicator/NY.GDP.MKTP.KD.ZG?end=2021&locations=TR&start=1961.

World Bank. 2023b. "Unemployment, Total, Turkiye". Accessed 13 March 2023, https://data.worldbank.org/indicator/SL.UEM.TOTL.ZS?end=2008&locations=TR&start=2001.

YSK (Supreme Election Council). 2023a. "Karar No. 2023/1255". Accessed 14 June 2023, www.ysk.gov.tr/doc/karar/dosya/45639002/2023-1255.pdf.

YSK. 2023b. "Karar No. 2023/1269". Accessed 14 June 2023, www.ysk.gov.tr/doc/karar/dosya/46610370/2023-1269.pdf.

Secondary Sources

Books

Acemoğlu, Daron and James A. Robinson. 2006. *Economic Origins of Dictatorship and Democracy*. New York: Cambridge University Press.

Achcar, Gilbert. 2013. *Marxism, Orientalism, Cosmopolitanism*. London: Saqi.

Adar, Sinem and Günter Seufert. 2021. *Turkey's Presidential System after Two and a Half Years*. Berlin: Centre for Applied Turkey Studies.

Ahmad, Feroz. 1977. *The Turkish Experiment in Democracy 1950–1975*. London: C. Hurst & Company.

Ahmad, Feroz. 2003. *The Making of Modern Turkey*. London: Routledge.

Ahmad, Feroz. 2008a. *From Empire to Republic: Essays on the Late Ottoman Empire and Modern Turkey*, vol. 1. Istanbul: Bilgi University Press.

Ahmad, Feroz. 2008b. *From Empire to Republic: Essays on the Late Ottoman Empire and Modern Turkey*, vol. 2. Istanbul: Bilgi University Press.

Ahmad, Feroz. 2014. *The Young Turks and the Ottoman Nationalities: Armenians, Greeks, Albanians, Jews, and Arabs, 1908–1918*. Salt Lake City: University of Utah Press.

Akdoğan, Yalçın. 2004. *AK Parti ve Muhafazakar Demokrasi*. Istanbul: Alfa.

Akkaya, Yüksel. 2010. *Cumhuriyet'in Hamalları: İşçiler*. Istanbul: Yordam.

Akkoyunlu, Karabekir. 2007. *Military Reform and Democratisation*. London: International Institute for Strategic Studies.

Akşin, Sina. 1980. *100 Soruda Jön Türkler ve İttihat ve Terakki*. Istanbul: Gerçek Yayınevi.

Akşin, Sina. 2001. *Ana Çizgileriyle Türkiye'nin Yakın Tarihi*. Istanbul: İmaj Yayınevi.

Akyaz, Doğan. 2002. *Askeri Müdahalelerin Orduya Etkisi*. Istanbul: İletişim.

Allen, William Edward David and Paul Muratoff. 2011. *Caucasian Battlefields: A History of the Wars on the Turco-Caucasian Border, 1828–1921*. Cambridge: Cambridge University Press.

Althusser, Louis. 2014. *On the Reproduction of Capitalism*. London: Verso.

Amin, Samir. 1976. *Unequal Development: An Essay on the Social Formations of Peripheral Capitalism*. Hassocks: Harvester Press.

Amin, Samir. 2009. *Eurocentrism: Modernity, Religion, and Democracy*. New York: Monthly Review Press.

Anievas, Alexander and Kerem Nişancıoğlu. 2015. *How the West Came to Rule: The Geopolitical Origins of Capitalism*. London: Pluto.

Arat, Yeşim. 2005. *Rethinking Islam and Liberal Democracy: Islamist Women in Turkish Politics*. Albany, NY: SUNY Press.

Atay, Falih Rıfkı. 2009. *Çankaya*. Istanbul: Pozitif.

Avcı, Akif. 2022. *Unravelling the Social Formation: Free Trade, the State and Business Associations in Turkey*. Leiden: Brill.

Avcıoğlu, Doğan. 1996. *Türkiye'nin Düzeni: Dün, Bugün, Yarın*, vol. 1. Istanbul: Tekin.

Aydemir, Şevket Süreyya. 1991. *İkinci Adam, 1938–1950*. Istanbul: Remzi.
Aydemir, Şevket Süreyya. 1993. *Menderes'in Dramı*. Istanbul: Remzi.
Aydın, Zülküf. 2005. *The Political Economy of Turkey*. London: Pluto.
Ayubi, Nazih N. 2009. *Over-Stating the Arab State: Politics and Society in the Middle East*. London: I.B.Tauris.
Azak, Umut. 2010. *Islam and Secularism in Turkey: Kemalism, Religion and the Nation State*. London: I.B.Tauris.
Bağımsız Sosyal Bilimciler [BSB]. 2007. *IMF Gözetiminde On Uzun Yıl, 1998–2008*. Istanbul: Yordam.
Başkaya, Fikret. 1999. *Yediyüz, Osmanlı Beyliğinden 28 Şubata: Bir Devlet Geleneğinin Anatomisi*. Ankara: Ütopya.
Beaud, Michel. 1984. *A History of Capitalism, 1500–1980*. London: Macmillan.
Berberoglu, Berch. 1982. *Turkey in Crisis: From State Capitalism to Neo-Colonialism*. London: Zed.
Berkes, Niyazi. 1998. *The Development of Secularism in Turkey*. London: Hurst & Company.
Block, Fred L. 1977. *The Origins of International Economic Disorder*. Berkeley: University of California Press.
Bloxham, Donald. 2005. *The Great Game of Genocide: Imperialism, Nationalism, and the Destruction of the Ottoman Armenians*. Oxford: Oxford University Press.
Bora, Tanıl and Kemal Can. 2004. *Devlet, Ocak, Dergah*. Istanbul: İletişim.
Boratav, Korkut. 1980. *Tarımsal Yapılar ve Kapitalizm*. Ankara: AÜSBF Yayınları.
Boratav, Korkut. 2014. *Türkiye İktisat Tarihi, 1908–2002*. İmge: Ankara.
BSB. 2009. *Türkiye'de ve Dünyada Ekonomik Bunalım, 2008–2009*. Istanbul: Yordam.
BSB. 2011. *Derinleşen Ekonomik Kriz ve Türkiye'ye Yansımaları: Ücretli Emek ve Sermaye*. Istanbul: Yordam.
BSB. 2015. *AKP'li Yıllarda Emeğin Durumu*. Istanbul: Yordam.
Buğra, Ayşe and Osman Savaşkan. 2014. *New Capitalism in Turkey: The Relationship between Politics, Religion and Business*. Cheltenham: Edward Elgar Publishing.
Bulut, Faik. 1997. *Tarikat Sermayesinin Yükselişi*. Doruk: Ankara.
Çakır, Ruşen. 1991. *Ayet ve Slogan: Türkiye'de İslami Oluşumlar*. Istanbul: Metis.
Cammack, Paul, David Pool, and William Tordoff. 1993. *Third World Politics: A Comparative Introduction*. Basingstoke: Macmillan.
Carnoy, Martin. 1984. *The State and Political Theory*. Princeton, NJ: Princeton University Press.
Cemal, Hasan. 1989. *Özal Hikayesi*. Istanbul: Doğan Kitap.
Cengiz, Fatih Çağatay. 2020. *Turkey: The Pendulum between Military Rule and Civilian Authoritarianism*. Boston, MA: Brill.
Çeviker-Gürakar, Esra. 2016. *Politics of Favoritism in Public Procurement in Turkey: Reconfigurations of Dependency Networks in the AKP Era*. New York: Palgrave.

Cevizoğlu, Hulki. 2001. *Generalinden 28 Şubat İtirafı: "Postmodern Darbe"*. Ankara: Işık.
Çöklü, Şenol. 2014. *1. Meşrutiyet'ten Cumhuriyet'e Asker Alma Usulleri (Ahz-ı Asker)*. Ankara: Atatürk Araştırma Merkezi Yayınları.
Demirağ, Yavuz Selim. 2015. *İmamların Öcü*. Istanbul: Kırmızı Kedi.
Diamond, Larry and Marc F. Plattner (eds). 1996. *Civil-Military Relations and Democracy*. Baltimore, MD: Johns Hopkins University Press.
Divitçioğlu, Sencer. 1981. *Asya Üretim Tarzı ve Osmanlı Toplumu*. Kırklareli: Sermet.
Dowd, Douglas. 2004. *Capitalism and Its Economics: A Critical History*. London: Pluto.
Dunn, Bill. 2009. *Global Political Economy: A Marxist Critique*. London: Pluto.
Dunn, Bill. 2014. *The Political Economy of Global Capitalism and Crisis*. New York: Routledge.
Eligür, Banu. 2010. *The Mobilization of Political Islam in Turkey*. New York: Cambridge University Press.
Erdost, Muzaffer İlhan. 2005. *Asya Üretim Tarzı ve Osmanlı İmparatorluğunda Mülkiyet İlişkileri*. Ankara: Sol Yayınları.
Erickson, Edward J. 2021. *The Turkish War of Independence: A Military History, 1919–1923*. Santa Barbara, CA: Praeger.
Escobar, Arturo. 1995. *Encountering Development: The Making and Unmaking of the Third World*. Princeton, NJ: Princeton University Press.
Finer, Samuel E. 1969. *The Man on Horseback: The Role of the Military in Politics*. London: Pall Mall Press.
Frank, Andre Gunder. 1982. *Dependent Accumulation and Underdevelopment*. London: Macmillan.
Ganser, Daniele. 2004. *NATO's Secret Armies: Operation Gladio and Terrorism in Western Europe*. Abingdon: Frank Cass.
Gerger, Haluk. 1999. *Türk Dış Politikasının Ekonomi Politiği: Soğuk Savaş'tan "Yeni Dünya Düzeni"ne*. Istanbul: Belge.
Gözler, Kemal. 2000. *Türk Anayasa Hukuku*. Bursa: Ekin Yayınevi.
Grüsshaber, Gerhard. 2018. *The "German Spirit" in the Ottoman and Turkish Army, 1908–1938*. Berlin: De Gruyter.
Gürcan, Efe Can and Efe Peker. 2015a. *Challenging Neoliberalism at Turkey's Gezi Park*. New York: Palgrave.
Haldon, John. 1993. *The State and the Tributary Mode of Production*. London: Verso.
Hale, William. 1994. *Turkish Politics and the Military*. New York: Routledge.
Hale, William. 2013. *Turkish Foreign Policy since 1774*. Abingdon: Routledge.
Hanioğlu, M. Şükrü. 2001. *Preparation for a Revolution: The Young Turks, 1902–1908*. Oxford: Oxford University Press.
Hanioğlu, M. Şükrü. 2008a. *A Brief History of the Late Ottoman Empire*. Princeton, NJ: Princeton University Press.

Hasanli, Jamil. 2011. *Stalin and the Turkish Crisis of the Cold War, 1945–1953*. Plymouth: Lexington Books.
Haspolat, Evren. 2012. *Neoliberalizm ve Baskı Aygıtının Dönüşümü*. Ankara: Notabene.
Harvey, David. 2007. *A Brief History of Neoliberalism*. New York: Oxford University Press.
Harvey, David. 2010. *The Enigma of Capital and the Crises of Capitalism*. New York: Oxford University Press.
Heper, Metin. 1985. *The State Tradition in Turkey*. Beverley: Eothen Press.
Heper, Metin and Nur Bilge Criss. 2009. *Historical Dictionary of Turkey*. Toronto: Scarecrow Press.
Heywood, Andrew. 2017. *Political Ideologies: An Introduction*. London: Palgrave.
Hilferding, Rudolf. 1981. *Finance Capital: A Study of the Latest Phase of Capitalist Development*. London: Routledge & Kegan Paul.
Hilton, Rodney, Paul Sweezy, Maurice Dobb, Kohachiro Takahashi, Christopher Hill, Georges Lefebvre, Giuliano Procacci, Eric Hobsbawm, and John Merrington. 1978. *The Transition from Feudalism to Capitalism*. London: Verso.
Hobsbawm, Eric. 1995. *Age of Extremes: The Short Twentieth Century, 1914–1991*. London: Abacus.
Huntington, Samuel P. 1973. *Political Order in Changing Societies*. New Haven, CT: Yale University Press.
Huntington, Samuel P. 1991. *The Third Wave: Democratization in the Late Twentieth Century*. Norman: University of Oklahoma Press.
Hurewitz, Jacob Coleman. 1956. *Diplomacy in the Middle East: A Documentary Record, 1914–1956*, vol. 2. Princeton, NJ: D. van Nostrand Company.
İnsel, Ahmet. 1996. *Düzen ve Kalkınma Kıskacında Türkiye: Kalkınma Sürecinde Devletin Rolü*. Istanbul: Ayrıntı.
Janowitz, Morris. 1971. *The Military in the Political Development of New Nations: An Essay in Comparative Analysis*. Chicago, IL: University of Chicago Press.
Janowitz, Morris. 1977. *Military Institutions and Coercion in the Developing Nations*. Chicago, IL: University of Chicago Press.
Jenkins, Gareth. 2008a. *Political Islam in Turkey: Running West, Heading East?* New York: Palgrave.
Jessop, Bob. 1985. *Nicos Poulantzas: Marxist Theory and Political Strategy*. Basingstoke: Macmillan.
Jessop, Bob. 2008. *State Power: A Strategic-Relational Approach*. Cambridge: Polity.
Juvenal. 1998. *The Sixteen Satires*. London: Penguin.
Kansu, Aykut. 1997. *The Revolution of 1908 in Turkey*. Leiden: Brill.
Kansu, Aykut. 1999. *Politics in Post-Revolutionary Turkey, 1908–1913*. Leiden: Brill.
Karpat, Kemal H. 2013. *Türk Siyasi Tarihi*. Istanbul: Timaş.
Kasaba, Reşat. 1988. *The Ottoman Empire and the World Economy*. Albany, NY: SUNY Press.

Kazgan, Gülten. 2005. *Türkiye Ekonomisinde Krizler, 1929–2001*. Istanbul: Bilgi University Press.
Kazgan, Gülten. 2006. *Tanzimat'tan 21. Yüzyıla Türkiye Ekonomisi*. Istanbul: Bilgi University Press.
Kepenek, Yakup and Nurhan Yentürk. 2001. *Türkiye Ekonomisi*. Istanbul: Remzi.
Keyder, Çağlar. 1987. *State and Class in Turkey: A Study in Capitalist Development*. London: Verso.
Kiely, Ray. 2005a. *Industrialization and Development: A Comparative Analysis*. Bristol: Taylor & Francis.
Kiely, Ray. 2007. *The New Political Economy of Development: Globalization, Imperialism, Hegemony*. Basingstoke: Palgrave.
Kiely, Ray. 2010. *Rethinking Imperialism*. Basingstoke: Palgrave.
Kiely, Ray. 2015. *The BRICs, US "Decline" and Global Transformations*. New York: Palgrave.
Kirby, Fay. 1962. *Türkiye'de Köy Enstitüleri*. Ankara: İmece.
Koç, Yıldırım. 2012. *AKP ve Emekçiler*. Ankara: Epos.
Köymen, Oya. 2007. *Sermaye Birikirken: Osmanlı, Türkiye, Dünya*. Istanbul: Yordam.
Krueger, Anne O. 1974. *Foreign Trade Regimes and Economic Development: Turkey*. New York: National Bureau of Economic Research.
Krueger, Anne O. 2020. *International Trade: What Everyone Needs to Know*. New York: Oxford University Press.
Küçük, Yalçın. 1980. *Türkiye üzerine Tezler*, vol. 1. Istanbul: Tekin.
Küçük, Yalçın. 1985. *Planlama, Kalkınma ve Türkiye*. Istanbul: Tekin.
Kuru, Ahmet T. 2009. *Secularism and State Policies toward Religion: The United States, France, and Turkey*. Cambridge: Cambridge University Press.
Lewis, Bernard. 1968. *The Emergence of Modern Turkey*. New York: Oxford University Press.
Liebknecht, Karl. 1917. *Militarism*. New York: B. W. Huebsch.
Linz, Juan J. and Alfred Stepan. 1996. *Problems of Democratic Transition and Consolidation: Southern Europe, South America, and Post-Communist Europe*. Baltimore, MD: Johns Hopkins University Press.
Lipset, Seymour Martin. 1960. *Political Man: The Social Bases of Politics*. New York: Doubleday & Company.
Löwy, Michael. 2010. *The Politics of Uneven and Combined Development*. Chicago, IL: Haymarket.
Mango, Andrew. 1999. *Atatürk*. London: John Murray.
Marois, Thomas. 2012. *States, Banks and Crisis: Emerging Finance Capitalism in Mexico and Turkey*. Cheltenham: Edward Elgar.
Marx, Karl. 1976a. *Capital: A Critique of Political Economy*, vol. 1. London: Penguin.
Marx, Karl. 1977a. *Critique of Hegel's "Philosophy of Right"*. Cambridge: Cambridge University Press.

REFERENCES

Marx, Karl. 1991. *Capital: A Critique of Political Economy*, vol. 3. London: Penguin.
Marx, Karl. 1992a. *Capital: A Critique of Political Economy*, vol. 2. London: Penguin.
Marx, Karl and Friedrich Engels. 1998. *The German Ideology*. New York: Prometheus Books.
McGhee, George. 1990. *The US-Turkish-NATO Middle East Connection: How the Truman Doctrine Contained the Soviets in the Middle East*. New York: Palgrave.
McMichael, Philip. 2017. *Development and Social Change: A Global Perspective*. Los Angeles, CA: Sage.
Meşe, Ertuğrul. 2016. *Komünizmle Mücadele Dernekleri Türk Sağında Antikomünizmin İnşası*. Istanbul: İletişim.
Müderrisoğlu, Alptekin. 1990. *Kurtuluş Savaşı'nın Mali Kaynakları*. Ankara: Atatürk Araştırma Merkezi.
Nordlinger, Eric A. 1977. *Soldiers in Politics Military Coups and Governments*. New York: Prentice-Hall.
Okutan, M. Çağatay. 2004. *Bozkurt'tan Kur'an'a Milli Türk Talebe Birliği, 1916–1980*. Istanbul: Bilgi University Press.
Ollman, Bertell. 1996. *Alienation: Marx's Conception of Man in Capitalist Society*. Cambridge: Cambridge University Press.
Ollman, Bertell. 2003. *Dance of the Dialectic: Steps in Marx's Method*. Chicago: University of Illinois.
Olson, Robert. 1989. *The Emergence of Kurdish Nationalism and the Sheikh Said Rebellion, 1880–1925*. Austin: University of Texas Press.
Oyan, Oğuz. 1998. *Feodalizm ve Osmanlı Tartışmaları*. Ankara: İmaj.
Oyan, Oğuz. 2016. *Feodalizmden Kapitalizme, Osmanlı'dan Türkiye'ye*. Istanbul: Yordam.
Öz, İlkay. 2020. *Mülksüzleştirme ve Türkleştirme: Edirne Örneği*. Istanbul: İletişim.
Özbek, Kadir and Ali Suat Ertosun. 2010. *Hakimler ve Savcılar Yüksek Kurulu'na ilişkin Anayasa Değişikliği konusunda Analitik bir İnceleme*. Ankara: Adalet Bakanlığı Yayınları.
Özbudun, Ergun. 2000. *Contemporary Turkish Politics: Challenges to Democratic Consolidation*. Boulder, CO: Lynne Rienner.
Pamuk, Şevket. 1987. *The Ottoman Empire and European Capitalism, 1980–1913*. Cambridge: Cambridge University Press.
Pamuk, Şevket. 2018. *Uneven Centuries: Economic Development of Turkey since 1820*. Princeton, NJ: Princeton University Press.
Park, Bill. 2012. *Modern Turkey: People, State and Foreign Policy in a Globalized World*. Abingdon: Routledge.
Pehlivan, Barış and Barış Terkoğlu. 2012. *Sızıntı: Wikileaks'te Ünlü Türkler*. Istanbul: Kırmızı Kedi.
Peköz, Mustafa. 2009. *İslamcı Cumhuriyete Doğru: Türkiye'de Siyasal İslamın Dünü, Bugünü ve Yarını*. Istanbul: Kalkedon.

Perlmutter, Amos. 1977. *The Military and Politics in Modern Times: On Professionals, Praetorians and Revolutionary Soldiers.* New Haven, CT: Yale University Press.

Politzer, Georges. 1976. *Elementary Principles of Philosophy.* New York: International Publishers.

Poulantzas, Nicos. 1976a. *Classes in Contemporary Capitalism.* London: New Left Books.

Poulantzas, Nicos. 1976b. *The Crisis of Dictatorships: Portugal, Greece, Spain.* London: New Left Books.

Poulantzas, Nicos. 1978. *Political Power and Social Classes.* London: Verso.

Poulantzas, Nicos. 1979. *Fascism and Dictatorship: The Third International and the Problem of Fascism.* London: Verso.

Poulantzas, Nicos. 2000. *State, Power, Socialism.* London: Verso.

Przeworski, Adam. 1985. *Capitalism and Social Democracy.* Cambridge: Cambridge University Press.

Przeworski, Adam. 1991. *Democracy and the Market.* Cambridge: Cambridge University Press.

Quataert, Donald. 2002. *Ottoman Manufacturing in the Age of the Industrial Revolution.* Cambridge: Cambridge University Press.

Quataert, Donald. 2005. *The Ottoman Empire, 1700–1922.* New York: Cambridge University Press.

Rabasa, Angel M., Cheryl Benard, Peter Chalk, C. Christine Fair, Theodore Karasik, Rollie Lal, Ian Lesser, and David Thaler. 2004. *The Muslim World after 9/11.* Santa Monica, CA: RAND.

Rey, Pierre-Philippe. 1971. *Les Alliances de Classes.* Paris: François Maspero.

Riddell, John. 2012. *Toward the United Front: Proceedings of the Fourth Congress of the Communist International, 1922.* Leiden: Brill.

Riddell, John. 2015. *To the Masses: Proceedings of the Third Congress of the Communist International, 1921.* Leiden: Brill.

Rodinson, Maxime. 1973. *Islam and Capitalism.* New York: Pantheon.

Rostow, Walt W. 1991. *The Stages of Economic Growth: A Non-Communist Manifesto.* Cambridge: Cambridge University Press.

Roxborough, Ian. 1979. *Theories of Underdevelopment.* Atlantic Highlands, NJ: Humanities Press.

Saad-Filho, Alfredo. 2002. *The Value of Marx: Political Economy for Contemporary Capitalism.* London: Routledge.

Salt, Jeremy. 2019. *The Last Ottoman Wars: The Human Cost, 1877–1923.* Salt Lake City: University of Utah Press.

Savran, Sungur. 2016. *Türkiye'de Sınıf Mücadeleleri, 1908–1980.* Istanbul: Yordam.

Şener, Mustafa. 2010. *Türkiye Solunda Üç Tarz-ı Siyaset: Yön, MDD ve TİP.* Istanbul: Yordam.

Shaw, Stanford J. 2006. *The Ottoman Empire in World War I.* Ankara: Türk Tarih Kurumu.

Shaw, Stanford J. and Ezel Kural Shaw. 1977. *History of the Ottoman Empire and Modern Turkey: Reform, Revolution, and Republic: The Rise of Modern Turkey, 1808–1975*. Cambridge: Cambridge University Press.

Şık, Ahmet. 2011. *Dokunan Yanar*. Istanbul: Postacı.

Sönmez, Mustafa. 1987. *Türkiye'de Holdingler: Kırk Haramiler*. Ankara: Arkadaş.

Sönmez, Sinan. 2005. *Dünya Ekonomisinde Dönüşüm*. Ankara: İmge.

Tanör, Bülent. 1994. *İki Anayasa: 1961–1982*. Istanbul: Beta.

Taylor, John G. 1983. *From Modernisation to Modes of Production: A Critique of the Sociologies of Development and Underdevelopment*. London and Basingstoke: Macmillan.

Timur, Taner. 1998. *Osmanlı Çalışmaları: İlkel Feodalizmden Yarı Sömürge Ekonomisine*. Ankara: İmge.

Timur, Taner. 2003. *Türkiye'de Çok Partili Hayata Geçiş*. Ankara: İmge.

Timur, Taner. 2004. *Türkiye Nasıl Küreselleşti?* Ankara: İmge.

Timur, Taner. 2012. *Marx-Engels ve Osmanlı Toplumu*. Istanbul: Yordam.

Timur, Taner. 2013. *Türk Devrimi ve Sonrası*. Ankara: İmge.

Timur, Taner. 2014. *AKP'nin Önlenebilir Karşı-Devrimi*. Istanbul: Yordam.

Toprak, Binnaz. 1981. *Islam and Political Development in Turkey*. Leiden: Brill.

Toprak, Zafer. 1995. *Milli İktisat–Milli Burjuvazi*. Istanbul: Tarih Vakfı Yayınları.

Toprak, Zafer. 2019. *Türkiye'de Milli İktisat, 1908–1918*. Istanbul: İş Bankası Yayınları.

Trotsky, Leon. 1957. *The Third International after Lenin*. New York: Pioneer Publishers.

Trotsky, Leon. 1972. *Writings of Leon Trotsky, 1932–1933*. New York: Pathfinder Press.

Trotsky, Leon. 1979. *Writings of Leon Trotsky, Supplement, 1934–1940*. New York: Pathfinder Press.

Trotsky, Leon. 2008. *History of the Russian Revolution*. Chicago, IL: Haymarket.

Turfan, M. Naim. 2000. *Rise of the Young Turks: Politics, the Military and Ottoman Collapse*. London: I.B.Tauris.

Türkmen, Zekeriya. 2001. *Mütareke Döneminde Ordunun Durumu ve Yeniden Yapılanması, 1918–1920*. Ankara: TTK.

Uyar, Mesut. 2021. *The Ottoman Army and the First World War*. Abingdon: Routledge.

Wallerstein, Immanuel. 2006. *World-Systems Analysis: An Introduction*. Durham, NC: Duke University Press.

Weber, Max. 1947. *The Theory of Social and Economic Organization*. New York: Oxford University Press.

Weeks, John. 2018. *Limits to Capitalist Development: The Industrialization of Peru, 1950–1980*. New York: Routledge.

Yalçın, Soner and Doğan Yurdakul. 2003. *Reis: Gladio'nun Türk Tetikçisi*. Istanbul: Kırmızı Kedi.

Yavuz, M. Hakan. 2003. *Islamic Political Identity in Turkey*. New York: Oxford University Press.

Yavuz, M. Hakan. 2005. *Modernleşen Müslümanlar: Nurcular, Nakşiler, Milli Görüş ve AK Parti*. Istanbul: Kitap.

Yavuz, M. Hakan. 2013. *Toward an Islamic Enlightenment: The Gülen Movement*. New York: Oxford University Press.

Yeldan, A. Erinç. 2001. *Küreselleşme Sürecinde Türkiye Ekonomisi*. Istanbul: İletişim.

Yerasimos, Stefanos. 1975. *Azgelişmişlik Sürecinde Türkiye: Tanzimattan 1. Dünya Savaşına*, vol. 2. Istanbul: Gözlem.

Yerasimos, Stefanos. 1989. *Azgelişmişlik Sürecinde Türkiye: Dünya Savaşından 1971'e*, vol. 3. Istanbul: Belge.

Yılmaz, Murat. 2010. *2010 Referandumu: Siyasi Partilerin Tutumları*. Ankara: SETA.

Zürcher, Erik J. 1984. *The Unionist Factor: The Role of the Committee of Union and Progress in the Turkish National Movement, 1905–1926*. Leiden: Brill.

Zürcher, Erik J. 2007. *Turkey: A Modern History*. London: I.B.Tauris.

Zürcher, Erik J. 2010. *The Young Turk Legacy and Nation Building: From the Ottoman Empire to Atatürk's Turkey*. London: I.B.Tauris.

Book Chapters

Adaman, Fikret, Murat Arsel, and Bengi Akbulut. 2021. "Neoliberal Developmentalism, Authoritarian Populism, and Extractivism in the Countryside: The Soma Mining Disaster in Turkey". In *Authoritarian Populism and the Rural World*, edited by Ian Scoones, Marc Edelman, Saturnino M. Borras Jr., Lyda Fernanda Forero, Ruth Hall, Wendy Wolford, and Ben White, 154–176. Abingdon: Routledge.

Ahmad, Feroz. 2010. "Military and Politics in Turkey". In *Turkey's Engagement with Modernity*, edited by Celia Kerslake, Kerem Öktem, and Philip Robins, 92–116. London: Palgrave.

Akça, İsmet. 2010. "Ekonomide Askerin Varlığı, Askeri Sermaye, OYAK". In *Türkiye Siyasetinde Ordunun Rolü: Asker-Sivil İlişkileri, Güvenlik Sektörü ve Sivil Denetim*, edited by Nihal Boztekin, 17–26. Istanbul: Heinrich Boll Stiftung.

Akça, İsmet. 2013. "Türkiye'de Darbeler, Kapitalizm ve Demokrasi(sizlik)". In *Cumhuriyet Tarihinin Tartışmalı Konuları*, edited by Bülent Bilmez, 49–71. Istanbul: Tarih Vakfı Yayınları.

Akça, İsmet and Evren Balta-Paker. 2013. "Beyond Military Tutelage? Turkish Military Politics and the AKP Government". In *Debating Security in Turkey: Challenges and Changes in the Twenty-First Century*, edited by Ebru Canan Sokullu, 77–92. Plymouth: Lexington.

Akşin, Sina. 1988. "Siyasal Tarih, 1789–1908". In *Osmanlı Devleti, 1600–1908*, edited by Sina Akşin, 72–190. Istanbul: Cem.

Akşin, Sina. 2011. "Siyasal Tarih, 1995–2003". In *Bugünkü Türkiye, 1980–2003*, edited by Sina Akşin, 163–186. Istanbul: Cem.

REFERENCES

Alavi, Hamza. 1982. "The Structure of Peripheral Capitalism". In *Introduction to the Sociology of "Developing Societies"*, edited by Hamza Alavi and Teodor Shanin, 172–192. London: Macmillan.

Alemdar, Zeynep. 2020. "Courtrooms as Solidarity Spaces and Trials as Sentences: Defending Your Rights and Asking for Accountability in Turkey". In *Turkey's New State in the Making*, edited by Pınar Bedirhanoğlu, Çağlar Dölek, Funda Hülagü, and Özlem Kaygusuz, 206–225. London: Zed.

Ankarloo, Daniel. 2012. "The Welfare State". In *The Elgar Companion to Marxist Economics*, edited by Ben Fine, Alfredo Saad-Filho, and Marco Boffo, 379–383. Cheltenham: Edward Elgar.

Apeldoorn, Bastiaan van and Henk Overbeek. 2012. "Introduction: The Life Course of the Neoliberal Project and the Global Crisis". In *Neoliberalism in Crisis*, edited by Henk Overbeek and Bastiaan van Apeldoorn, 1–20. New York: Palgrave.

Atılgan, Gökhan. 2015a. "Tarımsal Kapitalizmin Sancağı Altında, 1950–1960". In *Osmanlı'dan Günümüze Türkiye'de Siyasal Hayat*, edited by Gökhan Atılgan, Cenk Saraçoğlu, and Ateş Uslu, 387–514. Istanbul: Yordam.

Atılgan, Gökhan. 2015b. "Sanayi Kapitalizminin Şafağında". In *Osmanlı'dan Günümüze Türkiye'de Siyasal Hayat*, edited by Gökhan Atılgan, Cenk Saraçoğlu, and Ateş Uslu, 515–656. Istanbul: Yordam.

Aykut, Ebubekir and Kansu Yıldırım. 2016. "Türkiye ve Körfez 'Sermaye'sinin Sınıfsal ve Siyasal Etkileri". In *Stratejik Barbarlık*, edited by Özay Göztepe, 143–160. Ankara: Nota Bene.

Aytekin, E. Attila. 2015. "Kapitalistleşme ve Merkezileşme Kavşağında, 1703–1908". In *Osmanlı'dan Günümüze Türkiye'de Siyasal Hayat*, edited by Gökhan Atılgan, Cenk Saraçoğlu, and Ateş Uslu, 39–88. Istanbul: Yordam.

Babacan, Errol. 2021. "Hegemony and Privileges: Reproduction of Islamism in Turkey". In *Regime Change in Turkey: Neoliberal Authoritarianism, Islamism and Hegemony*, edited by Errol Babacan, Melehat Kutun, Ezgi Pınar, and Zafer Yılmaz, 123–142. Abingdon: Routledge.

Balkan, Erol and Erinç Yeldan. 2002. "Peripheral Development under Financial Liberalization: The Turkish Experience". In *The Ravages of Neo-Liberalism: Economy, Society and Gender in Turkey*, edited by Neşecan Balkan and Sunger Savran, 39–54. New York: Nova Science.

Baubérot, Jean. 2001. "Laicisation, History of". In *International Encyclopaedia of the Behavioural and Social Sciences*, vol. 20, edited by Neil J. Smelser and Paul B. Baltes, 8238–8242. Amsterdam: Elsevier.

Bedirhanoğlu, Pınar. 2013. "Türkiye'de Neoliberal Otoriter Devletin AKP'li Yüzü". In *AKP Kitabı: Bir Dönüşümün Bilançosu*, edited by İlhan Uzgel and Bülent Duru, 40–65. Ankara: Phoenix.

Bedirhanoğlu, Pınar. 2020. "Social Constitution of the AKP's Strong State through Financialization: State in Crisis, or Crisis State?" In *Turkey's New State in the Making*, edited by Pınar Bedirhanoğlu, Çağlar Dölek, Funda Hülagü, and Özlem Kaygusuz, 23–40. London: Zed.

Bhargava, Rajeev. 1998. "What Is Secularism for?" In *Secularism and Its Critics*, edited by Rajeev Bhargava, 486–546. Delhi: Oxford University Press.

Bora, Tanıl. 2020. "Narrating the Enemy: Image and Perception of the 'Communists' among the Radical Right". In *Turkey in Turmoil: Social Change and Political Radicalization during the 1960s*, edited by Berna Pekesen, 137–151. Berlin: De Gruyter.

Bora, Tanıl and Yüksel Taşkın. 2009. "Sağ Kemalizm". In *Modern Türkiye'de Siyasi Düşüncenin Gelişimi: Kemalizm*, vol. 2, edited by Tanıl Bora and Murat Gültekingil, 529–554. Istanbul: İletişim.

Boratav, Korkut and Erinç Yeldan. 2006. "Turkey, 1980–2000: Financial Liberalization, Macroeconomic (In)-Stability, And Patterns of Distribution". In *External Liberalization in Asia, Post-Socialist Europe and Brazil*, edited by Lance Taylor, 417–455. New York: Oxford University Press.

Boratav, Korkut and Özgür Orhangazi. 2022. "Neoliberal Framework and External Dependency Versus Political Priorities, 2009–2020". In *Political Economy of Development in Turkey: 1838–Present*, edited by Emre Özçelik and Yonca Özdemir, 287–314. Singapore: Palgrave.

Bozarslan, Hamit. 2008. "Kurds and the Turkish State". In *The Cambridge History of Turkey: Turkey in the Modern World*, vol. 2, edited by Reşat Kasaba, 333–356. Cambridge: Cambridge University Press.

Bulaç, Ali. 2009. "Medine Vesikası ve Yeni bir Toplum Projesi: Tarihsel ve Sosyal Çevre". In *Modern Türkiye'de Siyasi Düşüncenin Gelişimi: İslamcılık*, vol. 6, edited by Tanıl Bora and Murat Gültekingil, 503–513. Istanbul: İletişim.

Bulut, Faik. 1999. "Örgütün Ekonomik Kaynakları". In *Batı ve İrtica*, 361–385. Istanbul: Kaynak.

Çakır, Ruşen. 2009. "Milli Görüş Hareketi". In *Modern Türkiye'de Siyasi Düşüncenin Gelişimi: İslamcılık*, vol. 6, edited by Tanıl Bora and Murat Gültekingil, 544–575. Istanbul: İletişim.

Çelik, Aziz and Emrah Altındiş. 2019. "The Labor Movement". In *Authoritarianism and Resistance in Turkey Conversations on Democratic and Social Challenges*, edited by Esra Özyürek, Gaye Özpınar, and Emrah Altındiş, 133–146. Cham: Springer.

Çelik, Nur Betül. 2009. "Kemalizm: Hegemonik bir Söylem". In *Modern Türkiye'de Siyasi Düşüncenin Gelişimi: Kemalizm*, vol. 2, edited by Tanıl Bora and Murat Gültekingil, 75–92. Istanbul: İletişim.

Çitak, Zana. 2020. "The Transformation of the State–Religion Relationship under the AKP: The Case of the Diyanet". In *Turkey's New State in the Making*, edited by

Pınar Bedirhanoğlu, Çağlar Dölek, Funda Hülagü, and Özlem Kaygusuz, 167–187. London: Zed.

Cizre-Sakallıoğlu, Ümit. 2002. "The Military and Politics: A Turkish Dilemma". In *Armed Forces in the Middle East: Politics and Strategy*, edited by Thomas Keaney and Barry Rubin, 189–205. London: Routledge.

Cohn, Lindsay, Damon Coletta, and Peter Feaver. 2018. "Civil–Military Relations". In *The Oxford Handbook of International Security*, edited by Alexandra Gheciu and William C. Wohlforth, 711–727. Oxford: Oxford University Press.

Çolak, Yılmaz and Ertan Aydın. 2004. "Dilemmas of Turkish Democracy: The Encounter between Kemalist Secularism and Political Islamism in the 1990s". In *Democracy and Religion: Free Exercise and Diverse Visions*, edited by David Odell-Scott, 202–220. Kent, OH: Kent State University Press.

Cornell, Vincent J. 1999. "Fruit of the Tree of Knowledge: The Relationship between Faith and Practice in Islam". In *The Oxford History of Islam*, edited by John L. Esposito, 63–106. Oxford: Oxford University Press.

Coşar, Simten. 2021. "Regime Change in Turkey: Old Symbols into New Settings". In *Regime Change in Turkey: Neoliberal Authoritarianism, Islamism and Hegemony*, edited by Errol Babacan, Melehat Kutun, Ezgi Pınar, and Zafer Yılmaz, 143–159. Abingdon: Routledge.

Coşkun, Mustafa Kemal and Burcu Şentürk. 2012. "The Growth of Islamic Education in Turkey: The AKP's Policies toward *Imam-Hatip* Schools". In *Neoliberal Transformation of Education in Turkey: Political and Ideological Analysis of Educational Reforms in the Age of the AKP*, edited by Kemal İnal and Güliz Akkaymak, 165–178. New York: Palgrave.

Demirel, Tanel. 2004. "Türk Silahlı Kuvvetlerinin Toplumsal Meşruiyeti üzerine". In *Bir Zümre, Bir Parti: Türkiye'de Ordu*, edited by Ahmet İnsel and Ali Bayramoğlu, 345–381. Istanbul: Birikim.

Diamond, Larry. 1989. "Introduction: Persistence, Erosion, Breakdown, and Renewal". In *Democracy in Developing Countries: Asia*, edited by Larry Diamond, Juan J. Linz, and Seymour Martin Lipset, 1–52. Boulder, CO: Lynne Rienner.

Diamond, Larry. 1997. "Introduction: In Search of Consolidation". In *Consolidating the Third Wave Democracies: Regional Challenges*, edited by Larry Diamond, Marc F. Plattner, Yun-han Chu, and Hung-mao Tien, xiii–xlvii. Baltimore, MD: Johns Hopkins University Press.

Diamond, Larry, Juan J. Linz, and Seymour Martin Lipset. 1995. "Introduction: What Makes for Democracy?" In *Politics in Developing Countries: Comparing Experiences with Democracy*, edited by Larry Diamond, Juan J. Linz, and Seymour Martin Lipset, 1–66. Boulder, CO: Lynne Rienner.

Dinler, Demet Şahende. 2017. "New Workers' Struggles in Turkey since the 2000s: Possibilities and Limits". In *The Class Strikes Back: Self-Organised Workers'*

Struggles in the Twenty-First Century, edited by Dario Azzellini and Michael G. Kraft, 217–237. Leiden: Brill.

Doğan, Ali Ekber. 2013. "İslamcı Sermayenin Gelişme Dinamikleri ve 28 Şubat Süreci". In *AKP Kitabı: Bir Dönüşümün Bilançosu*, edited by İlhan Uzgel and Bülent Duru, 283–306. Ankara: Phoenix.

Duménil, Gérard and Dominique Lévy. 2012. "Neoliberalism". In *The Elgar Companion to Marxist Economics*, edited by Ben Fine, Alfredo Saad-Filho, and Marco Boffo, 240–245. Cheltenham: Edward Elgar.

Edmunds, Timothy. 2013. "Security Sector Reform". In *The Routledge Handbook of Civil-Military Relations*, edited by Thomas C. Bruneau and Florina Cristiana Matei, 48–60. Abingdon: Routledge.

Eligür, Banu. 2014. "Turkey's Declining Democracy". In *Current Trends in Islamist Ideology*, vol. 17, edited by Hillel Fradkin, Husain Haqqani, Eric B. Brown, and Hassan Mneimneh, 151–175. Washington, DC: Hudson Institute.

Engels, Friedrich. 1975. "The Condition of England I & II". In *Marx-Engels Collected Works*, vol. 3, 469–513. Moscow: Progress Publishers.

Engels, Friedrich. 1987. "Dialectics of Nature". In *Marx-Engels Collected Works*, vol. 25, 313–590. Moscow: International Publishers.

Engels, Friedrich. 1988. "On Authority". In *Marx-Engels Collected Works*, vol. 23, 422–425. Moscow: International Publishers.

Ercan, Fuat and Şebnem Oğuz. 2020. "Understanding the Recent Rise of Authoritarianism in Turkey in Terms of the Structural Contradictions of the Process of Capital Accumulation". In *Turkey's New State in the Making*, edited by Pınar Bedirhanoğlu, Çağlar Dölek, Funda Hülagü, and Özlem Kaygusuz, 97–117. London: Zed.

Erdem, Nilgün. 2007. "A 'Hot' Debate: Financial Crises in Turkey, Mexico and South Korea". In *Neoliberal Globalization as New Imperialism: Case Studies on Reconstruction of the Periphery*, edited by Ahmet Köse, Fikret Şenses, and Erinç Yeldan, 129–152. New York: Nova.

Eres, Benan. 2007. "Economic Policy Regimes and the Profitability: The Turkish Economy, 1968–2000". In *Neoliberal Globalization as New Imperialism: Case Studies on Reconstruction of the Periphery*, edited by Ahmet Köse, Fikret Şenses, and Erinç Yeldan, 115–128. New York: Nova.

Evin, Ahmet. 1988. "Changing Patterns of Cleavages Before and After 1980". In *State, Democracy and the Military in Turkey in the 1980s*, edited by Metin Heper and Ahmet Evin, 201–214. Berlin: De Gruyter.

Gallissot, R. 1999. "Colonisation/Colonialisme". In *Dictionnaire critique du marxisme*, edited by Gérard Bensussan and Georges Labica, 189–193. Paris: PUF.

Garnett, Mark. 2010. "Conservatism". In *Encyclopedia of Political Theory*, edited by Mark Bevir, 282–286. Thousand Oaks, CA: Sage.

Gereffi, Gary. 1990. "Paths of Industrialization: An Overview". In *Manufacturing Miracles: Paths of Industrialization in Latin America and East Asia*, edited by Gary Gereffi and Donald L. Wyman, 3–31. Princeton, NJ: Princeton University Press.

Gramsci, Antonio. 1992a. "The Intellectuals". In *Selections from the Prison Notebooks of Antonio Gramsci*, edited by Quintin Hoare and Geoffrey Nowell Smith, 5–23. New York: International Publishers.

Gramsci, Antonio. 1992b. "State and Civil Society". In *Selections from the Prison Notebooks of Antonio Gramsci*, edited by Quintin Hoare and Geoffrey Nowell Smith, 206–276. New York: International Publishers.

Güney, Aylin. 2002. "The Military, Politics and Post-Cold War Dilemmas in Turkey". In *Political Armies: The Military and Nation Building in the Age of Democracy*, edited by Kees Koonings and Dirk Kruijit, 162–179. London: Zed.

Güngen, Ali Rıza and Ümit Akçay. 2016. "2007–2009 Krizi Sonrası Dünya Ekonomisinde Gelişmeler ve Türkiye'nin Siyasal-İktisadi Yönelimi". In *Stratejik Barbarlık*, edited by Özay Göztepe, 17–44. Ankara: Nota Bene.

Gürel, Burak. 2015a. "Türkiye'de Kırda Sınıf Mücadelelerinin Tarihsel Gelişimi". In *Marksizm ve Sınıflar*, edited by Sungur Savran, Kurtar Tanyılmaz and E. Ahmet Tonak, 303–385. Istanbul: Yordam.

Gürel, Burak. 2015b. "Islamism: Comparative-Historical Overview". In *The Neoliberal Landscape and the Rise of Islamist Capital in Turkey*, edited by Neşecan Balkan, Erol Balkan, and Ahmet Öncü, 13–40. New York: Berghahn.

Hanioğlu, M. Şükrü. 2008b. "The Second Constitutional Period, 1908–1918". In *The Cambridge History of Turkey: Turkey in the Modern World*, vol. 2, edited by Reşat Kasaba, 62–111. Cambridge: Cambridge University Press.

Harris, George S. 1988. "Role of the Military in Turkey in the 1980s: Guardians or Decision-Makers?" In *State, Democracy and the Military in Turkey in the 1980s*, edited by Metin Heper and Ahmet Evin, 177–200. Berlin: De Gruyter.

Harvey, David. 2011. "The Enigma of Capital and the Crisis This Time". In *Business as Usual: The Roots of the Global Financial Meltdown*, edited by Craig Calhoun and Georgi Derluguian, 89–112. New York: New York University Press.

Hendrick, Joshua D. 2015. "Globalization, Islamic Activism, and Passive Revolution in Turkey: The Case of Fethullah Gülen". In *The Neoliberal Landscape and the Rise of Islamist Capital in Turkey*, edited by Neşecan Balkan, Erol Balkan, and Ahmet Öncü, 235–271. New York: Berghahn.

Hoare, Quintin and Geoffrey Nowell Smith. 1992. "The Intellectuals: Introduction". In *Selections from the Prison Notebooks of Antonio Gramsci*, edited by Quintin Hoare and Geoffrey Nowell Smith, 3–4. New York: International Publishers.

Hoşgör, Evren. 2015a. "Islamic Capital". In *The Neoliberal Landscape and the Rise of Islamist Capital in Turkey*, edited by Neşecan Balkan, Erol Balkan, and Ahmet Öncü, 142–165. New York: Berghahn.

Hoşgör, Evren. 2015b. "The Question of AKP Hegemony: Consent without Consensus". In *The Neoliberal Landscape and the Rise of Islamist Capital in Turkey*, edited by Neşecan Balkan, Erol Balkan, and Ahmet Öncü, 201–234. New York: Berghahn.

İslamoğlu, Huri. 2017. "The Politics of Agricultural Production in Turkey". In *Neoliberal Turkey and its Discontents: Economic Policy and the Environment under Erdogan*, edited by Fikret Adaman, Bengi Akbulut, and Murat Arsel, 75–102. London: I.B. Tauris.

Johnston, David. 2010. "Liberalism". In *Encyclopedia of Political Theory*, edited by Mark Bevir, 795–802. Thousand Oaks, CA: Sage.

Jongerden, Joost. 2003. "Violation of Human Rights and the Alevis in Turkey". In *Turkey's Alevi Enigma*, edited by Paul J. White and Joost Jongerden, 71–89. Boston, MA: Brill.

Kalaycıoğlu, Ersin. 2006. "The Mystery of the Turban: Participation or Revolt?" In *Religion and Politics in Turkey*, edited by Ali Çarkoğlu and Barry Rubin, 91–110. Abingdon: Routledge.

Karaosmanoğlu, Ali. 1988. "Turkey and the Southern Flank: Domestic and External Contexts". In *NATO's Southern Allies: Internal and External Challenges*, edited by John Chipman, 287–353. London: Routledge.

Karaosmanoğlu, Ali. 1993. "Officers: Westernization, and Democracy". In *Turkey and the West: Changing Political and Cultural Identities*, edited by Metin Heper, Ayşe Öncü, and Heinz Kramer, 19–34. London: I.B.Tauris.

Karpat, Kemal H. 1988. "Military Interventions: Army–Civilian Relations in Turkey before and after 1980". In *State, Democracy and the Military in Turkey in the 1980s*, edited by Metin Heper and Ahmet Evin, 137–158. Berlin: De Gruyter.

Kayalı, Hasan. 2008. "The Struggle for Independence". In *The Cambridge History of Turkey: Turkey in the Modern World*, vol. 2, edited by Reşat Kasaba, 112–146. Cambridge: Cambridge University Press.

Keyman, E. Fuat. 2010. "Assertive Secularism in Crisis: Modernity, Democracy, and Islam in Turkey". In *Comparative Secularisms in a Global Age*, edited by Linell E. Cady and Elizabeth Shakman Hurd, 143–158. New York: Palgrave.

Kiely, Ray. 2005b. "The Crisis of Global Development". In *Globalisation and the Third World*, edited by Ray Kiely and Phil Marfleet, 25–46. London: Routledge.

Köker, Levent. 2009. "Kemalizm/Atatürkçülük: Modernleşme, Devlet ve Demokrasi". In *Modern Türkiye'de Siyasi Düşüncenin Gelişimi: Kemalizm*, vol. 2, edited by Tanıl Bora and Murat Gültekingil, 97–112. Istanbul: İletişim.

Kuehn, David. 2018. "Democratic Control of the Military". In *Handbook of the Sociology of the Military*, edited by Giuseppe Caforio and Marina Nuciari, 161–178. Cham: Springer.

Kuru, Ahmet T. 2007. "Changing Perspectives on Islamism and Secularism in Turkey: The Gulen Movement and the AK Party". In *The Muslim World and Politics in Transition: Contributions of Gulen Movement*, edited by Greg Barton, Paul Weller, and İhsan Yılmaz, 140–151. London: Leeds Metropolitan University Press.

Kutun, Melehat. 2020. "The AKP's Move from Depoliticization to Repoliticization in Economic Management". In *Turkey's New State in the Making*, edited by Pınar Bedirhanoğlu, Çağlar Dölek, Funda Hülagü, and Özlem Kaygusuz, 134–150. London: Zed.

Laçiner, Ömer. 2004. "Türk Militarizmi 1". In *Bir Zümre, Bir Parti: Türkiye'de Ordu*, edited by Ahmet İnsel and Ali Bayramoğlu, 13–28. Istanbul: Birikim.

Lenin, Vladimir Ilyich. 1974. "Imperialism, the Highest Stage of Capitalism". In *Lenin Collected Works*, vol. 22, 185–304. Moscow: Progress Publishers.

Lenin, Vladimir Ilyich. 1977. "The Development of Capitalism in Russia". In *Lenin Collected Works*, vol. 3, 21–607. Moscow: Progress Publishers.

Lipset, Seymour Martin. 1995. "Development, Economic". In *Encyclopaedia of Democracy*, vol. 2, edited by Seymour Martin Lipset, 350–356. Washington, DC: Routledge.

Looney, Robert E. 2014. "Introduction". In *Handbook of Emerging Economies*, edited by Robert E. Looney, 3–12. New York: Routledge.

Luce, Mathias. 2015. "Sub-Imperialism, the Highest Stage of Dependent Capitalism". In *BRICS: An Anti-Capitalist Critique*, edited by Patrick Bond and Ana Garcia, 27–44. London: Pluto.

Luxemburg, Rosa. 1971. "Order Reigns in Berlin". In *Selected Political Writings of Rosa Luxemburg*, edited by Dick Howard, 409–415. New York: Monthly Review Press.

Marx, Karl. 1975. "Economic and Philosophic Manuscripts of 1844". In *Marx-Engels Collected Works*, vol. 3, 229–346. Moscow: International Publishers.

Marx, Karl. 1976b. "The Poverty of Philosophy: Answer to the Philosophy of Poverty by M. Proudhon". In *Marx-Engels Collected Works*, vol. 6, 105–212. Moscow: International Publishers.

Marx, Karl. 1976c. "Moralising Criticism and Critical Morality". In *Marx-Engels Collected Works*, vol. 6, 312–340. Moscow: Progress Publishers.

Marx, Karl. 1977b. "The Bourgeoisie and the Counter-Revolution". In *Marx-Engels Collected Works*, vol. 8, 154–178. Moscow: Progress Publishers.

Marx, Karl. 1979. "The Eighteenth Brumaire of Louis Bonaparte". In *Marx-Engels Collected Works*, vol. 11, 99–197. Moscow: International Publishers.

Marx, Karl. 1980. "The Greek Insurrection". In *Marx-Engels Collected Works*, vol. 13, 70–72. Moscow: International Publishers.

Marx, Karl. 1992b. "A Contribution to the Critique of Hegel's Philosophy of Right". In *Early Writings*, 243–258. London: Penguin.

Marx, Karl. 1992c. "Preface to a Contribution to the Critique of Political Economy". In *Early Writings*, 424–428. London: Penguin.

Marx, Karl. 2018. "The Secret of Primitive Accumulation". In *Class: The Anthology*, edited by Stanley Aronowitz and Michael J. Roberts, 383–392. Oxford: Wiley Blackwell.

Matei, Florina Cristiana. 2013. "A New Conceptualization of Civil–Military Relations". In *The Routledge Handbook of Civil-Military Relations*, edited by Thomas C. Bruneau and Florina Cristiana Matei, 26–38. Abingdon: Routledge.

Mertcan, Hakan. 2021. "Laicism and the Struggle of Alevis against the Rise of Political Islam". In *Regime Change in Turkey: Neoliberal Authoritarianism, Islamism and Hegemony*, edited by Errol Babacan, Melehat Kutun, Ezgi Pınar, and Zafer Yılmaz, 179–195. Abingdon: Routledge.

Morrison, Kevin M. 2018. "The Washington Consensus and the New Political Economy of Economic Reform". In *The Oxford Handbook of the Politics of Development*, edited by Carol Lancaster and Nicolas van de Walle, 73–87. New York: Oxford University Press.

Oğuz, Şebnem. 2016. "'Yeni Türkiye'nin Siyasal Rejimi". In *'Yeni' Türkiye?: Kapitalizm, Devlet, Sınıflar*, edited by Tolga Tören-Melehat Kutun, 81–127. Istanbul: SAV.

Öngen, Tülin. 2002. "Political Crisis and Strategies for Crisis Management: From 'Low Intensity Conflict' to 'Low Intensity Instability'". In *The Politics of Permanent Crisis: Class, Ideology and State in Turkey*, edited by Neşecan Balkan and Sungur Savran, 55–84. New York: Nova Science Publishers.

Öniş, Ziya. 2006. "The Political Economy of Islam and Democracy in Turkey: From the Welfare Party to the AKP". In *Democratization and Development: New Political Strategies for the Middle East*, edited by Dietrich Jung, 103–128. New York: Palgrave.

Öniş, Ziya, and Fikret Şenses. 2009. "The new phase of neo-liberal restructuring in Turkey: an overview". In *Turkey and the Global Economy: Neo-liberal restructuring and integration in the post-crisis era*, edited by Ziya Öniş and Fikret Şenses, 1–10. New York: Routledge.

Öniş, Ziya, and Fikret Şenses. 2022. "Turkey's Encounter with Neoliberal Globalization and the Logic of Washington Consensus, 1980–1990". In *Political Economy of Development in Turkey: 1838–Present*, edited by Emre Özçelik and Yonca Özdemir, 197–226. Singapore: Palgrave.

Oran, Baskın. 2013. "2001–2012: 11 Eylül Olayı Ertesinde AKP Donemi: Uluslararası Ortam ve Dinamikler". In *Türk Dış Politikası*, vol. 3, edited by Baskın Oran, 11–50. Istanbul: İletişim.

Örnek, Cangül and Çağdaş Üngör. 2013. "Introduction: Turkey's Cold War: Global Influences, Local Manifestations". In *Turkey in the Cold War*, edited by Cangül Örnek and Çağdaş Üngör, 1–18. London: Palgrave.

Ozan, Ebru Deniz. 2015. "İki Darbe arasında Kriz Sarmalı". In *Osmanlı'dan Günümüze Türkiye'de Siyasal Hayat*, edited by Gökhan Atılgan, Cenk Saraçoğlu, and Ateş Uslu, 657–746. Istanbul: Yordam.

Özcan, Gencer. 2001. "The Military and the Making of Foreign Policy in Turkey". In *Turkey in World Politics: An Emerging Multiregional Power*, edited by Barry M. Rubin and Kemal Kirişçi, 18–30. Boulder, CO: Lynne Reiner.

Özdemir, Hikmet. 1990. "Siyasal Tarih, 1960–1980". In *Çağdaş Türkiye, 1908–1980*, edited by Sina Akşin, 191–263. Istanbul: Cem.

Özdemir, Hikmet. 2002. "1980 ve Sonrası". In *Türkler*, vol. 17, edited by Hasan Celal Güzel, Kemal Çiçek, and Salim Koca, 125–161. Ankara: Yeni Türkiye.

Özden, Barış Alp, İsmet Akça, and Ahmet Bekmen. 2017. "Antinomies of Authoritarian Neoliberalism in Turkey: The Justice and Development Party Era". In *States of Discipline*, edited by Cemal Burak Tansel, 189–210. London: Rowman & Littlefield.

Özel, Işık. 2010. "Political Islam and Islamic Capital: The Case of Turkey". In *Religion and Politics in Europe, the Middle East and North Africa*, edited by Jeffrey Haynes, 139–161. Abingdon: Routledge.

Öztürk, Özgür. 2015. "The Islamist Big Bourgeoisie in Turkey". In *The Neoliberal Landscape and the Rise of Islamist Capital in Turkey*, edited by Neşecan Balkan, Erol Balkan, and Ahmet Öncü, 117–141. New York: Berghahn.

Pelt, Mogens. 2008. "Adnan Menderes, Islam and his Conflict with the One-Party Era Establishment". In *Religion, Politics and Turkey's EU Accession*, edited by Dietrich Jung and Catharina Raudvere, 91–116. Basingstoke: Palgrave.

Pınar, Ezgi. 2021. "A Labour-Oriented Perspective on Regime Discussions in Turkey". In *Regime Change in Turkey: Neoliberal Authoritarianism, Islamism and Hegemony*, edited by Errol Babacan, Melehat Kutun, Ezgi Pınar, and Zafer Yılmaz, 32–48. Abingdon: Routledge.

Poulantzas, Nicos. 2008. "The Political Crisis and the Crisis of the State". In *The Poulantzas Reader: Marxism, Law and the State*, edited by James Martin, 294–322. London: Verso.

Pye, Lucian W. 1967. "Armies in the Process of Political Modernization". In *The Role of the Military in Underdeveloped Countries*, edited by John J. Johnson, 69–90. Princeton, NJ: Princeton University Press.

Rapoport, David C. 1962. "A Comparative Theory of Military and Political Types". In *Changing Patterns of Military Politics*, edited by Samuel P. Huntington, 71–100. New York: Free Press of Glencoe.

Rapoport, David C. 2021. "The Praetorian Army: Insecurity, Venality, and Impotence". In *Soldiers, Peasants, and Bureaucrats: Civil-Military Relations in Communist and Modernizing Societies*, edited by Roman Kolkowicz and Andrzej Korbonski, 252–280. New York: Routledge.

Rukavishnikov, Vladimir O. and Michael Pugh. 2018. "Civil–Military Relations". In *Handbook of the Sociology of the Military*, edited by Giuseppe Caforio and Marina Nuciari, 123–144. Cham: Springer.

Saleh, Mohamed. 2021. "The Middle East: Decline and Resurgence in West Asia". In *The Cambridge Economic History of the Modern World: 1870 to the Present*, edited by Stephen Broadberry and Kyoji Fukao, 213–250. Cambridge: Cambridge University Press.

Saraçoğlu, Cenk. 2015. "Tank Paletiyle Neoliberalizm". In *Osmanlı'dan Günümüze Türkiye'de Siyasal Hayat*, edited by Gökhan Atılgan, Cenk Saraçoğlu, and Ateş Uslu, 747–870. Istanbul: Yordam.

Saraçoğlu, Cenk and Melih Yeşilbağ. 2015. "Minare ile İnşaat Gölgesinde". In *Osmanlı'dan Günümüze Türkiye'de Siyasal Hayat*, edited by Gökhan Atılgan, Cenk Saraçoğlu, and Ateş Uslu, 871–957. Istanbul: Yordam.

Savran, Sungur. 2004. "20. Yüzyılın Politik Mirası". In *Sürekli Kriz Politikaları*, edited by Neşecan Balkan and Sungur Savran, 13–43. Istanbul: Metis.

Savran, Sungur. 2015. "Class, State, and Religion in Turkey". In *The Neoliberal Landscape and the Rise of Islamist Capital in Turkey*, edited by Neşecan Balkan, Erol Balkan, and Ahmet Öncü, 41–88. New York: Berghahn.

Schick, Irvin C. and E. Ahmet Tonak. 1987. "The International Dimension: Trade, Aid, and Debt". In *Turkey in Transition*, edited by Irvin C. Schick and E. Ahmet Tonak, 333–363. New York: Oxford University Press.

Schnabel, Albrecht. 2015. "Security Sector Reform as a Manifestation of the Security-Development Nexus? Towards building SSR Theory". In *Handbook of International Security and Development*, edited by Paul Jackson, 115–134. Cheltenham: Edward Elgar Publishing.

Şener, Mustafa. 2015. "Burjuva Uygarlığının Peşinde". In *Osmanlı'dan Günümüze Türkiye'de Siyasal Hayat*, edited by Gökhan Atılgan, Cenk Saraçoğlu, and Ateş Uslu, 195–340. Istanbul: Yordam.

Shils, Edward. 1967. "The Military in the Political Development of the New States". In *The Role of the Military in Underdeveloped Countries*, edited by John J. Johnson, 7–68. Princeton, NJ: Princeton University Press.

Şık, Ahmet and Deniz Çakırer. 2019. "The Gülen Community and the AKP". In *Authoritarianism and Resistance in Turkey Conversations on Democratic and Social Challenges*, edited by Esra Özyürek, Gaye Özpınar, and Emrah Altındiş, 81–92. Cham: Springer.

Stiglitz, Joseph E. 2008. "Is There a Post-Washington Consensus Consensus?" In *The Washington Consensus Reconsidered: Towards a New Global Governance*, edited by Narcís Serra and Joseph E. Stiglitz, 41–56. Oxford: Oxford University Press.

Strothmann, R. and Moktar Djebli. 2000. "Takkiyya". In *Encyclopaedia of Islam*, vol. 10, edited by Peri Bearman, Thierry Bianquis, Edmund Bosworth, E. J. van Donzel, and Wolfhart Heinrichs, 134–135. Leiden: Brill.

Sunar, İlkay. 1983. "Demokrat Parti ve Popülizm". In *Cumhuriyet Dönemi Türkiye Ansiklopedisi*, vol. 8, edited by Murat Belge, 2076–2086. Istanbul: İletişim.

Tanör, Bülent. 2011. "Siyasal Tarih, 1980–1995". In *Bugünkü Türkiye, 1980–2003*, edited by Sina Akşin, 27–162. Istanbul: Cem.

Tanyılmaz, Kurtar. 2015. "The Deep Fracture in the Big Bourgeoisie of Turkey". In *The Neoliberal Landscape and the Rise of Islamist Capital in Turkey*, edited by Neşecan Balkan, Erol Balkan, and Ahmet Öncü, 89–116. New York: Berghahn.

Taymaz, Erol and Ebru Voyvoda. 2022. "From Domestic to Global Crisis: Turkey During the 2001–2009 Period". In *Political Economy of Development in Turkey: 1838–Present*, edited by Emre Özçelik and Yonca Özdemir, 257–286. Singapore: Palgrave.

Tella, Torcuato S. Di. 1995. "Military Rule and Transition to Democracy". In *Encyclopaedia of Democracy*, vol. 3, edited by Seymour Martin Lipset, 836–841. Washington, DC: Routledge.

Toprak, Binnaz. 1988. "The State, Politics, and Religion in Turkey". In *State, Democracy and the Military in Turkey in the 1980s*, edited by Metin Heper and Ahmet Evin, 119–136. Berlin: De Gruyter.

Tünay, Muharrem. 1993. "The Turkish New Right's Attempt at Hegemony". In *The Political and Socioeconomic Transformation of Turkey*, edited by Atila Eralp, Muharrem Tünay, and Birol A. Yeşilada, 11–30. Westport, CT: Praeger.

Uslu, Ateş and E. Attila Aytekin. 2015. "Burjuva Devriminin ve Savaşın Belirsiz Sınırlarında". In *Osmanlı'dan Günümüze Türkiye'de Siyasal Hayat*, edited by Gökhan Atılgan, Cenk Saraçoğlu, and Ateş Uslu, 89–194. Istanbul: Yordam.

Uysal, Gönenç. Forthcoming. "Turkey's Foreign Policy in Sub-Saharan Africa: A Case of Sub-Imperialism". In *Turkey and the Global Political Economy: Geographies, Regions, and Actors in a Changing World Order*, edited by Mehmet Erman Erol, Görkem Altınörs, and Gönenç Uysal. London: I.B.Tauris.

Uzgel, İlhan. 2009. "ABD ve NATO'yla İlişkiler". In *Türk Dış Politikası*, vol. 2, edited by Baskın Oran, 34–82. Istanbul: İletişim.

Volpe, Tristan. 2010. "Modernization Theory". In *Encyclopedia of Political Theory*, edited by Mark Bevir, 895–899. Thousand Oaks, CA: Sage.

Weber, Max. 1994. "The Profession and Vocation of Politics". In *Weber: Political Writings*, edited by Peter Lassman and Ronald Speirs, 309–369. Cambridge: Cambridge University Press.

Weeks, John. 2012. "Dependency Theory". In *The Elgar Companion to Marxist Economics*, edited by Ben Fine, Alfredo Saad-Filho, and Marco Boffo, 96–101. Cheltenham: Edward Elgar.

Williamson, John. 2008. "A Short History of the Washington Consensus". In *The Washington Consensus Reconsidered: Towards a New Global Governance*, edited by Narcís Serra and Joseph E. Stiglitz, 14–30. Oxford: Oxford University Press.

Wilson, Bryan R. 1992. "Reflections on a Many-Sided Controversy". In *Religion and Modernization: Sociologists and Historians Debate the Secularization Thesis*, edited by Steve Bruce, 195–210. Oxford: Clarendon Press.

Wolpe, Harold. 1980. "Introduction". In *The Articulation of Modes of Production*, edited by Harold Wolpe, 1–44. London: Routledge & Kegan Paul.

Yalman, Galip. 2002. "The Turkish State and Bourgeoisie in Historical Perspective: A Relativist Paradigm or a Panoply of Hegemonic Strategies?" In *The Politics of Permanent Crisis: Class, Ideology and State in Turkey*, edited by Neşecan Balkan and Sungur Savran, 21–54. New York: Nova Science Publishers.

Yavuz, M. Hakan. 2009a. "Bediüzzaman Said Nursi ve Nurculuk". In *Modern Türkiye'de Siyasi Düşüncenin Gelişimi: İslamcılık*, vol. 6, edited by Tanıl Bora and Murat Gültekingil, 75–92. Istanbul: İletişim.

Yavuz, M. Hakan. 2009b. "Milli Görüş Hareketi: Muhalif ve Modernist Gelenek". In *Modern Türkiye'de Siyasi Düşüncenin Gelişimi: İslamcılık*, vol. 6, edited by Tanıl Bora and Murat Gültekingil, 591–603. Istanbul: İletişim.

Yeldan, A. Erinç. 2022. "The Era of Speculation-Led Growth and the 2001 Crisis, 1990–2001". In *Political Economy of Development in Turkey*, edited by Emre Özçelik and Yonca Özdemir, 227–256. Singapore: Palgrave.

Yıldırım, Deniz. 2013. "AKP ve Neoliberal Popülizm". In *AKP Kitabı: Bir Dönüşümün Bilançosu*, edited by İlhan Uzgel and Bülent Duru, 66–107. Ankara: Phoenix.

Yılmaz, Koray R. 2005. "Türkiye'de Kapitalizmin Gelişim Evreleri: Sermaye Birikimi/Sınıf Merkezli bir Çerçeve". In *Kapitalizm ve Türkiye*, vol. 1, edited by Fuat Ercan ve Yüksel Akkaya, 211–238. Ankara: Dipnot.

Yörük, Erdem. 2022. "The Politics of Welfare in Turkey". In *The Oxford Handbook of Turkish Politics*, edited by Güneş Murat Tezcür, 187–204. New York: Oxford University Press.

Journal Articles

Ahmad, Aijaz. 2016. "India: Liberal Democracy and the Extreme Right". *Socialist Register* 52: 170–192.

Akçay, Ümit. 2021. "Authoritarian Consolidation Dynamics in Turkey". *Contemporary Politics* 27(1): 79–104.

Akçay, Ümit and Ali Rıza Güngen. 2022. "Dependent Financialisation and Its Crisis: The Case of Turkey". *Cambridge Journal of Economics* 46: 293–316.

Akkaya, Yüksel. 2002a. "Türkiye'de İşçi Sınıfı ve Sendikacılık, I". *Praksis* 5: 131–176.

Akkaya, Yüksel. 2002b. "Türkiye'de İşçi Sınıfı ve Sendikacılık, II". *Praksis* 6: 63–101.

Akpınar, Nazlı and Sinan Araman. 2011. "Din ve Kapitalizm Sarmalında Milli Görüş Hareketi". *Praksis* 26: 77–100.

Albo, Gregory. 2004. "The Old and New Economics of Imperialism". *Socialist Register* 40: 88–113.

Allinson, Jamie C. and Alexander Anievas. 2009. "The Uses and Misuses of Uneven and Combined Development: An Anatomy of a Concept". *Cambridge Review of International Affairs* 22(1): 47–67.

Altınörs, Görkem and Ümit Akçay. 2022. "Authoritarian neoliberalism, crisis, and consolidation: the political economy of regime change in Turkey". *Globalizations* 19(7): 1029–1053.

Amin, Samir. 1991. "The Ancient World-Systems versus the Modern Capitalist World-System". *Review* 14(3): 349–385.

Angın, Merih and Pınar Bedirhanoğlu. 2012. "Privatization Processes as Ideological Moments: The Block Sales of Large-Scale State Enterprises in Turkey in the 2000s". *New Perspectives on Turkey* 47: 139–168.

Anievas, Alexander. 2015. "Revolutions and International Relations: Rediscovering the Classical Bourgeois Revolutions". *European Journal of International Relations* 21(4): 841–866.

Ardıçoğlu, M. Artuk. 2017. "Cumhurbaşkanlığı Kararnamesi". *Ankara Barosu Dergisi* 3: 23–25.

Ashman, Sam. 2009. "Capitalism, Uneven and Combined Development and the Transhistoric". *Cambridge Review of International Affairs* 22(1): 29–46.

Atlı, Altay. 2011. "Businessmen as Diplomats: The Role of Business Associations in Turkey's Foreign Economic Policy". *Insight Turkey* 13(1): 109–128.

Aydınlı, Ersel. 2009. "A Paradigmatic Shift for the Turkish Generals and an End to the Coup Era in Turkey". *Middle East Journal* 63(4): 581–597.

Aydınlı, Ersel. 2011. "Ergenekon, New Pacts, and the Decline of the Turkish 'Inner State'". *Turkish Studies* 12(2): 227–239.

Azeri, Siyaves. 2016. "The July 15 Coup Attempt in Turkey: The Erdogan–Gulen Confrontation and the Fall of 'Moderate' Political Islam". *Critique* 44(4): 465–478.

Barın, Taylan. 2022. "Cumhurbaşkanlığı Kararnamesi Uygulaması ve Hükümet Sisteminin Tahlili". *Yıldırım Beyazıt Hukuk Dergisi* 7(2): 289–314.

Bashirov, Galib and Caroline Lancaster. 2018. "End of Moderation: The Radicalization of AKP in Turkey". *Democratization* 25(7): 1210–1230.

Başkan, Filiz. 2005. "The Fethullah Gülen Community: Contribution or Barrier to the Consolidation of Democracy in Turkey?" *Middle Eastern Studies* 41(6): 849–861.

Belge, Murat. 2009. "Nationalism, Democracy and the Left in Turkey". *Journal of Intercultural Studies* 30(1): 7–20.

Berberoglu, Berch. 1981. "Turkey: The Crisis of the Neo-Colonial System". *Race and Class* 22(3): 277–291.

Berktay, Halil. 1987. "The Feudalism Debate: The Turkish End—is 'Tax—vs.—Rent' Necessarily the Product and Sign of Modal Difference?" *Journal of Peasant Studies* 14(3): 291–333.

Bilgin, Hasret Dikici. 2008. "Foreign Policy Orientation of Turkey's Pro-Islamist Parties: A Comparative Study of the AKP and Refah". *Turkish Studies* 9(3): 407–421.

Bina, Cyrus and Behzad Yaghmaian. 1990. "Post-War Global Accumulation and the Transnationalization of Capital". *Review of Radical Political Economics* 22(1): 78–97.

Boix, Carles and Susan Carol Stokes. 2003. "Endogenous Democratization". *World Politics* 55(4): 517–549.

Bölme, Selin M. 2007. "The Politics of Incirlik Air Base". *Insight Turkey* 9(3): 82–91.

Boran, Behice. 1962. "Metod Açısından Feodalite ve Mülkiyet: Osmanlılarda Mülkiyet Meselesi". *Yön* 1(51): 13.

Boratav, Korkut. 2022. "Kriz Ortamı ve Toplumsal Bunalım". *Mülkiye Dergisi* 46(2): 612–618.

Boukalas, Christos. 2014. "No Exceptions: Authoritarian Statism. Agamben, Poulantzas and Homeland Security". *Critical Studies on Terrorism* 7(1): 112–130.

Bozkurt, Umut. 2013. "Neoliberalism with a Human Face: Making Sense of the Justice and Development Party's Neoliberal Populism in Turkey". *Science and Society* 77(3): 372–396.

Brown, James. 1989. "The Military and Society: The Turkish Case". *Middle Eastern Studies* 25(3): 387–404.

Bryan, Dick. 1995. "The Internationalisation of Capital and Marxian Value Theory". *Cambridge Journal of Economics* 19: 421–440.

Buğra, Ayşe. 1998. "Class, Culture, and State: An Analysis of Interest Representation by Two Turkish Business Associations". *International Journal of Middle East Studies* 30(4): 521–539.

Buğra, Ayşe and Ayşen Candaş. 2011. "Change and Continuity under an Eclectic Social Security Regime: The Case of Turkey". *Middle Eastern Studies* 47(3): 515–528.

Callinicos, Alex. 1989. "Bourgeois Revolutions and Historical Materialism". *International Socialism* 2(43): 113–171.

Callinicos, Alex and Justin Rosenberg. 2008. "Uneven and Combined Development: The Social-Relational Substratum of 'The International'? An Exchange of Letters". *Cambridge Review of International Affairs* 21(1): 77–112.

Çarkoğlu, Ali. 2002. "Turkey's November 2002 Elections: A New Beginning?" *Middle East Review of International Affairs* 6(4): 30–41.

Çavdar, Ayşe. 2014. "Gülen Sect: Reached for the State, Got Capital Instead". *Perspectives* 8: 8–12.

Çeçen, A. Aydın, A. Suut Doğruel, and Fatma Doğruel. 1994. "Economic Growth and Structural Change in Turkey 1960–88". *International Journal of Middle East Studies* 26(1): 37–56.

Çelik, Aziz. 2010. "Muhafazakar Sosyal Politika Yönelimi: Hak Yerine Yardım-Yükümlülük Yerine Hayırseverlik". *Ankara Üniversitesi Siyasal Bilgiler Fakültesi Dergisi* 42: 63–81.

Çelik, Aziz. 2015a. "Turkey's New Labour Regime Under the Justice and Development Party in the First Decade of the Twenty-First Century: Authoritarian Flexibilization". *Middle Eastern Studies* 51(4): 618–635.

Çelik, Aziz. 2015b. "The Wave of Strikes and Resistances of the Metal Workers of 2015 in Turkey". *Research Turkey* 4(10): 21–37.

Çelik, Aziz. 2021. "Labour in Turkey during the 1960s: The Long Hot Decade of the Working Class". *Turkish Historical Review* 12(2/3): 265–293.

Cizre-Sakallıoğlu, Ümit. 1997. "The Anatomy of the Turkish Military's Political Autonomy". *Comparative Politics* 29(2): 151–166.

Cizre, Ümit. 2003. "Demythologyzing the National Security Concept: The Case of Turkey". *Middle East Journal* 57(2): 213–229.

Cizre, Ümit. 2004. "Problems of Democratic Governance of Civil–Military Relations in Turkey and the European Union Enlargement Zone". *European Journal of Political Research* 43: 107–125.

Coş, Kıvanç and Pınar Bilgin. 2010. "Stalin's Demands: Constructions of the 'Soviet Other' in Turkey's Foreign Policy, 1919–1945". *Foreign Policy Analysis* 6(1): 43–60.

Dalay, Galip and Dov Friedman. 2013. "The AK Party and the Evolution of Turkish Political Islam's Foreign Policy". *Insight Turkey* 15(2): 123–139.

Davidson, Neil. 2005. "How Revolutionary Were the Bourgeois Revolutions?" *Historical Materialism* 13(3): 3–33.

Davison, Andrew. 2003. "Turkey, a 'Secular' State? The Challenge of Description". *South Atlantic Quarterly* 102(2/3): 333–350.

Demiralp, Seda. 2016. "The Breaking Up of Turkey's Islamic Alliance: The AKP-Gülen Conflict and Implications for Middle East Studies". *Middle East Review of International Affairs* 20(1): 1–7.

Demirel, Tanel. 2005. "Lessons of Military Regimes and Democracy: The Turkish Case in a Comparative Perspective". *Armed Forces and Society* 31(2): 245–271.

Demirel, Taner. 2001. "Turkey's Troubled Democracy: Bringing the Socioeconomic Factors Back In". *New Perspectives on Turkey* 24: 105–140.

Denoeux, Guilain. 2002. "The Forgotten Swamp: Navigating Political Islam". *Middle East Policy* 9(2): 56–81.

Dirlik, Arif. 2007. "Global South: Predicament and Promise". *The Global South* 1(1): 12–23.

Doğan, Ali Ekber. 2011. "1994'ten Bugüne Neoliberal İslamcı Belediyecilikte Süreklilik ve Değişimler". *Praksis* 26: 55–76.

Dos Santos, Theotonio. 1970. "The Structure of Dependence". *American Economic Review* 60(2): 231–236.

Dufour, Mathieu and Özgür Orhangazi. 2009. "The 2000–2001 Financial Crisis in Turkey: A Crisis for Whom?" *Review of Political Economy* 21(1): 101–122.

Ehrenfeld, Rachel. 2011. "The Muslim Brotherhood Evolution: An Overview". *American Foreign Policy Interests* 33(2): 69–85.

Eley, Geoff. 2016. "Fascism Then and Now". *Socialist Register* 52: 91–117.

Elveren, Adem Y. 2008. "Social Security Reform in Turkey: A Critical Perspective". *Review of Radical Political Economics* 40(2): 212–232.

Ercan, Fuat and Şebnem Oğuz. 2015. "From Gezi Resistance to Soma Massacre: Capital Accumulation and Class Struggle in Turkey". *Socialist Register* 51: 114–135.

Ergüneş, Nuray. 2009. "Banka Sermayesi Üzerinden Sınıf İçi Çatışmaları Anlamak". *Praksis* 19: 133–156.

Esen, Berk and Şebnem Gümüşçü. 2016. "Rising Competitive Authoritarianism in Turkey". *Third World Quarterly* 37(9): 1581–1606.

Fine, Ben. 2014. "Financialization from a Marxist Perspective". *International Journal of Political Economy* 42(4): 47–66.

Fine, Ben and Laurence Harris. 1987. "Ideology and Markets: Economic Theory and the "'New Right'"". *Socialist Register* 23: 365–392.

Foster-Carter, Aidan. 1978. "The Modes of Production Controversy". *New Left Review* 107: 47–77.

Frank, Andre Gunder. 1966. "The Development of Underdevelopment". *Monthly Review* 18(4): 17–31.

Ganser, Daniele. 2005. "Terrorism in Western Europe: An Approach to NATO's Secret Stay-Behind Armies". *Whitehead Journal of Diplomacy and International Relations* 6(1): 69–96.

Göle, Nilüfer. 1997. "Secularism and Islamism in Turkey: The Making of Elites and Counter-Elites". *Middle East Journal* 51(1): 46–58.

Göle, Nilüfer. 2000. "Snapshots of Islamic Modernities". *Daedalus* 129(1): 91–117.

Göle, Nilüfer. 2012. "Post-Secular Turkey". *New Perspectives Quarterly* 29(1): 7–11.

Gözaydın, İştar. 2009. "The Fethullah Gülen Movement and Politics in Turkey: A Chance for Democratization or a Trojan Horse?" *Democratization* 16(6): 1214–1236.

Gülalp, Haldun. 1985. "Patterns of Capital Accumulation and State–Society Relations in Turkey". *Journal of Contemporary Asia* 15(3): 329–348.

Gülalp, Haldun. 1987. "Capital Accumulation, Classes and the Relative Autonomy of the State". *Science and Society* 51(3): 287–313.

Gültekin-Karakaş, Derya. 2009. "Sermayenin uluslararasılaşması sürecinde Türkiye banka reformu ve finans kapital-içi yeniden yapılanma". *Praksis* 19: 95–131.

Güneş-Ayata, Ayşe. 2002. "The Republican People's Party". *Turkish Studies* 3(1): 102–121.

Gunter, Michael M. 1998a. "Susurluk: The Connection between Turkey's Intelligence Community and Organized Crime". *International Journal of Intelligence and CounterIntelligence* 11(2): 119–141.

Gunter, Michael M. 1998b. "The Silent Coup: The Secularist–Islamist Struggle in Turkey". *Journal of South Asian and Middle Eastern Studies* 21(3): 1–12.

Gunter, Michael M. and M. Hakan Yavuz. 2007. "Turkish Paradox: Progressive Islamists versus Reactionary Secularists". *Critique: Critical Middle Eastern Studies* 16(3): 289–301.

Gürcan, Efe Can and Efe Peker. 2015b. "A Class Analytic Approach to the Gezi Park Events: Challenging the 'Middle Class' Myth". *Capital and Class* 39(2): 321–343.

Gürgen, Melahat Kutun. 2012. "Neoliberal Politikalar üzerinde Kimlik Politikalarının İdeolojik İşlevi: Ana-Akım Söylemin Eleştirel bir Değerlendirmesi". *Toplum ve Demokrasi* 6(13/14): 1–24.

Hanieh, Adam. 2009. "Forum Hierarchies of a Global Market: The South and the Economic Crisis". *Studies in Political Economy* 83(1): 61–84.

Hanioğlu, M. Şükrü. 2011. "Civil–Military Relations in the Second Constitutional Period, 1908–1918". *Turkish Studies* 12(2): 177–189.

Harris, George S. 2011. "Military Coups and Turkish Democracy, 1960–1980". *Turkish Studies* 12(2): 203–213.

Haspolat, Evren. 2011. "Meşrutiyetin Üç Halkçılığı ve Kemalist Halkçılığa Etkileri". *Atatürk Yolu Dergisi* 47: 557–584.

Heper, Metin. 2005. "The Justice and Development Party Government and the Military in Turkey". *Turkish Studies* 6(2): 215–231.

Heper, Metin. 2011. "Civil–Military Relations in Turkey: Toward a Liberal Model?" *Turkish Studies* 12(2): 241–252.

Heper, Metin and Aylin Güney. 2000. "The Military and the Consolidation of Democracy: The Recent Turkish Experience". *Armed Forces and Society* 26(4): 635–657.

Heper, Metin and Şule Toktaş. 2003. "Islam, Modernity, and Democracy in Contemporary Turkey: The Case of Recep Tayyip Erdogan". *The Muslim World* 93(2): 157–185.

Hoşgör, Evren. 2011. "Islamic Capital/Anatolian Tigers: Past and Present". *Middle Eastern Studies* 47(2): 343–360.

Hurewitz, Jacob Coleman. 1968. "The Beginnings of Military Modernization in the Middle East: A Comparative Analysis". *Middle East Journal* 22(2): 144–158.

İnanç, Gül. 2006. "The Politics of 'Active Neutrality' on the Eve of a New World Order: The Case of Turkish Chrome Sales during the Second World War". *Middle Eastern Studies* 42(6): 907–915.

İnsel, Ahmet. 2003. "The AKP and Normalizing Democracy in Turkey". *South Atlantic Quarterly* 102(2/3): 293–308.

Işık, Ayhan. 2021. "Pro-State Paramilitary Violence in Turkey since the 1990s". *Southeast European and Black Sea Studies* 21(2): 231–249.

İslamoğlu, Huri and Çağlar Keyder. 1977. "Agenda for Ottoman History". *Review* 1(1): 31–55.

Janowitz, Morris. 1964. "The Military in the Political Development of New Nations". *Bulletin of the Atomic Scientists* 20(8): 6–10.

Jenkins, Gareth. 2008b. "Turkey's Latest Crisis". *Survival* 50(5): 5–12.

Jenkins, Gareth. 2011. "Ergenekon, Sledgehammer and the Politics of Turkish Justice: Conspiracies and Coincidences". *Middle East Review of International Affairs* 15(2): 1–9.

Jessop, Bob. 1983. "Accumulation Strategies, State Forms, and Hegemonic Projects". *Kapitalistate* 10–11: 89–111.
Jones, Gareth Stedman. 1977. "Society and Politics at the Beginning of the World Economy". *Cambridge Journal of Economics* 1(1): 77–92.
Karaçimen, Elif. 2014. "Financialization in Turkey: The Case of Consumer Debt". *Journal of Balkan and Near Eastern Studies* 16(2): 161–180.
Karaömerlioğlu, M. Asım. 1998. "The Village Institutes Experience in Turkey". *British Journal of Middle Eastern Studies* 25(1): 47–73.
Karaosmanoğlu, Ali. 2000. "The *Evolution* of the National Security Culture and the Military in Turkey". *Journal of International Affairs* 54(1): 199–217.
Karaosmanoğlu, Ali and Behice Özlem Gökakın. 2010. "Türkiye'de Sivil-Asker İlişkisinin Unutulan Boyutları". *Uluslararası İlişkiler* 7(27): 29–50.
Karataşlı, Şahan Savaş and Şefika Kumral. 2019. "Capitalist Development in Hostile Conjunctures: War, Dispossession, and Class Formation in Turkey". *Journal of Agrarian Change* 19(3): 528–549.
Karpat, Kemal H. 1963. "The People's Houses in Turkey: Establishment and Growth". *Middle East Journal* 17(1/2): 55–67.
Kaynar, Ayşegül Kars. 2022. "Post-2016 Military Restructuring in Turkey from the Perspective of Coup-Proofing". *Turkish Studies* 23(3): 383–406.
Keyder, Çağlar. 2004. "The Turkish Bell Jar". *New Left Review* 28: 65–84.
Kiely, Ray. 2012. "Spatial Hierarchy and/or Contemporary Geopolitics: What Can and Can't Uneven and Combined Development Explain?" *Cambridge Review of International Affairs* 25(2): 231–248.
Koelle, Peter Brampton. 2000. "The Inevitability of the 1971 Turkish Military Intervention". *Journal of South Asian and Middle Eastern Studies* 24(1): 38–56.
Köni, Hakan. 2012. "Saudi Influence on Islamic Institutions in Turkey Beginning in the 1970s". *Middle Eastern Journal* 66(1): 97–110.
Kumar, Deepa. 2011a. "Political Islam: A Marxist Analysis, I". *International Socialist Review* 76. Accessed 30 October 2022, https://isreview.org/issue/76/political-islam-marxist-analysis/index.html.
Kumar, Deepa. 2011b. "Political Islam: A Marxist Analysis, II". *International Socialist Review* 78. Accessed 30 October 2022, https://isreview.org/issue/78/political-islam-marxist-analysis/index.html.
Kuru, Ahmet T. 2012. "The Rise and Fall of Military Tutelage in Turkey: Fears of Islamism, Kurdism, and Communism". *Insight Turkey* 14(2): 37–57.
Laclau, Ernesto. 1971. "Feudalism and Capitalism in Latin America". *New Left Review* 67: 19–38.
Lapavitsas, Costas. 2013. "The Financialization of Capitalism: 'Profiting without Producing'". *City* 17(6): 792–805.

Leffler, Melvyn P. 1985. "Strategy, Diplomacy, and the Cold War: The United States, Turkey, and NATO, 1945–1952". *Journal of American History* 71(4): 807–825.
Lerner, Daniel and Richard D. Robinson. 1960. "Swords and Ploughshares: The Turkish Army as a Modernizing Force". *World Politics* 13(1): 19–44.
Linden, Marcel van der. 2007. "The 'Law' of Uneven and Combined Development: Some Underdeveloped Thoughts". *Historical Materialism* 15(1): 145–165.
Lipset, Seymour Martin. 1959. "Some Social Requisites of Democracy: Economic Development and Political Legitimacy". *American Political Science Review* 53(1): 69–105.
Luckham, A. Robin. 1971. "A Comparative Typology of Civil–Military Relations". *Government and Opposition* 6(1): 5–35.
Mardin, Şerif. 1973. "Center–Periphery Relations: A Key to Turkish Politics?" *Daedalus* 102 (1): 169–190.
Mardin, Şerif. 2005. "Turkish Islamic Exceptionalism Yesterday and Today: Continuity, Rupture and Reconstruction in Operational Codes". *Turkish Studies* 6(2): 145–165.
Müderrisoğlu, Alptekin. 1994. "Kurtuluş Savaşının Mali Kaynakları". *Atatürk Yolu Dergisi* 4(13): 27–53.
Müftüler-Baç, Meltem. 2005. "Turkey's Political Reforms and the Impact of the European Union". *South European Society and Politics* 10(1): 17–31.
Narlı, Nilüfer. 1999. "The Rise of the Islamist Movement in Turkey". *Middle East Review of International Affairs* 3(3): 38–48.
Narlı, Nilüfer. 2000. "Civil–Military Relations in Turkey". *Turkish Studies* 1(1): 107–127.
Narlı, Nilüfer. 2011. "Concordance and Discordance in Turkish Civil–Military Relations, 1980–2002". *Turkish Studies* 12(2): 215–225.
Oğuz, Şebnem. 2011. "Krizi Fırsata Dönüştürmek: Türkiye'de Devletin 2008 Krizine Yönelik Tepkileri". *Amme İdaresi Dergisi* 44(1): 1–23.
Oğuz, Şebnem. 2012. "Türkiye'de Kapitalizmin Küreselleşmesi ve Neoliberal Otoriter Devletin İnşası". *Mesleki Sağlık ve Güvenlik Dergisi* 45/46: 2–15.
Oğuz, Şebnem. 2023. "AKP'li yıllarda siyasal rejimin dönüşümü: Çelişkili bir süreç olarak yeni faşizm". *Toplum ve Hekim* 38(2): 106–125.
Ökçün, Gündüz. 1968. "1923 Yılında İzmir'de Toplanan Türkiye İktisat Kongresi'nde Kabul Edilen Esaslar". *AÜSBF Dergisi* 23(1): 54–100.
Öniş, Ziya. 1996. "Globalization and Financial Blow-Ups in the Semi-Periphery: Perspectives on Turkey's Financial Crisis of 1994". *New Perspectives on Turkey* 15: 1–23.
Öniş, Ziya. 1997. "The Political Economy of Islamic Resurgence in Turkey: The Rise of the Welfare Party in Perspective". *Third World Quarterly* 18(4): 743–766.
Öniş, Ziya. 2004. "Turgut Özal and his Economic Legacy: Turkish Neo-Liberalism in Critical Perspective". *Middle Eastern Studies* 40(4): 113–134.

Öniş, Ziya. 2009. "Beyond the 2001 Financial Crisis: The Political Economy of the New Phase of Neo-Liberal Restructuring in Turkey". *Review of International Political Economy* 16(3): 409–432.

Öniş, Ziya. 2015. "Monopolising the Centre: The AKP and the Uncertain Path of Turkish Democracy". *International Spectator* 50(2): 22–41.

Öniş, Ziya and Ahmet Faruk Aysan. 2000. "Neoliberal Globalisation, the Nation-State and Financial Crises in the Semi-Periphery: A Comparative Analysis". *Third World Quarterly* 21(1): 119–139.

Öniş, Ziya and Caner Bakır. 2007. "Turkey's Political Economy in the Age of Financial Globalization: The Significance of the EU Anchor". *South European Society and Politics* 12(2): 147–164.

Öniş, Ziya and Mustafa Kutlay. 2021. "The Anatomy of Turkey's New Heterodox Crisis: The Interplay of Domestic Politics and Global Dynamics". *Turkish Studies* 22(4): 499–529.

Orhangazi, Özgür. 2002. "Turkey: Bankruptcy of Neoliberal Policies and the Possibility of Alternatives". *Review of Radical Political Economics* 34(3): 335–341.

Orhangazi, Özgür and A. Erinç Yeldan. 2021. "The Re-Making of the Turkish Crisis". *Development and Change* 52(3): 460–503.

Overbeek, Henk. 1980. "Finance Capital and the Crisis in Britain". *Capital & Class* 4(2): 99–120.

Özbek, Nadir. 2008. "Policing the Countryside: Gendarmes of the Late 19th-Century Ottoman Empire, 1876–1908". *International Journal of Middle East Studies* 40(1): 47–67.

Özbudun, Ergun. 2006. "From Political Islam to Conservative Democracy: The Case of the Justice and Development Party in Turkey". *South European Society and Politics* 11(3/4): 543–557.

Özbudun, Ergun. 2015. "Turkey's Judiciary and the Drift Toward Competitive Authoritarianism". *International Spectator* 50(2): 42–55.

Özcan, Gül Berna and Murat Çokgezen. 2003. "Limits to Alternative Forms of Capitalization: The Case of Anatolian Holding Companies". *World Development* 31(12): 2061–2084.

Özçelik, Pınar Kaya. 2010. "Demokrat Parti'nin Demokrasi Söylemi". *AÜSBF Dergisi* 65(3): 163–187.

Özçelik, Pınar Kaya. 2011. "12 Eylül'ü Anlamak". *AÜSBF Dergisi* 66(1): 73–93.

Özdemir, Yonca. 2020. "AKP's Neoliberal Populism and Contradictions of New Social Policies in Turkey". *Contemporary Politics* 26(3): 245–267.

Öztürk, Özgür. 2006. "Emperyalizm Kuramları ve Sermayenin Uluslararasılaşması". *Praksis* 15: 271–309.

Öztürk, Özgür. 2009. "Türkiye'de Sendikal Mücadele, Sermaye Birikimi, MESS ve Koç Holding". *Praksis* 19: 337–361.

Öztürk, Özgür. 2011. "Türkiye finans kapitalinin dışa açılması". *Devrimci Marksizm* 13/14: 106–132.

Palloix, Christian. 1974. "Impérialisme et Mode d'Accumulation International du Capital: Essai d'une approche du néo-impérialisme". *Revue Tiers Monde* 15(57): 233–252.

Palloix, Christian. 1977. "The Self-Expansion of Capital on a World Scale". *Review of Radical Political Economics* 9(2): 3–28.

Park, Bill. 2008. "The Fethullah Gulen Movement". *Middle East Review of International Affairs* 12(4). Accessed 21 May 2013, www.gloria-center.org/2008/12/park-asp-2008-12-08/.

Parla, Taha. 1998. "Mercantile Militarism in Turkey, 1960–1998". *New Perspectives on Turkey* 19: 29–52.

Parsons, Talcott. 1964. "Evolutionary Universals in Society". *American Sociological Review* 29(3): 339–357.

Perlmutter, Amos. 1969. "The Praetorian State and the Praetorian Army: Toward a Taxonomy of Civil–Military Relations in Developing Polities". *Comparative Politics* 1(3): 382–404.

Perlmutter, Amos. 1986. "The Military and Politics in Modern Times: A Decade Later". *Journal of Strategic Studies* 9(1): 5–15.

Polat, Necati. 2011. "The Anti-Coup Trials in Turkey: What Exactly is Going On?" *Mediterranean Politics* 16(1): 213–219.

Poulantzas, Nicos. 1973. "On Social Classes". *New Left Review* 78: 27–54.

Przeworski, Adam and Fernando Limongi. 1997. "Modernization: Theories and Facts". *World Politics* 49(2): 155–183.

Raj, K. N. and A. K. Sen. 1961. "Alternative Patterns of Growth under Conditions of Stagnant Export Earnings". *Oxford Economic Papers* 13(1): 43–52.

Robinson, William I. 2019. "Global Capitalist Crisis and Twenty-First Century Fascism: Beyond the Trump Hype". *Science and Society* 83(2): 481–509.

Rosenberg, Justin. 2006. "Why Is There No International Historical Sociology?" *European Journal of International Relations* 12(3): 307–340.

Rustow, Dankwart A. 1959. "The Army and the Founding of the Turkish Republic". *World Politics* 11(4): 513–552.

Rutz, Henry J. 1999. "The Rise and Demise of Imam-Hatip Schools: Discourses of Islamic Belonging and Denial in the Construction of Turkish Civic Culture". *Political and Legal Anthropology Review* 22(2): 93–103.

Şahin, Osman. 2021. "How Populists Securitize Elections to Win Them: The 2015 Double Elections in Turkey". *New Perspectives on Turkey* 64: 7–30.

Sarıgil, Zeki. 2007. "Europeanization as Institutional Change: The Case of the Turkish Military". *Mediterranean Politics* 12(1): 39–57.

Sarıgil, Zeki. 2011. "Civil–Military Relations Beyond Dichotomy: With Special Reference to Turkey". *Turkish Studies* 12(2): 265–278.

Savran, Arin. 2020. "The Peace Process between Turkey and the Kurdistan Workers' Party, 2009–2015". *Journal of Balkan and Near Eastern Studies* 22(6): 777–792.

Savran, Sungur. 1985. "Osmanlı'dan Cumhuriyete: Türkiye'de Burjuva Devrimi Sorunu". *11. Tez* 1: 172–214.

Savran, Sungur. 2006. "Burjuva sosyalizminin düşman kardeşleri: Liberal sol ve ulusal sol". *Devrimci Marksizm* 2: 50–114.

Savran, Sungur and E. Ahmet Tonak. 1999. "Productive and Unproductive Labour: An Attempt at Clarification and Classification". *Capital and Class* 23(2): 113–152.

Sayarı, Sabri. 1996. "Turkey's Islamist Challenge". *Middle East Quarterly* 3(3): 35–43.

Schick, Irvin Cemil and E. Ahmet Tonak. 1981. "The Political Economy of Quicksand: International Finance and the Foreign Debt Dimension of Turkey's Economic Crisis". *Critical Sociology* 10(3): 59–79.

Selwyn, Ben. 2011. "Trotsky, Gerschenkron and the Political Economy of Late Capitalist Development". *Economy and Society* 40(3): 421–450.

Şenses, Fikret. 1999. "Yoksullukla Mücadele ve Sosyal Yardımlaşma ve Dayanışmayı Teşvik Fonu". *ODTÜ Gelişme Dergisi* 26: 427–451.

Sevim, Medine. 2007. "Türkiye'de Cumhuriyet Dönemi Din Eğitimi ve Öğretimi Kronolojisi (1923'den Günümüze)". *Değerler Eğitimi Merkezi Dergisi* 1(2): 64–71.

Sezen, Seriye. 2000. "Milli Güvenlik Kurulu Üzerine". *Amme İdaresi Dergisi* 33(4): 63–83.

Tachau, Frank and Metin Heper. 1983. "The State, Politics, and the Military in Turkey". *Comparative Politics* 16(1): 17–33.

Taş, Hakkı. 2018. "A History of Turkey's AKP–Gülen Conflict". *Mediterranean Politics* 23(3): 395–402.

Taylan, Turgut. 1984. "Capital and the State in Contemporary Turkey". *Khamsin* 11: 5–46.

Tekin, Ali. 2006. "Turkey's Aborted Attempt at Export-Led Growth Strategy: Anatomy of the 1970 Economic Reform". *Middle Eastern Studies* 42(1): 133–163.

Toktaş, Şule and Ümit Kurt. 2010. "The Turkish Military's Autonomy, JDP Rule and the EU Reform Process in the 2000s: An Assessment of the Turkish Version of Democratic Control of Armed Forces (DECAF)". *Turkish Studies* 11(3): 387–403.

Toprak, Binnaz. 2005. "Islam and Democracy in Turkey". *Turkish Studies* 6(2): 167–186.

Toprak, Zafer. 1982. "Unutulan Kongre: 1948 Türkiye İktisat Kongresi". *İktisat Dergisi* 211/212: 37–42.

Turan, Mahsun. 2016. "Legal Barriers to Freedom of Association and Collective Bargaining". *International Union Rights* 23(3): 10–11, 28.

Uyar, Mesut and Serhat Güvenç. 2022. "A Tale of Two Military Missions: The Germans in the Ottoman Empire and the Americans in the Republic of Turkey". *War and Society* 41(2): 85–106.

Uysal, Gönenç. 2018. "'Left-of-Centre' in Turkey: A Critical Approach to the Impasses of Social Democracy". *OKU Journal of Economics and Administrative Sciences* 2(1): 37–53.

Uysal, Gönenç. 2019a. "Secularism as a Field of Class Struggle: State, Religion, and Class Relations in Turkey". *Journal of Historical Sociology* 32(3): 331–344.

Uysal, Gönenç. 2019b. "Charity State: Neoliberalism, Political Islam, and Class Relations in Turkey". *New Proposals: Journal of Marxism and Interdisciplinary Inquiry* 10(1): 16–28.

Uysal, Gönenç. 2019c. "Türkiye'nin AKP Dönemi Orta Doğu ve Kuzey Afrika'da İzlediği Alt-Emperyalist Dış Politika". *Praksis* 51(3): 141–158.

Uysal, Gönenç. 2020. "Unevenness, (Under)development, and Resistance in the Middle East and North Africa: An Introduction". *New Middle Eastern Studies* 10(2): 132–146.

Uysal, Gönenç. 2021. "Turkey's Sub-Imperialism in Sub-Saharan Africa". *Review of Radical Political Economics* 53(3): 442–461.

Uzgel, İlhan. 2003. "Between Praetorianism and Democracy: The Role of the Military in Turkish Foreign Policy". *Turkish Yearbook of International Relations* 34: 177–212.

Weeks, John. 1976. "Crisis and Accumulation in the Peruvian Economy, 1967–1975". *Review of Radical Political Economics* 8: 56–72.

Weeks, John. 1977. "Backwardness, Foreign Capital, and Accumulation in the Manufacturing Sector of Peru, 1954–1975". *Latin American Perspectives* 4(3): 124–145.

Weeks, John. 1981. "The Differences between Materialist Theory and Dependency Theory and Why They Matter". *Latin American Perspectives* 8(3/4): 118–123.

Weeks, John. 1985. "Epochs of Capitalism and the Progressiveness of Capital's Expansion". *Science and Society* 49(4): 414–436.

Weeks, John. 1997. "The Law of Value and the Analysis of Underdevelopment". *Historical Materialism* 1(1): 91–112.

Weeks, John. 2001. "The Expansion of Capital and Uneven Development on a World Scale". *Capital and Class* 25(9): 9–30.

Weeks, John and Elizabeth Dore. 1979. "International Exchange and the Causes of Backwardness". *Latin American Perspectives* 6(2): 62–87.

Wright, Erik Olin. 1980. "Varieties of Marxist Conceptions of Class Structure". *Politics and Society* 9(3): 323–370.

Yaghmaian, Behzad. 1990. "Development Theories and Development Strategies: An Alternative Theoretical Framework". *Review of Radical Political Economics* 22(2/3): 174–188.

Yalman, Galip L. and Aylin Topal. 2019. "Labour Containment Strategies and Working-Class Struggles in the Neoliberal Era: The Case of TEKEL Workers in Turkey". *Critical Sociology* 45(3): 447–461.

Yaman-Öztürk, Melda and Fuat Ercan. 2009. "1979 krizinden 2001 krizine Türkiye'de sermaye birikimi süreci ve yaşanan dönüşümler". *Praksis* 19: 55–93.

Yankaya, Dilek. 2012. "28 Şubat, Islami burjuvazinin iktidar yolunda bir milat". *Birikim* 278/279: 29–37.

Yavuz, M. Hakan. 1997. "Political Islam and the Welfare (Refah) Party in Turkey". *Comparative Politics* 30(1): 63–82.

Yavuz, M. Hakan and Rasim Koç. 2016. "The Turkish Coup Attempt: The Gülen Movement vs. The State". *Middle East Policy* 23(4): 136–148.

Yeğen, Mesut. 1996. "The Turkish State Discourse and the Exclusion of Kurdish Identity". *Middle Eastern Studies* 32(2): 216–229.

Yeldan, A. Erinç. 1998. "On Structural Sources of the 1994 Turkish Crisis: A CGE Modelling Analysis". *International Review of Applied Economics* 12(3): 397–414.

Yeldan, A. Erinç. 2006. "Neoliberal Global Remedies: From Speculative-Led Growth to IMF-Led Crisis in Turkey". *Review of Radical Political Economics* 38(2): 193–213.

Yeldan, A. Erinç and Burcu Ünüvar. 2016. "An Assessment of the Turkish Economy in the AKP Era". *Research and Policy on Turkey* 1(1): 11–28.

Yeşilada, Birol A. 2016. "The Future of Erdoğan and the AKP". *Turkish Studies* 17(1): 19–30.

Yılmaz, Şuhnaz. 2012. "Turkey's Quest for NATO Membership: The Institutionalization of the Turkish–American Alliance". *Southeast European and Black Sea Studies* 12(4): 481–495.

Yılmaz, İhsan and Galib Bashirov. 2018. "The AKP after 15 Years: Emergence of Erdoganism in Turkey". *Third World Quarterly* 39(9): 1812–1830.

Yılmaz, Koray R. 2011. "Türkiye'de Kapitalizmin Gelişme Süreci ve Krizler: Tarihsel bir Bakış". *İktisat Dergisi* 519: 95–109.

Yılmaz, Koray R. and Demet Özmen Yılmaz. 2018. "Sermayenin Uluslararasılaşması Bağlamında Geç Kapitalist Gelişme: Kuramsal Bir Çerçeve". *Fiscaoeconomia* 1/2: 141–166.

Theses

Avcı, Akif. 2019. "Unravelling the Social Formation: Free Trade, the State, and Business in Turkey". PhD thesis, University of Nottingham.

Çitak, Zana. 2004. "Nationalism and Religion: A Comparative Study of the Development of Secularism in France and Turkey". PhD thesis, Boston University.

Nişancıoğlu, Kerem. 2013. "The Ottomans in Europe: Uneven and Combined Development and Eurocentrism". PhD Thesis, University of Sussex.

Oğuz, Şebnem. 2008. "Globalization and the Contradictions of State Restructuring in Turkey". PhD thesis, York University.

Öztürk, Özgür. 2008. "Türkiye'de Büyük Sermaye Grupları: Finans Kapital ve Faaliyet Çeşitliliği üzerine bir İnceleme". PhD thesis, Marmara University, Istanbul.

Pamuk, Şevket. 1978. "Foreign Trade, Foreign Capital and the Peripheralization of the Ottoman Empire, 1830–1913". PhD thesis, University of California, Berkeley.

Uysal, Gönenç. 2016. "The Interaction between Secularism and Civil–Military Relations in Turkey, 1908–2010". PhD thesis, King's College London.

Working Papers and Papers Presented at Meetings

Akçay, Ümit. 2018. "Neoliberal Populism in Turkey and Its Crisis". Working Paper, No. 100/2018. Berlin: Institute for International Political Economy.

Akçay, Ümit and Ali Rıza Güngen. 2019. "The Making of Turkey's 2018–2019 Economic Crisis". Working Paper No. 120/2019, Institute for International Political Economy, Berlin.

Dölek, Levent. 2016. "'Metal Fırtına' Işığında İşçi Sınıfı ve Sendikal Hareket". Paper presented at the DISK-AR Workshop in the 10th Karaburun Congress, Izmir, August–September 2016.

Oğuz, Şebnem. 2009. "The Response of the Turkish State to the 2008 Crisis: A Further Step towards Neoliberal Authoritarian Statism". Paper presented at the 3rd IIPPE International Research Workshop, Ankara, September 2009.

Soysal, Mümtaz. 2005. "Özelleştirmeler ve Hukuksal Savaşım". Paper presented at TMMOB Symposium on the Privatisations in Turkey, Ankara, September 2005.

Blogs and Websites

Çubukçu, Suat. 2018. "The Rise of Paramilitary Groups in Turkey". Small Wars, 3 March. Accessed 21 May 2023, https://smallwarsjournal.com/jrnl/art/rise-paramilitary-groups-turkey#_edn20.

Dinçer, Hülya. 2020. "Kalıcı Olağanüstü Halin Yeni Cezasızlık Rejimi: Adaletin Yasa Eliyle İlgası". Ayrıntı, 1 August. Accessed 21 May 2023, https://ayrintidergi.com.tr/kalici-olaganustu-halin-yeni-cezasizlik-rejimi-adaletin-yasa-eliyle-ilgasi/.

Göle, Nilüfer. 2013. "Public Space Democracy". Eurozine, 29 July. Accessed 3 May 2023, www.eurozine.com/public-space-democracy/.

Jessop, Bob. 2014. "Poulantzas's State, Power, Socialism as a Modern Classic". BobJessop.Org, 27 March. Accessed 17 April 2023, https://bobjessop.wordpress.com/2014/03/27/poulantzass-state-power-socialism-as-a-modern-classic/.

Keyder, Çağlar. 2013. "Yeni Orta Sınıf". Bilim Akademisi, 1 August. Accessed 3 May 2023, https://bilimakademisi.org/yeni-orta-sinif-caglar-keyder/.

Rodrik, Dani. 2016. "Turkey's Baffling Coup". Project Syndicate, 17 July. Accessed 20 July 2016, www.project-syndicate.org/commentary/turkey-coup-erosion-of-law-by-dani-rodrik-2016-07.

Savran, Sungur. 2010. "The Tekel Strike in Turkey". Socialist Project, 16 March. Accessed 1 May 2023, https://socialistproject.ca/2010/03/b326/.

Uysal, Gönenç. 2013a. "Unrest in Turkey: from '3 or 5 Trees' to 'Democracy'". Strife, 5 June. Accessed 1 May 2023, www.strifeblog.org/2013/06/05/unrest-in-turkey-from-3-or-5-trees-to-democracy/.

Uysal, Gönenç. 2013b. "From the Gezi Parki Protests to the Democratisation Package". Strife, 10 December. Accessed 1 May 2023, www.strifeblog.org/2013/12/10/from-the-gezi-parki-protests-to-the-democratisation-package/.

Newspapers and News Services

Balbay, Mustafa. 2003. "Genç Subaylar Tedirgin". *Cumhuriyet*, 23 May, 1.

Bardakçı, Murat. 2002. "Şiiri böyle montajlamışlar". *Hürriyet*, 22 September. Accessed 18 September 2023, www.hurriyet.com.tr/siiri-boyle-montajlamislar-99109.

BBC Türkçe. 2010. "'FETÖ'nün siyasi ayağı' tartışması: İlker Başbuğ'un ifadeye çağrıldığı süreç nasıl gelişti?" 10 June. Accessed 6 February 2020, www.bbc.com/turkce/haberler-turkiye-51398517.

BBC Türkçe. 2018. "Sivas 1993: Madımak Oteli'nde ne oldu". 2 July. Accessed 10 November 2022, www.bbc.com/turkce/haberler/2015/07/150702_sivas_1993.

BirGün. 2016. "F-16'lara yakıt ikmali yapan Üsteğmen, İncirlik Komutanını yalanladı". 28 July. Accessed 24 May 2023, www.birgun.net/haber/f-16-lara-yakit-ikmali-yapan-ustegmen-incirlik-komutanini-yalanladi-121994.

Bolaç, Efkan. 2013. "Ergenekon bir Bağırsak Temizliğidir". *Vagus*, 7 August. Accessed 9 October 2014, http://vagus.tv/2013/08/07/efkan-bolac-ergenekon-bir-bagirsak-temizligidir/.

Boratav, Korkut. 2023. "Korkut Boratav seçim sonrası Türkiye'yi değerlendirdi, Cenk Saraçoğlu ve Fırat Çoban". *İleri Haber*, 7 June. Accessed 13 June 2023, www.ilerihaber.org/icerik/korkut-boratav-secim-sonrasi-turkiyeyi-degerlendirdi-155447.

Çelik, Aziz. 2023. "Boş tencere ve sandık!" *BirGün*, 29 May. Accessed 10 June 2023, www.birgun.net/makale/bos-tencere-ve-sandik-441081.

CNN Türk. 2023. "Türk savunma sanayinin gözbebekleri Üsküdar'da sergileniyor". 10 May. Accessed 10 June 2023, www.cnnturk.com/turkiye/turk-savunma-sanayinin-gozbebekleri-uskudarda-sergileniyor.

Cumhuriyet. 1997. "Ecevit: Refah Militan Yetiştiriyor". 11 February, 17.

Cumhuriyet. 2001. "Hükümetin uyguladığı IMF programları kepenk kapattırıyor". 22 October, 1.

Cumhuriyet. 2003. "Şeriat isteyenler var". 26 August, 1.

Diken. 2016. "Cumhurbaşkanı, muhtarların oyuyla OHAL'i uzattı: Belki 12 ay da yetmeyecek". 29 September. Accessed 15 May 2023, www.diken.com.tr/erdogan-muhtarlarin-oylariyla-ohali-uc-ay-uzatti-belki-12-ay-da-yetmeyecek/.

Evrensel. 2015. "Metal grevi de yasaklandı!" 30 January.

Evrensel. 2017. "Erdoğan'dan itiraf: OHAL'le grevlere müsaade etmiyoruz". 12 July. Accessed 16 May 2023, www.evrensel.net/haber/326078/erdogandan-itiraf-ohalle-grevlere-musaade-etmiyoruz.

Gürsel, Kadri. 2013. "AKP-Cemaat savaşında neyi savunmalıyız?" *Milliyet*, 8 December. Accessed 4 May 2023, www.milliyet.com.tr/yazarlar/kadri-gursel/akp-cemaat-savasinda-neyi-savunmaliyiz-1804154.

Habertürk. 2014. "İşte Tankların Yürütülmesinin Nedeni". 7 January. Accessed 9 November 2014, www.haberturk.com/gundem/haber/910441-iste-tanklarin-yurutulmesinin-nedeni.

Hürriyet. 1997a. "RP'ye ikinci şok". 16 October. Accessed 20 November 2022, www.hurriyet.com.tr/gundem/rpye-ikinci-sok-39269035.

Hürriyet. 1997b. "Bu Defa İşi Silahsız Kuvvetler Halletsin". 20 December, 1.

Hürriyet. 1998a. "En Büyük İrtica Darbe". 14 March. Accessed 28 May 2014, http://webarsiv.hurriyet.com.tr/1998/03/14/32707.asp.

Hürriyet. 1998b. "Sivil Plan Devrede". 17 March. Accessed: 29 May 2014, http://webarsiv.hurriyet.com.tr/1998/03/17/33268.asp.

Hürriyet. 2003. "Siyasetteki Boşluğu Bazen Ordu Doldurdu". 25 January. Accessed 5 September 2014, http://hurarsiv.hurriyet.com.tr/goster/haber.aspx?id=123843.

Hürriyet. 2011. "İşte Susurluk Tutanakları". 22 September. Accessed 18 November 2022, www.hurriyet.com.tr/iste-susurluk-tutanaklari-18797756.

Hürriyet. 2012. "Dindar Gençlik Yetiştireceğiz". 2 February. Accessed 12 June 2014, www.hurriyet.com.tr/gundem/19825231.asp.

Hürriyet. 2013a. "Fethullah Gülen'den Gezi Parkı değerlendirmesi". 6 June. Accessed 5 May 2023, www.hurriyet.com.tr/kelebek/fethullah-gulenden-gezi-parki-degerlendirmesi-23446001.

Hürriyet. 2013b. "Başbakan Recep Tayyip Erdoğan eylemcilere seslendi". 11 June. Accessed 5 May 2023, www.hurriyet.com.tr/gundem/basbakan-recep-tayyip-erdogan-eylemcilere-seslendi-23468516.

Hürriyet. 2014. "Balyoz Davası'nda Hak İhlali". 18 June. Accessed 20 October 2014, www.hurriyet.com.tr/gundem/26637844.asp.

Hürriyet. 2018. "Milli Savunma Bakanı Orgeneral Hulusi Akar oldu". 9 July. Accessed 23 May 2023, www.hurriyet.com.tr/gundem/milli-savunma-bakani-orgeneral-hulusi-akar-oldu-40891653.

Hürriyet Daily News. 1996. "The Secret of Hoca's Position in the 'Islamic Command' Unravelled". 13 October. Accessed 4 March 2014, www.hurriyetdailynews.com/turkish-press-scanner.aspx?pageID=438&n=turkish-press-scanner-1996-10-14.

Hürriyet Daily News. 2013. "2.5 million People Attended Gezi Protests across Turkey: Interior Ministry". 24 June. Accessed 1 May 2023, www.hurriyetdailynews.com/25-million-people-attended-gezi-protests-across-turkey-interior-ministry--49292.

İlter, Balçiçek. 2016. "Ahmet Zeki Üçok: O dönem hazırladığım liste maalesef bugün tulum çıkardı". Habertürk, 25 July. Accessed 23 May 2023, www.haberturk.com/gundem/haber/1271387-ahmet-zeki-ucok-o-donem-hazirladigim-liste-maalesef-bugun-tulum-cikardi.

Kasapoğlu, Çağıl. 2016. "15 Temmuz darbe girişiminin arkasında kim var?" BBC Türkçe, 20 July. Accessed 18 September 2023, www.bbc.com/turkce/haberler-turkiye-36843901.

Memurlar.Net. 2010. "CHP, MHP, BDP, HSYK ve YARSAV red cephesinde buluştu". 9 July. Accessed 29 September 2014, www.memurlar.net/haber/171449/.
Milli Gazete. 1991. "Cübbeli Ahmet Hoca: İnananlar Refah'ta Toplanmaya Mecbur". 18 September, 6.
Milliyet. 1958. "Söz Düellosu Tekrar Başladı". 13 October, 5.
Milliyet. 1960. "Yayınlanan Tebliğler". 28 May, 5.
Milliyet. 1968a. "Mecliste Kanlı Kavga: AP'liler TIP'lileri Dövdü". 21 August, 7.
Milliyet. 1968b. "Demirel: 'Sokaklar eskimez takati olan yürür' dedi". 9 November, 1.
Milliyet. 1982. "'Çıkarları Bozulanların Propagandalarına Kanmayın'". 27 October, 9.
Milliyet. 1994. "Erbakan 'Kanlı' Konuştu". 14 April, 1.
Milliyet. 1996a. "'Demokrasi Bizim için Araçtır'". 14 July, 20.
Milliyet. 1996b. "Ağar'ın fezlekesi iade edildi". 14 December. Accessed 8 April 2016, www.milliyet.com.tr/1996/12/14/siyaset/agar.html.
Milliyet. 1997a. "Sincan Manevrası İktidarı Sarstı". 5 February, 1.
Milliyet. 1997b. "İki Gensoru Geliyor". 5 February, 1.
Milliyet. 1997c. "Sönen Her Mum Hükümeti Tüketiyor". 13 February. Accessed 6 March 2014, www.milliyet.com.tr/1997/02/13/siyaset/mum.html.
Milliyet. 1997d. "Ordu: Öncelik İç Tehdit". 30 April, 18.
Milliyet. 1997e. "Gövde Gösterisi". 12 May, 1.
Milliyet. 1997f. "Erbakan İmzaladı". 27 May, 1.
Milliyet. 1997g. "RP'li Erdoğan: Camiler Kışlamız". 7 December, 1.
Milliyet. 2001. "Gül: Partimiz Hazır". 22 June, 16.
Milliyet. 2002. "Askerler MGK'da 'Dikkat' Çekti". 1 December, 20.
Milliyet. 2003a. "Milli Görüş elbisesini çıkardık". 17 May, 1.
Milliyet. 2003b. "Genç-Yaşlı Yok". 27 May, 1.
Milliyet. 2003c. "Emekli Paşalar Muhtırası". 23 August, 16.
Milliyet. 2003d. "Özkök: Doğan Sonra Konuşsaydı İyiydi". 26 August, 1.
Milliyet. 2007a. "Orgeneral Büyükanıt Hayalindeki Cumhurbaşkanının Portresini Çizdi". 12 April. Accessed 17 September 2014, www.milliyet.com.tr/2007/04/12/son/sonsiy24.asp.
Milliyet. 2007b. "Sezer Son Konuşmasında Sert Uyarılarda Bulundu". 13 April. Accessed 11 September 2014, www.milliyet.com.tr/2007/04/13/son/sonsiy19.asp.
Milliyet. 2007c. "Ankara'da Miting Olaysız Sona Erdi". 14 April. Accessed 1 October 2014, www.milliyet.com.tr/2007/04/14/son/sontur07.asp.
Milliyet. 2007d. "Arınç: Dindar Cumhurbaşkanı Seçeceğiz". 16 April. Accessed 11 September 2014, www.milliyet.com.tr/2007/04/16/son/sonsiy21.asp.
Milliyet. 2007e. "Erdoğan grup toplantısında Gül'ün ismini açıkladı". 24 April. Accessed 11 September 2014, www.milliyet.com.tr/2007/04/24/son/sonsiy09.asp.
Milliyet. 2007f. "Baykal: Zafer Havası Taşımıyorum". 27 April. Accessed 11 September 2014, www.milliyet.com.tr/2007/04/27/son/sonsiy36.asp.

Milliyet. 2007g. "Gerektiğinde Tavır Koyarız". 28 April. Accessed 12 October 2014, www.milliyet.com.tr/2007/04/28/siyaset/asiy.html.

Milliyet. 2007h. "Hükümetin Açıklaması: Zamanlama Dikkat Çekici". 28 April. Accessed 12 October 2014, www.milliyet.com.tr/2007/04/28/son/sonsiy12.asp.

Milliyet. 2007i. "Anayasa Mahkemesi Cumhurbaşkanlığı Seçimini Durdurdu". 1 May. Accessed 11 September 2014, www.milliyet.com.tr/2007/05/01/son/sonsiy25.asp.

Milliyet. 2010. "Rodrik'e göre İddianame Delik Deşik". 16 December. Accessed 29 June 2011, www.milliyet.com.tr/rodrik-e-gore-iddianame-delik-desik/asli-aydintasbas/siyaset/siyasetyazardetay/16.12.2010/1326884/default.htm.

Milliyet. 2011. "Orgeneral Işık Koşaner İstifa Etti". 29 July. Accessed 30 July 2011, www.milliyet.com.tr/orgeneral-isik-kosaner-istifa-etti/siyaset/siyasetdetay/29.07.2011/1420393/default.htm.

NTV. 2010. "Erdoğan: 'Hayır' diyen Darbecidir". 7 September. Accessed 28 September 2014, www.ntv.com.tr/arsiv/id/25129484/.

NTV. 2023. "Kılıçdaroğlu'ndan TCG Anadolu tepkisi: Ordunun gemisini seçim otobüsü yaptılar". 4 May. Accessed 10 June 2023, www.ntv.com.tr/turkiye/kilicdaroglundan-tcg-anadolu-tepkisi-ordunun-gemisini-secim-otobusu-yaptilar,hYVFKJOVLEWn3DewRCqkQg.

NTVMSNBC. 2014. "Ergenekon'da Tahliyeler Bugün de Sürdü". 12 March. Accessed 20 October 2014, www.ntvmsnbc.com/id/25503881/.

OdaTV. 2010. "Zombileri Yardıma Niçin Çağırdılar". 5 September. Accessed 11 May 2016, http://odatv.com/zombileri-yardima-nicin-cagirdilar-0509101200.html.

OdaTV. 2012. "İşte Ergenekon ve Balyoz'un Bilançosu". 15 May. Accessed 10 April 2023, www.odatv4.com/guncel/iste-ergenekon-ve-balyozun-bilancosu--1505121200-23698.

Orhangazi, Özgür. 2022. "Sorunu çözme, seçime kadar hafiflet taktiğinin sonucu, Cihan Çelik". *Evrensel*, 13 October. Accessed 10 June 2023, www.evrensel.net/haber/472104/sorunu-cozme-secime-kadar-hafiflet-taktiginin-sonucu-once-gecici-rahatlama-ardindan-buyuk-sanci.

Radikal. 2009. "Başbuğ'dan Evren'e Ziyaret". 4 August. Accessed 11 January 2013, www.radikal.com.tr/turkiye/basbugdan_evrene_ziyaret-948184.

Radikal. 2011a. "Savcı Öz, Şener ve Şık'a Kitaplarını Sordu". 6 March. Accessed 30 July 2014, www.radikal.com.tr/turkiye/savci_oz_sener_ve_sika_kitaplarini_sordu-1041974.

Radikal. 2011b. "Necdet Özel Genelkurmay Başkanı Oldu". 29 July. Accessed 30 July 2011, www.radikal.com.tr/turkiye/necdet_ozel_genelkurmay_baskani_oldu-1058141.

Reuters. 2021. "Turkish Minister Says US behind 2016 Failed Coup—*Hurriyet*". 4 February. Accessed 23 May 2023, www.reuters.com/article/turkey-security-usa-int-idUSKBN2A41NF.

RT. 2016. "NATO Officers Caught in Turkey's Post-Coup Crackdown". 8 December. Accessed 24 May 2023, www.rt.com/news/369565-nato-officers-turkey-purges/.

Sabah. 1997. "MÜSIAD özelleştirme sahnesinde". 3 March. Accessed 5 November 2022, http://arsiv.sabah.com.tr/1997/03/03/e04.html.

Şahin, Uğur. 2017. "Bekçiler yaşam tarzına karışacak". *BirGün*, 14 August. Accessed 20 May 2023, www.birgun.net/haber/bekciler-yasam-tarzina-karisacak-174622.

Sayın, Ayşe. 2022. "Kılıçdaroğlu: Erdoğan sokağa çıkmamızı istiyor; zorlayacak, baskı kuracak ama çıkmayacağız". BBC Türkçe, 5 January. Accessed 18 September 2023, www.bbc.com/turkce/haberler-dunya-59881472.

soL. 2013. "#unutMADIMAKlımda Sivas Katliamı AKP ile sürüyor". 2 July. Accessed 10 November 2022, http://haber.sol.org.tr/devlet-ve-siyaset/unutmadimaklimda-sivas-katliami-akp-ile-suruyor-haberi-75640.

Soylu, Ragıp. 2016. "NBC News Asked to Issue an Apology over False Erdoğan Report during Coup Attempt". *Daily Sabah*, 25 July. Accessed 23 May 2023, www.dailysabah.com/diplomacy/2016/07/25/nbc-news-asked-to-issue-an-apology-over-false-erdogan-report-during-coup-attempt.

Sözcü. 2014. "Cemaat 15 kat büyüdü". 11 January. Accessed 15 May 2023, www.sozcu.com.tr/2014/gundem/cemaat-15-kat-buyudu-439588/.

Sözcü. 2016. "Necdet Özel'den tarihi 15 Temmuz 'itirafları'". 12 August. Accessed 10 April 2023, www.sozcu.com.tr/2016/gundem/necdet-ozelden-15-temmuz-aciklamasi-1349287/.

Sözcü. 2019. "İlker Başbuğ'u yargılayan FETÖ'cü hakim: Hatırlamıyorum". 27 March. Accessed 10 April 2023, www.sozcu.com.tr/2019/gundem/ilker-basbugu-yargilayan-fetocu-hakim-hatirlamiyorum-4155150/.

Taraf. 2010. "Darbenin Adı Balyoz". 20 January. Accessed 12 October 2014, www.taraf.com.tr/haber-darbenin-adi-balyoz-46614/.

Terkoğlu, Barış. 2020. "Menzil Bakanlığı'nın Recep Abisi". *Cumhuriyet*, 8 October. Accessed 24 May 2023, www.cumhuriyet.com.tr/yazarlar/baris-terkoglu/menzil-bakanliginin-recep-abisi-1771894.

The Guardian. 2001. "Turkish Government Devalues Lira". 22 February. Accessed 10 March 2023, www.theguardian.com/world/2001/feb/22/1.

Toker, Çiğdem. 2016. "Denetlenmeyen bir savaş şirketi: SADAT". *Cumhuriyet*, 11 July. Accessed 23 May 2023, www.cumhuriyet.com.tr/yazarlar/cigdem-toker/denetlenmeyen-bir-savas-sirketi-sadat-565548.

Uludağ, Alican. 2023. "Vahdet Kitabevi'nden domuz bağı cinayetlerine: Hizbullah". DW, 30 March. Accessed 14 June 2023, www.dw.com/tr/vahdet-kitabevinden-domuz-ba%C4%9F%C4%B1-cinayetlerine-hizbullah/a-64973270.

Vatan. 2008. "'Evet Ergenekon'un Savcısıyım'". 16 July. Accessed 11 January 2013, www.gazetevatan.com/-evet-ergenekon-un-savcisiyim--189246-siyaset/.

Yaşlı, Fatih. 2008. "Dolmabahçe Mutabakatından Ergenekon Mutabakatına". Sendika. Org, 21 November. Accessed 11 November 2013, http://sendika1.org/2008/07/dolmabahce-mutabakatindan-ergenekon-mutabakatina-fatih-yasli/.

Yaşlı, Fatih. 2011. "İstifalar: Bugüne Nasıl Gelindi?" *soL*, 2 August. Accessed 12 April 2014, http://haber.sol.org.tr/yazarlar/fatih-yasli/istifalar-bugune-nasil-gelindi-45052.

Yeni Akit. 2016. "Merve Kavakçı: Hepimiz İsmail Kahraman'ız". 29 April. Accessed 1 May 2016, www.yeniakit.com.tr/yazarlar/merve-kavakci-islam/hepimiz-ismail-kahramaniz-14783.html.

Yeni Şafak. 2023. "15 Temmuz Darbe Girişimi". 20 March. Accessed 23 May 2023, www.yenisafak.com/15temmuz/haberler.

Yıldız, Müyesser. 2014. "Erdoğan ve Necdet Özel'den Balyoz sanıklarına bir darbe daha". OdaTV, 5 August. Accessed 10 April 2023, www.odatv4.com/yazarlar/muyesser-yildiz/erdogan-ve-necdet-ozelden-balyoz-saniklarina-bir-darbe-daha-0508141200-62702.

Zaman. 2010. "Davutoğlu: Referandumda hayır çıkarsa bunu dünyaya anlatamayız". 8 September. Accessed 28 September 2014, www.zaman.com.tr/politika_davutoglu-referandumda-hayir-cikarsa-bunu-dunyaya-anlatamayiz_1025561.html.

Index

Abdülhamid II 28, 31, 32, 37, 38
  Hamidian 28–29, 31
Akar, Hulusi 185
AKP 8–9, 22, 23, 112, 139, 140, 141, 142, 143, 144, 145–147, 148–149, 150–151, 152, 153, 154, 155, 156, 157, 158, 159, 160, 161, 162, 163–165, 166–167, 168, 169–170, 171–172, 173, 174, 175, 176, 177–179, 180, 182, 184–185, 186–188, 190, 196, 197, 198, 199, 200–201
ANAP 22, 103–104, 105, 106, 107, 109, 112, 121, 122, 124, 134, 135, 136, 140, 151, 195
AP 8, 21, 81, 85, 86, 88, 89, 91, 94, 95, 97, 195
Atatürk, Mustafa Kemal 42, 47, 48, 51, 52, 66, 129
  Kemalism/Kemalist 48, 49, 177
authoritarian/authoritarianism 4, 7, 9, 22, 38, 64, 71, 72, 73, 74, 83, 100, 102, 103, 105, 107, 108, 110, 139, 150, 153, 154, 159, 161, 163, 165, 167, 190, 194, 196–197

Başbuğ, İlker 162
bourgeois revolution 29, 32–33, 35
  revolution of 1908 21, 24, 29, 31, 32, 33, 35, 36, 37–38, 39, 40, 194
  revolution of 1923 21, 24, 33, 40, 42, 50, 194
Britain/British 25, 26, 30, 32, 39, 41, 43, 55, 68, 71, 83, 194
Büyükanıt, Yaşar 155, 156, 157, 162

capital 9, 10, 12, 14–18, 19, 22, 36, 59, 61, 62, 78, 82, 85, 88, 94, 97, 100, 101, 102, 106, 107, 109, 111, 112, 113, 114, 115, 119, 120, 121, 124, 125, 140, 141, 142, 143, 146, 147, 148, 148, 151, 167, 168, 175, 176, 179, 180, 189, 191, 192–193, 195, 197, 198; *See also* foreign capital
  commercial/commodity capital 14, 15, 16, 17, 104, 120, 125, 174, 192
  finance capital 15–16, 17, 19, 21, 93, 97, 101, 104, 111, 112, 113, 114, 115, 116, 120, 124, 134, 143, 146, 147, 151, 152, 168, 175, 176, 192, 195, 196, 199
  financial/money capital 14, 15, 16, 17, 100, 114, 115, 116, 120, 140, 167, 168, 174, 192
  industrial/productive capital 14, 15, 16, 17, 34, 61, 77, 79, 86, 93, 100, 125, 146, 174, 192
  internal capital 17, 18, 19, 21, 141, 192
  internationalisation of capital 14, 15, 16, 17, 77, 100, 101, 104, 114, 116, 124, 125, 146, 147, 150, 168, 192, 193
  Islamic capital 22, 94, 106, 107, 108, 111–112, 113, 115, 117, 118, 123, 124, 125–126, 131, 134, 135, 142, 147, 168, 175, 181–182, 195–196, 199
capital accumulation 9, 10, 12, 14, 16, 17, 18, 19, 20, 33, 36, 40, 45, 48, 55, 76, 82, 83, 92, 95, 100, 101, 104, 105, 113, 114, 116, 118, 134, 139, 166, 167, 171, 182, 186, 187, 191, 192, 193, 194
  agricultural production 6, 15, 21, 26, 27, 33, 44, 45, 56, 59, 60–61, 62, 71, 83, 168, 194
  commercial capital accumulation 15, 21, 26, 45, 93, 192
  export-led/export-oriented industrialization 16, 17, 21, 97, 100, 101, 102, 104, 113, 114, 120, 192
  fictitious/financial capital accumulation 17, 136, 192
  financialisation/financial liberalisation 17, 22, 111, 114, 115, 116, 119, 147, 192, 195
  import-substitution industrialization 16, 17, 21, 45, 61, 63, 70, 71, 76–77, 78, 82, 87, 92, 94, 96, 97, 100, 192, 194, 195
  industrial/productive capital accumulation 15, 16, 17, 22, 34, 45, 78, 83, 84, 146, 167, 194, 196
CHP 6, 7, 21, 44–45, 46, 47, 48, 49, 50, 51, 52, 56–57, 59–60, 63, 65–66, 68, 69, 72, 73, 74, 81, 85, 87, 94, 97, 98, 123, 131, 155, 156, 164, 194, 195, 199
class/class relations 6, 9, 13, 14, 18–20, 21, 22, 29, 31, 32, 33, 36, 37, 41, 42, 44, 48, 49, 51, 55, 56, 57, 59, 60, 62–63, 64, 65, 69, 71, 72, 74, 76, 77, 78, 79, 82, 83, 84, 85, 86, 88, 89, 90–91, 92–93, 94, 98, 99, 100, 101, 102, 103, 104, 105, 106, 107, 108, 111, 117, 118, 119, 121, 122, 124, 127, 133, 135, 137, 139,

class/class relations (*cont.*)
    141, 143, 144, 148, 150, 151, 152, 156, 158, 166, 167, 168–169, 174, 175, 178, 182, 189, 190–191, 193, 194, 195, 196, 200
    commercial bourgeoisie/merchants   8, 26, 30, 32, 34, 41, 42, 44, 45, 51, 56, 57, 59, 60, 62, 63, 71, 73, 75, 85, 88, 91, 94, 97, 112, 194, 195
    financial bourgeoisie   84
    industrial bourgeoisie/industrialists   7, 34, 37, 44, 45, 46, 62, 71, 76, 77, 78, 81, 83, 85, 88, 91, 93, 94, 97, 102, 195
    intelligentsia   28, 33, 37, 41, 42, 59–60, 63, 71, 75, 84, 85, 90, 118, 164, 195
    landlords   8, 21, 29, 32, 41, 42, 44, 45–46, 47, 48, 51, 56, 57, 59–60, 63, 64, 65, 71, 73, 75, 84, 85, 86, 88, 91, 94, 97, 194, 195
    local religious constituents   8, 35–36, 41, 42, 66
    Muslim/Anatolian bourgeoisie   21, 33, 34, 36, 37, 41, 42, 44, 45, 56
    non-Muslim bourgeoisie   30, 32, 34, 37, 56
    notables   8, 25, 28, 32, 37, 41, 47, 64
    peasants   31, 36, 41, 42, 46, 47, 48, 57, 62–63, 64, 73, 76, 84, 85, 86, 94, 102, 107, 148
    petty bourgeoisie   33, 37, 42, 59–60, 63, 94, 117, 118, 180, 195
    smallholders   29, 41, 42, 46, 47, 48, 57, 62–63, 64, 73, 76, 84, 85, 148
    ulama   35–36, 41, 42
    workers/working class   8, 21, 30, 31, 34, 41, 42, 44, 46, 48, 56, 62, 63, 64, 70, 71, 78, 84, 85, 86, 87, 88, 89, 90, 91, 92, 93, 94, 95, 97, 98, 99, 101, 105, 106, 107, 108, 113, 115, 117, 118, 121, 123, 124, 125, 141, 148, 149, 151, 167, 168, 169, 170, 171–172, 175, 176, 178, 179, 180, 195, 197, 199, 200, 201
counter-guerrilla   70, 87, 90, 98, 160, 161, 175; *See also* paramilitary/paramilitary forces

Demirel, Süleyman   86, 88, 89, 97, 121, 122, 131, 135
dependency/dependence/dependent   9, 12–13, 16, 17, 19, 21, 22, 24, 26, 28, 29, 30, 34, 39, 42, 55, 58, 60, 62, 64, 65, 66, 76, 79, 83, 87, 93, 96, 100, 102, 104, 111, 114, 115, 120, 136, 140, 143, 158, 167, 168, 182, 187, 190–191, 193, 194, 195, 197, 198

development   3, 4–6, 7, 9–10, 11, 12, 14, 19, 25, 26, 27, 31, 32, 34, 35, 44, 47, 49, 55, 62, 63, 76, 77, 89, 114, 117, 133, 136, 158, 189–190, 191, 192
    late developer/late-developing   3, 12, 13, 14, 16, 17, 18, 19, 24, 77, 95, 96, 100, 145, 189, 191, 192, 193, 194
    late development   9–10, 11–12, 14, 18, 20, 23, 24, 25, 117, 190–191, 195
    uneven and combined development   11, 12, 190
DP   6, 7, 8, 21, 55, 57, 59, 60–63, 64, 65–66, 68, 69, 70–72, 73–74, 75–76, 77, 81, 85, 194
DSP   121, 124, 131, 135, 136, 140
DYP   121, 124, 127, 135, 161

Ecevit, Bülent   94, 97, 121, 134, 136, 137, 141
Erbakan, Necmettin   94, 118, 121, 124, 125, 126, 128–129, 130, 131, 132, 135
Erdoğan, Recep Tayyip   128, 129, 142, 144–145, 147, 156, 159, 161, 164, 170, 173, 174, 177–178, 179, 180, 181, 182, 184, 187, 199, 200, 201
Ergenekon trials   22, 157, 159–162, 172, 174, 196
EU   9, 86, 116, 118, 126, 133, 140, 142, 143, 145, 146, 149, 150, 153, 187–188, 196, 197
    EEC   86, 90, 94
Evren, Kenan   99, 103, 106, 108, 109, 162

fascism/fascist   22, 23, 53, 93, 98, 166, 175–176, 178, 179, 180, 181–183, 184, 187, 197, 200–201
foreign capital   13–14, 16, 17, 19, 26, 27, 29, 34, 41, 44, 61–62, 77, 83, 89, 96, 100, 104, 105, 113, 114, 119, 120, 142, 147, 158, 164, 168, 186, 191, 192, 193, 195
    Gulf capital   105, 106, 115, 168, 175
    Western capital   6, 59, 62, 93, 111, 118, 121, 124, 125, 168, 175, 176, 178, 196
France/French   25, 26, 41, 43, 53, 55, 172, 194

General Staff   38, 40, 52, 53, 54, 67, 68, 79, 80, 89, 91, 108, 126, 130, 131, 132, 153, 154, 185
    chief of the General Staff   52, 53, 54, 67, 68, 80, 89, 90, 91, 99, 100, 109, 154, 155, 156, 157, 162, 185, 186
Germany   25, 28, 30, 34, 39–40, 53, 55–56, 68, 95, 105, 125, 178

Gül, Abdullah   142, 144–145, 153, 155, 156
Gülen, Fethullah   86, 143, 165, 173
 See also Gülen congregation
Gulf countries/states   107, 115
Gürsel, Cemal   80, 87

hegemony/hegemonic   4, 9, 19, 20, 21, 22, 28, 34, 39, 51, 52, 55, 57, 58, 60, 63, 64, 65, 66, 68, 70, 71, 72, 73, 75, 76, 81, 82, 85, 86, 87, 88, 90, 93, 94, 95, 97, 104, 107, 111, 116, 117, 118, 119, 121–122, 123, 124, 126, 127, 134, 136, 137, 139, 141, 142, 144, 145, 146, 148, 149, 150, 151, 157, 158, 159, 167, 168, 172, 173, 178, 187, 188, 190, 193, 194, 195, 196, 200

IMF   22, 57, 59, 62, 70, 88, 95, 97, 100, 120, 136–137, 139, 140–141, 145, 146, 149, 150, 158, 196
İnönü, İsmet   47, 52, 60, 68, 72, 73, 81, 87, 94
ITC   6, 7, 32, 33, 34, 35–36, 38, 39, 40, 42, 50, 51
 Unionist   32, 37, 38, 39, 42

MBK   74, 75, 76, 80–81
Menderes, Adnan   59–60, 68, 71, 73
MGK   99–100, 102, 103, 105
MHP   85, 87, 95, 136, 140, 164, 199
military   2–5, 6, 7, 8, 9–10, 14, 15, 18, 19, 20, 21, 22, 24, 25, 27–28, 29, 31, 32, 33, 37, 38, 39, 40, 42, 43, 44, 47, 50–52, 53–54, 55, 56, 66, 67, 68, 69, 70, 73–74, 75, 76, 79–81, 82, 85, 86, 88, 89, 90, 92, 93, 99, 100, 107, 108, 109, 110, 112, 126, 127, 129, 130, 131, 132, 133–134, 135, 137, 138, 139, 143–144, 152, 153–154, 155, 156–157, 158, 160, 162–163, 164, 166, 173, 177, 178, 181, 183–185, 186–188, 189–191, 193, 194–195, 196, 197, 200, 201
 civil-military bureaucracy in Turkey   7–8, 28, 33, 42, 44, 48, 55, 62, 63, 65, 73, 77, 79–81, 144, 154, 155
 civil-military relations   2, 3, 4, 5, 6, 7, 33, 51, 63, 139, 166, 189, 190, 191
 military's guardianship role   5, 6, 8, 15, 21, 22, 24, 33, 37, 38, 50, 51, 55, 79, 80, 82, 89, 91, 102, 107, 108, 109, 128, 130, 133, 138, 139, 153, 156, 158, 188, 190, 194, 195
Military Court of Appeal   80, 92, 144, 186

military intervention   4, 5, 8, 9, 18, 20, 72, 74, 81, 82, 89, 94, 99, 109, 133, 149, 156, 184, 189, 190, 193, 196
 abortive/failed coup of 2016   9, 22, 81, 142, 166, 173, 177, 178, 180, 184, 185, 187, 197
 coup/junta of 1960   7, 21, 55, 62, 68, 73, 74, 75, 76, 77, 78, 79, 80, 81, 194, 195
 coup/junta of 1980   21, 82, 97, 99–100, 101, 106, 107, 108, 109, 112, 118, 154, 162, 175, 190, 195
 e-memorandum of 2007   22, 139, 154, 156, 196
 memorandum of 1971   21, 82, 88, 89, 90, 91, 92, 94, 96, 99, 100, 107, 195
 memorandum/process of 28 February/memorandum of 1997   8, 22, 111, 112, 119, 130, 132, 133, 134, 135, 137, 138, 141, 143, 144, 159, 196
Military Supreme Court of Administration   92, 186
Milli Görüş   8, 22, 85, 87, 94, 111, 112, 116–118, 119, 123, 127–129, 130, 133, 141, 142, 184, 195, 196, 199
MNP   8, 85, 87, 88, 94
mode of production   13
 articulation of modes of production   12–13, 190–191
 capitalist forms/mode of production/relations   10, 11–12, 13, 14, 19, 21, 24, 25, 26, 27, 28, 29, 31, 32, 33–34, 40, 44, 45, 49, 78, 79, 89, 116, 167, 190, 191, 192, 194
 precapitalist forms/modes of production/remnants   13, 27, 29, 36, 41, 42, 49, 65, 90
modernisation/modernity   4–5, 6, 7–8, 21, 25, 27, 28, 33, 37, 39, 40, 44, 46–47, 48, 50, 51, 66, 67, 73, 107, 141, 189–190, 194
modernised/modernist   6, 7, 8, 38, 42, 65, 194
MSP   8, 87, 94, 95, 97, 118

National Security Council   79–80, 99, 108–109, 130, 131–132, 133, 135, 137, 138, 153–154, 157; *See also* Supreme Defence Assembly
NATO   9, 68–69, 73, 76, 86, 87, 99, 131, 160, 187, 197

INDEX

neoliberal/neoliberalism   17, 21, 22, 82, 95,
    100–102, 103, 104, 105, 106, 123, 124, 135,
    139, 140, 141, 142, 148, 149–152, 153, 157,
    159, 163, 166, 167, 168, 169–172, 173, 175,
    178, 186, 192, 195, 196, 199, 201

Ottoman/Ottoman Empire   6, 7, 21, 24, 25–
    28, 29–32, 33–36, 37–40, 42–45, 50, 54,
    66, 184, 194
    Young Turks   28–29, 31
OYAK   79, 89, 93, 110, 152–153, 172
Özal, Turgut   103, 104, 106, 121
Özel, Necdet   162–163, 185
Özkök, Hilmi   157

paramilitary/paramilitary forces   54, 70, 88,
    183–184, 200; See also counter-guerrilla
periphery/peripheral/peripheralisation   3–
    4, 5, 7, 8, 9–10, 11, 12, 13–14, 15, 16, 17, 18,
    26, 33, 59, 76, 95, 101, 104, 114, 188, 189,
    191, 192, 193
political Islam/Islamism   7, 8, 22, 65, 94, 111,
    116–118, 122, 131, 139, 141, 142, 150, 151,
    152, 153, 155, 159, 161, 163, 166, 167, 168,
    169, 171, 172, 173, 175, 178, 190, 195–196,
    199, 201
    Islamisation/Islamise   111, 112, 118, 122,
        129, 142, 151, 155, 181, 183, 187, 196
    Islamist   8, 65–66, 70, 85, 86, 87, 105, 111,
        112, 116, 117, 118–119, 121, 122, 123, 128, 130,
        131, 132, 133, 134, 135, 137, 143, 146–147,
        148, 155, 156, 160, 163, 171, 182, 184, 187,
        195, 199

religious brotherhoods   35, 51, 65–66, 75, 85,
    86, 106–107, 112, 113, 123, 125, 128, 130,
    131, 135, 142, 144, 152, 157, 159, 162, 163,
    164, 195–196, 199
    Gülen congregation   22, 125, 135, 139,
        142–144, 152, 158, 159, 160, 161, 162, 163,
        164–165, 166, 167, 172–173, 174, 176, 177,
        178, 180, 185, 196, 197
    İskenderpaşa congregation   106, 112, 164
    İsmailağa congregation   123, 133, 161, 164

Menzil order   164, 187
Nakşibendi order   50, 51, 87, 106, 123
Nurcu congregation   66, 86, 106
Süleymancı order   106
RP   8, 22, 87, 118–119, 122, 123–130, 131, 132, 133,
    134, 137, 161, 195–196

Saudi Arabia   87, 105
Sezer, Ahmet Necdet   145, 155
Sledgehammer trials   22, 157, 159, 160, 161,
    162, 172, 196
Soviet Union   4, 6, 43, 45, 58, 59, 65, 66, 67,
    69, 87, 99, 105, 116, 117, 118, 125
state   2, 3, 4, 5–6, 7, 8, 9–10, 14, 15, 18–19, 20,
    21, 22–23, 24, 26, 27, 28, 29, 30, 31, 35, 36,
    39, 40, 43, 44, 45, 46, 47–48, 49, 53, 54,
    55, 59, 60, 65, 69, 72, 73, 75, 76, 77, 78,
    83, 87, 92, 93, 97, 99, 100, 102–103, 104,
    106, 107, 108, 109, 111–112, 114–115, 118,
    122, 127, 128, 129–130, 131, 132, 134, 135,
    136, 137, 139, 140, 142, 143, 144, 146, 147,
    148, 150, 151, 152, 153, 154, 155, 156, 158,
    159, 161, 163, 166–167, 169, 170, 172, 173,
    174, 175, 177, 179, 181, 182, 183, 184–185,
    189, 190, 191, 193, 194, 195, 196–197, 199,
    200, 201
    exceptional state   22, 23, 48, 163, 166,
        167, 169, 172, 174–176, 181, 184, 190, 196–
        197, 200
    normal state   75, 150, 196, 200
State Security Courts   92, 98, 109, 144,
    153, 154
Supreme Defence Assembly   52–53, 67, 79
Supreme Military Council   53, 67, 91–92, 109,
    132, 153, 157, 162–163, 164, 186

TSKGV   110, 187

United States/American   4, 6, 21, 57–58, 62,
    66, 68–69, 70, 72, 76, 86, 93, 95, 99, 104,
    105, 117, 118, 125, 126, 142, 143, 149, 157,
    158, 160, 172, 187–188, 194–195, 196, 197

World Bank   57, 59, 95, 97, 100, 141, 146, 150

www.ingramcontent.com/pod-product-compliance
Lightning Source LLC
Chambersburg PA
CBHW062123040426

42337CB00044B/3814